BLACK ARMADA

Rupert Lockwood

BLACK ARMADA
AUSTRALIA AND THE STRUGGLE
FOR INDONESIAN INDEPENDENCE
1942-49

EQUINOX
PUBLISHING
JAKARTA   KUALA LUMPUR

Equinox Publishing (Asia) Pte Ltd
No 3. Shenton Way
#10-05 Shenton House
Singapore 068805

www.EquinoxPublishing.com

BLACK ARMADA:
Australia and the Struggle
for Indonesian Independence 1942-49
by Rupert Lockwood

ISBN 978-979-3780-94-8

First Equinox Edition 2013

Originally published in 1982 by
Hale & Ironmonger Pty Limited, Sydney
under ISBN 0-86806-0004-6

Printed in the United States

1 3 5 7 9 10 8 6 4 2

Contents

Illustrations

Abbreviations

ACTU: Australian Council of Trade Unions
ALP: Australian Labor Party
CPA: Communist Party of Australia
NEI: Netherlands East Indies
NICA: Netherlands Indies Civil Administration
NSW: New South Wales
PKI: Partai Kommunis Indonesia — Communist Party of Indonesia
RAAF: Royal Australian Air Force
RAN: Royal Australian Navy
RAPWI: Release of Allied Prisoners of War and Internees
SEAC: South-East Asia Command
SWPA: South-West Pacific Area (Command)
TLC: Trades and Labor Council
WWF: Waterside Workers' Federation of Australia

Note: Names and titles have been used as they stood at the time: Batavia (Djakarta), Borneo (Kalimantan), Celebes (Sulawesi), Netherlands New Guinea (Irian Jaya), Mr R. G. (Sir Robert) Menzies, Mr R. G. (Lord) Casey, Mr P. C. (Sir Percival) Spender and so on.

Introduction: War Without Shooting

In 1787, the year the First Fleet embarked enchained British colonisers for Botany Bay, *Discourse on Banishment*, a pamphlet attributed to William Eden (Lord Auckland), prophesied that the new settlement on the coast of what Captain James Cook named New South Wales "would be of great advantage to our cause in the event of a future war, particularly if our ancient friends the Dutch should happen to be the adverse party".

In 1947, 160 years after the strategic speculation inspired by Captain Arthur Phillip's transports, Mr Robert Menzies, Leader of the Opposition, was complaining to the Australian Parliament: "Australia has virtually been at war with the Dutch for two years, except for the shooting".[1]

War without shooting—overlooking a few shots fired by the Dutch in New South Wales—was in truth being waged on our ancient friends the Dutch, in validation of the old Roman formula of *non solo armis*—not by arms alone. On this unscheduled Australian battlefield, Indonesian mutineers and Australian boycotters, drawing occasional aid and comfort from the Chifley-Evatt Government, paralysed vital initial military operations to restore Dutch rule in the Indies, helped significantly in the diplomatic isolation of Dutch recolonisers and speeded the Indonesian Republic's victory.

The head of the Netherlands Indies Government-in-Exile established in Australia after the Dutch surrender to Japan, Dr Johannes Hubertus Van Mook, who moved from Brisbane to Batavia to act as Governor-General in 1945, was quite

1

definite as to which nation had inflicted the deepest wounds on the Dutch Empire in its war with the new-born Indonesian Republic. "Their greatest grievance was against Australia," wrote Dr Van Mook,[2] protesting for Netherlanders dismissed from their Indies constituency.

The Dutch in March 1942 navigated most of their Indies shipping through the bombs and torpedoes to crowd Brisbane, Sydney and Fremantle ports, and key colonial administrators flew from Tjilatjap in Java down the Zero-infested route to Broome, until a Japanese air-raid wrecked and burned the evacuation flying-boats in Roebuck Bay. This traumatic debut of the Dutch on the north-west Australian coast was followed by a regrouping at Melbourne of 15 members of the Netherlands East Indies Governing Council, military and economic leaders and a token representation of loyal Indonesians, and then by the setting up on Brisbane's outskirts, at the unlikely address of Wacol, of the Netherlands East Indies Government-in-Exile.* Not far from the temporary South-West Pacific Command headquarters of a more exalted evacuee, General Douglas MacArthur, Dr Van Mook transformed the wooden barracks of Wacol camp to an imperial capital without an empire.

In this South Seas diaspora the bread of banishment was seldom bitter to Dutch taste. Australia provided the Wacol establishment with military camps, housing, armaments, officers to train its armed forces, hospitals, shipyard berths, airfields, workshops, clothing, food and drink, some of the latter in the comfort of beer gardens. The Australian Government also gave the Dutch access to prison cells for the punishment of disobedient Indonesians. The Australian Government proclaimed more than once that the Government-in-Exile and its armed forces were, by invitation, making Australia their base from which they would move north to resume control of the Indies. Neither hosts nor guests noted the symptoms that a terminal condition approached for South-East Asian empires.

---

*While its role from the beginning was that of Government-in-Exile, the Australian Government delayed giving full statutory recognition to the first foreign government allowed to operate on its territory till later in the war.

The refugee Dutch brought with them to Australia, in merchant ships, warships and aircraft, thousands of Indonesian servicemen, clerks, medical orderlies and merchant seamen. With the Indonesians were imported the frictions of a stratified colonial society. It should have been quickly obvious to both Australian and Dutch authorities that an insubordinate spirit reticulated the Indonesian crews and military formations. Some two thousand Indonesian seamen were on strike and mostly in gaol or internment camp before they had been in the country a month. Indonesian servicemen were, like the merchant seamen, demanding Australian standards of pay.

Official Australian hospitality to the Netherlands Indies Government should have known more reservations and fewer superlatives, as the Canberra Government began to realise when it had to act as gaoler of a foreign empire's discontented subjects and to accept the transplant from Netherlands New Guinea of an ill-reputed concentration camp, Tanah Merah or Boven Digul, resited at Compound D, Cowra prisoner-of-war camp, New South Wales, and, in smaller part, at Liverpool, outer Sydney. The Tanah Merah prisoners, released after agitation by Australians, created in Australia a system of republican power, long before the Indonesian Republic was proclaimed in August 1945. Indonesian independence organisations, sponsored in Sydney, Melbourne, Brisbane and Mackay by Tanah Merah ex-internees, supplanted Dutch authority. The Indonesian Independence Committee in Sydney issued a 1945 ruling that anyone who did not support boycott of the Dutch would no longer be regarded as an Indonesian subject. The warning was hardly necessary. Nearly all Indonesians in Australia, with the exception of the Ambonese janissaries, were disaffected.

Yet the Hollanders in Australia, except for a few of the more enlightened around Dr Van Mook, could not be shaken in their confidence that their predominantly Indonesian ships' crews would, under Anglo-American protection, ensure them an easeful return journey to the Indies treasure-house. They arranged to rendezvous with Lord Louis Mountbatten's South-East Asia Command at Batavia in October 1945, to enjoy again the sweet colonial life. Indonesian mutinies and Australian boycotts struck like a thunderclap in September, converting it to a rendezvous with history.

Indonesian troops mutinied, refusing orders from Dutch officers to prepare to fight the Indonesian Republic. Indonesian seamen walked off ships, refusing to carry troops, munitions, archives, currency and other paraphernalia of colonial rule. Indian, Chinese and Malayan seamen joined the Indonesians' boycott. Waterside workers, first at Brisbane then at other ports round the coast, refused to load Dutch cargoes, tug-crews would not provide tow-ropes, shipyard unions denied repairs to Dutch ships, Royal Netherlands Indies Air Force aircraft and Navy craft were sometimes kept out of the Java battle zones by bans. The boycott extended to Dutch transport, stores and depots ashore. Some 31 Australian trade unions and four unions of Asian seamen temporarily organised in Sydney imposed boycotts on any Dutch activity likely to aid the war on the Indonesian Republic.

Black Armada is not a title that inflates actualities. Subject in some manner to black bans in Australia were 36 Dutch merchant ships, passenger-liners and troopships, two tankers and 35 other oil industry craft, 450 power and dumb barges, lighters and surf-landing craft—essential to landing troops and stevedoring in shallow Indies waters—and aircraft and a vast land transport fleet. Nine corvettes, two submarines (one stayed for good, to rust on a Fremantle breakwater) and seven submarine-chasers of the Royal Netherlands Navy, two British troopships under Admiralty orders and three Royal Australian Navy vessels were also listed as black. In the later crisis over Holland's attempt to retain West Irian, the boycott was revived to embrace at Fremantle the aircraft-carrier *Karel Doorman* and her destroyer escorts. The identifiable total of ships of war and war-supply and medium and smaller craft in the black armada reached 559.

The Netherlands Sea Transport Officer in Australia conceded that 1,000 trucks were still held in Australia by boycott at March 1946. Netherlands Indies Government executives, their archives and reoccupation guilders were prevented from arriving in time, along with troops and munitions.

The boycott in Australia not only temporarily incapacitated

4

a Dutch war machine slim in resources; the Australian example influenced bans on Dutch war services in several other key countries.

The plight of officers aboard the Netherlands war transport *Bontekoe*, denied by boycott at Brisbane, the port where Australian unions opened their anti-Dutch campaign, coal for its boilers and galleys, stevedores and tugs, illustrated how tight was the immobilising grip of the maritime unions on Dutch shipping. Dutch officers wrote from the boycotted *Bontekoe* to the Queensland Trades and Labor Council Secretary, Belfast-born Michael Healy:

> The situation is thus, Mr Healy, that, if you more-over succeed in coaxing the bakers, butchers and grocers in Brisbane not to sell us any food and you can persuade the Harbour Board to have us shifted to a berth where no fresh water is available, you will really have created a very unpleasant situation for an Allied unit. Besides meddling with the Indonesian question, upon which we deny you capacity to pass judgment, you are trying to make life unbearable for us in your country.[3]

Boycott's Military Damage

Six months after the first Dutch ships were black-banned in the Brisbane River Lord Louis Mountbatten found the boycott still so hurtful to his South-East Asia Command operations that he flew into Sydney to appeal, in vain, to maritime unionists to release the Dutch ships.

The Black Armada represents the greatest boycott demonstration of its kind in Australian history. It is difficult to recall a boycott anywhere in the world comparable in character and scope.

Political and strategic consequences of the Australian boycott of the Dutch were substantial. The postwar shipping famine, the distractions and deflections of the first cold war strategies in Europe and Washington's China obsession multiplied the havoc arising from immobilisation of Dutch ships, soldiers, munitions and other war necessities in Australia.

As poets and generals tell us, all delays are dangerous in

war. When delays are compounded and integrated and of qualitative emphasis, they are devastating. The first blow is half the battle if the enemy is ill-prepared, and the first blow for the Republic of Indonesia against the Royal Netherlands armed forces, delivered at Australian wharves, warehouses, military camps, airports, naval depots and shipyards, was one from which the Dutch could not recover in time. Each day's hold-up of the Dutch colonial apparatus in Brisbane, Sydney, Melbourne or Fremantle could be measured in ground won for the new Republic. Dutch warriors were too few and the dimensions of the battlefield too vast for timely redress of boycott damage.

The Dutch failure was not one of nerve: they showed dogged resource in negotiating the reefs with which the Australian boycotters studded their course back to the Indies. Dutch skippers navigated Australian harbours and estuaries without tugs or pilots. Sometimes they burned wood like Murray River paddle-steamers to overcome trade union denials of fuel, and contrived to have colliers awaiting them outside harbour heads.

The Netherlands Indies Government-in-Exile recruited Italian prisoners-of-war in Western Australia and Dutch internees flown from Japanese horror camps to stevedore ships. Dutch soldiers made up scratch crews to replace mutinous Indonesian seamen.

These Caesarian outlets were too late to prevent the Indonesian Republic's consolidation, which went ahead while the Dutch war-supply fleet was held by boycott in Australian ports. The imperial superstructure of what the Dutch regarded as their hereditary fief was near to dust and bone before they could range their ordnance against the revolution.

Australian Awakening

In Australian politics the boycott challenge to colonialism in the 3,000 islands strung across the northern sea frontier tested and revealed, as no other domestic postwar event, the official alignments and attitudes to the upheavals in Asia.

Mr Menzies, Opposition Leader, drew on postulates that became *démodé* in a short season in his efforts to reconcile a nineteenth century empire mythos with the dynamics of

6

mid-twentieth century Asia. To Mr Menzies, Asia without European superintendence spelled danger. Australian intervention against Holland in the Indies would encourage foreign intervention against the White Australia policy. Without European colonies in the Near North, Mr Menzies prophesied in doom-laden phrases, Australians would be lonely, in hazardous isolation, shorn of body armour.

One of the guiding predilections in Mr Menzies' outlook was that Indian, Malayan, Indo-Chinese and Indonesian attempts to expel the British, French and Dutch could never be majoritarian. Australian practitioners of a more Platonic relationship with Asia were singularly ill-informed about developments as the Opposition Leader understood them. The Indonesian Republic was merely the outcome of a revolt by a clique of pro-Japanese collaborators, and those agitating against the Dutch did so against overwhelming Indonesian sentiment. Louis XVI had to be told on the Bastille's fall that it was not a revolt — it was a revolution. In both cases confirmation was not long withheld.

Australia is not a land of fast learners in Asian studies. Past interest in Asian nationalism had been fretful, seldom sympathetic or informed. Prime Minister Joseph Benedict Chifley led a Labor Party whose attitudes to colonial Asia had been mere appendices to relations with metropolitan Britain. Restless Asia poised above the Arafura Sea was more prone to create paranoic emergencies among Labor's vocal White Australia advocates than among many conservatives. Before the Indonesians touched on this tenderest national nerve, partnership with independent Asian regimes seemed light-years away.

Mr Chifley sensed the awakening concerns that rose from the ashes of defeat: no colonial empire of South-East Asia could command in 1941-42 the support of its subjects or delay for long the capitulation ceremonies.

The Prime Minister, unremarked over his years in politics for attention to Asian wants, read with some perception the meanings for Australia in the colonial debacle and the volcanic flow of the postwar revolutions. Though syndromes of the old imperial environment remained, Mr Chifley showed during the debates on trade union boycotts of Dutch ships

7

more appreciation than most members of his party that Australian foreign policy could not stay within its old configurations. He was, without question, the first of Australian Prime Ministers to promote publicly the redefinitions and reformulations demanded in policies toward Asia. Mountains of prejudice stood in the way: these were not all moved by the time he was voted to the Opposition benches in December 1949.

Many Australians far removed from the labor movement sympathised with the boycott of Dutch ships, realising that the outworn superstructures built by the Europeans in Asia must dematerialise, and anticipating the end of constricting Netherlands trade practices in the nearest export market.

Before parliament on 6 March 1946 Mr Chifley assessed Australian support for the anti-Dutch boycott as running "much wider than the trade union movement". He would have been aware of market ambitions in business and farming communities, of Australian soldiers' resentments against the Dutch whose rule they were delegated to restore in East Indonesia and of their illicit aid to the Indonesians, and of a rising tide of protest against colonialism in Sydney and Melbourne universities. (The first significant student demonstration in the cause of Asian independence, turned to a riot by a police attack, was in Wynyard Square, Margaret Street, Sydney, immediately after the First Police Action of the Dutch against the Indonesian Republic in July 1947.)

Conflict and Contradiction

The Australian trade unions' boycott of the Netherlands Indies Government-in-Exile and its sinews of war was, to Mr Chifley, the most contentious sign of readjustment in Australian postures toward Asia. The prophet was without honour abroad as well as in his own country: the stones thrown at Mr Chifley for his accommodations to the Asian nationalist revolutions were enough to build his monument.

Australian intervention in the Dutch-Indonesian confrontation evoked the first major foreign policy clash with Britain, the first heated protest from Australia's new ally in Washington. The Commonwealth, ready to succour the mother country on the battlefield "to the last man and the last

8

Mick Healy, Queensland TLC Secretary, photographed in 1947 farewelling Slamet, a foundation member of the Brisbane Indonesian Independence Committee. Slamet and two other Indonesians, Pakato and Bondan, stayed behind in Australia in 1945 to look after the interests of repatriates

Jim Healy, leader of the Waterside Workers' Federation from 1937 until his death in 1961

E. V. Elliott, Federal Secretary of the Seamen's Union for more than 45 years

Indonesia in 1945.

- - - - International Borders

\ Borders of the Republic

///// British

///// Portuguese

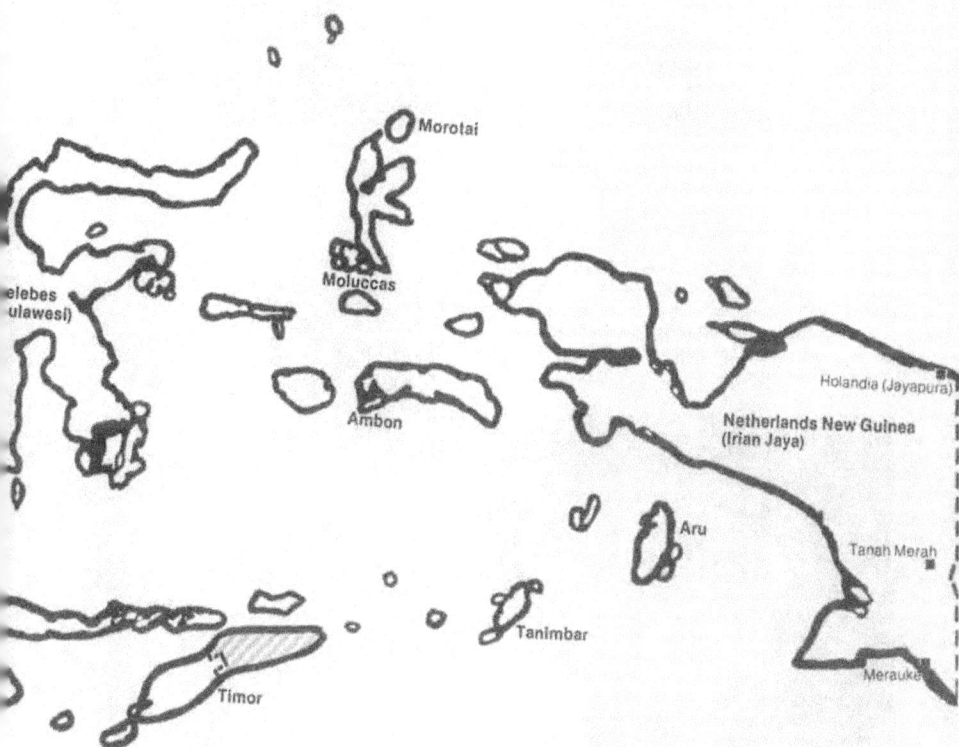

Ben Chifley, Prime Minister 1945-49 and Arthur Calwell, Minister for Immigration 1945-49. Calwell was responsible for the repatriation of Indonesians from Australia to Indonesia where they were delivered to supporters of the revolution, and not to the Dutch

H. V. Evatt, Australian Minister for External Affairs in the Curtin and Chifley governments. He was opposed to Dutch attempts to use armed force to restore their rule in Batavia, and actively supported the Indonesian cause in the United Nations

Lord Louis Mountbatten, head of South-East Asia Command. Mountbatten opposed the repatriation of Indonesian revolutionaries because their return would impede Dutch recolonisation of Indonesia

shilling" — as Labor Prime Minister Andrew Fisher put it in 1914—for the first time evaded engagement in a British war. Mr Chifley declined to marshal troops for South-East Asia Command's condemned cause in Java.

Mr Chifley was bound by pledge and protocol to espousal of Holland's reinstatement at Batavia. He handed the Netherlands Indies Government-in-Exile all the arms, supplies and services to which it was entitled under treaty—and more. But the press and pull of nationalist revolution in the Indies led him at the same time to comfort the trade union boycotters of the Dutch and to subvert, in alliance with his External Affairs Minister, Dr H. V. Evatt, Anglo-American plans to install the Dutch with pre-war prerogatives.

Challenged by the Opposition in parliament to prosecute the law-breaking boycotters of Dutch ships Mr Chifley proclaimed from the Government benches his conviction that "the old order in Indonesia will not go on".[4] The Prime Minister's policy of giving the NEI Government-in-Exile an arsenal and laboring to defuse it was not easy to understand in his time. Politics is the science of the possible, and Mr Chifley could see no escape from the manoeuvre of keeping one foot in the old world while shuffling the other into the new.

During a turbulent transition he led a society of European-Australians habituated to the imperial "umbrella" above the northern sea frontiers, a society prone in its Asian environment to the psychosomatic disorder that caused the illusion to linger that a restoration of fugitive and perishable colonial regimes would immobilise "the hordes". In their antipathy to Asia many Australians, including statesmen and newspaper proprietors, would not believe that the "umbrella" was blown to tatters in the gale force of Japanese conquest.

Mr Chifley was not in 1945 an abolitionist. He wanted British, American and European influences to survive and Australian influences to grow in Asia. He felt that these influences could not endure unless the Dutch plan to replicate the confining structures of pre-war days was ostentatiously discarded. Thus followed his abetment of the trade unions in applying their muscle against a colonialist restoration.

External Affairs Minister H. V. Evatt was less of an abol-

9

itionist than his Prime Minister. Asia was changing guard more swiftly and raggedly than Dr Evatt found comfortable. He graduated cautiously from the milder metaphors of colonialism during welcomes to the Netherlands Indies refugee leaders in 1942 to cautious tilting at Dutch windmills in 1943, when he helped to secure the release of the transferred Tanah Merah political prisoners. Dr Evatt always had a firmer dedication to civil liberties than to trade union action. It was not until the 1947 Dutch Police Action against the Republic that he connived at a boycott in breach of the laws he administered as Attorney-General. Appalled at the Dutch attempt to restore their rule at Batavia by military onslaught, Dr Evatt promoted the Indonesian cause at the United Nations and, in 1948, boldly criticised Washington for sustaining Dutch attacks on the Republic.

The Minister for Commerce, Mr R. G. Pollard, sought a sublimity for the boycott movement. Mr Pollard saw the Australian trade unionists who black-banned Dutch ships as being, years hence, "in the same category as the Dorchester Labourers"[5] — the Tolpuddle Martyrs transported to Van Diemen's Land for having organised to seek a wage rise in the 1830s.

The Dawning Realism

For those who hold that a strong undercurrent of sympathy for the downcast and dispossessed runs through Australian society, that the egalitarian politic is the clue to resentments and actions against colonialism and racism, it would be gratifying to have the Black Armada presented as the symbol of selfless sacrifice to aid an Asian people to independence.

True, many Australians did lose wages and risk penalties with no other consideration in mind. The trade union boycotters of the Dutch and the significant groupings that underwrote their efforts will not, nevertheless, be remembered when martyrs from Tolpuddle or other addresses are mentioned. There are additional explanations of the wider range of sympathy for the boycott of the Dutch that Mr Chifley noted.

Many, still viewing through the foggy dews of White Australia mentality, felt that the independent Asian power

10

emerging within the husks of the European empires offered a rising prosperity and industrial opportunity for the deprived millions. The satisfactions thus engendered would relieve Australia of the nightmare of southward-migrating millions, and multiply her exports.

The Black Armada boycott helped materially to advance the debate as to whether Australian ideas about Asia were to remain in mortgage to the past, to a Malthusian determinism that surpluses of coloured men would spill through the islands into Australia's empty north unless a white man's surveillance continued, or whether Australia should take initiatives to speed self-government for Asians.

The clutter of black war cargoes and the smokeless stacks of Dutch ships intruded this question to parliamentary debates and to trade union meetings.

The scriptural, century-old White Australia propaganda, directed to the threat of Asian immigration to white men's living standards, seemed to rebound in the trade union movement, in which William Lane and other labor pioneers, the Sydney *Bulletin* and at times Henry Lawson had lent pervasive force to fears of "cheap coloured labor".

The writer addressed many meetings to incite and maintain boycott of the Dutch. The rationalisation had clearly entered numerous Australian minds that, if Asians could rid themselves of imperial tolls and improve their living standards by industrialisation and literacy, they would no longer cast covetous eyes at Australian bounty.

Dr Van Mook was bewildered that Australia, rigidly excluding Asian immigrants, should have made cause with Asians against Europeans by boycott of Dutch shipping and services and by diplomatic backing to the Indonesian nationalist revolution. Not all Australians could have found answers to ameliorate the Acting Governor-General's bewilderment.

The main strand of sentiment that evoked the wider support or passivism that allowed the trade union boycotters of the colonial Dutch to succeed in their bold enterprise owed much to a dawning Australian realism and self-reliance. Theorists of varied stripes arose to seek attunement to Asian inquietudes, rejecting Mr Menzies' Delphic conclusions on the inevitability and necessity of empire. They held that

11

national interest, maybe survival, depended on friendly co-existence with independent Asian nations.

The colonial bureaucracies had clotted Australia-Asia trade arteries and, by their notorious derelictions, left Australia with no choice but to plead for an American umbrella as South-East Asian outposts were handed, one after the other, to small Japanese forces by Europeans, amid a flutter of white flags.

Union Intervention in Foreign Policy

In the Black Armada years the trade unions, presenting themselves as conscious instruments of history, reached the zenith of their capacity to intervene in Australian foreign policy. This intervention brought upon the trade unions, particularly of the maritime industry, the wrathful charge that they were "dictating foreign policy". Mr Menzies and his parliamentary followers, the press and Dr Evatt laid the charge.

Mr Chifley commanded adequate contrivances of authority to resist "dictation" from the unions, though the cost might be temporary industrial dislocation. His rejoinder to the 1949 coal strike was merciless: trade union leaders directly and indirectly involved were transported, without recourse to conventional legal practice, through the gates of Long Bay Gaol in Sydney.

In contrast to his violent assaults on labor tradition during the 1949 coal strike were his tolerances and aids for the boycotters of the Dutch. It is difficult to avoid the conclusion that Mr Chifley unofficially endorsed this trade union usurpation in the hazardous arena of relations with old and new orders in Asia, where he himself had to tread much more warily.

Australian Ambitions

The imperial forfeit in South-East Asia, the drooping of white flags before Japanese generals by French, British and Dutch military commanders, the disorderly arrival of the Netherlands Indies administration and the popular resistance to European colonialism that emerged in Australia for the first time were to cast subdued light on Australia's ambitions in

12

the Near North. A bitter Dr Van Mook, the fallen viceroy on his way back to Holland from his native Java, said in an attack on "impulsive actions", such as the ban on Dutch shipping, that Australia had no foreign policy "apart from personal ambitions and ideas".[6]

Ambition was bi-partisan. There were no disputes in parliament over the wartime thesis of Mr P. C. Spender, to be the Menzies Government's External Affairs Minister, that Australia had an "overriding interest"[7] in the islands north of Australia, with Mr Menzies' placing of these islands "among our first regional responsibilities",[8] or with Dr Evatt's definition that they came "within an extended Australian zone".[9] The Allied Commander-in-Chief in the Pacific War, General Douglas MacArthur, claimed that Australia had Indies annexation designs, according to Dr Van Mook's deputy, Dr Charles Van Der Plas. However, Canberra, at a time when Anglo-Dutch military incapacity suggested opportunity, shied away from Dr Evatt's bold plan to give armament to ambition by ordering the Australian Army then based in East Indonesia to invade Java. Which was just as well, for the invasion order to the war-weary, homesick Australian soldiers, many of them pro-Republic, could have left the Government with a mutiny on its hands.

13

1   Shipload of Sedition

The Dutch steamer *Both*, named after a Dutch viceroy of the Indies, sailed in mid-1943 through Torres Strait and into the dry tropics above Capricorn, unrecognised, until she navigated her way through Barrier Reef coral islands to the Port of Bowen, North Queensland, as the first ship destined to land convicts in Eastern Australia for nearly a century.

The fog of censorship that screened the *Both*'s mission to Australia began to lift soon after mooring ropes were cast ashore. A scribbled note, fluttering to the feet of one of the Bowen waterside workers engaged to load bunker coal and provisions, explained that confined aboard were more than 500 Indonesian men, women and children from the Dutch prison camp of Tanah Merah, often called Boven Digul, up the Digul River from Merauke, Netherlands New Guinea. The Indonesian political prisoners were to be re-interned in Australia. The note hinted strongly that Australian help to free them would be welcome.

Perhaps there are still many Australians, well versed in the cruelties suffered by those exiled and enserfed to colonise the land, who retain a special sensitivity about convict transportation. Sydney citizens rioted in arms to end the traffic to New South Wales. Demonstrations of sympathy and succour greeted the men and women who fought on the barricades of the 1871 Paris Commune, when French transports brought them in iron cages to Melbourne and Sydney, on their way to the Isle des Pins penal colony in New Caledonia. The Bowen waterside worker who picked up the note thrown from a *Both* porthole was sufficiently moved to give the plight of captive human freight in the ship immediate political attention. The note went by courier to Brisbane, then on to Sydney. The English learned by an Indonesian in the steaming jungle of Boven Digul opened the first chapter of the story of the most effective and significant boycott movement in Australian history.[1]

The Indonesian prisoners aboard the smoky tramp berthed in Edgecumbe Bay, Bowen in 1943 were resurrected from a jungle tomb, created by the Dutch to sepulture the Indonesian nationalist rebellion that flared in 1926-27. By chance of Japanese invasion they were moved down the Digul River to Liverpool and Cowra internment camps in New South Wales. In this shipload of sedition were the most politically experienced of the Indonesians forced to Australia by the 1942 surrender to Japan. Identification of these Tanah Merah deportees, via the note tossed ashore at Bowen and then by a second note to a Sydney railwayman from a prison train passing through Liverpool station on the way to a camp nearby, marked the foundation of an Indonesian-Australian front against Dutch destruction of the Republic and the first Netherlands-Australian frictions at government level. Mutterings behind barbed wire at Liverpool and Cowra camps became a program of action. The convicts from the *Both's* holds were the initiators of the movements in Australian ports and at Dutch bases that impeded Dutch retrieval of the fabled Indies and helped Australia some way along the road to an entirely new relationship with Asian neighbours.

The "Specially Appointed Place"

Tanah Merah on the Digul River, with its malaria, blackwater fever, nutritional diseases, maltreatment by guards, exposure to monsoonal rain and heat, despair and appalling death rates, put a word into the Indonesian language: *Di-digul-kan*, to be "Digulled".

Tanah Merah was some 200 miles up the Digul River from Merauke, in south-east New Guinea, which the Japanese did not occupy. The camp was established under the *Indische*

Staatregeling, Article 37 of which allowed the NEI Government to exile to "a specially appointed place" for an indefinite period those it considered as disturbers of "the public peace and order". One of the printed pamphlets[2] issued by the Indonesians in Australia after the Republic's proclamation on 17 August 1945 described Tanah Merah as being "in the worst malarial district of the island . . . surrounded by thick jungle and head-hunting tribes"

Five hours up the Digul River from Boven Digul, first camp of the Tanah Merah system, where a future Republican Premier, Dr Sutan Sjahrir, spent his brief exile, was Tanah Tinggi. To Tanah Tinggi were deported the "incorrigible and troublesome cases". These had recidivated, or continued subversive activities in camp. In the steaming, fever-racked Tanah Tinggi sector, Indonesian internees seemed doomed to living death, without hope of escape.

Dr Sjahrir gave an unforgettable description[3] of Tanah Merah to which the Dutch exiled him in March 1935. Sjahrir sailed to his exile at Tanah Merah over blue and emerald seas, past the near-derelict Bandas where the East India Company of Holland had fertilised clove and nutmeg with Indonesian blood, past Dobo in the Aru Islands where Australian pearling schooners fished, and then up the deep and tortuous Digul River. Rank tropical foliage overhung the dark waters and brushed the prison steamer. Sjahrir noted that the gaol, camp and staff buildings were under a Dutch Army officer. No housing was provided for exiles. By their own hands they cut down jungle timber to build huts. Dr Sjahrir found the conditions of exile produced "profound spiritual misery":

> The weary faces, the shy, sometimes queer-looking eyes, with deep, dark lines under them, bear testimony to this suffering. Most of them appear to be permanently broken in spirit . . .

This remote jungle camp was as escape-proof as Devil's Island. Usually, those attempting to escape died in the dark jungle. For those who reached the coast, a short sea voyage to nearby NEI islands meant capture and recidivist penalties at Tanah Tinggi. The line northward was blocked by mountains

17

so high that equatorial snows capped their peaks, by unbridgeable ravines and unfordable rivers. Not only the feverous afflictions, hunger and dense jungle awaited those essaying southward escape: primitive tribesmen, their Stone Age isolation barely ruffled, still prone to cannibalism, seldom offered mercy. "The tropical jungle and arrows of the headhunters made prison walls or barbed wire unnecessary", said the Indonesians' Australian-printed pamphlet on Tanah Merah. "Those who did try to escape met their inevitable fate."

To Australia and Back Again

But the taper of hope flickered. By miracle, three Tanah Merah escapees enjoyed fleeting liberty on Australian soil, more than a decade before the *Both* steamed into Bowen harbour.

Four Indonesians, interned for their part in the 1926-27 strikes and riots, made a break from the Digul River after some three years in the camp. They floundered out into wildly inhospitable jungle and on the first day were harried by Dutch pursuers. The patrols withdrew to leave the reckless four to death. By miracle the four encountered sympathetic tribesmen. Further on they steered clear of tribes opposing by arms any intrusion of their preserves. In hostile country they sometimes hid in the jungle by day and felt their way painfully along the tribesmen's trails by night. One was speared by a tribal warrior. The other three helped him along, day after day, until, far from medical aid, he died lingeringly.

The Tanah Merah escapees would seek shelter in vain from the monsoonal downpours that pelted through the green canopy. On the mountain heights they shivered in their rags. Mostly they hungered, but found enough jungle produce to sustain them. On occasions they had to take a chance, stagger into a village and beg refreshment from tribesmen who were unaware that they were Dutch subjects and had never seen either a Dutchman or a Javanese. Guided by Melanesian natives on paths southward, through country not yet explored by the Dutch, three of the four Tanah Merah prisoners arrived, naked, thorn-torn and emaciated, on the

Dutch New Guinea south coast near Merauke. They had crossed some of the world's most formidable terrain.

Coastal Melanesians helped to restore them to health and allowed them a small canoe. They navigated the tiny craft with the skill of ancestors who centuries before rode the monsoons of the Arafura Sea to Australia. They sailed round the southern bulge or under-belly of New Guinea, on to the south-west coast of Australian-ruled Papua.

The coastal Papuans, at home on these shallow, reef-studded seas, gave the Indonesians passage in a fishing boat to Torres Strait and Thursday Island, at the tip of Cape York, the north-east extremity of the continent, where the Queensland State Government's writ runs.

On Australia's Thursday Island the three ex-prisoners, who survived an unprovidored navigation of desperate daring, were accorded no garlands. Canberra was contacted and deportation to the NEI authorised.

The three found friends, however, among Indonesian pearl-divers at Thursday Island. The intention to deport the three men was conveyed to trade unionists in Darwin. Darwin trade unionists asked the Commonwealth Government that the Tanah Merah ex-prisoners be granted political asylum. The Scullin Government refused.

Mr Gerald Peel, a Cambridge University Master of Arts graduate (of the same family that produced Sir Robert Peel, British Prime Minister) and an active supporter of the Indonesian Republican cause in Australia, wrote that "the Scullin Labor Government put them on a ship and packed them back to a Dutch concentration camp".[4] There they joined, no doubt, the recidivists of Tanah Tinggi.

By the perversity of White Australia politics one of the three Indonesians who made the voyage from Tanah Merah to Thursday Island as a free man, to return as a prisoner, was transported to Australia in 1943, when he did not seek admission or asylum. He was Abdul Rachman[5] who battled miserably for life after his escape to Thursday Island and re-internment in New Guinea.

Mission to Tanah Merah

Lieutenant-Colonel J. H. Jones, District -Officer of the

19

Australian New Guinea Administration for the Sepik River District, heard on 19 May 1942 that the Japanese had occupied Hollandia, capital of Dutch New Guinea. Colonel Jones left Wewak on 25 May, with three men of the New Guinea Volunteer Rifles. Scouts sent from Wutong on the Dutch-Australian border reported that "the Japanese had been in Hollandia and had gone again".

The Australian party learned in Hollandia that the Japanese had come there on 6 May in an aircraft carrier and two destroyers, landed several officers and about 200 marines. The episode is more or less dismissed in a footnote of the official war history[6] :

> The Japanese raided the Government stores, killed all the livestock they could find, "drank the town dry" and then went away, taking with them the Dutch Controleur, his wife and child and a Dutch priest, saying they would be back in three weeks.

While the Dutch forgot to scorch the earth at Hollandia they did not forget Tanah Merah over the mountains. Tanah Merah internees knew less about what was happening than did the Australians at Wewak. Occasional war planes were seen, but the Indonesians in camp could only speculate. Dutch guards would not enlighten them. If they had known of the war and the Dutch forfeit, they would, their spokesmen in Australia later claimed, have made a break and organised guerilla bands.

The Dutch feared the consequences of partisan armies, likely to prejudice postwar arrangements. Their decision to rescue the Tanah Merah prisoners and bring them to Australia had more fateful repercussions than if they had been left to their own devices. The Dutch sent Dr Charles Van Der Plas, head of the Netherlands East Indies Commission in Australia, to Merauke and up the Digul River to organise their deportation to New South Wales. The Tanah Merah exiles later reported[7] that Dr Van Der Plas, "with fine irony" addressed the prisoners assembled to hear him as "fellow-countrymen". (Dr Van Der Plas was born in Java.) He liked the Indonesian people, a tribute which a recidivist from Tanah Tinggi told the writer was accepted in the same spirit as if the cannibal chief in the surrounding jungle had said that he, too, was fond of Indonesians. More than conciliatory phrases were needed to assuage the bitterness of the Digul River veterans. Except for a few, chiefly the old and the sick (who, said the pamphlet on Tanah Merah published in Australia by the Indonesians, "reasoned that their deaths would not help the oncoming Japanese"), the internees were moved down the Digul River, Sydney-bound.

According to the Indonesian Independence Committee formed in Melbourne in 1944-45, 507 were transported from Tanah Merah to Australia. A Brisbane Indonesian Independence Committee Bulletin of 16 October 1945 said that 295 political exiles "together with families numbering 212" were evacuated from the Digul. The prisoners and families on their voyage from Merauke to Bowen and Sydney slept on mats, used their miserable rolls of worldly possessions as pillows and ate little but rice.

The overcrowded *Both*, refreshed at Bowen, attracted little notice as she steamed down Sydney Harbour. Wartime Sydney was accustomed to massive movements of warships, troopships and transports disembarking enemy prisoners of war. While some maritime unionists had been alerted on the voyage of the prison ship *Both,* they had obviously not been made conscious of any duty to demonstrate or assist. The Indonesian men, women and children were landed without incident from the *Both,* and conveyed by road transport from the Sydney waterfront to Central Station, there to entrain for internment, some in the Liverpool complex of military camps, and the remainder at Cowra, the site in central south-western New South Wales for prisoner-of-war camps holding Italians, Japanese and other Asians.

Dr Van Der Plas's friendly words on the eve of the voyage down the Digul River to Australia culminated not in freedom but in encirclement by barbed wire under the brand of treason. The Netherlands Indies Government, in its approach to the Australian Government for internment facilities, had been less than honest: the Indonesians from the Digul were designated by the Dutch as enemies of the Allied cause, to be treated as prisoners of war. The Curtin Government accepted the transplant of Tanah Merah concentration camp on that basis.

However, it could have been charged with negligence for failure to verify, for the Indonesian women and young children from the *Both* should have aroused suspicions and inquiries about "enemy prisoners" status. (Wives, if they insisted, were allowed to join husbands in Tanah Merah; likewise a husband could join an interned wife. Children were born in Tanah Merah, many to die and some to come to Australia in a convict ship.)

Liverpool station staff, on duty for the arrival of a trainload of "enemy prisoners of war", were puzzled. When the train stopped at Liverpool station the railwaymen noted that carriages held captives darker and thinner than Japanese. Some prisoners lay on seats or floors, exhausted or sick.

Here at Liverpool station the Tanah Merah prisoners launched their second note, addressed to any Australians who might sympathise with their plight. The note was scribbled in pencil and thrown to the platform, near a railwayman's feet. The writer of the note was a Javanese railway worker, whose name was pronounced as Jo-Jo by Australians who later came to know him. Since the 1926 Java rail strike he had been in the Digul River camp. Jo-Jo's note, in English, identified the prisoners on the train as Indonesian prisoners of the colonial Dutch. It reported that those aboard the train had mostly been in Tanah Merah since 1926-27, that many of their companions had died on the Digul, that some of those destined for re-internment in Australia were very sick with malaria, tuberculosis and other ailments. The writer expressed on behalf of his fellow-captives a determination to fight for release from continued imprisonment in Australia and for medical attention to the sick.

The thin, ailing, poorly dressed Indonesians were transferred to military trucks and driven off to a prison camp in the Liverpool military zone. The Liverpool station staff member who picked up Jo-Jo's note was a militant unionist. When he finished working his shift that day he took the note to Mrs Laura Gapp[8], of the Civil Rights League, then Sydney's leading civil-libertarian organisation. While the Bowen wharf note had served as forewarning, it was the Liverpool station note that sparked immediate action.

Mrs Gapp and trade union friends traced the Tanah Merah

22

exiles, with the help of Australian soldiers, to the Liverpool area internment camp. Others—the main body of the prisoners—were located in Compound D of the prisoner-of-war camp at Cowra. (Compound A was for Italian prisoners, B for Japanese, C for Koreans, Chinese, Taiwanese and other Asians who had served the Japanese.) The Indonesians of D Compound were put on the same footing as the enemy war captives. They were guarded by the 22nd Garrison Battalion of the Australian Army and some Dutch soldiers.

Hospitality Behind Barbed Wire

Soldiers detailed to guard the Indonesians at Cowra and Liverpool were mostly veterans of the 1914-18 world war— middle-aged civilians donning uniforms for behind-the-lines service in the war against Japan. Many had been trade unionists on enlistment. They soon discovered that the Indonesians were anything but friends of Japan: they learned the Tanah Merah story and passed word on to trade union contacts. Mrs Laura Gapp confirmed that Australian soldiers guarding the Indonesians had been men of compassion. Though admission of parcels of fruit, cakes, canned milk, sweets and other gifts for the prisoners was not legal, soldiers allowed her to carry these into camp. The Australian guards also allowed her to take in medicines for the sick Indonesians. Sardjono[9], one of the leaders of the 1926 movement against the Dutch in Java, while critical of the Australian authorities' failure to ensure earlier medical relief for the sick, recorded "heartfelt gratitude" for the kindness received from Australian guards by him and the other Tanah Merah deportees in Cowra Compound D.

Very soon after the railwayman from Liverpool brought to her office in George Street, Sydney, the note thrown by Jo-Jo from the train at Liverpool station, Mrs Laura Gapp was in the office of the Minister for External Affairs and Attorney-General, Dr Herbert Vere Evatt, in Parliament House, Canberra. This was the beginning of Australian-Indonesian collaboration against the Dutch at the higher political levels.

Dr Evatt, according to Mrs Gapp, was already worried

23

and "somewhat conscience-stricken" at the continued imprisonment of the Indonesians disembarked from the *Both*, and tried to wash his hands of responsibility. "Don't come here and kick me in the pants!" he told Mrs Gapp. "Go to the Dutch and kick them in the pants!" He quietly urged her to go right ahead with a campaign for the Indonesians' release, to help him win the necessary support in a cautious Cabinet to defy the Dutch and order releases from Cowra and Liverpool if the Netherlands Indies authorities refused. It was later apparent, said Mrs Gapp, that Dr Evatt made personal representations to the Netherlands Indies leaders to grant freedom to the Tanah Merah internees. The late Mr Bartlett Adamson, Australian poet and writer and a former President of the Fellowship of Australian Writers, was of considerable help. He enlisted the aid of cultural bodies and prominent writers in the campaign to free the Indonesian prisoners.

With Mrs Gapp, Bartlett Adamson raised a storm in the Dutch Consulate, Margaret Street, Sydney. They found diplomats there still inclined to wander in the backwoods of colonial politics.

Next Mrs Gapp and Bartlett Adamson gate-crashed the medical clinic run by Netherlands Indies emigre forces in Kent Street, near Sydney Harbour Bridge. They fronted a statuesque Dutch doctor, over six-feet tall and generously fleshed, but, as Mrs Gapp would have it, not fat. The two gate-crashers insisted the doctor should do something about the sick Tanah Merah prisoners at Liverpool—admit them to the medical clinic or free them to an Australian hospital.

The doctor was undistracted from first loyalties. "How dare you interfere in the affairs of the Netherlands!" he demanded. It was not hard for the two Australian interviewers to think of the answer—that what went on in an Australian prison camp was the affair of Australians. Mrs Gapp continued her report:

Bartlett Adamson calmly but firmly argued with the Dutch doctor, whose pink health contrasted so glaringly with the condition of the prisoners at Liverpool. Bartlett wanted to know what right the Dutch had to intern in

24

(*above*) Ted Englart, former WWF Brisbane Branch Secretary and a leader of the first Australian boycott of Dutch ships, being escorted off the Brisbane wharves (*below*) WWF Secretary Ted Roach in 1946 at the first national congress of SOBSI, the Indonesian trade union federation, with Tukliwon, Secretary of the Sea and River Workers' Union. Tukliwon — later known as Tuk Subianto — played a leading role among Indonesian exiles in Australia and became a member of the first Indonesian parliament.

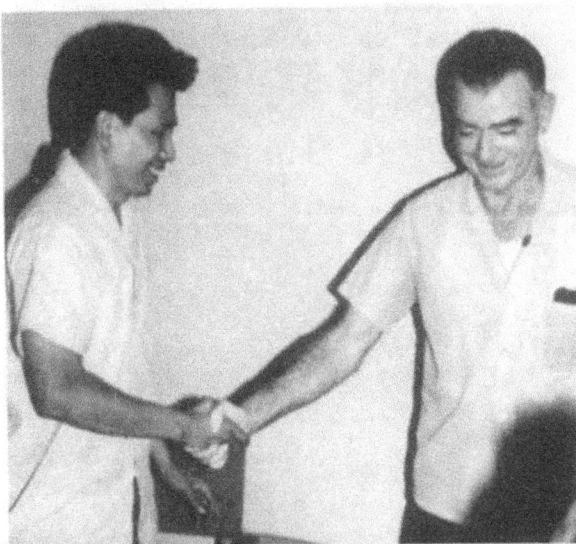

(*above*) Proclamation of the Indonesian Republic on 17 August 1945 was monitored by Indonesians listening round the clock to Batavia Radio on a receiver they had built from components 'borrowed' from the Dutch (*Indonesia Calling*). (*below*) Soekarno, first President of the Republic

an Australian prison camp men completely innocent of any offence against Australian law or persons. The Dutch doctor only began to register when Bartlett told him that the issue of Indonesians held prisoner by the Dutch in Australia and refused proper medical attention would be given the widest publicity throughout Australia, that we were reporting this scandal to Commonwealth and State Governments, political parties, trade unions and cultural bodies.

The Dutch doctor tried to give the impression that his stand was irreversible, but he was obviously concerned. Pressure soon became too strong, and the mounting agitation caused the Curtin Government to make firm representations to the Netherlands Indies leaders.

First Taste of Merdeka

Dr Evatt helped to free the access routes to the Indonesians: he contrived the removal of Dutch guards from the camps in favour of all-Australian supervision, soon after Mrs Gapp made her first report on the sick prisoners at Liverpool. Advanced tuberculosis sufferers and other seriously ill Tanah Merah survivors were moved from Liverpool to the Dutch-run Princess Juliana Hospital at Turramurra on Sydney's North Shore. Numbers of Australians, reading in the Indonesians' plight the indices of colonial deprivation, brought them gifts and news of the war. Some patients quickly recovered under medical treatment and went to various industrial, construction and office jobs to assist the anti-Japanese war effort.

Release of the ailing prisoners from Liverpool reinforced demands that all Indonesians should be freed immediately. The adversities suffered by the Indonesians in the enemy prisoner-of-war camp at Cowra, in the rugged, wind-swept inland of New South Wales, where winters played havoc with Javanese health, affronted Dr Evatt, a lawyer distinguished in the field of civil liberties, though he had to overcome resistance from uncaring colleagues.

First, the Netherlands Indies Commission, serving as the government-in-exile in Australia, was induced to free the rest of the Liverpool internees. Then the gates of D Compound at

Cowra finally swung open to the Indonesians on 7 December 1943—second anniversary of Pearl Harbor. This first taste of *merdeka* in Australia, Tanah Merah exiles' spokesmen acknowledged, was won "after some agitation by the labor movement".[10]

To Australians, their democratic system has inhibitive boundaries. But to the Digul ex-convicts, particularly those in travail since 1926, Australia seemed a libertarian, egalitarian society. They said that they found great inspiration in the Australian democratic example. They had emerged into a society where, for the first time in 17 years for some, they could read this and say that, deliver speeches from public platforms, join trade unions, take white girls to the cinema, catch up on past news. It soon mattered little to them that Dutch and Australian intelligence agents were observed tailing them to trade union offices, to homes of Leftwing Australians and to political meetings. They were confident that after the war the world would know no such place as the Netherlands East Indies. When they accepted service under the Dutch in Australia, it was not only to aid the anti-Japanese war effort but to sabotage the Dutch reoccupation of the Indies, to be launched from Australian bases.

The refugee Netherlands Indies administration had been in Australia for 15 months before the unwilling immigrants from the Digul River were unloaded from trucks in D Compound, Cowra. To mark the unique visitation Prime Minister John Curtin in March 1942 invoked in overkill oratory Henry Lawson's doctrine of mateship to assure the Lieutenant Governor-General of the Netherlands East Indies, Dr Hubertus Johannes Van Mook, that Australia was a land fit for emigre colonial regimes. The Australian national poet had not seen mateship as the consonance of a Labor Government and imperial vice-royalty. Nor would the drift and drag of Asia's winds of change — nor the upheavals plotted by the transplanted Tanah Merah prisoners for Australian wharves, military camps and airfields used by the Dutch — allow the compact for a colonial restoration to prevail.

2   Imported Revolution

By evacuating the political prisoners from the Digul, the Dutch introduced to the Indonesian community established in Australia after Japan's lightning conquest of the Indies a corps of seasoned revolutionaries. Without the Digul prisoners to organise, conspire, lead and propagandise and form liaisons with trade unions and other allies, it is doubtful that there would have been a boycott movement launched, as in September 1945, able to hobble and tether the colonial re-occupation forces at the most crucial period.

Few moderate Indonesian nationalists were brought to Australia by the Netherlands Indies Government to provide checks and balances against the Digul revolutionaries. While the air escape route from Tjilatjap in Java to north-west Australia was still open, the NEI Government offered Dr Sutan Sjahrir and other nationalist leaders passage to Australia. These nationalists stipulated that the Tanah Merah prisoners must be released before the offer could be considered. Dr Sjahrir would not accept safety for himself while men and women he had suffered with remained in the green hell of Tanah Merah and Tanah Tinggi. A few days after the offer of passage to safety, Dr Sjahrir and his friends unexpectedly received a message from the Dutch authorities on Ambon that "the exiles in New Guinea would also be cared for". However, Sjahrir and his nationalist colleagues decided, in the fateful last days, to remain to face the Japanese occupation.[1] Had the Tanah Merah inmates been given free choice they, too, would have refused passage to Australia. As it was they

27

were delivered, only half-understanding by what bells they they were called to an Australia of which they knew little, to the Australian and Dutch guards at Liverpool and Cowra. The Dutch had only themselves to blame for loading into the *Both* well-springs of revolutionary ardour that burst out of their control.

Aboard the *Both* was the leadership core of the Communist Party of Indonesia (PKI).[2] They brought to Australia their experiences of struggle against the Dutch, their ideological deprivations, memories of maltreatment, and hopes resurrected from the graveyard of the 1926 uprising that had cost many their liberty. High on the list of Tanah Merah deprivations they placed news of the wide world from which they were segregated. Sardjono, the leading PKI identity landed in Australia from the Digul, told the writer in Sydney that when Dr Van Der Plas and party arrived at the huts on the Digul River banks he and other prisoners did not know what the second world war was all about. They had only the vaguest idea of Japanese operations and intentions in the Netherlands Indies. Sardjono was the only revolutionary leader in the world who did not know that Trotsky had left the Soviet Union and was dead, that Hitler had seized power in Germany, that Italians had colonised Abyssinia, that Spain had suffered a civil war, that Japan had conquered much of China and that Germany had invaded the USSR.

Revolutionaries Confronted the Past

Dr Van Der Plas and his party had not let much light into this half-lost human congregation on the Digul. Once outside the barbed wire in Australia, the ex prisoners mostly showed diligence in catching up on reading of past events, organising political study groups and learning or improving English. They not only had their bitter memories of Tanah Merah for company in Australia, but the knowledge and damage of past errors of the PKI. These errors they discussed freely with their Australian sympathisers, and their advance from a bottomless marsh of enforced ignorance, sectarian wrangling and mangled lives to an understanding of the new approaches demanded in the era of the second world war were to have decisive influence in triggering the Indonesian mutinies and boycotts against the Netherlands forces mobilised in Australia and, indirectly, on Australian Government policy toward the Dutch-Indonesian confrontation.

Among the ex-prisoners were men of considerable intellect, able to reorientate, relate and understand the past mistakes of the PKI and the requirements of anti-colonial revolution. These Indonesian intellectuals gave to Australian sympathisers their version of the history of a party that was almost to drown in blood two decades later, after the events of 1965.

The version brought to Australia from the Digul by Tanah Merah exiles was that the PKI emerged after the 1917 Russian Revolution. The newly-founded PKI knew only ragged Marxism and less Leninism. Although affiliated to the Communist (Third) International in Moscow, the PKI was more akin to a social democratic than to a communist party. It was influenced by what the PKI intellectuals in Australia regarded as "reformist" theories, sometimes degenerating into a jumble of anarchic tactics. Peasant groups and some shopkeeper-small business organisations were incorporated in or affiliated to the PKI.

The PKI became the spearhead force in the fight to overthrow Dutch rule. In 1926 the PKI raised the slogan of "Soviet Power" instead of "National Independence". This sectarianism and revolutionary romanticism opened the way for effective Dutch offensives against the PKI. Wholesale arrests to crush the 1926 strikes and riots were followed by a thinning-out process, with new leaders and new branches being constantly grabbed by the colonial police, preventing any significant restoration of PKI strength. The most intractable PKI members were sent to the Digul River; those given more moderate ratings by the Dutch Intelligence were held in prisons or less onerous camps.

The "New PKI"

In the efforts to rebuild the PKI after the 1926 debacle, emphasis was on a more modern Marxist-Leninist party, on the Soviet model. Close attention was now given to the theories of Marx, Lenin and Stalin on the colonial question. Attrition by internment remained an acute problem, but there was enough organisation in Java for two groupings to be identified — the "Old PKI" and the "New PKI'.

The Old PKI tended to remain locked in the cages of dogmas that contributed to the 1926 defeat, and neglected to adjust to changes made necessary by the rampages of Japan, Hitler's Germany and Mussolini's Italy. This PKI sector relied too narrowly on simplistic resentments of Dutch colonial rule to furnish the steam for the engines of revolutionary upheaval.

The New PKI forces were dedicated to throwing off the old "reformist" and anarchist influences and to building a broad alliance of Indonesian independence supporters to find a national alternative to Dutch rule acceptable to the Indonesian majority. In Java the inner party conflict was muffled and distorted by Dutch censorship and the beheading of the party by constant arrests. The inner party struggle moved to Tanah Merah, where leaders of the New PKI were joining the veterans of 1926.

The New PKI reinforcements to the Tanah Merah exiles were mostly enthusiasts who had become party members in full awareness of internment dangers. They were usually tough in nerve and spirit. Some were among the most highly educated men in the NEI. Stumbling barefooted down the *Both's* gangplank at Sydney were graduates of Netherlands and Asian universities, including Leyden university in Holland, where a radical academic group had been directing attention to Indies grievances, and Peking and Canton, then centres of nationalist ferment. Others had managed to enter select higher schools in Java. A few had degrees equivalent to Bachelor of Arts, Bachelor of Engineering or Bachelor of Science. A sizable group from the Digul commanded artisan skills in electrical, engineering and metal trades. One of the internees in Cowra's D Compound spoke eleven languages; another six. Sufficient of the New PKI internees spoke English and Dutch to hold language classes in Tanah Merah. Hence the Indonesians sent to Australia from New Guinea were blessed by a high quota with a working knowledge of English, including Sardjono and other PKI leaders, while some spoke German, French, English, Chinese or Hindi. Engineers and electricians conducted technical classes, which explains why Tanah Merah men were able, from components bought in Australian shops or removed from Dutch stores, to put together radio receivers and monitor broadcasts from the Japanese-occupied Indies.

The New PKI intellectuals in Tanah Merah propagandised among Muslims as well as the Old PKI members. Muslim nationalist leaders were sent to Tanah Merah along with PKI activists, and were not ready listeners to PKI advice. One Muslim group wanted restoration of rajah power and feudal relations and a theorcratic state to rule an independent Indonesia. Another Muslim grouping was more democratic, and in favour of unity with politically diverse forces in a republican coalition.

The New PKI inevitably rose to the top among the political groupings in Tanah Merah; it commanded the support of most of the interned intellectuals, whose experiences were more recent and whose capacities for conspiratorial organisation more sophisticated. The New PKI intellectuals' education drive in Tanah Merah won over many non-party prisoners, fractured the dogmas of those of Old PKI orientation, and earned gratitude and prestige. Education classes had been essential relief from the stark and austere existence; they had modified the stringencies of life in the fetid jungle and had sustained morale. Nevertheless, many prisoners could not answer the roll call for the *Both*'s journey. They had succumbed to the despair and mental stresses portrayed by Dr Sjahrir. Suicides and mental breakdowns, so the Tanah Merah survivors told friends in Australia, were common. Prisoners were known to rush off into the jungle where, as reports fostered by Dutch guards had it, they became cannibal diet. The influx of New PKI intellectuals, from the time of the Great Depression in the early 'thirties up to Japan's move into South-East Asia, prevented worse deterioration of morale and, thanks to an historic Dutch blunder, set in motion the fateful disruptions suffered by the Netherlands armed forces and supply ships mobilised in Australia for the march back.

Illegal Organisation in Australia

Once ordered up the gangway of the *Both*, berthed in the Digul, the new PKI began to regroup, to establish a directing leadership and grouplets that would make illegal work possible, once they were in Australia. All this did not mean that the PKI members had a ready-made organisation in good shape when they settled into D Compound at Cowra. The jungle tomb of Tanah Merah was too isolated for prisoners to follow the march of events in the outside world. Theory was divorced from practice and experience, and therefore was often barren. Ideas withered because they could not be applied, or refreshed as new political situations developed in the world. In Cowra and Liverpool, the censorship curtain was thin; they became better informed and better organised.

The Tanah Merah prisoners were infinitely more advanced and richer in political experience and cadres than were the Indonesians already in Australia as members of the Netherlands Indies armed forces, government-in-exile staffs, shipping companies and ships' crews. These pre-*Both* Indonesians were virtually leaderless. Republican sentiment was strong, but they had no apparent republican-orientated organisation nor the nucleus of one. When the Tanah Merah prisoners signed the release documents in 1943, this was soon altered.

Liberty for the Tanah Merah prisoners, won by trade union, civil-libertarian and Australian Government pressures on the Netherlands emigre regime, helped to tear down some of the remaining barriers between the various political groupings. In breach of the general rule, disunity in servitude began to give way to unity in freedom. Thus ended the segregation of the politically conscious prisoners from the Indonesian seamen, soldiers, aircrewmen, civil servants, shipping clerks and others in the NEI Government service in Australia.

There was hardly any need to refer to the "New PKI" when the releases were won. The Old PKI forces were fading fast and by mid-1944 had ceased to count for much. The PKI came out of Cowra with a central organisation, headed by Sardjono, and incorporating various branches or units. Once established in New South Wales and Queensland, with members here and there in other States, it was easy enough to recruit to membership or win the support of Indonesians who had been free since their arrival early in 1942.

Various claims have been made on how and when the decision to boycott Dutch shipping, supplies and services was taken. One claim was that it began with a resolution of Sydney waterside workers, another by an approach from an Indonesian representative to the Seamen's Union head office in Sydney, and conclusions were drawn from the fact that the boycott first began at Brisbane wharves. The Menzies-led Opposition and the metropolitan press blamed the Communist Party of Australia and Communist trade union officials. Mr J. C. Henry[3], the Australian most active among the Indonesian community in Australia, particularly Queensland and New South Wales, who had more knowledge of their planning than any other Australian, and was a member of the Communist Party National Secretariat and learned to speak Indonesian, said that the boycott did not begin in any decision taken by any Australian organisation. "The intention to act," he said, "was there from the day the Tanah Merah prisoners arrived in Australia, as evidenced by the note thrown to the wharf at Bowen. The plan to sabotage Dutch reoccupation of the Indies was in the minds of the Tanah Merah prisoners from the start: it was just a question of the action unfolding."

Key Jobs for Ex-Prisoners

None could accuse the colonial Dutch of political sophistication. They were hooked on the idea that they had devised the most successful, most benevolent form of colonialism in the world, and the natives could not but be grateful for the blessings. The rising of 1926 had been a nasty aberration, but the ex-Tanah Merah prisoners, now working for the Dutch and their allies in Australia on good wages, must see the error of their ways. Or perhaps the Dutch were lulled to a false sense of security by the backing of America, now the mightiest power on earth, of Britain and other powers pledged to help reinstall them in the Indies. In any event, the Netherlands Indies authorities had no due appreciation of the threat the ex-Tanah Merah prisoners represented to their postwar ambitions. They had asked the Australian Government for re-internment facilities so that dangerous subversives could not lend aid and comfort to the enemy, once they shifted them from New Guinea to New South Wales. The Dutch opposed the release of these security risks. After release against the Dutch will, the Netherlands authorities contrived, oddly, to place many of them where they could do the colonial interest the greatest harm.

The liberated Indonesians were sent to civil and military jobs, mostly through the agency of the Allied Works Council, the wartime employment directorate set up by the Government. Queensland was recognised as the most amenable climate for Javanese who had not fared well in the forests and cold winds of Cowra and Liverpool. Mackay, in north-central Queensland, saw the biggest ex-Tanah Merah concentration. Here the Dutch had offices where the better educated ex-prisoners worked as clerks, handling documents. Some were in north Queensland sugar mills. Others went to the Netherlands Indies Government-in-Exile's offices at Brisbane, to the Royal Netherlands Indies Air Force station at Bundaberg as aircrewmen, mechanics and airport labourers; to labouring and technical jobs in munitions factories and depots, foundries, construction, service and railway maintenance work at Blackbutt, Toowoomba and Helidon, Queensland. The Dutch saw nothing incongruous in using technical skills learned on the Digul at their Casino military base in northern New South Wales, or at their Bundaberg air base. In Brisbane, Sydney and Melbourne, Tanah Merah men joined other Indonesians in sea transport services related to supply of Dutch ships and military units as they moved into the islands north of Australia, and in clerical and technical occupations.

Tanah Merah rebels were thus in jobs productive in knowledge of Dutch air, sea and land movement, whereabouts of munitions stores and nature of ships' cargoes. They had access to the contents of messages to the Netherlands Indies apparatus in Australia from General Douglas MacArthur's Southwest Pacific Command, from the Royal Netherland Government-in-Exile in London, from Australian Government departments in Canberra and other suppliers of vital intelligence.

The ex-Tanah Merah men were also within speaking range of Labor Party and Communist Party organisations, Trades and Labor Councils in Brisbane and north Queensland and trade union shop stewards. Those allotted to industrial jobs won, with Australian support, Australian standards in hours and working conditions, and joined Australian trade unions.

These contacts were to prove of great importance in the coming Indonesian struggle against the Dutch establishment in emigration.

The Tanah Merah men worked alongside Indonesians who had come to Australia with the Netherlands Indies administration, armed forces and shipping fleet, propagating among them the idea of postwar revolution against the Dutch. The deep undertow of hatred and resolve imported from New Guinea drew in many Indonesian exiles of less bruising experience. The pitch of feeling was infectious.

For a "Democratic People's Republic"

The Communist Party of Indonesia was, in all its effective forms and personnel, based in Australia and not in the Japanese-occupied Netherlands East Indies, where it could scarcely claim a surviving unit. The Dutch had sent the party's cadres to Tanah Merah and the Japanese terror was all-pervasive. The Communist Party of Australia was faced with a problem unique in its experience: a foreign Communist Party operated within its territorial preserves. The PKI based in Australia was the only decisive organisation and representation of the Indonesian Communist movement, and it had no contact with or direction from the occupied Indies. As a concession to the Communist Party of Australia's territorial rights, the PKI agreed to function under the title of "Foreign Section of the PKI operating among the Indonesian People in Australia". This semantic elasticity did not alter the fact that the operational headquarters of the PKI was on Australian soil. The PKI was never incorporated in any way in the CPA structure. Though advised by the CPA, the PKI retained its independence, and at first made sectarian errors that made CPA hairs stand on end.

The PKI brought many problems with it from behind the barbed wire of D Compound. Not a few of its members still spoke in the warmed-up cliches of 1926, and resisted cooperation with the NEI Government-in-Exile. There were numerous discussions between CPA and PKI leaders: the Australian advice was delivered in firm terms, that support of the war against the Axis was essential, because victory would spark anti-colonial revolutions in Asia. This line won overwhelming majority support in PKI ranks, and it was carried through the Indonesian community.

Sardjono, sprung from the Old PKI, had ameliorated his views sufficiently to lead the PKI in Australia, as President. He came to understand that Japan's defeat would open the road toward republican power. The Javanese who had been a leader of the disorganised assault on Dutch authority in 1926 and came to an intensity of hatred in Tanah Merah, set an example in the tactic of "one step backward for two steps forward" by donning a Dutch uniform, as Netherlands Indies Government-in-Exile Public Relations Officer.

It was a fragile commitment that Sardjono and his party made to the Dutch. The spirit of rebellion ran deep, and the Dutch reinforced it by arrogant paternalism. By mid-1944 republican groups, called Indonesian Independence Committees, embracing PKI members, Muslims and non-affiliated Indonesians, were formed, semi-secretly. The slogan was for a republic, not for soviet or socialist power as in the sectarian days of 1926. The future regime would be, the PKI in Australia preached, a "democratic people's republic" that would be "bourgeois democratic". The nucleus of a republican command structure, destined to supplant Dutch authority over the Indonesians in Australia, was taking shape in the middle of 1944.

Intelligence Leaks

Through its own widespread organisation of branches and contacts, the CPA gave special assistance in establishing for the Indonesian Independence Committees communication between the various Indonesian groups in Australia, separated often by vast distances and not able to trust the mails. The ex-Digul internees at Mackay speedily approached the local CPA branch; they did the same at Helidon (Toowoomba branch), at Bundaberg air base where there were communists among the Australian Air Force men, and, of course, in the state capitals of Brisbane, Sydney, Melbourne and Perth, whose port, Fremantle, served as a Dutch Navy base. CPA branches acted as post offices for the Indonesians, delivering their communications by hand, usually through communists in the railways, maritime transport and the armed forces.

Surprisingly, the Indonesians found a few sympathisers among non-executive Dutch clerical staff and rank-and-file members of the Dutch armed forces. These Dutchmen kept their opinions from NEI Government officialdom and armed forces officers, but provided to the PKI and Indonesian Independence Committees information of material benefit in the assessment of Dutch policies and reoccupation plans.

With Australian standard wages the Indonesians were able to afford radio receivers or components to assemble them. They regularly monitored radio stations in the occupied Indies. The Indonesians in Australia were quick to grasp that in the broadcasting services of the Japanese-sponsored Soekarno regime were some well clued-up Indonesians who, by various ruses, were releasing information of guidance to Indonesian exiles in Australia. Indonesians working in the NEI Government offices also had access to Allied radio monitoring reports and to what intelligence could be collected on the Indies by Colonel Simon H. Spoor's department, set up to establish intelligence contact with the occupied Indies.

Denial of replenishments from Holland, held tight in the Nazis' grip, forced the NEI Government into heavy reliance on Indonesians for key clerical and technical posts. Thus intelligence leaks to the Indonesian republican forces in Australia were facilitated. With republican sympathisers in all the Dutch departments in Australia, and several cooperative Hollanders ready to help, the PKI and Independence Committees often knew the contents of messages from the Royal Netherlands Government in London, and later in reconquered Holland, before the NEI Government, its armed forces commanders and diplomatic and supply services in Australia.

The Indonesian independence forces in Australia learned enough to feel certain that when Japan was defeated Dutch rule would be forcibly rejected by a newly established national government. In their discussions with Australian friends the Indonesians predicted that the battle for the republic would be long and bloody. Their part of the action would, in the opening stages, not be in Indonesia but in Australia, disrupting Dutch shipping, aircraft and other transport movements to inhibit the return of the Netherlands Indies Government and its reoccupation apparatus. They could not start the

37

Indonesian revolution but they would be the first republicans to give battle to the colonial regime. But republican power in Australia was not to come out of the barrel of a gun.

From the beginning the PKI advised — commanded might be the better word — the Indonesians in Australia that they were to refrain strictly from use of arms or other violence when the time came for strikes and mutinies, even if provoked by the Dutch. They were tutored on this point by the CPA. Armed action in Australia, the Indonesians were told, would affront Australian tradition: though they were temporarily resident in a land that knew massive strike movements and demonstrations, all disputes tended to be solved without bloodshed. Armed action, even in self-defence, would be used by the pro-Dutch forces in Australia to rouse a scare-and-hate campaign against the Indonesians. The Indonesian community faithfully followed this advice, which originated with the CPA, when the Dutch reacted violently to mutinies at Casino military camp and Bundaberg air base.

Hope, conspiracy and intent were translated to action when Dutch ships in the Brisbane River, having begun loading munitions and embarking Netherlands Indies Government and Royal Netherlands Indies Army troops, got up a head of steam for a rendezvous with Lord Louis Mountbatten's Southeast Asia Command forces in Batavia. They were PKI men from aboard the ships in the Brisbane River who brought word to the Queensland Trades and Labor Council that the Indonesian crews would not take the Dutch ships to sea.

3 The Dutch Rediscover Harmonyland

Off Dampier Land coast, 60 miles or so north of Broome, a king's ransom lies in the crystalline deeps. Less than half an hour from the safety of Broome's airfield the last aircraft to leave Java with Dutch refugees, a DC3, was shot into the sea by Japanese Zeros. The Dutch DC3 "happened to be carrying a valuable consignment of diamonds".[1]

Diamonds cut in Amsterdam and viceroys from Batavia, bank drafts and police archives, ships of war and commerce, soldiers and civil servants came in haste to Australia from a Dutch Empire of the East that was in darkening eclipse. These arrivals of February and March 1942 were the panoply and personnel of the first and only government-in-exile to which Australia gave sanctuary. Giant Dutch Dornier and Qantas flying-boats, Royal Air Force, Royal Australian Air Force and American bombers and transport planes were pressed into a shuttle service to Broome to clear the last evacuation centre at Tjilatjap in Java. As the Japanese invading force ran like a stain over the Indies archipelago, Broome, the dilapidated, dozing pearling port, was swiftly converted to a hustling international airport.

Fremantle, the Brisbane River and Sydney Harbour were host to warships, passenger and cargo vessels, fleeing south from what had been the Netherlands East Indies, now in the Japanese Co-Prosperity Sphere. On the Australian waterfront the ships were called the "Flying Dutchmen".

Dutch refugees clambering from the flying-boats in Broome's Roebuck Bay were ferried in small craft to a shore of schoolbook memories. As children they had studied Dutch cartography that converted *Terra Australis Incognita* from the elusive wonderland of the ancients to faltering lines on the route to the Spiceries.

United East India Company skipper Dirk Hartog was first to make a landfall, leaving his plate in 1616 on the west coast's central bulge and naming his discovery Eendrachtsland (Harmonyland), after his ship *Eendracht*. Other Dutch explorers followed to strew the Australian coast with Dutch names, but, failing to pass the South Australian gulfs or Cape York, found neither trade goods nor an adobe hamlet to plead with the solitudes of Harmonyland.

The Dutch, who by the ironies of history rediscovered Harmonyland in 1942, understood readily why their ancestors aboard East Indiamen relinquished their undeveloped estate. Alighting, hungry and shaken, from aircraft at Broome, they gazed inland at desolate wastes where goats and kangaroos competed for sparse desert shrubbery. Their tribulations in Australia were to mock the name Dirk Hartog bestowed on the coastline.

Broome's hotels and private homes were thrown open to the unexpected guests. The school became a canteen. But while Broome offered hospitality there was little of the old romance and deviltry. Around them in the sunbaked town the Dutch from Tjilatjap saw testimony to the fading lure of Australian pearls. Pearls two decades before had been been Western Australia's fifth industry. Four-hundred luggers put out from Broome. Some 2,300 divers were employed, of whom about 1,700 were Indonesians and quite a few Japanese. Only a few hundred now remained of all the Malays and Manilamen, Koepangers and Timorese, Sinhalese and South Sea Islanders who provided the grisly martyrology of the north-west Australian pearling industry. The Japanese divers left before the war, to serve their own pearling luggers.

As evidence of a quaint contradiction in the White Australia Policy — a policy which the Dutch guests were soon to misinterpret — the Japanese "geisha house" still stood above the desolate horizon. For most pearl-divers relief of this kind ashore was a must. They would sometimes surface from the pearl and trocus beds of the Indian Ocean floor, bleeding from ears and noses, eyes bulging from sockets, and feeling the first twinges of divers' paralysis, a condition remote from the necklaces that graced women's necks in London, New York or Paris.

In their charity administrators of the White Australia Policy allowed Japanese "geisha girls" — the occupation must have read better than "whore" on an immigration form — to land at Broome, though Chinese girls were rigidly excluded. Japanese prostitutes, the Department of Immigration no doubt concluded, knew the facts of life and were not so likely to breed little non-white Australians as the less sophisticated Chinese women. (The "geisha house" which the Dutch refugees saw at Broome in 1942 was being advertised for sale "with an ocean view" in 1960.) Some of the girls who served for pounds and pearls in a sellers' market at Broome mothered children. Babies of mixed race were conceived amid sand and scrub or on the mangrove-fringed bayside. There were respectable inter-race marriages, too. Broome knew an easier tolerance than other Australian frontier towns, and racial affront was rare. The Java Dutch who flew in over the Roebuck Deeps and Buccaneer Rocks — reminders of the *Roebuck's* navigator, William Dampier, of the tough Yucatan pirate school who had spread sail to depart a coast offering no Santa Martas to sack, and to trade two years in Indies islands of a proximity to north-west Australia now proving fateful — had little time to study at Broome a unique community. South Sea Islanders, Indonesians and Aborigines were soon digging a mass grave for numbers of them in Broome cemetery, next to those who did not survive the pearl-beds.

Tjilatjap to Broome

Admiral Nagumo's fast carrier group, fresh from its shoddy triumph at Pearl Harbor, turned into the wind in the Timor Sea on 19 February 1942. Two hours later the Japanese 21st Flotilla's warplanes followed from Kandari in the Celebes. Darwin became a shambles in this first bombardment of Australia from the air, deliverable because Netherlands Indies bases had fallen so easily. The escape route from Java was switched from the shattered Darwin base to poorly equipped, undefended Broome.

As Java's time ran out, Tjilatjap, the Dutch-British-American-Australian war base on the south-central coast facing North-West Australia, became the main escape port. Javanese crowding the streets and saronged women doing their daily marketing as they had for a thousand years saw a stream of jeeps and trucks hustling their way to the waterfront. The little carriages that looked like toy trains on the narrow-gauge railway to Tjilatjap disembarked crowds of hot, dishevelled women and crying children. Aircraft carried more civilian and uniformed refugees hoping against hope for passage to Australia. Many got aboard HMAS *Bendigo* and the Dutch ships *Zaandam* and *Khoen Hoa*. Some of the ships in Tjilatjap harbour had lost their Dutch and Indonesian crews; among them, *General Verspijck* was manned by survivors from sunken British warships. The last ships got away for Western Australia late on the night of March 1, when the Japanese were near. Ships still arriving off Tjilatjap in the few days left were ordered to scurry for Fremantle or Colombo. A few refugee ships were lost by enemy action, but most of the seaborne Dutch refugees made it to Western Australia.

The Qantas and British, Dutch and American air force pilots stepped up the escapes by air before Admiral Nagumo followed up his Darwin carnage by bombarding Tjilatjap, causing 17 ships to be sunk or scuttled and many despairing refugees and Indonesian civilians to die.

The official chronicler of the Australian Air Force contribution in the Pacific War, Douglas Gillison, gave an idea of the scope of this emergency evacuation service:

> As many as 57 aircraft arrived in Broome in one day, and in 14 days between 7,000 and 8,000 passengers passed through the base. The strain on aircrew was severe, some of them remaining on the ground only to eat a hurried meal and make ready for take-off as soon as their aircraft had been refuelled; one pilot even recorded 84 hours' duty without rest.[2]

Priorities for the Dutch

The splash and roar of the great Qantas and Dornier flying-boats on Tjilatjap's calm waters drew Australians as well as Hollanders, but evacuation priorities seemed for the Dutch. Lieutenant-General H. Gordon Bennett, Australian military commander in Malaya, who cheated Japanese gaolers by an epic boat voyage from Singapore, hitch-hiked a ride to Tjilatjap from Bandung and approached a Qantas pilot for a lift to Australia. The Qantas pilot, under charter for Dutch refugees, could not take the Australian commander. General Bennett stowed away on a plane on the night of 26 February, reached Broome next day and on 28 February was aboard a Dutch aircraft for Charleville in Queensland.

The 160 officers and airmen of No.1 Squadron, RAAF, were too late in reaching Tjilatjap. On 5 March Japanese bombers devastated the port. Most of them, under Wing-Commander R.H.S. Davis, spent the rest of the war in prison camps. Unable to find air passage, Wing-Commander J. R. Jeudwine, Pilot-Officer M. S. MacDonald and Sergeants G. W. Sayer, W. N. Cosgrove, J. A. Lovegrove, A. C. Longmore, A. C. E. Snook, P. A. Haynes and P. M. Corney accomplished a Bligh-style open-boat navigation, leaving Java on 7 March and reaching north-west Australia on 18 April. They covered 1,500 miles in 44 days, happy to be ignored by a Japanese submarine but watched over "for what seemed a lifetime" by a big whale.[3]

The Australian Army's 2/2nd Pioneers were not aware that the Dutch Commander-in-Chief in the Indies, General Hein ter Poorten, had met the Japanese Commander-in-Chief at Kalidjati on the afternoon of 8 March, and surrendered to Japan all Dutch and Allied troops in the Netherlands Indies. Dutch Intelligence and liaison with British and Australian allies was always deficient: General ter Poorten had not consulted them on capitulation.

The Australians remained at their battle stations on three days after the surrender — 9, 10 and 11 March. They tried to contact the Australian Government for instructions, but all radio communication was at an end. Seeking escape routes, the Pioneers set off for the sea. At Tjibadak on the road to Buitenzorg they were told the Dutch had surrendered. Some 67 of them tried to battle through to Tjilatjap, not knowing the Japanese had destroyed the port on 5 March. On 13

March they slogged wearily into nearby Palabuhan and went to the KPM shipping office to inquire about sailings to Australia. No more ships would sail. The Pioneers divided up into guerilla bands and fought on in the mountains. The last Australian guerilla band was captured by the Japanese on 2 August 1942.[4]

Another straggling band of Australian soldiers narrowly escaped the same fate, after a long retreat from Singapore. They were sappers of the 2/10th Field Company, Royal Australian Engineers, of the Eighth Division lost by the British surrender at Singapore. Sapper Lewis Hillier,[5] then aged 20 and part of the defending force on the Straits of Johore, described how 14 of his unit, after being thrown into disorder by the Japanese, began their long journey to Tjilatjap and Western Australia. The confused 14, grouping in a church-yard near the Padang in central Singapore, were told by an Australian infantry officer: "Singapore has had it – everyone should fend for himself." The band of Australians got to an old pinnace-type boat with a Dodge motor engine, and per-suaded an obstinate Malay driver, at tommy-gun point, to change his mind about a passage out of doomed Singapore. The Australians put some European women and children aboard, took off into Keppel Harbor and into the eye of a Japanese bomb storm. The boat pulled alongside a small steamer. A Scots captain at the rail agreed to accept the women and children, then invited all into his ship, saying, "I'm getting out." Though machine-gunned by Japanese planes, the steamer got to Batavia.

A malaria-stricken Sapper Hillier, lying on a heap of bunker coal, woke from a fevered daze to see a green-uniformed, jackbooted officer in a cap like that of a panzer-korps man and thought he was in Nazi hands, but it slowly dawned on him that the officer was Dutch.

The Australians, mostly ragged and barefooted by this time, went ashore penniless. Geoffrey Tebbutt, the Melbourne *Herald* war correspondent, gave them six shillings. He didn't have much loose cash.

A detachment of the Seventh Australian Division, landed from the Middle East, was in Batavia. Officers paraded the bedraggled escapees and temporarily allotted them to ex-

Middle East units. "There'll be no escaping from here!" one Seventh Division officer warned the Singapore survivors. But the Eighth Division soldiers in the threatened Netherlands Indies capital were later given the choice of staying with their new units or moving on in a body. They chose to stay together and move on. After a slow train to Tjilatjap, they marched, or limped through streets of tropical foliage, atap huts, Dutch villas and office buildings, to the waterfront, attracting only a few glances from Indonesians by now accustomed to the flight of Europeans to Australia. Tjilatjap confirmed the verdict of too little, too late.

Sapper Hillier and his companions saw unused guns, vehicles and other military equipment and American planes still in wraps, waiting Japanese takeover. Sapper Hillier remembers leaving the teeming Tjilatjap streets, the carts drawn by oxen, the abandoned vehicles and armaments, to embark in a cockle-sized steamer. On the harbour were flying boats: the shuttle service to Broome was in its last hours.

For company aboard the steamer were British sailors, survivors of the battleships *Repulse* and *Prince of Wales*, defenceless, without air cover, when Japanese bombers sank them in the Gulf of Siam. Sailors and soldiers were down the cargo hold, living on hard biscuits, rice and bully beef.

The ship sailed from Tjilatjap into a setting sun — "a ball of red fire" as Sapper Hillier called it — and just in time. Flashes from explosions signalled the Japanese death sentence on the Tjilatjap evacuation base. Japanese planes shadowed the small steamer but it looked so nondescript that they did not waste bombs. Ten days out from Tjilatjap, Dutch-discovered Rottnest Island was in sight. In the warm sunshine of the Swan River at Fremantle, the unlisted passengers disembarked, only dimly aware that they had been witnesses to the decline and fall of the two greatest European empires in Asia.

Easy Targets for Zeros

Broome's Roebuck Bay moorings served only three flying-boats: the rest anchored. Big Dutch Dorniers and Qantas Empire flying-boats lay high and dry on mud from which a thirty-foot tide raced away. Disembarkation was slow and difficult. Some remained aboard for long periods. Fuelling was by drums from a lighter. On Broome's aerodrome, Flying Fortress, Liberator, Hudson, Douglas and other bombing and transport planes were landing the Dutch from Tjilatjap, along with a few Britons, Americans and Australians. Nearly 180 Aborigines, South Sea Islanders, Indonesians and other Asians whom pearl-diving had lured to Broome maintained the runway, sufficient for heavy bombers.

Japanese Zeros began to prowl the Tjilatjap-Broome escape route after the 19 February bombing of Darwin. Captain L. R. Ambrose, of Qantas Empire flying-boat *Coriolanus*, landing Dutch refugees at Broome from Tjilatjap on 27 February, reported that Japanese invasion of Java was near.

On that day the crew of Qantas flying-boat *Circe* (Captain W. B. Burton commander) died in action south of Tjilatjap on the way to pick up more Dutch evacuees. Flying-boats on the way back from Broome searched for *Circe*, but no trace was ever found. *Corio* was also lost, a sacrifice by Australians in the carriage of the Dutch from Java.

Java was invaded on 1 March and sentence was speedily carried out on Tjilatjap and Broome. On 2 March a Japanese reconnaissance aircraft came down over the Buccaneer Archipeligo and circled Broome three times at about nine thousand feet in the mid-afternoon. The pilot observed sufficient to invite his colleagues to follow next day.

Three flying-boats were in Roebuck Bay and thirteen more were on the way from Tjilatjap. Four of them alighted before dusk and nine arrived during the night. Big bombers and transport craft were on the aerodrome. With 16 flying-boats sitting like ducks on the harbour and stranded at low tide, captains were warned to be off as soon after daybreak as possible. From the lighter *Nicol Bay*, Captain H. Mathieson worked through the night to refuel three Dutch Dorniers by drums. The warnings were not heeded. Only a float-plane had taken off when Japanese Zeros swept down on Broome at 9.20 am on 3 March.

A Royal Australian Air Force flying-boat was shot up first. Other flying-boats were soon blazing or sinking and refugees were struggling in the sea. Of 24 aircraft lost in the 3 March raid on Broome, two were RAAF Empire flying-boats, three were Royal Netherlands Indies Air Force Dorniers, two were British and two were American Catalinas. There were seven other flying-boats, most of them, presumably, belonging to Qantas.

On Broome aerodrome were two American Flying Fortresses and two Liberator bombers, one Dutch Hudson bomber, one RAAF plane and, in the air, not far from Broome, was the Dutch DC3 transport loaded with refugees and diamonds from Java. The American crew of one Liberator managed to take off, but, like the diamond-carrying DC3 was shot down in the sea. All the big planes on the aerodrome were lost. The Japanese made quick work of Broome, the staging base for evacuation of the Indies Dutch. In 15 minutes they destroyed every sea and land aircraft.

Death and Courage in Roebuck Bay

Refugees had remained aboard some of the flying-boats, expecting to take off soon to Port Hedland on the next stage of the journey south. Men, women and children, wounded or shocked, were splashing in bloodied water to keep afloat.

For empire-minded people shrinking pains are more acute than growing pains. The colonial Dutch refugees, shaken by the predicaments of flight to a strange, desolate-looking land, their dream of safety after the demoralising military defeat of their arms in the Indies shattered by the Zeros' machine-guns, could have been forgiven had they panicked during the Broome ordeal. In disaster they found honour. The last resident white woman to leave Broome after the bombing, unnamed because of censorship, said:

> Those Dutch refugees were absolutely marvellous . . . They were left with nothing but the clothes in which they stood, but they endured the ordeal without a tear, without a word of complaint. One Dutchman left Java with six children and a brave wife. After the raid at Broome he was left with a wounded wife and two children. Another man lost his wife and two children.[6]

Captain Lester Brain, Australian air pioneer and at that time operations manager with Qantas, had contracted fever in Broome. But he rushed to the harbour front, shoved a small boat into the water with the aid of Mr Malcolm Millar, from the Qantas agency in Singapore, who had arrived that morning by US Flying Fortress, and began rescuing victims. Brain and Millar found a Dutchman supporting a Dutch girl near to collapse and drowning. Next they saved a man holding the woman's baby, then a Dutch boy; and four men trying to swim ashore were crowded into their boat.

Qantas flying-boat *Corinna's* crew dived into Roebuck Bay, grabbed a dinghy from one of the pearling luggers at anchor and went among refugees who were struggling for life in the harbour. They packed as many as they could find into the dinghy. Fortunately, the Japanese Zeros did not strafe those in the water. Captain Lester Brain thought 35 to 40 people were killed in the 3 March raid and as many wounded. But there were, too, the crew of the Liberator bomber and the refugees aboard the Dutch DC3 down in the ocean. Of the 33 Americans in the Liberator when it came down in flames in Roebuck Bay, only a US Army sergeant lived — after 30 hours in the sea.

There were no records for identification of most Dutch evacuees from Java who perished in the strafing of Broome. Twenty-nine of those buried in Broome cemetery over the next day or so are in nameless graves. The destructive Japanese bombing of Tjilatjap two days later was superfluous. The wrecked and burned flying-boats left high and dry by the Indian Ocean tide at Broome signalled the closing of the escape route to north-west Australia from the Netherlands Indies.

4   The Netherlands Indies Government-in-Exile

The Tjilatjap-Broome shuttle service and the Dutch warships and merchant fleet that crowded into Brisbane, Sydney and Fremantle and later spread to other ports carried to Australia a substantial nucleus of political, economic and military leaders.

Wartime censorship delayed news of their arrival for a few days, but the *Sydney Morning Herald* of 10 March 1942 carried a 9 March message from Adelaide, announcing the arrival of Dr Van Mook and "a party of high Indies officials".

The party, the *Herald* said, came by air, "escaping in the teeth of a Japanese attack from the last strip of runway available". It included members of the NEI Governing Council and "certain high officers of the fighting services with technical people".

Among names given were those of Dr Van Mook's deputy, Dr Charles Van Der Plas; General H. Van Oyen, Commander-in-Chief, Netherlands Indies Air Force; Messrs H. Greutsberg, C. Gisbel, Mr and Mrs Arens, Messrs S. Van Der Molen and P. Bouten. An Indonesian member of the Governing Council, Admiral C. E. L. Helfrich, Netherlands Indies Navy leader of valiant but hopeless sea battles against the Japanese, and various other service chiefs were already in Sydney.

Dr Van Mook was asked about wives and children. "We all had to leave them behind," he replied. "We do not know where they are or how long it will be before we hear of them again." Dr Van Mook's wife suffered till the war's end in a concentration camp, but numbers of Dutch women escaped to Australia — enough to form a Women's Auxiliary Force, attached to the armed forces.

The following day, 11 March, the *Sydney Morning Herald* noted that Dr Van Mook had come to Melbourne from Adelaide with General Van Oyen and Dr Van Der Plas. More names of Netherlands Indies leaders to reach Australia safely were given on 12 March. They comprised:

Messrs R. A. A. Soejono, member of the Council of the Indies; R. Loekman Djajadiningrat, Director of the Department of Education and Public Worship; N. S. Blom, Director of the Department of Justice; A. H. Lovink, Director of the Bureau of Far Eastern Affairs; P. H. Sitzen, head of the Industrial Section, Department of Economic Affairs; J. T. Creme, Director of Deli Tobacco Company; D. Crena de Iongh, Director of the Netherlands Indies Foreign Exchange Bureau; Professor J. Eggens, Professor of Civil Law at the University of Batavia, and W. Vogt, Manager of Javastaal Company.

Mr Vogt was attached to the Netherlands Purchasing Commission in Melbourne. This Commission had been established before Pearl Harbor, following the visit to Australia in October 1941 of a Netherlands Indies delegation led by Dr Van Der Plas.

Like Dr Van Der Plas, Dr Van Mook was no stranger in Australia. As the Japanese Army spilled down the Malayan Peninsula, invaded Borneo and bombed Indies bases, Dr Van Mook flew to Australia on 6 January for war talks with Mr Curtin. While in Canberra he arranged with Dr Evatt the first exchange of diplomats between Australia and the Netherlands Indies. Lieutenant-Colonel Eugene Gorman, in peacetime a wellknown Melbourne lawyer, reached Batavia as Australian Consul-General on 4 February, but, as the Dutch surrendered a month later, his mission was brief.

Dr Van Mook presumably discussed in January plans to use Australia as the Dutch recovery base should the Indies fall to Japan. On 6 March NEI Economic Affairs Director J. E. Van Hoogstraaden was in Australia: when he left Java Batavia and Bandung had yet to fall. Sufficient NEI representatives were in Melbourne to lay the foundations of an administration in exile before General ter Poorten offered capitulation to the Japanese Command in Java on 8 March. While Dr Van Mook and Dr Van der Plas were the recognised leaders, the Royal Netherlands Government in London at first nominated Dr Van Hoogstraaden as Netherlands Indies Commissioner for External and Maritime Affairs in Australia and New Zealand, pending the formation of the Netherlands Indies Commission for Australia and New Zealand, to be headed by the Viceroy, Dr Van Mook, and Dr Van Der Plas.

Australian Welcome to "Mates"

Mr Curtin received Dr Van Mook within a few days of his flight to Australia. Mr Curtin pledged to Dr Van Mook that "every facility will be given by the Australian Government to so gallant an ally to conduct its business". In offering Australia as the Dutch base and sanctuary, the Prime Minister said he used the word sanctuary "in the same way as the trade unionist uses the word 'mate' ".

Mr Curtin further promised that the Australian Government would "do all it can to help the Netherlands Administration in reorganising such forces as have reached Australia, or may do so in future, from Java".[1] In April he told parliament that a Netherlands East Indies Commission had been set up "to deal with matters affecting the Netherlands East Indies Government and to provide for refugees from the Indies in Australia".[2] Dr Evatt, in a statement to parliament later; sealed the contract with colonialism:

Australia will become a base from which the Dutch colonies will be finally regained . . . As in the case of New Caledonia, we visualise the restoration of the former sovereignty.[3]

Dr Van Mook announced the NEI Commission's formation on 8 April 1942. The Commission served as a provisional Government-in-Exile to handle Dutch affairs in Australia and New Zealand. While Dr Van Mook headed the Commission as Acting Governor-General — Governor-General Tjarda Van Starkenborgh Stachouwer spent the war in a Korea prison camp — Dr Van Der Plas took the title of NEI Chief Commissioner for Australia and New Zealand.

Regrouping for Reoccupation

By this time the remnants of the Royal Netherlands Indies Air Force had regrouped in Queensland, where they were allotted facilities at Brisbane and Bundaberg aerodromes, later, at Canberra, and, occasionally, Darwin. Australia and America assisted to train and re-equip the Dutch force. Admiral Helfrich, now Commander-in-Chief of Netherlands Forces Far East, set up his naval headquarters in Melbourne, with a liaison at the main Australian Defence Department in St. Kilda Road, close to the city, and depots at St. Kilda and Middle Park, nearby suburbs. Dutch submarines and other smaller warships used a naval base established for them on the Swan River at Fremantle.

The Royal Netherlands Indies Army Command's survivors briefly reassembled in Melbourne. The Dutch officers and troops were allotted barracks, training centres and equipment in Victoria, New South Wales and Queensland. Colonel Simon H. Spoor, who as Lieutenant-General Spoor was to command the Dutch "police actions" designed to wreck the Republic and restore the Dutch to their tenured posts, was allotted a key political-military role. He and other Dutch officers worked in Australia with the British, American, Australian and various Asian intelligence-gatherers, propagandists and planners of the Allied Intelligence Bureau. Colonel Spoor's main interest was directed to intelligence and propaganda in Japanese-occupied islands.

The Netherlands Indies Civil Administration (NICA) was originally set up in Melbourne. NICA began to train civil administrators to follow the Allied forces into Indonesia and there set up the first units of the restored colonial administration. As some of the Indies Dutch escaped to Colombo Dr Van Mook flew there in 1942 to organise an additional group of NICA civil servants.

Separatist Ambitions

The Dutch not only marshalled in Australia sufficient cadres

52

to form a plausible Government-in-Exile; they had two extremely able and experienced political leaders in Dr Van Mook and Dr Van Der Plas. Dr Van Mook's parents, both school teachers, emigrated from Holland to Java in 1893 and the next year Hubertus Johannes was born at Semarang. After schooling in Semarang he was sent to Amsterdam and Delft. On return to Java he joined the colonial civil service but returned to Holland to study law and Indology at Leyden University. There he joined a group called *Stuw*, favouring reforms in Indies administration. As an agitator at Leyden for NEI reforms Van Mook was to incur the enduring suspicions of Professor P. S. Gerbrandy, emigre Dutch Prime Minister in London, and other metropolitan hardliners. A term at Stanford University, California, gave Van Mook a broader political panorama than many at The Hague or Batavia and put a slight American inflection into his near-perfect English. In the early 1930's Dr Van Mook was founder in Java of the Society for Promotion of the Social and Political Development of the Netherlands East Indies. A decade before the Japanese attack he had developed theories of "Commonwealth," allowing the Indonesians to share in a tutelatory administration and the colonial Dutch many autonomous rights, including commercial arrangements with neighbours in South-East Asia and Australasia.

The main political interest, Dr Van Mook contended, should be shifted from The Hague to Batavia. His experiences in Java brought him to more profound estimations of the Indonesian nationalist movement's deep roots and potential. He was a very young Assistant President of Police in Batavia, food controller in Semarang, co-editor of a relatively radical bi-weekly and a monthly economics magazine, Chief of the Bureau of Economics (1934-37) and Director of Economic Affairs from 1937 till his war eve appointment as Lieutenant Governor-General. In Australia, dumpy of figure, bespectacled, of mountainous erudition in Indonesian culture, Dr Van Mook was a cheery mixer with Australian politicians and departmental chiefs and American staff officers. Of a race not celebrated for famous diplomats he was polished in this art.

Dr Van Der Plas, like his superior, represented the Indies rather than the metropolitan Dutch. Born at Buitenzorg,

Java, he had been in the NEI Government service since 1911, when he became District Officer at Bandung. He was Governor of East Java when he took the plane for Australia. His functions under the viceroy Van Mook resembled those of prime minister. Dr Van Der Plas wrote and spoke scholarly Indonesian and took deep interest in Indonesian dancing, folk culture and history. He was versed in Islamic culture, spoke Arabic and had served in Arabia, London and Paris. The cultivated, luxuriously bearded Charles Van Der Plas was not of the Bols gin and *rijs-taffel* society of the Hotel des Indes, like some of his colleagues. As the time to invade Java drew near, he became the official Netherlands representative at Lord Louis Mountbatten's South-East Asia Command in Colombo. He concluded his colonial career as adviser in Batavia to the Netherlands Indies Government, which was to discover that neither advice nor arms could restore administrative capability.

Omens of Australian-Dutch Conflict

The Hague statesmen who in May 1940 carried with them to London such light ideological baggage were determined to reduce Dr Van Mook's investment of time and energy for realisation of his postwar autonomy ambitions. To the ultras in London who refused to be coaxed into the new age, Van Mook was almost a bleeding-heart liberal. The London government made him Minister for Colonies in November 1941, and ordered him to Britain in 1942 to run the Ministry of Colonies there. This transfer strengthened those Dutch political navigators based in Australia who shot their albatrosses without thought. Their aims were expressed in the tired cliches of European empire in Asia. The Australian Government, sensing opportunities for Indies footholds in Dr Van Mook's separatism, read warnings of a return to Dutch colonial monopoly, and relations between Canberra and the Dutch began to deteriorate soon after Dr Van Mook was ordered out. Dr Evatt sailed boldly into choppy seas and began to stake Australian claims in Indonesia.

From London, neither Dr Van Mook nor any other Minister could supervise the march-back from Australia to

Batavia. Only the wraith of power remained to the Royal Government; the warplanes, soldiers and surviving warships and most available sources of replenishment were in Australia.

Dutch preparations in Australia moved sluggishly and the metropolitans were obliged to restore Dr Van Mook to Australia. Canberra was told in November 1943 that Dr Van Mook would be flying out to reorganise the government-in-exile's forces. By this time the Australian Government was not in a mood to accept a colonial government whose principal objective was restoration of Dutch rule without Australian partnership.

The Royal Government, its diplomacy becoming more blunt-edged, decreed on 23 December 1943 an official Netherlands Indies Government, under Dr Van Mook as Acting Governor-General, to be sited in Australia until the restoration of Dutch rule. The Australian hosts were by now not only restive but inclined to pull the 1942 red carpet from under Dutch feet. As unexpected standard-bearers of the rights of Indonesians, both Mr Curtin and Dr Evatt began trying to discourage use of Australia as the base for a government-in-exile dedicated to revival of the 1941 colonial system. The Dutch were contemptuous of Canberra sentiments and thus helped to convert Australia to a mortuary of colonial ambition rather than a springboard for reconquest.

Dr Van Mook was back at the end of 1943; the Royal Government in April 1944 set up seven government departments in Australia — defence, a NICA bureau for re-establishment of civil rule in reconquered areas, economic affairs, education, home affairs, finance, public works. On 14 September 1944 another royal decree formalised what had already been achieved — establishment on Australian soil of the Netherlands Indies Government. Exceptional temporary powers were made available to this provisional government by statute law of the Royal Government in London. The London Government, suspicious of Dr Van Mook's separatist spirit, was anxious to keep a tight rein on the colonials. The Netherlands Military Administration, back in liberated South Holland in March 1944, set up a special section of East and West Indian Affairs to provide more metropolitan personnel for the revived Indies administration and economic reconstruction.

Imperialism in the Eucalypts

The main organs of the Dutch emigre regime were brought together at Brisbane in June 1942. The NICA organisation moved to Brisbane two years later, but Admiral Helfrich's naval headquarters remained in the Melbourne area. Minor government agencies and various branches of the armed forces were dispersed at other points. Camp Columbia was the irrelevant name given to the capital in exile of the Dutch Empire of the East. The offices and barracks were in the Wacol military camp area of outer Brisbane, on the main Brisbane-Ipswich line. Wacol was, as many Australian and American soldiers knew it in wartime, a flat generously covered with eucalyptus scrub and some tall gums. To this day Wacol retains, along with its memories of the Dutch visitation, much scrub and timber land, though the suburb has been built up. Cape Columbia was enclosed by wire, guarded at its main entrance from Wacol station by Dutch and Ambonese soldiers. In the central administrative block Dr Van Mook bent his head over his desk long into the humid Brisbane nights, planning his return, the training of officials for liberated areas, the despatch of Dutch troops to Netherlands New Guinea, Morotai, Tarakan and Balikpapan, and marshalling munitions — Australian and US lend-lease — and transport.

Though loyal Indonesians of influence were in short supply, Dr Van Mook tried to demonstrate that the Dutch were now more inclined to share power. Two Indonesian members of the NEI Governing Council had come to Australia with him, though moderates like Dr Sutan Sjahrir declined the invitation. His Highness the Sultan of Ternate, Iskander Mohamed Djabir Sjah XLVI, served under Van Mook at Wacol, and from Wacol Colonel Abdulkadir, who spent several years in America under Dutch sponsorship, flew to become Commanding Officer for Civil Affairs in the Netherlands New Guinea-Morotai zone.

Indonesians were initially in a majority in the armed forces readied in Australia. The four-day collapse of Holland in May 1940 left the Netherlands Indies Government-in-Exile with no metropolitan sources on which to draw. Dutch command-

Proclamation of the Republic of Indonesia over the names of Soekarno and
Mohammed Hatta on 17 August 1945. The proclamation was nailed up on walls,
poles, and trees throughout what had been the Netherlands East Indies

Republican slogans in Java shortly after the declaration of independence. The swords are kris, the wavy bladed Indonesian dagger used as a nationalist symbol. In the top picture the reference is to the Dutch contention that the Indies were the life-blood of the nation. These photographs are from an album presented to Australian trades unions by the newly founded Republic

ers quested for recruits among the small Dutch community in Australia. A Sydney *Bulletin* writer[4] said that the Netherlands Indies Government "found it necessary to enlist some aged people and children in their armed forces in exile".

Contingents from the Dutch West Indies began to arrive in Australia in June 1942: numbers of the blacks from Surinam and Curacao served as Dutch provosts. With war winding up in Europe the percentage of Dutch troops in the NEI Government's forces began to rise. Dutch soldiers and airmen trained under Allied supervision during the exile of the Royal Netherlands Government were released, where transport could be arranged, to the NEI establishment in Australia.

When the flyingboats from Tjilatjap flopped down on Roebuck Bay in 1942, few besides Dr Van Mook appeared to realise what dismembering blows the Dutch Empire of the East had suffered and how awesome were the tasks of reclamation. The weight of American arms pouring into Australia probably aided in desensitising the Dutch to gathering popular momentum in Asia. They certified their confidence that they would march back from Australia, faultlessly in file, to govern as before. They gave no more credence to warnings of wrath to come than would Louis XVI if he had been told in 1789 that soon the faubourgs mobs would be addressing him as *Citoyen*.

However, by 1945, when aroused nations were tearing the Axis to pieces, the sighting shots aimed by Indonesians at the NEI Government-in-Exile in Australia, foretokening an independence struggle, had helped to invigilate a minority around Dr Van Mook. Dutch Intelligence in Australia began to shadow Indonesian leaders, and in archives now in Holland are surveillance reports on contacts between Indonesians and various Australians who were later to discommode the Dutch by boycott.

5 Resumed Indonesian Voyages to Marega

Bara, the north-west monsoon, was blowing steadily when Lieutenant-Colonel J. R. L. Kapitz, Royal Netherlands Indies Army, surrendered Ambon to General Takeo Ito, 38th Japanese Division. Australian allies were not consulted; they and some Indonesians fought a little longer, hopelessly, in south-east Indonesia.

Bara caused Indonesian sea-rovers of old to think of *Marega,* their name for North Australia, as the land at the end of the wind. In *Marega,* long before the Europeans sighted the southern continent's coasts, Indonesians established Australia's first secondary industry — the processing of trepang or beche-de-mer for export to China through the Macassar entrepot, hiring Aboriginal labor in return for iron axes, metal fish-hooks, Celebes fruits, rice and other trade goods. Indonesian voyages to *Marega* were banned, early in this century, under the White Australia policy.

Indonesians, no doubt aware of the legendary road to *Marega,* helped some Australians to escape the terror the Japanese launched in a fury of mass executions in February 1942. They piloted escaping Australians to praus. Some landed at Dobo in the Aru Islands. From the Arus, one party, along with 72 Indonesian soldiers, used two motor-launches to reach Merauke and pick up another prau.

The monsoon by its timeless rhythm carried 16 Australians and 72 Indonesian soldiers across the Arafura Sea into the Gulf of Carpentaria and right down to Karumba, now a prawn-fishing port in the Gulf's south-east pocket. Other Indonesians, sometimes accompanied by escaped Australians, moved from Japanese clutches in praus, luggers and launches to North Australian beaches. The Indonesians escaping on the old monsoon route were taken south from North Australia. They found that greater numbers of their compatriots had arrived on busier escape routes.

Indonesian soldiers, sailors, marines, aircraftsmen, merchant seamen, hospital attendants, civil servants and shipping clerks were aboard merchantmen and men-o'-war and aircraft. Surviving Dutch cruisers, destroyers, frigates, submarines, sub-chasers, passenger and cargo liners, hospital ships and a mosquito fleet of small craft that had maintained KPM inter-island services cluttered up major Australian ports already overtaxed by war traffic.

Nearly all the Dutch ships had Indonesian crews, under European officers, though some of the warships had substantial Dutch complements. The remnant of the Netherlands Indies Army that reached Australia was Dutch in little more than command. An Australian official war historian pointed out that in 1940 and 1941, after the fall of metropolitan Holland, "the proportion of Europeans to Indonesians in the army was reduced until it was about one in forty".[1]

In the confusion of war no precise statistics of Indonesian arrivals could be kept. The big majority of refugees from Asia were Indonesians and Dutch, for Hong Kong and Singapore had fallen too quickly and casualties among those seeking escape from Singapore over Japanese-controlled routes were terrible. The Bureau of Census and Statistics recorded 1,539 refugees from Asia in the three months ended 31 December 1941 and 8,138 for the year 1942, but correctly warned that "some thousands could have been missed from the records". The Queensland press reported 4,000 arriving in Queensland alone during the month of February 1942; there were the seven to eight thousand listed by war historian Douglas Gillison as flying into Broome in 14 days; others came to Darwin and Queensland bases, or in ships to Fremantle, Brisbane and Sydney. Many Indonesians serving with the Dutch forces were moved out to reconquered islands in 1944-45, before the Republic's proclamation; warships and merchantmen with Indonesians aboard sailed from Australia to war fronts in the Bay of Bengal and South-West Pacific; numbers of Indonesian seamen returned, not always willingly, to Java in Dutch ships at the war's end. The Curtin Government's Minister for Immigration, Mr Arthur Calwell, said Australia gave sanctuary during the war to 15,000 from nearby countries, of whom 5,437 were Europeans.[2] This, apparently, was his total of refugees, and did not include naval and merchant seamen and soldiers, or political prisoners. Mr Calwell said that up to February 1949 the Commonwealth Government repatriated 3,768 Indonesians to Republican territory and only 19 still awaited repatriation. Two thousand Indonesian seamen were involved in the first Dutch-Indonesian confrontation in Australia — the strike for non-colonial wages — in April 1945.

An Australian maritime union leader estimated that, in all, about 5,000 Indonesian seamen were in Australian ports between 1942 and 1945.[3] Lacking accurate statistics, it would be reasonable to estimate that the aggregate of Indonesian sailors, merchant seamen, soldiers, civil service and shipping company clerks, hospital staffs and political prisoners to spend varying periods in Australia between 1942 and 1945 would have reached 10,000.

Indonesians by mid-1942 were stationed at the naval, military and air depots and camps alloted to the Dutch along the Eastern Australian coast and at Fremantle. Indonesian clerks were in city offices, Indonesian craftsmen in war factories, Indonesian prisoners in gaols and internment camps.

The Australian Government diverted substantial resources to the Dutch to prepare Indies reoccupation. Ironically, the Government, continuing to view South-East Asia through a dusty haze of preconception, was also providing scarce resources to train the officers of a future Republican force to wage war on Dutch allies. The death in action on 14 December 1947 of the Deputy Chief of Staff of the first Republican Air Force, Vice-Air-Commodore Halim Perdana Kusuma, was a reminder of this service. The Republican Air Force deputy leader was one of the Indonesians brought here by the Dutch and given training.

Import of Colonialism Rejected

The embarrassments of playing host to a colonial government-in-exile and at the same time volunteering custodial care of its reluctant subjects were evident before some of the Netherlands plenipotentiaries could unpack their bags and re-file their archives. To the 2,000-odd Indonesian seamen carried unexpectedly to Australian ports the situation seemed stark and simple. They were commanded to sail among Japanese mines, torpedoes and bombs for about £2 (now four dollars) a month by Dutch officers who often bellowed at them. They would hazard their lives to re-impose Dutch rule on their families at home. Through the blurred light of nationalist emotion the Indonesians held that the war was a purposeless clash of empires, after which they would be asked to accept the familiar currency of authoritarian direction. In March 1942 they had no evidence that the Japanese were treating the Indonesians worse than had the Dutch: gruesome affirmation of this had to await the war's end.

Indonesian seamen in Australia were mostly illiterate. They may or may not have heard of Hitler and Tojo and had experienced no change of masters as had their compatriots at home. Many of them, precipitated from the tropics into the first autumn nip, shivered in sarongs and trod the decks in bare feet, too poor to buy temperate zone clothing. The refusal of such slight investment as trousers and woollen jumpers to replace sarongs and shoes for bare feet was interpreted as a Dutch stance against a new deal.

In the Australian society the Indonesians saw around them, of dazzling affluence by their own experience, they were expected to form a colonial enclave, a managed sub-society. Thus, while the demand for Australian-level wages instead of the £2 a month rice-bowl pittance was the public issue, anti-colonial overtones were apparent in the strike by over 2,000 Indonesian seamen in Australian ports, mostly at Sydney. As the ships they manned were for war duties their strike was mutiny.

On the Australian waterfront on April Fool's Day the count-down started for the explosion that blasted the Dutch out of the Indies.

Australian Help

While Australians, deeply alarmed at the Japanese thrust into an "island screen" that proved so flimsy, had scant sympathy with Indonesians holding up war shipping at the height of the South Pacific emergency, neither Australian officialdom nor Australian maritime unions were pleased at the Dutch graft of colonial customs. The Dutch, it appeared to their Australian critics, were seeking to bandage the mutilations of the military debacle by pomp and strut and the Dutch shipping masters were displaying a lubberly obstinacy to hints that they should improve accommodation and wages for their crews.

The mutinous Indonesian seamen sought help from the Seamen's Union of Australia. The Australian union faced a dilemma. On the one hand, its leaders had been giving unstinted support to the war against the Axis since the Nazi attack on the Soviet Union in June 1941. The union's members were keeping all possible ships moving to the South-West Pacific war fronts. On the other hand, the Seamen's Union could not ask Indonesian seamen to risk their lives in mine-strewn and bomber-patrolled seas for less than one-tenth of the wages paid to Australian merchant seamen.

Seamen's Union Federal Secretary E. V. Elliott inspected some of the "Flying Dutchmen", as the maritime workers called the ships from Java. Mr Elliott said that the skipper of the passenger-cargo ship *Swartenhondt*[4] behaved toward him in such a manner that he could only assume the Dutch master had been influenced by his ship's name (Black Hound). Indonesian seamen aboard *Swartenhondt,* said Mr Elliott, had only sarongs and scanty clothing; they slept on boards and ate with their hands.

As the Indonesians were on strike, the Dutch captain, not yet politically acclimatised, demanded that Mr Elliott authorise Australian seamen to man the *Swartenhondt,* accepting the same quarters, food standards and working conditions as the Indonesians. Instead of getting an Australian crew the captain got an order from the Australian maritime authorities to put his ship in dock for extensive reconstruction before

seamen of any nationality would be permitted to sail her out
of Sydney.

Gaol for Indonesian Strikers

Even before the Netherlands Indies surrender of 8 March
1942 and the seamen's strike of 1 April 1942, there had been
trouble between Indonesians and Australian unionists, working together, and the Dutch. Indonesians manning the
Boissevan demanded a war-risk bonus, as paid to seamen of
other nationalities, before they would carry munitions to
South-East Asia. The Seamen's Union of Australia backed
the demand and the war-risk bonus was successfully negotiated
with the Dutch in Sydney. But in Batavia the *Boissevan's*
crew was gaoled. They may have fallen into Japanese hands.
According to Mr Elliott, the imprisoned men were replaced
at Batavia by an "illiterate" crew.[5]

Australian trade unionists explained to the 2,000-odd
striking Indonesian seamen the gravity of the Japanese
threat. The enemy was advancing in New Guinea and had
bombed Darwin, Broome, Wyndham and Derby. They tried
to convince the Indonesians of the liberating energies that
would be unleashed by Allied defeat of the Berlin-Rome-
Tokyo Axis. At the same time the Australian unionists had to
support Indonesian economic demands.

A Dutch guarantee of improved working conditions would
have sent the ships to sea. The Dutch preferred to use the
extra-territorial powers they had been granted over Indonesian
subjects in Australia by the Curtin Government. The Netherlands Indies Commission made the alien colonial presence
more acutely felt by soliciting from Australian penal and
military bodies goal and internment camp space for its
mutinous subjects.

In reviewing this mutiny of April 1942 the Committee of
Indonesian Independence later set up in Brisbane said that
the seamen had no way of putting their case to the public and
"it was easy for the authorities to accuse them of breaking
the law of the country and of disrupting the Allied war
effort . . . "

The Indonesian deserters were taken to Long Bay Gaol,
Sydney, to Loveday (South Australia) and Liverpool and

Cowra camps. Mutiny and gaolings, only a month after the Netherlands Indies' fall, cast a shadow over the Dutch road back.

First Non-Colonial Wage

Japanese and puppet Taiwanese and Korean prisoners soon began to trickle into Australia, following sinkings of Japanese ships, downing of aircraft and Allied counter-attacks. Pressure on internment space caused penal and military authorities and the Government to lend more sympathetic ears to union and civil rights representations for release of the Indonesians. In any event the Allies were desperately short of seamen.

Indonesian seamen were released from prisons and camps, many to return to Dutch ships refitted and reconstructed in Australian dockyards to provide sleeping and messing facilities. Instead of a £2 a month and unlimited hours the Indonesian seamen, aided by the Seamen's Union of Australia, won £22 a month (44 dollars) and an eight-hour day.[6] These approximated the Australian standard of the time.

Other Indonesians in Australia could not be denied. Those working at Blackbutt, Ipswich area of Queensland, and Helidon, near Toowoomba, contacted the unions in 1944. The trade unions successfully backed their demands for equivalent pay. Some of these Indonesians joined the Australian Railways Union; they were working to maintain railways carrying American and Australian troops. Indonesian clerks and other employees at the Netherlands Indies administrative and shipping companies' offices followed the seamen in insisting on Australian economic standards. They could not, of course, have lived reasonably on less during wartime inflation.

Key craftsmen from technical battalions were transported to Australia by the Dutch. An Indonesian Technical Battalion was regrouped in Australia. They mutinied for higher pay and were speedily thrust behind barbed wire. A Netherlands captain offered them release if they would work under the direction of the Australian Government in its Army Engineering Corps. They would receive 6s. 6d. (65 cents) a day, he said. (Australian Army engineers got far higher pay.)

The Netherlands captain further told them that until the

64

war was over they would only receive 3s. 0d. (30 cents) of the 6s. 6d. and that the other 3s. 6d. (35 cents) would be deferred, and only paid over when the Dutch repatriated them to the Netherlands Indies. Such deferred pay, conditional on accepting the old status of Dutch subject, stoked the fires of Indonesian disaffection. The Indonesian Technical Battalion members finished their internment to work for the Australian Engineering Corps at something approaching Australian standards.

Indonesian aircraftsmen and aircrews at Royal Netherlands Indies Air Force stations at Bundaberg, Brisbane and Canberra also fought with some success to have their pay raised. Indonesians for the first time enjoyed non-colonial wages.

The New Life in White Australia

First contacts for many of the Indonesians in Australia were with prison warders and military provosts. Now, with civilised wages and greater freedom, they began to mix socially with Australians in the capital cities and in some provincial centres. With low-cost board and lodgings they could sometimes outspend Australians. Numbers of them boarded in city suburbs at hostels and hotels allotted to the Netherlands Indies administration; they went to dances with Australian girls and there were quite a few Indonesian-Australian marriages. The Indonesians were adaptable people. Men who sailed into Australian harbours in sarongs walked abroad in tailored suits, well-ironed shirts and bright-patterned ties. Some tailors in the localities of their hostels did well on Indonesian orders.

Despite the White Australia Policy Indonesians generally found Australians less inclined than the Dutch to discriminate. The latter sometimes complained that Australians were spoiling their subjects. Australian racism has different content and direction, not easily comprehensible to colonial Dutchmen. Certainly, the Dutch did not bear all the guilt for race discrimination against Indonesians; the Australian Government granted them the right to do so. And the inbuilt skeleton of the White Australia Policy occasionally rattled in the hearing of Asian guests.

Mr Maurice Blackburn, Labor Member of the House of

Representatives, protested in May 1942 that "the Commandant of the Royal Australian Air Force at Canberra had forbidden Javanese airmen to dance with Australian girls". The Commandant of the Women's Auxiliary Air Force at Canberra had also "forbidden girls under her control to meet the Javanese airmen on terms of social equality," Mr Blackburn said.[7] The Minister for Air, Mr Arthur Drakeford, formally denied the charge, but many others besides Mr Blackburn knew that Indonesians suffered discrimination at Australian as well as Dutch initiative. However, the wide Australian effort on behalf of Indonesian rebels in Australia and social contacts with the Indonesians during their stay showed that insensitivity to Asian aspirations and feelings was not general in Australian manners.

Australian girls serving at a Netherlands Forces canteen in Sydney joined in a protest against a fantastic example of Dutch race discrimination. The Dutch banned "coloured" Australian girls — part-Aboriginal — from entering the canteen with Indonesians or West Indians. Mr J. E. Govell, a West Indian, was stopped at the door when he tried to escort a part-Aboriginal girl inside the canteen. A mystified Negro from Surinam pleaded in vain that the ban be lifted on comparison of his girl friend's honey complexion with his own sable skin. The Australian waitresses at the canteen, members of the Hotel, Club and Restaurant Union, threatened to take action against colour discrimination at the canteen. The ban on girls of honey or olive complexion while admitting those of dark brown or black skins was too incongruous to prevail.

6 Anticipating the Republic

On 22 February 1944 a large American force seized Humbolt Bay and Hollandia, Netherlands New Guinea capital. On 29 February Biak Island off Geelvink Bay was heavily assailed and the Hollandia-Biak zone was converted to General MacArthur's base for re-entry to East Indonesia. Cape Sanapor, at the Bird's Head or extreme western tip of New Guinea was occupied on 1 August 1944. Two weeks later the Allies landed at Morotai. While the Supreme Commander had Japan and the Philippines most in mind, East Indonesia was on the route and Morotai in the Moluccas region became his temporary staging base.

Behind General MacArthur's American and Australian forces was the Netherlands Indies Civil Administration, given additional training in Australia as the spearhead of Dutch administration in areas cleared of Japanese. NICA men were startled to be greeted by the slogan: "Better to be in hell than colonised again." The NICA men should have read a clearer warning into the first strikes and mutinies among the Indonesians in Australia and the plottings and preparations for their overthrow among Tanah Merah exiles, soldiers, sailors and merchant seamen. Dr Van Mook was apparently too busy in Australia to brief them adequately.

Dr Van Mook, before the Japanese invaded, had seen Dutch rule disintegrating until "all of a sudden we realised that . . . authority was in rags . . . . Gone overnight was a structure that had seemed solid and trustworthy and as immovable as granite". He noted that because of this disintegration "the conception of the colonial government and government in general, as a kind of natural force, could not be easily restored". The force of Indonesian nationalism was offering itself "with much more persistence and persuasion in its stead . . . ".[1]

Dr Van Mook's forebodings did not attract much attention among the eucalypts of Wacol or at the emigre court in London. However, his fears were passed on to some in the apparatus of the Netherlands Indies Government-in-Exile.

In premonition of turmoil emissaries of the Netherlands Indies Government Information Service in Sydney — two men and a woman, polite, cultured and seemingly liberal-minded — paid a visit to the office of the Communist *Tribune* in George Street, Sydney, in the late summer of 1945. They were received by the writer, then Associate Editor of the *Tribune*. The purpose of the mission was to seek Australian Communist sympathy with what someone called "the Dutch leap back into the seventeenth century". The NEI Information Service in Sydney could not help but be aware of a chain of communication between Australian Communists and the Indonesian communities.

The NEI representatives did not feel that any sweeping postwar reforms were necessary: Dutch rule had been exemplary and, obviously, the Indies treasure lode was far from worked out. They gave estimates in figures of the enormous stockpiles of Indies commodities that must be awaiting export, for the Japanese merchant marine was mostly at the bottom of the sea and little of the Indies production had been moved abroad. Eager buyers would be making their bids when the war ended. They stressed that the Netherlands Indies Government, drawing on supplies based in Australia, would bend every effort to relieve the plight of Indonesians groaning under three years of Japanese occupation, by shipping food, clothing and medical care, once the islands were liberated. The inference was that Australian Leftwing cooperation with the Dutch in this effort would be of great benefit to the Indonesians.

The *Tribune* was placed on the Netherlands Indies Government Information Service mailing list. The Service's bulletins arrived, occasionally useful in giving clues to Dutch intentions.

This approach to the Australian Communists was obviously a reflection of dawning concern among a minority of political sophisticates in Dr Van Mook's administration at the possibility of difficulties with the Indonesian soldiers, seamen and civil servants of the reoccupation force and with the Communist-led maritime unions.

Dutch Skippers Sound Alert

More effective than this attempt to disarm the Leftist planners would have been an instruction to Dutch sea captains not to bare the traps which Indonesians suspected were being laid for them, for in three-and-a-half years of Australian exile many of the Dutch must have lost sense of strategem: the shipping masters behaved like cat burglars who wear Dutch clogs, noisily alerting intended victims.

In May 1945 Notice No.62 was issued to captains of KPM ships in Australian harbours. The KPM executives neglected to take into account that the Indonesian petty-officers and clerks employed in the KPM office at Sydney would see Notice No.62 and circulate its contents to Indonesian seamen, nor did the Dutch contemplate that this trouble-inciting document would become one of the first entries in the Waterside Workers' Federation Indonesian File.

Notice No.62 of the KPM said that deferred pay set aside for Indonesian petty-officers and seamen since June 1943 at the rate of 25 guilders a month would be paid to each seaman or his dependants "after the Netherlands East Indies has been liberated from the Japanese". Notice 62 added:

> It is important to remember that only those seamen whose service is continuous and satisfactory to their captains and/or the KPM as from June 1943 will be entitled to receive this deferred pay. The deferred pay of 25 guilders to all seamen is to be regarded as a bonus for their services.

Deferred pay or war bonus to a merchant seaman is a legal wage entitlement and not a good conduct bonus, particularly when good conduct is construable as loyalty to restored Dutch rule in Indonesia. In any event the deductions from wages of Indonesian seamen sailing to war zones from

Australian ports were in the main intended as family allotments, to be used for rehabilitation of families at home after liberation.

Indonesian seamen operating from Australian ports were earning £22 (44 dollars) a month, of which £17 was paid them in cash and £5 deducted for family allowances and deferred pay. A considerable accumulation of these family allowances and deferred pay had been paid by Dutch shipowners into their own accounts in Australian banks. The Dutch, it was obvious, intended to use the "continuous" and "satisfactory" service proviso to withhold from seamen and their families substantial sums held in trust, should any of them resist restoration of Dutch rule or reduction of pay to the old colonial standards.

KPM executives informed Indonesian petty-officers, temporarily employed as shipping clerks because their vessels were war casualties, that their wages would be cut by £12 (24 dollars), leaving them £15 (30 dollars) a month. In cost-inflated wartime Australia the cut would have spelled catastrophe. The petty-officers struck work and the Dutch retreated. This attack on the petty-officers' wages and deferred pay alienated those previously inclined to accept Dutch sovereignty. The petty-officers were to play a major role in the strikes and mutinies that later tied up Dutch ships. Indonesian seamen similarly gave notice that they would not accept wage cuts and that their deferred pay must be freed of political conditions. Notice 62 compounded economic grievance with the independence aims of Indonesians in Australia.

As Holland was liberated before May 1945, when Notice 62 was issued, metropolitan directors were no doubt responsible for this particular forewarning that the investing corporations based in Holland would not set their sails to new Indies breezes.

"A State of Great Alarm"

A May 1945 statement by Mr Alan Fraser (Labor, NSW) to Federal Parliament[2] indicated that the Dutch in Australia were moving toward a showdown with the more troublesome Indonesians. Mr Fraser appears to have been the first

70

Australian parliamentarian, after Dr Evatt's 1943 efforts for the Tanah Merah internees, to intervene on behalf of the Indonesians, against the Dutch colonial interest. He said that Indonesians employed by the Dutch in Australia, particularly seamen, were in "a state of great alarm", and were "very much afraid of what may happen to them after the Japanese have been driven back and the Dutch regain possession of their territories". After noting that before the war trade union organisation had not been permitted to Indonesians Mr Fraser said:

> But during the war Indonesian seamen have, for the first time, been gaining some measure of freedom of expression and enjoyed reasonable standards of living. They now seem to have cause to fear that they will soon have to return to the extremely unsatisfactory conditions under which they existed prior to the war and, moreover, action will be taken against those who have shown any progressive political spirit during their stay in Australia.

Mr Fraser wanted the Curtin Government to extract assurances from the Dutch that the Indonesians would not be victimised. Victimisation was, however, already under way. Two petty-officers of the NEI merchant service, Max Soeprapto and Willi Pande Iroot, were arrested immediately after the dispute with the KPM. Soeprapto was Vice-President and Iroot Secretary of the Indonesian Club in Sydney and both were active in the local independence movement. The two men, held under the Commonwealth Immigration Act, were first put in Long Bay Gaol, then transported in a closed prison van to Central Railway and taken north for deportation from Queensland to Netherlands New Guinea.

Queensland trade unions brought the Soeprapto-Iroot case to the attention of the Minister of the Interior, Senator J. S. Collings. The Minister, though his past associations with the Queensland unions had been close, took no action and the deportations proceeded. Likewise, the Minister for the Navy, Mr Norman Makin, when pressed by Mr Fraser to intervene for Indonesian seamen, observed the committal to Dutch sovereignty. Mr Makin said:

71

Mr Fraser would not wish the Government to take any imprudent action in connection with people under the jurisdiction of a friendly neighbour. It would be an extremely delicate matter to raise; indeed, any such action might be regarded as highly improper.[3]

But action designated highly improper in May was respectable by October.

Republican Organisation

From the Office of the Central Committee of Independence in Brisbane and from the Tanah Merah exiles' organisation at Mackay, contact was maintained with Indonesians at various Queensland camps, air stations and projects and with the Indonesian soldiers in the Dutch military camp at Casino, northern NSW. Just as the Dutch established their Government-in-Exile at Brisbane, the Indonesians made Brisbane a shadow capital for Republicans outside their native islands. The Central Committee of Indonesian Independence, reviewing six months of Republican activity here in the pamphlet *Republic of Indonesia*, printed at Brisbane in February 1946, revealed that from Australia the Republicans "strongly advised the Indonesian people in America, the Middle East and India to form similar organisations and from all quarters we received support for this suggestion".

The Indonesian Independence Committee of Sydney maintained an office at 16 Sir John Young Crescent and in 1947 was still printing the *Free Indonesia Bulletin*. It gave monitored radio news from Djogjakarta, temporary Republican capital, speeches by Indonesian leaders and other information features. The Independence Committee at Mackay provided Queensland unions with much information about Dutch moves in Australia, through agents in the NEI Government-in-Exile's service. The Melbourne Committee was a busy publisher of Republican propaganda.

The Indonesian Independence Committees which began to take shape in Australia in 1944 were fairly vigorous bodies by September 1945. Indonesian servicemen also joined the Independence Committees, against Dutch military regulations.

The Indonesians in Australia enjoyed, in the more permissive atmosphere of the last year or so of the war against the Axis, considerable freedom to discuss their independence aims with and seek advice from Australians. Mrs Gwyn Williams, who taught English in Sydney to former Tanah Merah internees and other Indonesians, said:

In 1944 these Indonesians at the English class talked incessantly of the independent Indonesia that would arise. A few pro-Dutch Indonesians occasionally found their way to English classes, but were soon excluded by the Republicans. As I taught English to these exiles in Sydney I could see the Republic growing before my eyes.[4]

Mrs Laura Gapp, who played her part in winning release of Tanah Merah internees, said:

The theme of their conversation from the first days when I met them behind barbed wire at Liverpool was: "We shall return to Indonesia — but the Dutch? Never!"[5]

Australian Preparations to Aid Indonesia

Mobilisation of Indonesian Independence Committees without any Australian penal action should have served as another warning to the Netherlands Indies Government-in-Exile to improve its diplomatic engineering. Indonesian independence activities in Australia, while in accord with the Allies' war aims, were in breach of protocol and sometimes of the Commonwealth Crimes Act's political clauses. The Netherlands Indies draconic legal code, applicable to Indonesians in Australia by Curtin Government consent, was also seditiously defied. This Australian Government ambivalence — provision of arms, training facilities and diplomatic support for Dutch reconquest and toleration of Indonesian planning to frustrate this reconquest — was clearly evident before the war ended.

Netherlands Navy officers made merry in Sydney when news of Japan's capitulation was flashed to the world. "We'll soon be back!" said a Dutch officer, raising his glass of gin in a toast. An Indonesian naval petty-officer, member of Mrs Williams' class who was attending the officers, was confident enough to interrupt: "Yes, we will be back but you will not be there."[6]

Australian export interests were also beginning to readjust their sights. A leading Victorian agricultural machinery and implement manufacturer showed two Indonesians known to the writer over its factory, to the accompaniment of suggestions on how Australian industry could help modernise Indonesian agriculture. Several businessmen in Sydney joined the Australia-Indonesia Association, launched about a month before the war ended as the first public organisation of citizens ever to arrange contact and exchanges with Asians conspiring to end colonial rule. Others on the Australia-Indonesia Association Executive, elected in July 1945 after several preliminary meetings of interested people, included Professor A. P. Elkin (Anthropology, University of Sydney), Bishop Cranswick of the Church of England, the Secretary of the NSW Trades and Labor Council, Mr Guy Anderson (a Labor Party member) and activists in women's movements.

The Association, in outlining the reasons for its foundation, said:

> The Association's objects are to foster friendly cultural, sporting, educational and trade relationships with Indonesia. Its formation was a natural result of existing friendships (and some marriages) between Indonesians and Australians, and it linked together various groups, such as the Indonesian Petty Officers' Social Club, language study circles, those Australians entertaining Indonesians in their homes, Indonesian Seamen's Union and Independence Committee.
> Of prime importance is the gathering of publicity material for dissemination through the more progressive Labor press and by booklet and leaflet distribution, in order to combat ignorance and prejudice sedulously fostered by a large section of the general press.[7]

When news of the Indonesian Republic's proclamation on 17 August reached Australia, the Australia-Indonesia Association was able to arrange pro-Indonesian broadcasts from several Sydney radio stations. The Association printed 20,000 copies of the Political Manifesto of the Republic of Indonesia for distribution to representative citizens. In

Melbourne and Brisbane there were similar propaganda efforts through the Indonesian Independence Committees.

While the Association enjoyed some support in academic and business circles, it had to rely mostly on trade unionists. "The Association," said a report on its activities, "arranged a conference between religious leaders and other humanitarians to discuss the position of Indonesians here and in their own country. The attendance was moderate only. It appears that the greatest support for Indonesia is amongst working people. However, we shall continue our efforts with the religious bodies."[8]

Directive for Action

The Communist Party of Australia, with its intimate contacts, aiding organisation among the exiles and providing courier services and sometimes finance, anticipated the Republican revolution ahead of other political groupings. It gave advance warning of action against the Dutch, through the trade unions it influenced, in December 1944. Mr R. Dixon, then Assistant General Secretary and soon to be President of the party, wrote an article[9] declaring that the "various sections of the Labor movement must stand together and with the progressive forces among other sections of the people show that Australia stands irrevocably for the freedom and independence of the oppressed peoples". He said that "the old order in South-East Asia must go", and that "we in Australia cannot stand idly by and see the old imperialist order restored in the colonies". When the Japanese were driven from Indonesia it would be more as a result of the efforts of the Australians, Americans and British and of the Indonesians themselves than of the Dutch. "Our contribution to the Pacific War entitles Australia to a major say in the final settlement," Mr Dixon added, reaffirming a national interest in South-East Asia's future already promoted in Federal Parliament.

Mr Dixon's article was tantamount to a directive to clear decks for broadsides against Dutch shipping in Australian ports and an appeal for Australian official intervention. Mr Dixon told the writer, in March 1972, that this article foreshadowing action on behalf of an independent Indonesia was written after approaches from leaders of Indonesian exiles who, monitoring the broadcasts from the Japanese-occupied Indies, were certain of a revolt against Dutch rule immediately the war ended.

7   Return to Tanah Merah

The first confrontation between Indonesian Republicans and the Netherlands East Indies Government, whose life lingered on an alien couch, was, naturally, in Australia. No Netherlands authority could reach Java till well after the Republic's 17 August proclamation in Batavia, occupied by a defeated Japan.

The NEI Government-in-Exile struck the first physical blow by deporting key Indonesian cadres to a reopened Tanah Merah Digul camp. This regress to the Netherlands New Guinea internment system, the employment of violence to force resisting Indonesians aboard Dutch planes for deportation fused the vigilance of Indonesians in Australia and swelled the ranks of their Australian allies.

The Netherlands military officers in Australia were by 1945 mostly metropolitans, though usually of Indies service. They were far less discreet than Dr Van Mook and seemed to have used much of their own initiative in answering the Indonesians' ebullient expectations by muscle rather than manoeuvre. In the weeks before the Japanese surrender of 15 August 1945 the Dutch military officers and provost corps in Australia began arresting and air-lifting Indonesian rebels to Hollandia and Merauke for internment.

These deportations to Tanah Merah further scarred the Dutch reputation. They indicated that the Netherlands Indies rulers could not rise above their biases to go some way toward tranquilising the smothered discontents of centuries that had now found voice and aim. For too long, it seemed, the Dutch

77

officers had dwelled in zones beyond reach of logic and reality; they could not discern that imperial momentum was failing not only in South-East Asia but in the whole world.

Dr Van Mook must have known of the Tanah Merah deportations and the harm they would do. Whether or not he tried to halt them is not on record. The reopening of Tanah Merah did not fit the philosophies which he soon after put down on paper. He complained that Dutch colonial government had never descended from its seat of power to take counsel with its subjects. The substitute for negotiation was internment which, he admitted, was "resorted to an unprecedented scale" after the 1926-27 rebellion. He acknowledged that the camp that was their journey's end on the Digul River was "ill-reputed".

If Dr Van Mook proposed to cross the shadow line from the old colonial severities and enlist Indonesian administrators, then the fracas at Hinkler airport, Bundaberg, when violence was used to put Indonesians aboard Dutch planes and members of the Australian Air Force made their indignation known, was no aid to credibility.

Though the Japanese-held Indies had been in oppressive silence, Republican propaganda resounded loudly enough in Australia for Dr Van Mook to have heard and have taken a stand against the rough-house tactics of Dutch officers who, over-confident in the flush of Allied victories, were paying too much attention to the statistics of Anglo-American arms and not enough to political changes that were making impossible a return to colonial power in Asia, Africa and the Middle East. The Indonesians were giving vociferous publicity to the reopening of Tanah Merah and the deportations and interpreted these as evidence that even the Acting-Governor-General had now excluded compromise from his precautions.

The deportations for internment worsened relations — already becoming abrasive — between the Australian Government and the colonial Dutch. Mr Arthur Calwell, speaking from Melbourne to the writer on 9 April 1971, described one deportation incident that angered Ministers:

A blue-eyed, fair-haired Dutch colonel demanded of me that a number of Indonesian servicemen interned for mutiny near Alice Springs should be handed over for removal to the Netherlands Indies. I said I would not let him send them back to Dutch custody. He was very arrogant — I found out later that he had been an executive of Royal Dutch Shell — and — clicking his heels, so it seemed — declared: "If you don't let me get them, I'll take them!" He did. Australian Army officers arranged for the Indonesians to be flown out, behind my back. Although I was Minister for Immigration, responsible for any such movement of aliens out of Australia, I did not know these Indonesian internees were gone until some time later.

Trade Union Intervention

The large group of ex-Tanah Merah internees employed on projects related to the Allied war effort in Mackay quickly initiated action designed to prevent further deportations. Mr Alexander Patty, President of the Indonesian organisation in Mackay, warned on 21 August that the Netherlands Indies Government intended to remove speedily to New Guinea the politically active Indonesians. Mr Patty demanded that Indonesian exiles be returned to "the islands of their birth and not New Guinea, and that they be protected against Dutch persecution".

The Tanah Merah veterans also set Australian trade union machinery in motion. On 22 August 1945, only a week after Japan's surrender, the Queensland Trades and Labor Council had before it a telegram sent by Mackay Trades and Labor Council to the Minister for External Affairs, Dr Evatt, to the Minister for External Territories, Mr E. J. Ward, and Mr G. W. Martens, Labor MHR for the local electorate of Herbert. The telegram, signed A. Carvloth, said:

> Mackay Trades and Labor Council protests against deportation of Indonesians from this country to prison camps and requests that they be allowed here until they can be returned to Java, Sumatra, Ambon and the Celebes as free people.

Queensland TLC, in a resolution arising from the Mackay telegram, asked the Federal Government that the Indonesians "should be allowed to remain in Australia until they are repatriated to their home areas with complete political freedom and the right to form their own trade unions". The Council sent protests to the Prime Minister, Minister for the Interior, and the Netherlands Indies Government-in-Exile at Brisbane. The Australian Council of Trade Unions and other State Trades and Labor Councils were also asked to protest. Also on 22 August Mr Gerald Peel, the active supporter from England of the Indonesian cause, said in Sydney that "Tanah Merah concentration camp in Western New Guinea is again being used by the Dutch authorities to house Indonesian political prisoners". In Tanah Merah there were already 16 Indonesian prisoners from Australia. Most of them had served up to 17 years in the camp before the war and since their arrival in Australia had been "giving their all for the war effort". "This is their reward," Mr. Peel added.

The Battle of Bundaberg

The Netherlands Indies Command in Australia selected Bundaberg's Hinkler Airport on the Central Queensland coast as a main jumping-off place for bombers, fighters and transport planes bound north-west to the Indies and Dutch New Guinea. Here at Bundaberg, Colonel Van Haselen commanded a mixed Dutch and Australian squadron.

Indonesians at Bundaberg began demonstrating their support for the Republic in September. Leaders of this demonstration, were, according to the Indonesians' version, forced into a Dutch plane and whisked away to the islands north of Australia. Indonesians left behind claimed the destination was Tanah Merah prison camp in New Guinea. Later, when Dutch officers and provosts tried to force more Indonesians aboard planes, the Dutch, it was alleged, fired shots. The Council for Civil Liberties repeated in print the charge that the Dutch fired shots at the Indonesians. Queensland Trades and Labor officials who travelled to Bundaberg to investigate the affray reported that 10 Indonesians who refused to enter a Dutch plane had been hit with batons, kicked and punched by Dutch provosts. The mutineers had then been flown to Casino for internment. Some of the Indonesian soldiers who served as guards for the Dutch-Australian squadron at Bundaberg were flown to Camp Lytton, Brisbane, and interned.

A pamphlet titled "Action", issued by the Bundaberg branch of the Communist Party, late in October 1945 said:

> The Dutch bashed and kicked the men into a bomber. What will be their fate now?
>
> Australian RAAF personnel on our aerodrome stopped working when they saw the open brutality of Dutch Fascism practised here on the Bundaberg drome.
>
> RAAF personnel are working under protest and are demanding that the Dutch, or they, be removed from the Bundaberg aerodrome.

The *Bundaberg News-Mail* of 29 October 1945 claimed that RAAF men questioned "denied seeing the incident". They considered that "reports of the incident were spread in an exaggerated form by Communist-influenced groups at the station". An incident could hardly be dismissed as non-existent and then rated as exaggerated.

The Dutch commander at the Bundaberg station, Colonel Van Haselen, similarly followed denial with confirmation of an incident. According to the same article in the *Bundaberg News-Mail* the commander said that "nothing out of the ordinary had happened . . . It was just a case of men under military law refusing their duty and being arrested". He had told them they would have to be sent to the prison camp at Casino. When they were ordered into the plane they refused and had to be forced in. "Some of the men," he said, "had to be dragged in by the arms. There was no one injured and definitely no shots were fired. One man who struggled was hit behind the leg with a baton. He fell to the ground, and when he refused to get up, had to be picked up and put into the plane."

Colonel Van Haselen conceded that there was some objection from Air Force men ". . . some little reaction from a little group who did not like the way the men were put into the plane, but they were very few". He claimed that the Dutch bombers going north had been stripped to carry supplies and were not armed. One plane sent north not long before had carried several Indonesian armorers who had completed a training course at Melbourne to Biak.

Mr C.W. Johnson, who with Mr F. Weigel was a delegate from Queensland Trades and Labor Council to investigate the Bundaberg incident, asked if they could inspect the planes. "Colonel Van Haselen," said the *Bundaberg News-Mail*, "indignantly asked was his word not enough."

The Dutch Commandant, who had been in Australia since Java's fall in 1942 and previously commanded the mixed Netherlands-Australian No.18 Squadron at Darwin, threw further doubts on denials that there had been no hostile reaction from Australian Air Force men when he told the *Bundaberg News-Mail*:

> This was the first case of any alleged ill-feeling. It was probably due to the men's own desire for demobilisation coupled with seeds of propaganda sown from outside.

According to the *Bundaberg News-Mail* of 29 October about 40 more Indonesians left Bundaberg on the night of 28 October under arrest and "in charge of Australian Army authorities". The Australian Army guards seemed to have interpreted the Army Regulations liberally. The *Bundaberg News-Mail* said:

> The men were in a special carriage and seemed a happy group. They were allowed to talk freely with the public and to their own countrymen who were there to see them off. Members of the Bundaberg Branch of the Communist Party were also there; also Messrs Weigel and Johnson.
>
> The Indonesians all wore red and white rosettes, colors of the Indonesian Republic. When the train moved off, led by Mr Johnson, the Indonesians shouted, "Long live the Indonesian Republic," then broke into a song in their own language.

For the quiet town of Bundaberg, all this scarcely fitted Colonel Van Haselen's description of "nothing out of the ordinary".

By no means all Bundaberg trade unionists sympathised with Indonesian insurgence. On 12 November 1945 Queensland Trades and Labor Council Executive had before it a resolution from Bundaberg Trades and Labor Council:

That the Bundaberg Trades and Labor Council deplores
the action of Brisbane Trades and Labor Council in allowing the Communist element in that body to use the
Trades and Labor Council movement as a cover for what
appears to be a communistic plot to bring discredit on
the whole of the working-class movement and the Labor
Party by stirring up racial hatred among the followers of
a self-confessed collaborator with the Japanese and our
Dutch allies at the Bundaberg aerodrome.

Bundaberg Branch of the Waterside Workers' Federation
expressed another view:

That we disassociate ourselves with the resolution passed
at the Trades and Labor Council meeting on Wednesday
30 October as reported in the *Bundaberg News-Mail* of
1 November 1945 re the Bundaberg aerodrome incident.

8 Reoccupation Forces Mutiny

On 1 September 1945 the Central Committee of Indonesian Independence Committees said in a manifesto:

> A reimposition of the undemocratic and ruthless Dutch rule over the peoples of Indonesia is not and never will be accepted by our people.

The manifesto appealed to both Australians and Indonesian exiles to assist "the struggle to win elementary rights".[1] It was circulated to Indonesians in ships, naval depots, military camps and shipping offices and to Australian maritime unions.

Indonesian response was tested as the ink dried on the Japanese signature to the surrender document put before them aboard USS *Missouri* in Tokio Bay on 2 September. General MacArthur's Command had ordered both the Dutch and Mountbatten not to move till the Japanese signed the capitulation articles. The Netherlands Navy cruiser *Tromp*, of 5,000 tons, heavily gunned and one of the swiftest cruisers afloat, repaired in Australian yards after heavy damage while serving in Java waters with Admiral Karel Doorman's ill-starred fleet, dashed for Batavia.

Sydney waterfront workers noted disturbances aboard *Tromp* as she steamed to the harbour heads. Indonesians in the crew may have been taken by surprise. The first mimeographed circular to Sydney waterside workers, asking them to boycott Dutch ships and issued in the week-end of September 22-23, mentioned this disturbance on the Dutch warship as an argument in favour of trade union support of the Indonesian

Republic. Indonesians aboard, the circular claimed, demonstrated against being carried to Java "to shoot their own brothers".[2]

Queensland Trades and Labor Council said in September that "Indonesian sailors have refused to man a Dutch warship returning to the Indies".[3] The unnamed warship was presumably at Brisbane and could not have been delayed for long, otherwise greater publicity would have resulted.

Netherlands Navy ships arriving off Tanjong Priok could not give the Indonesians their first postwar glimpse of the House of Orange ensign until the British landed. *Tromp*, anchoring off Tanjong Priok on 16 September, feared unswept minefields and officers were uncertain of their reception ashore. The first British warship, HMS *Cumberland*, did not appear until the end of September and escorts of the Seaforth Highlanders and other British spearhead units were not available until early October. Troops from Australia in the *Balikpapan* had to rely on British and Gurkha protection.

Indonesian Troop Mutinies

Once the Axis was shattered most of the Indonesian troops in Australia recognised no further obligation to the Allies -- only to the new-found Republic. They asked immediate discharge from the Royal Netherlands Indies armed forces and repatriation to Republican territory as Republican citizens. The Dutch were desperately situated. The only army of occupation for immediate deployment in the Indies was in Australia. No other substantial Dutch transport fleet was available except the ships in Brisbane, Sydney, Melbourne and Fremantle. Wartime shipping losses and Allied demands on tonnage meant that, even when Holland recovered sufficiently from the agony and ruin of battles and bombings on her soil, and trained a new army, transport to Indonesia would not be easy.

Indonesians in Netherlands uniforms were ready at various points for embarkation -- the greatest number in the camp system around Brisbane, engineers at Casino awaiting transport to Brisbane, a few units of army and navy men at Sydney, militia and marines at Middle Park and sailors at St. Kilda in Melbourne, sailors at the Fremantle naval depot and air-crew and ground staff men at Bundaberg, Brisbane and Canberra, to be sent north by ship, or by air from Bundaberg.

Early in September the Indonesian servicemen at Casino served demands on Dutch officers that they be discharged forthwith into civilian life, pending repatriation to the Republic, and that their deferred pay be promptly refunded. They notified the Netherlands Commandant that if their demands were not met within a reasonable time they would refuse orders. A few days later the Commandant paraded them and had them surrounded by soldiers and provosts carrying tommy-guns. The Commandant read the Netherlands Indies version of the Riot Act, delivered a panegyric to Dutch colonial benevolence in dense jargon and, as an irrelevant finale, expressed his extreme antipathy toward Soviet Russians.

According to the Brisbane Independence organisation the men came out on strike on 12 September "in sympathy with the independence movement".[4] The Commandant who had extolled colonial paternalism so prodigally interned the mutineers behind a 10 foot barbed wire fence, in an area 100 yards by 150 yards where they were crowded into small huts, overlooked by watch-towers and searchlit at night.

Casino Indonesians for some time had contact with Queensland Trades and Labor Council. The Council's General Secretary, Mr M. Healy, advised his Executive of information from Casino that 104 Indonesians were now interned there and that the Dutch had "completely rejected" their demands. The letter from Casino Indonesians was before a Council meeting on 17 September. Two days later Queensland TLC was informed that a further 100 Indonesians had been arrested at Casino. The remainder were disarmed. This was, for the Dutch, a loss of engineers, signallers and other skilled men from the Indonesian Technical Battalion.

The Labor Council meeting of 19 September proposed that the mutineers be transported to their homeland, or, if they remained for some time, should be employed as civilians discharged from the armed forces on Australian-standard wages and that those who had served the Australian Army Engineering Corps should immediately be paid their deferred earnings. These proposals and protests against internment were sent to

Mr Chifley and the Netherlands Indies Government-in-Exile.

Following the Casino refusals of duty mutiny flared among all units of militia and marines and at the Melbourne naval depot. The Central Committee of Indonesian Independence in Brisbane said that "hundreds of Indonesians unanimously gave up their jobs in Casino" and at Camp Columbia, Wacol. It claimed also that 230 soldiers "unanimously and outspokenly" told the Dutch at Camp Columbia that they supported the Republic. Their weapons were surrendered to the Dutch. (While the 230 were "unanimous", the Ambonese guards mostly remained in Dutch service.) Dutch authority at Wacol "was no longer capable of any control", the Central Independence Committee added, and the men from there were imprisoned at Camp Lytton not far away, under Australian guards. By October 1945 470 Indonesians were interned at Casino. Another 214 were in Gaythorne camp as deserters and "prohibited immigrants".

The Melbourne *Argus* of 2 October reported that 23 soldiers (these would have been marines) at Middle Park and 30 sailors at the St. Kilda naval depot had been arrested for mutiny and that nearly 60 Indonesians had resigned from their employment in Dutch establishments in Melbourne. Perhaps only the NEI Government-in-Exile archives would have the total of mutineers in Australia, but these archives went to Batavia and Holland. Although most of the Indonesian mutineers, deserters and strikers were by April 1946 back in Java, repatriated by the Chifley Government, there were still at this time about 100 Indonesian marines in Geelong Gaol, 480 soldiers interned at Casino and 240 at Camp Lytton.

First Dutch Defeat

Casino internment camp stood as the symbol of Holland's defeat in her first skirmish with the Republic of Indonesia. The gaoled Indonesian Technical Battalion members, by mutiny on 12 September, preceded their compatriots at home in action against the Dutch military command.

The engineers at Casino, the soldiers in the Brisbane camps, the handful of Indonesian servicemen in Sydney's Long Bay and the marines and sailors arrested at Melbourne and Geelong were essential to the Netherlands Indies Command if it was to establish its presence in key Indies centres before the Republic could muster military forces.

The transplanted garrisons, acting as the statutory support of Netherlands repossession, were to have been shielded by Mountbatten's SEAC until the freshly trained divisions arrived from Holland. The Indonesian mutinies in Queensland, New South Wales and Victoria meant that the Dutch were bereft of their spearhead at a decisive postwar period. Many of the Netherlands officers and soldiers due for reoccupation tasks had to remain in Australia to confront the mutineers, and even to load boycott-bound Dutch war-supply ships. These unexpected soldiers of the Republic, retaining their Netherlands uniforms and insignia, possessed of neither guns nor liberty, inflicted mortifying casualties. Unarmed, removed from any Republican command, surviving the severe penalties of mutiny, they could be credited with the first Republican military gain at Dutch expense.

History knows its unpredictable symmetries. The Netherlands and Netherlands Indies authorites invested millions of guilders to house, clothe, feed, train and equip the Indonesian servicemen in Australia. Government and taxpayers of Australia assisted in this Dutch reconquest exercise. Yet the Australian Government was later to repatriate the mutineers, at taxpayers' expense, into Republican hands. Schooled by Dutch and Australian officers, understanding Dutch and Anglo-Australian military methods and tactics, the Indonesians from Brisbane, Casino, Sydney and Melbourne made some of the Republic's most competent military officers.

The Casino Scandal

The Dutch vented a little of their anger at the barbed-wire compound two miles out on the Kyogle Road from Casino. Camp space was cramped and those Indonesians not under detention after the mutiny were still allowed passes to visit Australian friends in Casino.

Miss Marie Moran of Carlton Guest House, Casino, reported that in October 1945 she attended a house party where Indonesians were present. Two jeep-loads of Dutch military police arrived about midnight. Eight provosts surrounded the house, owned by an Australian, flourishing tommy-guns. Others

'OH, THERE YOU HAVE ME!'

Armstrong, *Argus*, 17 November 1945

On 5 and 8 November, two shortwave broadcasts by G. Sawer and M. Keon of the Australian Department of Information were strongly critical of the Dutch and accused Britain and the USA of hypocrisy. Prime Minister Chifley and Arthur Calwell both denied authorising the broadcasts

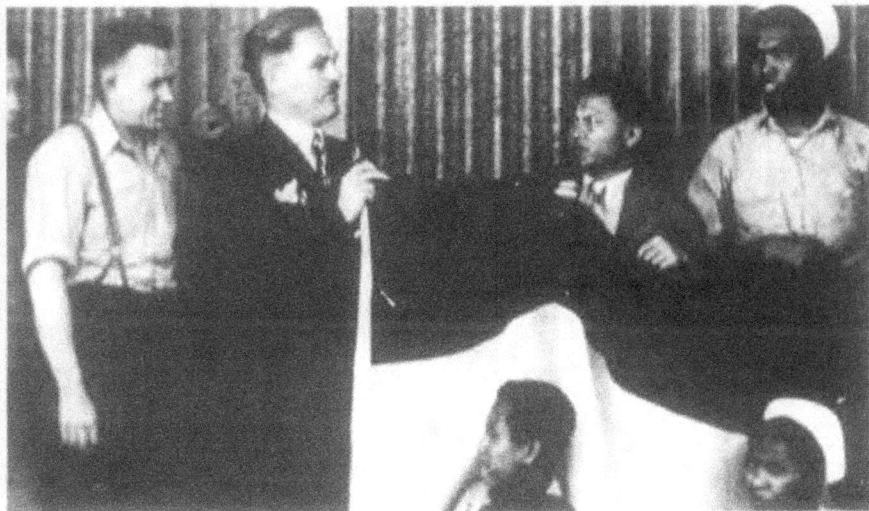

E. V. Elliott, Secretary of the Seamen's Union of Australia, presenting an Australian-made Republican flag to Indonesians about to be repatriated on board the *Esperance Bay*. (*Indonesia Calling*)

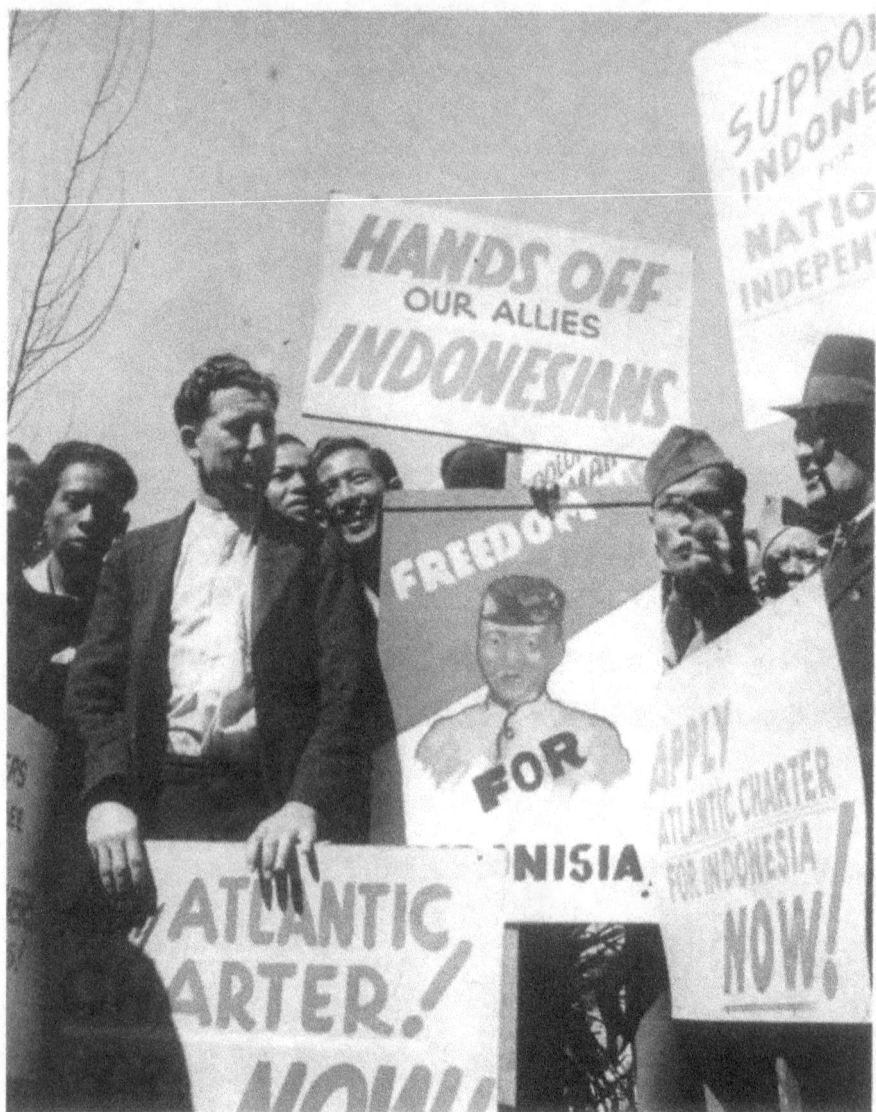

Indonesians and Australians marched together, for the first time, in the 1945 Six-Hour Day demonstration in support of Indonesian republic

rushed the verandah with drawn revolvers. A Dutchman threatened to shoot one resisting Indonesian. Several Indonesians were dragged out of the house, pushed into jeeps and taken back to camp.

On each Sunday for about 12 months Mr Robert Cooper, a railwayman, visited an Indonesian friend at Casino camp without interference from Dutch guards. One Sunday visit in October, Dutch guards with tommy-guns encircled the hut in which Mr Cooper was having a sing-song with his Indonesian friend. He complained that both were bustled into a jeep and driven to Casino police station, guns poked in their ribs all the way. The policeman on duty knew Mr Cooper and he knew that the Indonesians at the camp gave local police no trouble.

The policeman demanded to know of the Dutch why they had arrested an Australian citizen at gunpoint. A Dutch officer replied that Cooper had no permit to enter the camp. The policeman inquired if the girls who visited the Dutch in their camp quarters had permits. "That is different," was the predictable answer. Countering Dutch illegality with Australian illegality, the policeman ordered the Dutch to drive Mr Cooper back to Casino camp so he could get the car he had left there.[6]

Queensland Trades and Labor Council suspended business to discuss this Casino affair and called on the Australian Government immediately to disarm all Dutch personnel in Australia and to "investigate the arrest by the Dutch of the Casino railwayman Cooper on Sunday 14 October 1945, the entry by Dutch guards into an Australian home (Mr McGillicutt's) in Casino" and a further Dutch intrusion to a political meeting at Bundaberg.[7] (Dutch provosts raided a public meeting in support of the Indonesian Republic at Bundaberg, forcibly removed Indonesians from the audience, despite protests from Australians present, and later flew them to Camp Lytton for internment.)

Mr E.J. Hanson reported that he had visited Casino on behalf of the Queensland TLC, found the charges against the Dutch were correct and that the people concerned were prepared to sign affidavits.[8]

Indonesian internees could easily be seen by Casino residents from the Kyogle Road. They bathed and laundered in an open trough, used crude latrines and slept in crowded huts and tents. No lamps were provided in winter or mosquito nets in summer. The prisoners had little soap, less disinfectants and never adequate medical care. Many of the prisoners' personal possessions were taken from them, some burnt. Knowing the two daily camp meals were frugal, Casino residents, in a kind of guilty compassion, collected on Christmas Eve 1945 a truckload of fruit for the prisoners. Dutch guards refused entry to the truck. Residents' protests were vehement and insistent, so the fruit was allowed in but all conversation with the prisoners was banned.

The Dutch stopped the next day's rice ration. An Indonesians' Defence Committee was formed by Casino residents and Lismore Trades and Labor Council called a public meeting that demanded the Dutch concentration camp's closure.

Bloodshed in Camp Victory

The first known Casino killing, after several Indonesian suicides, was on 17 April 1946. The 480 prisoners demonstrated against bad food. Casino residents heard the camp alarm wailing and saw some 300 armed Dutch and Ambonese move against the protesters. The guards ordered the Indonesians to run for their tents. Last man to the tents, called Tazan, was shot dead and another prisoner, Lenkong, wounded, according to the version given by two internees released later.[9] The Sydney *Daily Telegraph* account said:

> A volley was fired over their heads but the men still refused to return to their huts. Another shot was fired, killing an Indonesian.[10]

Lengkong was wounded again in an affray at Casino on 12 September 1946. Serdo was killed by a spray of 18 bullets from an Austen sub-machine gun. Another Indonesian, Parta, was severely wounded late in 1946, in the last week of Casino camp's existence.

An Australia-Indonesian Association report of August 1946 said:

> We have endeavoured to persuade the Australian Govern-

ment to intervene on behalf of the Casino internees but so far with little success.[11]

Immigration Minister Calwell was by this time trying to free the Casino Indonesians and end this embarrassing overstretch of the extraterritorial powers his Government had granted the NEI Government-in-Exile. First Mr Calwell made polite representations to the Dutch, then heated protests and demands. Against the wishes of some of his Cabinet colleagues he sent a strongly worded cable to The Hague, demanding closure of the Casino camp. The language was so demanding that there was almost a diplomatic incident. Mr Calwell threatened that if the Dutch did not free the Casino prisoners from their guards then the Australian authorities would take action to remove those guards.[12]

The Casino inmate total had been augmented by transfers of mutineers from camps the Dutch were relinquishing as they moved out to Java. In November 1946, 562 were held at Casino. Mr Calwell's shock cable provoked action; 227 were transported to Chermside, Brisbane, in that month for repatriation. The remaining 335 were shipped to Republican territory soon after. These were the last Asian prisoners of colonialism for which the Commonwealth of Australia furnished an open-air bastille.

The Casino evacuation closed the file of Hollanders' incongruities in their Australian nomenclature. The first name the Dutch conferred was Dirk Hartog's Harmonyland. The last was Camp Victory, the Netherlands Indies Government-in-Exile's name for the barbed wire compound at Casino where the first mutiny for the Republic was staged.

9 Indonesians Initiate the Boycott

A group of Indonesians in Woolloomooloo, Sydney waterfront suburb where the Indonesian Seamen's Union had its office, kept ears glued to a short-wave radio that had come into their possession. They monitored every word from Batavia Radio after the Japanese surrender of 15 August 1945. Here in Woolloomooloo the emigre Indonesians first heard the Batavia broadcast of the Republic's August 17 proclamation. They danced for joy.

That night a young Indonesian of Mrs Gwyn Williams' English-language class burst into her flat in Darlinghurst, "terribly excited".[1] He was known as Tukliwon, or Tuk for short. Later he was to return to Australia as Tuk Subianto,[2] a leader of the Indonesian seamen and dockers and a member of the Republican Parliament. Tuk was so young-looking that Australians might have taken him for 16. He was 20 years of age when the Republic was born. Tuk had come to Australia as a seaman aboard one of the "Flying Dutchmen". Australian friends had arranged a course for him at Sydney Technical College and, after that, a maintenance mechanic's job on Sydney Harbour ferries.

Tukliwon was leader of the Indonesian Seamen's Union in Australia. He set out from his union's Woolloomooloo office on the first morning after the Batavia broadcast to tell the Seamen's Union of Australia, at the corner of Day and King Streets in Sydney, that the Indonesians in Australia "would actively support the new Republican Government". The Seamen's Union promised support.

Within a week Tukliwon was back at the Seamen's Union office to advise that the Dutch had indicated that they wanted Indonesian crews to take their ships back to Java from Australia. The Indonesian seamen intended to refuse duty. The Seamen's Union of Australia again promised support.[3]

Australian seamen, however, did not hold the decisive power. Loading Dutch cargoes was the task of Waterside Workers' Federation members. Tukliwon and Mr Elliott went to interview Mr James Healy, General Secretary of the Waterside Workers' Federation. Mr Healy offered "unstinted support" but his union's governing executive must approve first.[4] This approval – by the Waterside Workers' Federation Federal Council – was given.

Inspiration for the boycott in Australia of Dutch ships and other services did not begin, however, with Tukliwon's mission to Mr Elliott and Mr Healy: these visits were in the sequence of Indonesian resistance moves.

Australian Nationalist Angle

Indonesian initiatives had already evoked a decision in the Communist Party headquarters, George Street, Sydney, to marshal maritime, shipyard and land transport unions' support to Indonesian rebels. The Party by 1944 could claim about 23,000 members, many of them in the armed services or employed in enterprises associated with the Netherlands Indies Government-in-Exile's war mobilisation.

Indonesians at the Dutch establishment had intelligence access and so, from the Indonesians and its own members, the Communist Party had the very best of information on Dutch intentions and dispositions.

The *Tribune*, Communist Party organ, went to press in Sydney on 20 August (dated 21 August) with an article prepared by the writer, under policy direction, immediately after the Republic's proclamation:

Australia must raise the strongest voice to see that her 70 million Indonesian neighbours win their freedom. A fettered Indonesia in the Near North carries a constant threat of political and economic instability to Australian trade and foreign policy.

93

This was a wide cast for public sympathy in the coming operation to embargo the Dutch, suggesting to the then influential Party membership that appeals for support to the Indonesians should be angled to national interest. "International solidarity" was too fragile a strategy to stand alone before the stresses ahead. Sir Robert Peel, the British statesman who helped extend colonial controls in Asia, must have turned in his grave when his descendant, Mr Gerald Peel, wrote in the Communist *Tribune* on 23 August 1945:

The question of Indonesian independence is now definitely on the agenda. The Australian Labor Movement must stand foursquare behind the Indonesian people in their just demand for independence . . . The Australian Labor Movement must be very vigilant to see that there is no military intervention in Indonesia against the Indonesian people for restoration of Dutch rule.

The imperative mood was then employed *ad nauseam* in Communist journalism: in this instance use of *must* went hand in hand with concrete planning against the Dutch armada being mustered in Australian ports. In Brisbane, due in part to the persistence of Tanah Merah exiles, planning to boycott Dutch ships began early in September. In the Queensland Trades and Labor Council and the maritime unions militant influence was strong.

The man who, in the public eye, bore the main burdens in leading the unions in their first bans on the Dutch and caring for Indonesian deserters was Michael Healy,[5] timber-cutter, construction worker, coal-mine-trucker, an unemployed leader in the Great Depression, a cattle-station hand and then a waterside worker. In July 1943 he was elected unopposed as Queensland TLC Secretary. Talking to Indonesians in Brisbane he could smell gunpowder not far away. So convinced were they that revolution loomed in the Indies that in 1944 he and his wife learned the language. Their teacher was Prowito, interned in Tanah Merah since 1926. (Prowito, his health undermined at Tanah Merah, where he acted as school-teacher to the internees, died soon after his return to Java. A son, educated in Australia, flew in the Republican Air Force against the Dutch.)

Economic Issues

Brisbane was to see the first application of the boycott to Dutch ships. This was natural: the Queensland unions had well-briefed and committed leaders, Brisbane was the head-quarters of the Netherlands Indies Government-in-Exile, the depositary of archives and directives and in the area was the largest concentration of Indonesians. In Brisbane and other Queensland centres were most of the Tanah Merah men.

Two of these men, Prowito and Slamet, met secretly in Brisbane on Sunday morning, 23 September, with Mr Michael Healy, with the two principal officials of the Waterside Workers' Federation Brisbane Branch, Messrs E. Englart and A. Graham, and with a Building Workers' Industrial Union official, Mr Archie Nichol. Indonesian representatives from the Dutch ships in the Brisbane River came ashore on the Sunday evening and conferred with Australian union officials. The conference, which lasted from 8 pm to 1 am, put the finishing touches on the plan discussed at the morning meeting, on tactics to be employed in the Indonesian seamen's walk-off from Dutch ships.

The demands to be served by the Indonesians on the Dutch captains were typed out in the Brisbane Trades Hall. They were to be presented to the ships' captains on the following Monday morning, 24 September. It was arranged that Messrs Englart and Healy should address waterside workers assembled for the morning labor pick-up early on the Monday morning to enlist their support for the Indonesians. The Dutch ship-owners' threat to the Indonesians' deferred pay or "bonus" and to their wage rates reinforced Republican sentiment and allowed both Indonesians and their Australian supporters to present the walk-offs from Dutch ships not only as a political demonstration in favour of the Indonesian Republic but as a strike over economic grievances, legitimate in the Australian trade union tradition. The economic phase of the Indonesian seamen's mutinies made it easier for Australian militants to rally the support of Trades and Labor Councils and the central governing body, the Australian Council of Trade Unions.

The Indonesian seamen's delegates at their Sunday evening meeting in the Trades Hall carried both a political and an

95

economic resolution. The political resolution (in the Indonesians' own English) said:

> To prevent the Dutch Government exiled here in Australia to go back to Indonesia to interference with the Independent Indonesia, i.e. the Government of the Republic of Indonesia.

The economic resolution said that the money deducted by the Dutch shipowners from Indonesian seamen's wages each month should be refunded "here in Australia" and that minimum wages and hours should be fixed, otherwise they would not go to sea.[6] The Indonesian seamen, said Queensland Trades and Labor Council, "know from past experience that, if they are not paid this money while in Australia, they will never get it." The seamen were faced with "a return to the old rate" of £2 (4 dollars) a month gross.[7]

Indonesian resistance to regression to the squalid colonial wage had stronger appeal to many moderate Australian trade unionists, always wary of political manipulation, than did the issue of Indonesian independence.

First Boycott Resolution

While in Brisbane the unions felt the need to move circumspectly, the Sydney preparations against the Dutch were more public. Sydney Branch members of the Waterside Workers' Federation, at a meeting in their union hall in Sussex Street on 20 September, delivered a rugged denunciation of Dutch colonialism. The meeting unanimously carried a resolution moved by Mr Stanley Moran, the Sydney WWF Branch Treasurer, advising waterside workers "to place an embargo on all ships carrying munitions or any other war materials to be used against the Indonesian Government". The resolution continued:

> Further, we call on the Labor Council to support the struggle by deputation to the Dutch Consul, demanding that the Indonesian people should be given the right to elect their own government.[8]

This was the first public resolution for boycott of Dutch

96

ships. Promptly a circular was distributed on Sydney wharves, saying:

> Four ships, the *Japara*, *El Liberatador*, *General Verspijck* and *Patras*, are being loaded with supplies for the Dutch Army that is being brought from England for the purpose of waging war against the independence of the Indonesian people and to convey the Dutch East Indies puppet government to Indonesia.

After referring to trouble on a Dutch warship (*Tromp*) and, presciently and prematurely, to refusal of Indonesian seamen to sail Dutch ships to Indonesia, the circular to Sydney waterside workers said:

> The loading of these ships is a definite challenge to the democratic ideals of the Australian Labor Movement. To assist the Dutch in any way is to assist avaricious Dutch imperialism against Indonesian democracy.[9]

This brassy language could not be translated to union black bans till some days after the Brisbane walk-offs of Indonesian seamen opened the first chapter of the Black Armada story. On Monday 24 September Sydney waterside workers were on a strike on a conventional industrial issue.

In Melbourne, apparently without consulting Australian trade unions, Indonesian crews began refusing duty on 23 September. The Melbourne Branch of the Waterside Workers' Federation was under conservative leadership and was not at first officially involved.

Fremantle, the fourth main port to join this movement to ostracise the Netherlands Indies Government-in-Exile, its supplies and institutions, was mainly concerned with ships of war and no maritime unionists were engaged at the Royal Netherlands Navy base on the Swan River. No Dutch merchant ships were due for waterfront labor at Fremantle on 24 September.

97

10   Strike-Bound Government

According to plan, Indonesian seamen began to desert Dutch ships moored in the Brisbane River on the morning of Monday 24 September. The Indonesians were sometimes too faithful to compact: because captains were missing from two of the ships and they could not present the typed demands to them as agreed with Australian union officials they remained aboard. The Queensland Trades and Labor Council sent men down to the wharves in the evening to bring them off.

Brisbane waterside workers imposed an immediate black ban on all ships flying the Dutch flag. Six ships were denied stevedoring labor on the Monday: *Minyak-Terah*, *Janssens*, *Van Outhoorn*, *Van Heutz*, *Cawra* and *Khoen-Hoea*. The *Both*, which had carried the Tanah Merah inmates to Australia, coyly flying no flag at all, was listed as a suspect and black-banned on 25 September. The Dutch hospital ship *Oranje* was exempted.

Brisbane WWF Branch minutes reveal a remarkable unanimity among workers of Left, Right and Centre persuasions. On the Branch Executive the boycott resolution, moved by J. Doolan and seconded by J. Clancy, demanding wage justice for Indonesian seamen and "that the Dutch Government in Australia shall not interfere with the Government as at present established by the Indonesian people themselves", was carried unanimously. The 1,400 watersiders attending a mass meeting the following day, September 25, endorsed the black ban on Dutch ships without a dissentient. However, one member, named as Cummings in the minutes, offered for work at

98

Brett's Wharf. The mass meeting, still in session, heard of this and resolved that Mr Cummings should be expelled from the union unless he offered a satisfactory explanation. Mr Cummings explained that he "only vaguely understood the dispute" and, on reaffirming his ignorance of the issue, was allowed by a meeting of members to continue as a waterside worker.[1] This iron unanimity of men of mixed opinions could not but impress the former locomotive driver, Ben Chifley, who lost his job on the engine of the Forbes Mail in NSW when divided railwaymen staged a strike in 1917.

The watersiders' boycott of the seven Dutch ships in Brisbane was speedily extended to unions with members servicing the maritime industry — boilermakers, engineers, iron-workers, ship painters and dockers and carpenters of the repair yards, storemen and packers, tally clerks, and tug-crews.

The Fighting Ship

The Netherlands Indies Government Information Service in Sydney, unhelpful to its own cause, reported on 22 September that a ship scheduled to leave Brisbane for Java would carry "Netherlands Indies Civil Administration officials". Queensland Trades and Labor Council officials established that the "government ship" was the *Van Heutz*. Mr E.J. Hanson, Chairman of the TLC Disputes Committee set up to handle the Australian-Indonesian strikes, reported to the Council that "the Dutch Government wanted to get away on the *Van Heutz*".[2] Government-in-Exile officials, except for the skeleton staff required to handle remaining tasks in Australia, embarked in the *Van Heutz* in the week-end of 22-23 September, some of them with baggage and crates of documents.

It was desperately urgent for the Dutch to disembark this key administrative personnel and documents at strategic points in the Indies, under temporary British and Japanese protection, to get the machinery of Netherlands control operating again.

The Queensland Trades and Labor Council officials made sure that the Indonesians were all off the *Van Heutz* on 24 September. They were given emergency accommodation in the Brisbane Trades Hall. The trade union boycott of the *Van*

99

Heutz set the match to a short political fuse. As well as the 200 government officials from Camp Columbia, she had aboard 600 Dutch troops and their baggage and equipment and 200 tons of small arms and ammunition.

When the Waterside Workers' Federation refused the call to provide labor for the *Van Heutz*, the Australian and Netherlands Indies Governments selected her as the "fighting ship" in a trial of strength with the boycotting unions. Because of her vital importance to Dutch reoccupation plans, the Stevedoring Industry Commission, the Commonwealth Government's waterfront labor control body, was instructed to put the *Van Heutz* at the head of the list for labor pick-up. Then, to answer the wharfies' refusal to finish loading *Van Heutz*, the Stevedoring Industry Commission refused to call labor for any other ships in the Brisbane River. This meant that the whole port of Brisbane was locked out. The Government ultimatum to the waterside workers was, in effect: finish loading the *Van Heutz* or you'll get no other work.

With the whole port idle ships necessary to provision and repatriate Australian soldiers in South-East Asia and the Pacific Islands were delayed. This strengthened the union position: the Chifley Government could not afford to immobilise ships required to service Australian units of the armed forces in South-East Asia and the South Pacific. Waterside Workers' Federation General Secretary James Healy protested to the Minister for Shipping, Senator W.P. Ashley, with whom he was on good terms. Brisbane WWF Branch Secretary E. Englart also telegraphed Senator Ashley, urging "immediate action to prevent further unnecessary hold-ups in shipping in this port affecting Australian people and soldiers in Islands by instructing Stevedoring Industry Commission to accept labor offering for these vessels".[3]

The Chifley Government felt, apparently, that trade union strength was too formidable, that "colonial Dutch" prestige was not high and that soldiers awaiting supplies and repatriation ships would become restive. Many Australian soldiers, in fact, sent messages of support to the Waterside Workers' Federation during the boycott of the Dutch ships. The Government in Canberra, no doubt with some qualms, ordered the Stevedoring Industry Commission to remove *Van Heutz* from the top of the labor pick-up list, to call labor for non-Dutch ships and leave the Dutch ships without stevedoring labor.

The first round thus went to the trade unions and the rebellious Indonesian seamen. They had not only delayed the transport of the Netherlands Indies Government apparatus from Camp Columbia, but had forced the Australian Government into a strange official collaboration in the boycott of Dutch shipping.

Dutch Soldiers Break Strike

Mr E. Englart (WWF) reported to a 26 September meeting of the Labor Council Disputes Committee and representatives of unions involved in the boycott that the Netherlands Indies Government-in-Exile planned to load *Van Heutz* by using soldiers as wharf-laborers. *Van Heutz* was at a Brisbane berth controlled by Dalgety & Co., English-owned wool-broking, trading, shipping and stevedoring concern. The unions' meeting of 26 September warned Dalgety & Co. that if *Van Heutz* was loaded by Dutch soldiers at the Dalgety wharf, this wharf would be declared black for all stevedoring work. The unions also decided that labor—mostly covered by the Storemen and Packers' Union — would be withdrawn from Dalgety & Co.'s wool storage sheds.

The Waterside Workers' Federation sought Federal Government intervention to block use of Dutch troops on the wharves. Mr Englart telegraphed the Minister for the Army, Mr F.M. Forde, on 25 September, telling him that information had been received of Dutch Government and South-East Asia Command intentions to work *Van Heutz* with Dutch troops. "Such action if taken," said Mr Englart's telegram to Canberra, "will result in serious industrial unrest. Urge you take immediate action contact Dutch authorities to prevent their loading vessel with cargo consisting of small arms and ammunition."[4] Others of the unions involved, through Queensland Trades and Labor Council, also warned Army Minister Forde by telephone of "serious repercussions" if Dutch troops were permitted to load *Van Heutz*. Protests were sent directly to Prime Minister Chifley.[5]

On 27 September Labor Council General Secretary M. Healy advised a meeting of boycotting unions at the Trades Hall that

400 Dutch troops had been transported from Wacol camp, near Brisbane, on the previous afternoon. Soon these Dutch soldiers, officers included, began work as stevedores at *Van Heutz*. Some wrath was caused among Queensland trade unionists.

Now everyone seemed to be breaking the law. Stevedoring work, under Federal legislation to which the Chifley Government was a party, was the legally recognised preserve of members of the Waterside Workers' Federation, registered for waterfront loading and unloading operations under Act of Parliament. No emergency law or regulation had been issued to alter this arrangement. Mr Healy of the Labor Council confronted the Dutch soldiers who in defiance of law and tradition were breaking a strike on the Australian waterfront. The Dutch soldiers claimed they were working under "an agreement with the Australian Government". Mr Healy complained that neither the Labor Council Disputes Committee nor the unions concerned "possessed any knowledge of the terms contained in this agreement between the two Governments".[6]

Orders from Mountbatten?

The Dutch soldiers, Mr Healy of the Labor Council said, claimed to him that they had "definite orders from Major-General Stantke, acting on behalf of Lord Louis Mountbatten, to get this ship away to the north". (Major-General Victor Paul Hildebrand Stantke was General Officer Commanding Queensland Lines of Communication at the time, and from 1940 to 1943 he had been Adjutant-General at Australian Army Headquarters, Melbourne.) The meeting of unions to which Mr Healy reported on 27 September decided to protest to Prime Minister Chifley against the use of Dutch soldiers as strike-breakers and to seek from Major-General Stantke and from the Government in Canberra the terms of the agreement between the Netherlands Indies Government-in-Exile and the Australian Government.[7]

Lord Louis Mountbatten's SEAC, charged with preparing the way for the Dutch reoccupation, was desperately short of ships and no military action against the Indonesian Republic could have effective political sequel unless the Dutch administrative staffs were transported to their allotted posts. Hence it is more than likely that SEAC, through the Chifley Government and Major-General Stantke, did move for urgent breaking of the boycott on the "government ship", the *Van Heutz*, at Brisbane.

Australian Government assistance was given for the defeat of the *Van Heutz* black ban. The presence in Australia of a foreign emigre regime was providing another paragraph in the chronicle of unique historical experience: the widest Australian imagination had never conceived a Labor Government aiding the soldiers of a foreign army to break a strike of Australian trade unionists who contributed generously in funds and votes to put that Labor Government in office. Dutch military trucks poured in troops from Wacol Camp to the Brisbane wharves. Slowly, laboriously and incompetently, sweating Dutch officers and soldiers loaded lethal boxes of small arms and ammunition in *Van Heutz*. The Netherlands Indies Army stevedores were guarded from angry trade union pickets and demonstrators by officers in Dutch uniforms, carrying tommy-guns, armed Queensland State Police and Commonwealth Police. Brisbane waterside workers demanded in vain an end to this display of arms by foreign soldiers.

A trade union ban was imposed on all deliveries to and from Dalgety's Wharf. Feeling ran so high that non-unionists joined the anti-Dutch movement. At the Warry Street depot for receipt and despatch of Netherlands Indies Government stores, non-unionists accepted a Trades and Labor Council appeal and refused to touch goods marked for delivery to Dutch ships. Non-unionists employed at McWhirter's department store and merchandising concern in Valley, an inner Brisbane suburb, stopped work rather than handle goods for the Dutch and when they returned to their jobs pledged that they "would not in any circumstances" load materials for transfer to Dalgety's Wharf.[8]

Interrupted Voyage

Van Heutz was having trouble with Indonesians as well as Australians. The original crew of strikers was replaced by other Indonesian seamen. The second crew of Indonesians walked off. The Dutch tried to get 26 Indonesian soldiers aboard to act as seamen, but failed. Some 90 Indonesians were flown down from Netherlands New Guinea; they, too, joined the strikers. However, the Dutch were able to bring some Indonesians aboard under armed guard and hold them as prisoners.

The *Van Heutz* could not get all the cargo booked because some of it was under black ban in Brisbane storehouses. Nor could *Van Heutz* get enough coal for her voyage to Java, because of coal-lumpers' refusal to supply her. Seamen would not provide tugs. *Van Heutz*, tugless, lumbered down the Brisbane River about 1 October, while a launch loaded with Indonesians and Australians, shouting "Merdeka!" and "Down with Dutch colonialism!", circled round her. A week later *Van Heutz* put into Bowen Harbour, North-Central Queensland, about 72 hours' normal steaming time from Brisbane. There was no public explanation as to why the ship took so long to reach Bowen. The general surmise was that the Dutch officers had trouble with Indonesians held under duress. The Bowen Branch of the Waterside Workers' Federation black-banned *Van Heutz*. Collinsville miners, at the coal mines not far from Bowen, resolved they would not hew coal for Dutch ships. *Van Heutz* was delayed at Bowen for about a week. The *Van Heutz*, Waterside Workers' Fedération officials believed, was coaled by another Dutch ship at sea to enable her to complete her interrupted voyage and deliver personnel and equipage of the Netherlands Indies Government to British custody in Batavia.

11   Australian Navy Landed Black Guilders

Dutch officers were at hand as Melbourne waterside workers slung, lifted and stowed the cases of silver and copper coins and guilder notes, bearing engravings of the Netherlands Queen. The guilder notes and coins in the *Karsik*, berthed in Victoria Dock, were as strategic as bullets for disinheritance of the Indonesian Republic.

The *Karsik*'s Indonesian seamen debated on Saturday and Sunday, 22-23 September, whether they would sail the *Karsik* to Java. Dutch officers, aware of their disaffection, prepared a replacement crew of marines from the Middle Park depot. When the seamen made it clear that they would not sail the marines were ordered aboard on 24 September. They refused to man the *Karsik* and were lodged in Pentridge and Geelong Gaols. From a pool of Indian seamen established in Melbourne for wartime and postwar duties the Dutch were able to draw a crew.

Though Melbourne Branch of the Waterside Workers' Federation, under Rightwing leadership, did not immediately apply the boycott to Dutch ships, as did watersiders in Brisbane, numbers of Melbourne watersiders joined the striking Indonesian seamen, Australian seamen and other trade unionists in a demonstration against the Dutch aboard the *Karsik*. Indonesian seamen sang the new Republican anthem on the wharf and appealed to the Indian crew to desert. The Indians agreed to come ashore on 28 September, but they remained on the *Karsik*. Australian maritime unionists assumed that the Indians were under some pressure from the Dutch officers and from the Australian and British authorities concerned in their recruitment, and that these recent arrivals from India were confused and uncertain about the issues at stake.[1]

Karsik's captain called for tugs on 28 September. Tug-captains and crews refused to tow the "money ship" out of Victoria Dock into the Yarra River stream. *Karsik* also called for coal: this was refused by the "coalies" who in Melbourne were members of the Waterside Workers' Federation. The money-laden ship lurched out of Victoria Dock into the river, down the bay and through the Rip of Port Phillip heads. She was heading into worse trouble than she had struck at Melbourne.

The only other ship in Melbourne port identifiable as Dutch at this time was the *Merak*. *Merak*'s Indonesian crew of 62 joined 33 Indonesian strikers from the *Karsik*. The Dutch ship *Tjibesar* was under a maritime unions' black ban not long after.

Dutch ships black-banned in Melbourne were not listed by any trade union. The late Mr Charles Young,[2] a WWF Federal Councillor at the time the boycott began, claimed that Melbourne watersiders prevented considerable Dutch cargo from being shipped to Java and that the Transport Workers' Union, Federated Clerks' Union, Seamen's Union and Painters and Dockers' Union materially assisted in making the boycott effective. Denied military stevedoring labor as in Brisbane, Sydney and Fremantle, the Dutch captains had to leave much of their cargo on the wharves.

The Dutch, said Mr Young, changed port destinations marks or cut these port marks from bales and crates. "But the transport drivers", he added, "conveyed the information to the watersiders about the changed or missing marks and the cargo never left the berths, despite strong protests from Dutch ships' captains and Australian shipping agents".[3]

The Victorian Secretary of the Seamen's Union, Mr William Bird, was a key figure in the Melbourne boycott, ensuring that no tugs towed Dutch ships.

Trouble Ashore in Melbourne

Ashore in the city, the 33 *Karsik* and 62 *Merak* seamen tried to push their way into a hostel maintained by the Dutch for Indonesians in their employ. They brushed past supervisors but were soon served with eviction notices. Trade unionists and other sympathetic citizens found accommodation for them.

On 30 September a public rally in favour of Indonesian independence was held at the Savoy Theatre, Melbourne. So many attended that another meeting had to be organised for the overflow crowd. The Savoy Theatre meeting was addressed by an Indonesian sergeant from the Netherlands Indies Army, by a survivor of 17 years in Tanah Merah camp, two Indonesian girls and an Australian trade union representative. A collection to aid the Republican cause realised £240 (480 dollars). The meeting and its overflow called for withdrawal of British troops from Indonesia, protested at "Dutch intimidation" of Indonesians in Australia and the re-opening of Tanah Merah, and then formed a procession from the audience to march through Melbourne streets, headed by Australian and Republican flags. This was probably the first public procession of Australians and Asians for independence of an Asian nation. Opposite St. Paul's Anglican Cathedral in Flinders Street the assembly sang *Indonesia Raya*.

The Dutch were also at the Melbourne meetings. Next day, Monday 1 October, van-loads of Dutch military and plain-clothes police and West Indian provosts raided Indonesians billeted in the Metropole Hotel. The Dutch were accompanied by Victorian State and Commonwealth police and Australian Army provosts. Of the first four Indonesians arrested, two had spoken at the Savoy Theatre rally and two had been in the audience. The tumult of the arrests and Indonesian resistance drew a crowd. The *Sydney Morning Herald*[4] reported that "several onlookers were roughly handled", that one man had a knife brandished at him by a Dutch serviceman and that a Dutch provost stopped a photographer from taking a picture of the incident. The Council for Civil Liberties in Melbourne denounced use of armed force by a foreign power on Australian territory.

Victorian State police took over the task of arresting deserters from the *Karsik* and *Merak*. They were fined only £3 (6 dollars) with 5s. (50 cents) costs — a very light fine for "prohibited migrants" — by a Melbourne court. As in the *Karsik* case, Indonesian marines and Navy sailors refused to replace the *Merak* strikers. The *Sydney Morning Herald*[5] reported the arrest of 50 Indonesian servicemen for refusal to obey orders and their impending court-martial.

Navy to the Rescue

Meanwhile, *Karsik* was heading north, her treasure chests full but her bunkers nearly empty. The captain had hoped to make a non-Australian port with his limited supply of coal, but the Indian stokehold crew was apparently anything but thrifty in feeding the boilers. North of the Tropic of Capricorn, *Karsik* had to put into Bowen, seeking coal from the Collinsville field, railed to the port. Mr A. Little, Secretary of the Bowen WWF Branch, wired his national union leaders in Sydney on 4 October, asking the names of all Dutch ships to which labor should be refused in case any of them, denied coal at southern ports, should try to bunker at Bowen. Next day, when *Karsik* sailed into Bowen harbour, Secretary Little wired the WWF headquarters in Sydney: "*Karsik* here. Not supplying coal."[6]

The Miners' Federation members at Collinsville declared that they would not mine coal if it were for Dutch ships and the Australian Railways Union members said they would refuse to carry coal from Collinsville to Bowen unless they were assured it would not bunker the *Karsik*. *Karsik* was tied down at Bowen until at some future date she could be bunkered from a Dutch collier at sea.

The Netherlands Indies Government obviously appealed to the Chifley Government for help in repairing the damage inflicted by the Melbourne and Bowen boycotts of the *Karsik*. The Indonesian Republic had adapted the Japanese occupation currency; this was being widely recognised as a symbol of Republican power. The Dutch currency default thrust at the very heart of their economic and political recuperation plans. An embracing trade union boycott at Bowen would have made it virtually impossible to unload the currency notes and coins from the *Karsik* and re-load them on another ship or aircraft.

The Australian Government, therefore, made a warship available.

First, additional supplies of Netherlands Indies currency had to be marshalled before the Australian Navy could transport it to Batavia, so the Dutch faced nettlesome delay into the following year. In February 1946 Australian naval ratings loaded Netherlands Indies currency, brought to the berth by naval transport, aboard the sloop HMAS *Bungaree*. The *Bungaree* sailed at speed for Batavia. On 6 March 1946 the British and Dutch authorities in Batavia, knowing that the *Bungaree* would soon be off Tanjong Priok, ordered reintroduction of Netherlands Indies currency; there was to be an immediate changeover from Indonesian currency.[7] The Australian Associated Press Special Representative in Batavia reported on 7 March that the *Bungaree* was expected to reach Batavia on 8 March "with a load of Netherlands Indies paper money and silver coins . . . The money, printed and minted in the United States in 1943, has been stored in banks in Australia".[8]

The new Netherlands Indies currency was to have more substantial backing than gold bullion. A few days later the *Sydney Morning Herald*[9] reported the landing of 3,000 Dutch troops in Java, as forerunners of a Dutch force of 20,000. The Dutch soldiers were taken ashore in landing craft manned by British Marines.

Dr Sjahrir's Protest

The Dutch, however, were still heavily reliant on British arms in Java and Sumatra and on Australian arms in East Indonesia. Netherlands Indies currency could only be introduced by force of arms, mainly British.

As Republican Premier, Dr Sjahrir sent a bitter protest against HMAS *Bungaree*'s currency mission to the Commander of SEAC forces in Java, Lieutenant-General Sir Montagu Stopford. Dr Sjahrir said that the Republican Government held the British military responsible "for active intervention in the affairs of Java and for having failed to confine themselves to their allotted tasks". The landing and issue of the Dutch currency meant "a serious aggression against the sovereign power of the Republic of Indonesia". The British had broken their promise, Dr Sjahrir's note charged, that they would not issue a new currency while the political situation remained unsolved.

The British recognised the NICA-scrips, as they were called, in areas under their control. But Republican rule in the productive hinterland tended to confine NICA-scrips circulation to the Dutch themselves. The Dutch could get neither foodstuffs nor other necessities in return for NICA-scrips. The Indonesian population needed the adapted Japanese money to buy produce from the rich areas which neither the British nor the Dutch had, as yet, the forces to subjugate.

While the boycott of the *Karsik* had been circumvented and Netherlands Indies notes and coins landed at Tanjong Priok by the Australian Navy, the delays in Melbourne and Bowen gave the Republic time to prepare the launching of its own rupiah. On 15 March 1946 the American Associated Press correspondent reported from Batavia that Dutch efforts to reestablish their currency appeared to have failed. Workers and tradesmen were refusing to accept Dutch money as payment.

It required Dutch naval blockade and military occupation of substantial areas to undermine Republican currency, but this dubious economic success was to be short-lived. The same Australian Government that provided the naval sloop *Bungaree* to dash guilder notes to Anglo-Dutch-held Batavia, in an effort to cancel out the *Karsik* boycott and help restore Dutch rule, was soon providing naval auxiliary ships to repatriate *Karsik* strikers and mutineers to Republican territory, thus helping the Indonesians to prevent the Dutch from restoring their rule.

12   Atlantic Charter Strikers

Sydney trade unionists did not pretend that their strikes against the Dutch were first and foremost to protect Indonesians' wage rights. On the night of Thursday 27 September, the New South Wales Trades and Labor Council in Sydney resolved that Indonesia's claims were "in accordance with the Atlantic Charter", endorsed boycotts of Dutch ships and formed a deputation to the Dutch Consul-General to acquaint him with New South Wales trade unionists' opposition to colonialism.[1]

First strike action against the Dutch in Sydney was not, as in Brisbane and Melbourne, to back deserting Indonesian seamen, but as a demonstration for the Republic of Indonesia — and perhaps the only strike in history to proclaim the Atlantic Charter as its credential. Members of the Boilermakers' Society, Ship Painters and Dockers' Union and Federated Ironworkers' Association were on Tuesday 25 September giving a final refit to the *Swartenhondt*, the first Dutch ship to run into trouble with the Seamen's Union after its flight from the Indies in 1942. On that day these shipyard workers walked off the *Swartenhondt* as a demonstration of support for the Republic.

On 25 September, too, Sydney truck-drivers serving the waterfront (Transport Workers' Union) and tally clerks (Federated Clerks' Union) declared they would boycott Dutch shipping and services.

Sydney waterside workers were not immediately involved because of their industrial strike over methods of using forklift machines on the waterfront. No labor was called to continue stevedoring the *General Verspijck* after the Javanese and Timorese seamen deserted her on 24 September. On 28 September Sydney waterside workers were the main participants in a street demonstration outside Dutch shipping companies' and diplomatic offices in Kembla Building, Margaret Street and Wynyard Square. Police intervened, tried to seize "Hands off Indonesia" banners and were resisted in scuffles.

On 29 September, with industrial troubles receding on Sydney waterfront, the Commonwealth Government's Stevedoring Industry Commission made the first direct call for labor for Dutch ships. Wharfies were picked up to load *El Liberatador* with supplies for the Indies. Sydney watersiders had been forewarned by the Brisbane tactics of the Stevedoring Industry Commission. They knew that if they refused the call to *El Liberatador*, the ship would have been put at the head of the pick-up roster and the whole port locked out. Money was scarce after the industrial stoppage, so a ruse was applied to avoid lock-out. The required number accepted the engagement call for *El Liberatador*, travelled to the ship and went aboard at leisurely pace, prepared for work — and then walked off again. By the time the Stevedoring Industry Commission realised what had happened only about 500 of the port's 4,000 registered waterside workers remained at the pick-up centre. These were then locked out, because they rejected an order to replace the *El Liberatador* strikers.

Sydney maritime industry unionists — watersiders, seamen, truck-drivers, tally clerks, shipyard tradesmen and laborers — were, before September ended, all engaged in boycott of the Dutch. They had immobilised in Sydney the *El Liberatador*, *Japara*, *Maetsuycker*, *Patras*, *Van Swoll* and *Swartenhondt*. *General Verspijck* had almost completed loading just before the Indonesian crew walked off on 24 September, immobilising her without Australian trade union aid.

On 2 October Sydney waterside workers were called to load *Japara* and *El Liberatador* with supplies for the Indies. The Stevedoring Industry Commission had learned from the 29 September ruse at *El Liberatador*. The labor pick-up was slowed down until those assigned to *Japara* and *El Liberatador* began work. The wharfies proceeded as slowly as they could to the two ships and worked — or pretended to work — for about two hours. By then a courier informed them that labor had been allocated to all available jobs and so they walked off *Japara* and *El Liberatador.*

In a period of acute shipping shortage and heavy supply commitments, British and other shipowners, able to earn quick profits, and the Federal Government, conscious of soldiers' needs in the islands, were not keen to lock out whole ports for the sake of Dutch allies. Hence the Waterside Workers' Federation had partial success in its representations to the Minister for Shipping, Senator Ashley, to have the boycott movement against the Dutch isolated from general maritime activity.

"Everything Dutch Is Black"

New South Wales Trades and Labor Council, then representing about 250,000 unionists and the most influential State branch of the Australian Council of Trade Unions, had a delicate balance of Right, Centre and Left opinions and their shadings. Conflict was often bitter and during the emergencies of World War II there was not always agreement on whether strikes of workers in war industries and services should be condoned.

Yet this Council of such sharply divergent opinion was united in the first stages of the boycott of Dutch shipping. The Australian Council of Trade Unions Executive, which had a right-centre majority, also endorsed the boycott in its first months. Under the name of Mr Frank Kelly, Acting Secretary of the Trades and Labor Council, Labor Party member of the NSW Legislative Council and a trade union leader of consistently Rightwing views, a TLC leaflet was issued, saying:

Hands off Indonesia! All support for the demand of the Indonesians for independence! Stand by the Indonesian Trade Union Movement!

The official TLC leaflet referred to Indonesians sent to:

the ill-famed Tanah Merah in Dutch New Guinea, under conditions of the most savage treatment by the Dutch authorities, similar to conditions in Nazi concentration camps. Many Indonesians served 17 of the best years of

113

their lives in this hell-camp, and don't want to go back there.

The TLC instruction to unionists was in commanding tone:

Dutch soldiers and officers should not get transport. No Dutch munitions should be touched. Repairs on Dutch planes, ships, etc., must not be done. Dutch ships must not get coal. Tugs must not be made available to Dutch ships. Food, stores, etc., must not be provided to Dutch ships, offices, canteens or personnel. Dutch officers and seamen should not be taken to and from ships.

In fact everything Dutch is black.

The Council set up an Indonesian Sub-Committee, with Mr Hugh Grant, a Glasgow-born official of the Boilermakers' Society, as Chairman, and members of varied political affiliations, to police the trade union boycott of the Dutch.

No boycott could be more complete. An Australian trade unionist could not give a Dutchman in Australia a caraway seed without being rated as a blackleg. When the Australian Council of Trade Unions voted its support, some 1,500,000 Australian workers became subscribers to the slogan that "Everything Dutch Is Black!".

Over 30 trade unions were called on to take boycott measures against the Dutch in Australia. With them were the first trade unions of Asians ever formed in Australia – the Indonesian Seamen's Union, the Indian Seamen's Union, the Chinese Seamen's Union and the Malayan Merchant Navy Association.

The *Fort Renselaar* case in Sydney showed how rock-like was the authority of the trade unions in the early stages of the boycott. *Fort Renselaar*, American-owned but with a Dutch crew, was under black ban at Sydney early in October. *Fort Renselaar*'s agents meekly offered to unload munitions destined for Indonesia and reload her with coal for the Philippines if the ban was lifted. The ship was freed from union boycott on this condition: she promptly unloaded the Dutch-owned munitions and took on coal – under NSW Trades and Labor Council surveillance. She was then permitted to sail.

114

Craft Distinctions Forgotten

Shipyard workers do not cohere in their labors like a ship's crew and cannot be deployed in the para-military style of stevedoring gangs. Ship refit and repair required a multitude of distinct crafts and unlike-minded craftsmen. Jealousy over area of work rights has brought many a shipyard to a standstill. Among shipwrights, carpenters, fitters, plumbers, boilermakers, electricians, crane-drivers, painters and riggers of the shipyards there is far less congruity of union organisation and outlook than in wharf-laboring or ship-manning. Therefore, it was a surprise to both Australian and Dutch authorities to find the shipyard unionists taking the initiative against the Dutch, as when they walked off the *Swartenhondt* at Blue's Point yard, at the northern end of Sydney Harbour Bridge.

Swartenhondt had an Indian crew and, because the ship was under refit, there was no attempt to entice Indians ashore to join the striking Indonesian seamen. Thus there was no interlock between the shipyard unions' walk-off at Blue's Point and the Indonesian seamen's desertions of Dutch ships. The *Swartenhondt* strike was directly and exclusively in support of the Indonesian Republic.

Australia is very low on the list of world shipbuilders. Only shipyards large by Australian — not world — standards were those of Vickers of England at Cockatoo Island, Sydney; Mort's Dock, Sydney (since closed); Broken Hill Pty. Co., Whyalla (South Australia); New South Wales State Government Dockyard, Newcastle; Evans Deakin Ltd, Brisbane; and Walkers Ltd, Maryborough (Queensland); and the two Royal Australian Navy yards — Williamstown, Melbourne, and Garden Island, Sydney. Garden Island has extensive engineering facilities but lacks slipways. For ship repair, however, Australia then had a large total of smaller yards at both major and medium-sized ports round the coast. The Federated Ship Painters' and Dockers' Union and the then unaffiliated Docks Union of Fremantle, Leftist-led, held trump cards at yards needed by the Dutch. Painters and dockers supervised the docking of ships for repairs and, unless these men cooperated, the Dutch ships could not get into the docks.

When the Sydney members, directed by Federal Secretary

Terry Gordon, became involved in the *Swartenhondt* boycott, painters and dockers in other ports quickly followed them. From Newcastle the union's General President, Mr F.B. Roarty, reported backing from State Dockyard workers. Melbourne painters and dockers, their Secretary, Mr George A. Doyle, reported were "heartily in accord". Williamstown (Melbourne), Garden Island and Cockatoo Island (Sydney) and Whyalla (South Australia) followed with their endorsements.[3] Fremantle painters and dockers, their union still not federally affiliated, were involved in a black ban on two Dutch submarines, the corvette *Piet Hein* and the Royal Netherlands Navy auxiliary ship *Bonaire*.

The Dutch, no doubt briefed by Australians who understood the industrial scene, tried to exploit distinctions of craft and militancy in the various shipyards. *Curacao*, black at Sydney yards, was moved to Melbourne in October, only to come under ban there, along with *Wewak*. *Piet Hein*, black to Fremantle painters and dockers and boilermakers, sailed to Melbourne, then to Sydney, to suffer the same fate in each port.

Queensland Branch of the Federated Ironworkers' Association, while maintaining a ban on Dutch ships in Brisbane and other Queensland yards, air-freighted, at some expense, children's school-books to Indonesia, in 1945, to assist the Republic in its drive against illiteracy.

Some seven Dutch warships were directly affected by shipyard boycotts, and about a dozen merchant ships. In mid-1946 four Dutch submarine-chasers were nominally under boycott at the British naval depot, Rose Bay, Sydney Harbour. Eight Australian corvettes sold by the Chifley Government to the Dutch in 1946 were banned in the shipyards.

Airport Boycotts

The Dutch had squadrons of aeroplanes in Australia when the war ended and were soon supplied with surplus American military and transport aircraft. They began a shuttle service from Sydney and Queensland airbases, through Darwin, and sometimes used Broome, its runway restored after the 1942 Japanese bombings. Landing and servicing facilities available to them in South-East Asia were meagre. However, after the boycott of the *Van Heutz* at Brisbane, some of the top NEI Government officials and officers were flown out of Australia. Many released Dutch men and women from Japanese prison camps were flown to Australia for recuperation, some of the men for military training and stevedoring work where health permitted.

As extensive Air Force facilities remained for months after the Pacific War ended and the Dutch were using RAAF bases, Dutch aircraft could not often be held by Australian civilian mechanics' black bans. Members of the Amalgamated Engineering Union imposed a ban on Dutch aircraft at Mascot, the chief Sydney airport. On 31 October 1945, 16 Catalina flying-boats, supplied to the Dutch by the US Government, were put under boycott at the Rose Bay base by the Amalgamated Engineering Union, Australasian Society of Engineers, Electrical Trades Union, Sheetmetal Workers' Union and Transport Workers' Union. These unionists at Rose Bay flying base were employees of Qantas, the Australian international line, and had been loaned by Qantas to the Dutch to service the Catalinas. Qantas threatened dismissal of the strikers unless they repaired the aircraft, without result.

13   Troubled Dutch Naval Base

Fremantle, at the Dutch-discovered south-west corner of Australia, is nearest to Djakarta of all major Australian ports. The sea miles are less between Fremantle and Djakarta than between Fremantle and Melbourne.

Western Australia's leaders had often looked longingly to the Netherlands Indies as a source of cheap supplies, denied them by the State's 1900-01 adherence to the federation of the old semi-colonial States into the Commonwealth of Australia. Netherlands Indies sugar, cotton, coffee, cocoa, rubber, tea and oil could have been imported to Western Australia far more cheaply but for the national customs duties that followed federation; textiles and other Indies manufactured goods would have been cheaper than those from Eastern Australia.

Fremantle and Perth commercial and farm export interests continued, when World War II ended, to think of the cheaper supplies and the agricultural products outlet promised by Dutch rulers. Hospitality was assured at Fremantle to the Netherlands Navy and Army; for the reconquerors of the Indies it should have been a stable refit, refreshment, supply and mobilisation base. At the eastern end of Victoria Quay, in Beach Street, Fremantle, the Netherlands reoccupation forces had their arms deposit, their navy and army stores and officer-supervisors. Barbed wire and armed Dutch patrols surrounded the base, to guard munitions that were to savage the Indonesian Republic.

In Fremantle Harbour and the Swan River estuary when the

Republic was proclaimed were three Netherlands anti-submarine warships and a small submarine. The cruiser *Tromp*, damaged in the Java Sea battle, had stayed at Fremantle for a good portion of the war, moored in middle harbour, before she went to a Sydney yard. The Dutch submarine *K15* (*Tygerhadi*) came to Fremantle early in November 1945. The Royal Netherlands Navy corvette *Piet Hein* (ex-HMS *Serapis*, British Navy) arrived soon after.

The affair of the *Piet Hein* illustrated the Hollanders' vaunting confidence in Fremantle's potential as a boycott-free port. *Piet Hein* was damaged in the English Channel. Instead of sending the corvette to a British or West European or even Mediterranean or US Atlantic shipyard for repairs the Dutch ordered her 10,000 miles to the Antipodes — to Fremantle at the Swan River's mouth, where ship repair facilities were anything but adequate. *Piet Hein* had to limp all the way from Europe on her tank tops (exposed double bottom). Prime Minister Chifley made a puzzled protest against this provocative voyage to Australia, which happened at that time to be the only country in the world where shipyard workers banned Dutch warships.

Divided Unions Put to Test

Fremantle had an added attraction for the Netherlands authorities: its conservative central leadership of the trade unions and the secessionist spirit that in Western Australia spread from commercial, farm and manufacturing interest right down among the workers. While leaders in the WA economic field did not like Eastern Australian monopolies, so WA trade unions did not like the symbols of control in Sydney or Melbourne. The Fremantle Lumpers' Union broke away from the Waterside Workers' Federation in 1928 and did not re-affiliate till late in World War II. The Western Australian Docks, Rivers and Harbour Works Union (known for short as the Docks Union), covering painters and dockers and tug crews, was not affiliated with the federal union in Sydney. Nor were Western Australian carpenters in the Building Workers' Industrial Union, headquartered in Sydney.

A further complication for unions prone to join the boycott of Dutch ships was the Labor Party control of the central

119

trade union body in WA, the State Metropolitan Council. The Council was not only the State Branch of the Australian Council of Trade Unions, but also the WA Branch of the ALP. (This Labor Party supervision of the WA Branch of the Australian Council of Trade Unions has now ended, but it prevailed right through the period of the Dutch boycott.)

Fremantle ship repair unions had been put to test before *Piet Hein* sailed into the harbour. They were asked to service the submarine *K15* on 5 November 1945. Mr Paddy Troy, Vigilance Officer, Western Australian Docks, Rivers and Harbour Works Union, moved and Mr Parisi seconded a successful motion "that this union is not prepared to work on Dutch ships".[1] The "dockies" walked off the *K15* job. On 9 November the Western Australian Carpenters and Joiners' Union advised its members that the work of preparing the slip for *K15* was black.

On 19 November the Docks Union had before it a resolution from the State Disputes Committee, agency of the State Metropolitan Council and therefore of the Labor Party. The State Disputes Committee resolution was:

> That the matter of servicing vessels of any nationality which arrive in Australian ports is a question which can only be determined by the Commonwealth Labor Government excepting in those disputes which arise in the ordinary course of relationships between employees and employers.
>
> The States Disputes Committee is, therefore, of the opinion that no restriction in servicing such vessels should be initiated by units of the Australian Labor Party without a direction from the Federal Labor Government, and we strongly recommend to all unions and members therefore to engage and re-engage in their usual functions.[2]

There was not the slightest chance of the Federal Labor Government authorising a boycott of Dutch warships — those of a treaty ally. The Labor Party at this stage was supplying the Dutch with arms to snuff out the Republican revolution.

The moderate Federal and WA leadership of the Boilermakers' Society gave no support to the black ban. The boilermakers' Federal Secretary in Sydney, Mr John O'Toole,

NON-INTERVENTION!

Lusby, *Courier-Mail*, 24 July 1947

Indonesians and Australians march together through the streets of Sydney in 1945 and urge an end to Dutch rule. This was probably the first occasion on which Indonesians anywhere in the world outside the Indies marched to demand independence. (*Indonesia Calling*)

DUTCH COURAGE

announced that "the Western Australian industrial bodies had been opposed all along to any ban on Dutch ships in that State."[3] However, the Amalgamated Engineering Union's governing body, the Commonwealth Council, instructed its members in Fremantle not to repair Dutch naval craft or ships carrying arms to Indonesia.

When, at a meeting in Fremantle on 3 December of the Docks Union, Mr Paddy Troy moved that the union "reaffirm the decision not to work Dutch ships except hospital ships and proven mercy ships to or from Indonesia until the Indonesian issue had been settled," a Labor Party majority defeated the motion. But the minority carried on boycott activities despite the majority decision.

Obeying his State Management Committee, an organiser of the Carpenters and Joiners' Union stopped members from preparing slips for the submarine *K15*. The WA Labor Party leaders then summoned two delegates from the Carpenters and Joiners' Union to attend a State Disputes Committee meeting on 15 December. The union was disaffiliated from the Labor Party. But the union members were defiant: an aggregate meeting of members reaffirmed the boycott decision and expressed resentment at the Labor Party "departing from a basic principle of the labor movement — the right of self-determination".[4]

Though Fremantle trade unions faced more problems and difficulties than in other States in applying boycott, neither the *Piet Hein* nor the Dutch submarines could get sufficient labor to service them. *Piet Hein* lay idle, along with submarine *K15* at No.2 wharf, Fremantle. *Piet Hein*'s captain stuck it out until 14 May 1946, when she sailed for Melbourne. Workers at Williamstown Naval Dockyard and other Melbourne shipyards maintained a ban on repairs. *K15* sailed about the same time, in poor shape, for Sumatra. A smaller Dutch submarine was stranded at Fremantle by the boycott; she could not risk a sea voyage without refit and so, eventually, had to be dumped there. "Indeed," said Mr Paddy Troy, "I had the very great pleasure of putting her on the beach to be used as a breakwater".[5] This was something entirely new in trade union practice: converting a warship of a foreign navy, offered official hospitality, to a rusting breakwater.

Royal Netherlands Navy Stevedores

The Dutch had learned chastening lessons by the time the Royal Netherlands Navy Fleet auxiliary *Bonaire* arrived at the Dutch naval depot, Victoria Quay, Fremantle, in March 1946. The Indonesian islands were aswarm with revolutionaries, frustrating reoccupation. The groups of collaborators recruited offered only a thin and bloodless loyalty and Dr Van Mook could not be certain of the fealty of sultans and rajahs. The waterfronts of the main Australian base areas were almost enemy territory. The *Bonaire* came to load munitions and naval stores from behind the barbed wire and tommy-guns of Victoria Quay. She had to berth without tugs: the tug crews were then members of the Docks Union; they were transferred to the Seamen's Union in 1955. When *Bonaire* shifted berth tug crews again refused her tow-lines. The Fremantle Harbour Trust berthing staff were ordered to assist *Bonaire*, but refused to do jobs that tugmen of the Docks Union had black-banned. *Bonaire*'s officers and crew manoeuvred the vessel skilfully between berths without tugs. Fremantle lumpers, only recently in the Waterside Workers' Federation, banned all stevedoring work on *Bonaire*. As *Bonaire* was needed to run a shuttle service between Fremantle and Java, the Dutch authorities protested against the ban. Labor Party leaders in Perth intervened and heavy pressure was exerted on the waterside workers.

The Australian Council of Trade Unions Secretary, Mr A.E. Monk, according to the *West Australian*,[6] sent a telegram to Fremantle, saying that it was policy for the Waterside Workers' Federation to load ships in accordance with an agreement between External Affairs Minister Evatt and the Netherlands Minister in Australia, Baron Van Aerssen. The ACTU intervention widened the divisions in WA union ranks.

The Dutch aided the anti-boycott campaign considerably by reporting that they had cancelled £6 million worth of trade orders in WA because of trade union bans. As Perth and Fremantle interests were supplying food, clothing and other stores for the Royal Netherlands Navy, Army and Air Force, local businessmen reacted angrily against the boycotting unions. The Secretary of the Liberal Party in Western Australia, Mr C. Palmer, declared:

Cancellation by the Dutch Government of £6 million worth of orders placed in Australia, portion to come from Western Australia, is the climax of what may be claimed as one of the most deplorable episodes with which any Australian Government has been associated. That it would have been possible for a small section of the community to cause the cancellation of such an order is nothing short of amazing, particularly at a time when there are limitless possibilities of building up Australia's export trade with the Netherlands East Indies.[7]

In this prickly dispute the Waterside Workers' Federation could do little to prevent Royal Netherlands Navy sailors from loading munitions into *Bonaire*. Fremantle waterside workers were still poorly organised. About 660 were regular stevedores, in the Federation. Another 365 were outside the Federation, serving as registered casual waterside workers, but were members of other unions, particularly the Docks Union. These 365 could only get intermittent work. There was a third pool of unregistered casual labor that could be engaged after Federation members and registered casuals had been picked up for work. Organisation was so loose that the boycott was not easy to maintain. The Dutch Navy's stevedores finished loading *Bonaire* on 20 April 1946. She moved out from a Victoria Quay that was rain-swept and deserted, tugless, pilotless, loaded by the armed forces of a foreign power.

Bonaire was unloaded at Batavia by Japanese prisoners-of-war and Dutch soldiers. In July she was back in Fremantle, again under black ban, despite efforts of the State Industrial Court to have her worked by Australian unionists. Dutch Navy men did the stevedoring work and again she was unloaded by Japanese and Dutch soldiers in Java. The ban still applied on her third trip in October-November. Dutch Navy men were stevedores once more.

Shipment by Stealth

The *Bonaire* played a part in circumventing the boycott, because at the Dutch naval depot on the Fremantle wharves Royal Netherlands Navy stevedores could always be used, under extra-territorial privilege. The *Bonaire* could also pick up urgent goods shipped from Brisbane, Sydney and Melbourne to Fremantle — goods not marked for the Dutch or for Java. Federal Office of the Waterside Workers' Federation was warning its branches early in November 1945 to watch all cargoes loaded in East Coast ports for Fremantle because they might subsequently be loaded on to Dutch vessels for shipment to the Indies.[8] Unions in the Eastern States were often unaware that cargoes they loaded for Fremantle went to the Dutch Army in the Indies. Some ships, including the American *Henry Zetland*, gave non-Indies destinations and so got stevedoring labor without question. At sea these ships were rerouted to Dutch-held Indies ports.

14 Emergency Hospitality to Mutineers

Girls employed as typists and clerks in trade union offices at Brisbane Trades Hall came to work on Tuesday 25 September to find the place teeming with Indonesians. Mutineers, ship deserters, prohibited immigrants, doubly inadmissible because of their skin pigment, the Indonesian seamen were camped on the dance floor at the top of the Trades Hall. They had brought with them the properties and presents they intended to take back to Indonesia: sewing machines, bicycles, musical instruments, tin trunks of clothes, children's toys. Australian union officials could think of nowhere else to house the Indonesians but in the Trades Hall. September nights were too cool for tropical people to sleep without blankets, and there were over 150 Indonesians to bed down on the first Monday night.

Someone remembered that members of the Chinese Seamen's Union, formed in Australia during wartime, like the Indonesian Seamen's Union, were employed by the US Navy at Bulimba on the Brisbane River. These Chinese, led by a colourful character who remained in Australia to make a good living, arranged everything. Mr E.J. Hanson, Secretary of the Painters' Union, drove to Bulimba in a big lorry. The Chinese contrived an absence of guards at the gate. The truck drove to an appointed place at the US Navy base and Chinese seamen loaded the truck high with US Navy blankets. The Chinese then threw atop the blankets bags of US Navy rice and cartons of cigarettes for good measure. Thanks to the unwitting generosity of the US Navy, Indonesians mutinying against an allied government slept warmly, ate rice and smoked Chester-fields and Lucky Strikes while Australians were queuing for inferior brands of cigarettes.

The first night over, the swelling total of Indonesians must have their constant food supplies. The Trades and Labor Council launched an appeal for finance, and, with some of the money raised, paid Brisbane Chinese cafés to give the Indo-nesians one substantial meal each day. Some private accom-modation was found for Indonesians, but at the peak about 300 slept in the Trades Hall. This did not conform with health laws and certainly not with immigration laws. Press and radio opened an attack. The weekly newspaper *Truth* in Brisbane published a virulent attack on Sunday 30 September. *Truth* was threatened with reprisals by the Trades and Labor Council leaders. Girl clerks in the Trades Hall protested pub-licly against having to work with so many Indonesians crowded into the building. To keep up their morale the Indo-nesians had to be provided with writing paper, entertainment and recreation.

Over to Dr Van Mook

Queensland Trades and Labor Council Secretary Michael Healy[1] accepted the role as host-in-chief to the Indonesian guests. Mr Healy had already met Dr Van Mook and some of the other Dutch leaders at Wacol on union business. He per-suaded the Trades and Labor Council that the NEI Govern-ment-in-Exile, having brought the Indonesians to Australia, should be held responsible for their upkeep.

Mr Healy and others organised a fleet of big transport lorries to carry the Indonesians' belongings to Wacol. The Indonesians were deployed from the Trades Hall and other billets to five separate city and suburban railway stations for entrainment to Wacol. Trade union officials awaited them at Wacol. They loaded the Indonesians into the lorries with their luggage, ignored the challenges of the Dutch and Ambonese guards and drove straight into Wacol camp. They told the Dutch who stood around with rifles, revolvers and tommy-guns at the ready that they now had the responsibility of feeding and housing the Indonesians. The Dutch in Australia were never celebrated for their sense of humour. There was no sign of it when the Australian trade union officials bundled into their laps Indonesians who had refused to sail them back to Java.

The Queensland Trades and Labor Council arranged an interview at Wacol with Dr Van Mook, about the future of the Indonesian strikers. Ushered into the presence of the Viceroy were the Secretary and President of the Labor Council, Mr M. Healy and Mr G. Dawson, and the Queensland Secretary of the Seamen's Union, Mr W. Casey. Dr Van Mook, according to Mr Healy, was courteous, affable and an intent listener. He talked of the past and its errors and of the new life ahead for the Indonesian people. There would be no going back, Dr Van Mook said, to past poverty and lack of rights. Trade unions would be legalised, administrative posts given to Indonesians and Indonesians would appear at international bodies like the United Nations and International Labor Organisation.[2]

"They Have To Go Back"

Dr Van Mook wanted his Indonesians to return on Dutch ships. The Indonesians, backed by Australian trade unions, wanted to return to Republican-held territory on British or Australian ships. The Prime Minister, Mr Chifley, came to Brisbane around this time. Mr M. Healy and another Trades and Labor Council leader, Mr Harry Harvey (later an Arbitration Court judge), interviewed Mr Chifley at the Canberra Hotel in Brisbane. They asked Mr Chifley to repatriate the Indonesians to Republican territory. "Yes, we can't keep them here — they have to go back," Mr Chifley said. He conceded that the Republic had to be recognised.[3]

Dr Van Mook was not ready to give the Indonesians suddenly dumped back into his care at Wacol any instalment of the promised new freedom. Some of the Indonesians were shifted to Grovelly and other military prison camps and others to the cramped cells of the antiquated Boggo Road Prison in Brisbane. The chicken, prawns, duck, bamboo shoots and mushrooms of the Chinese restaurants gave way to the hominy of the prison mess-room. Numbers of the Indonesian mutineers were brought before Brisbane courts and gaoled as prohibited immigrants.

The trade unions asked Mr Chifley to waive the gaol penalties of the Commonwealth Immigration Act, pending repatriation. The Prime Minister was adamant. He said that "one thing is clear — there will be no waiving of any conditions of the Navigation Act for these seamen".[4] For the Liberal Party the Deputy Leader of the Opposition in Federal Parliament, Mr Eric Harrison, demanded penalties for the Indonesians as "prohibited migrants"[5] immediately the walk-offs from Dutch ships began. A *Sydney Morning Herald*[6] report showed that action was not long in coming:

> In Brisbane 200 striking Indonesian seamen were rounded up at the Dutch camp at Wacol. They will be charged tomorrow with being prohibited immigrants. They were taken in military trucks to the interment camps at Gaythorne and given a language test[7] by Immigration officers.

On 4 October 1945 Mr Max Julius, barrister, pleaded in vain for 214 Indonesian seamen charged before a court as "deserters". On 14 November Mr Julius was to appear for another 85. In his address to the court Mr Julius said that the Indonesian seamen had been faithful allies of Australians in the war and that they were "doing more at this moment in the struggle against Fascism than the shipping company [KPM] concerned". Some of the Indonesian seamen, Mr Julius said, had been as long as 10 years at sea, "and took risks along with British and Australian seamen during the war". He added:

> It is unreasonable to expect men to serve on a ship which belongs to their enemies. It is their national pride and their desire for freedom which made them commit this "offence" and no one should expect them to wage war on their own peoples.[8]

But gates at Boggo Road, Gaythorne, Grovelly, Camp Lytton and other places of internment swung open to receive Indonesian seamen.

Stately Mansions for Prohibited Immigrants

The Sydney boycotters were able to mobilise far more popular support and to prevent the mass gaolings of Indonesians that occurred in Brisbane and Melbourne. On 30 September 1945 a public rally for Indonesia, attended by some 5,000 people in the Sydney Domain, was addressed by three Indonesians — one a Tanah Merah survivor — and by NSW Trades and Labor spokesmen. A resolution from the meeting demanded release of all Indonesians held by or for the Dutch in Australian gaols and internment camps and asked the Federal Government to cease allowing Dutch troops to load ships.

On 1 October some 3,000 gathered in Wynyard Park, Sydney, in support of the Indonesian Republic. Police attacked the meeting, which was not authorised, smashed the speaker's microphone, tore up pro-Indonesian banners. A few people were knocked to the ground in scuffles. A Dutch official who tried to argue with Indonesians in the audience was hissed and hustled.

Early in October arrests of Indonesians began in Sydney, and 23 appeared in court as "deserters". They were defended in court by the Chairman of the TLC's Indonesian Sub-Committee, Mr Hugh Grant, and Mr Arthur Olive, an official of the Federated Ironworkers' Association and Military Medal winner of World War I. The Indonesians went to gaol, but not for long.

Pro-Indonesian rallies in Sydney continued. Bishop Cranswick of the Church of England chaired a meeting of Australians and Indonesians in Sydney Trades Hall. Many Australian soldiers attended. Cheers greeted a cable from the Dutch Seamen's Union branch in New York, pledging aid to the Indonesian Republic. On 12 October 1945 the Australia-Indonesia Association organised a public rally in Sydney Town Hall which unanimously urged the Australian Government and Allied Powers "to take needful action to enable the people of Indonesia to assume their right under the Atlantic Charter to choose the form of government under which they will live".[9]

The better-protected Indonesian mutineers from the Dutch ships in Sydney had to be fed and sheltered. With the aid of Australian trade union officials Indonesians illegally occupied the Lido private hotel in North Sydney and the Belvedere at King's Cross. The Belvedere was a stately old mansion that belonged to the pre-apartment house era of King's Cross, the brightest centre of Sydney nightlife. The Australian Govern-

129

ment had allotted the Belvedere to the Dutch as a club for their subjects on leave from ships and the armed forces. Led by Mr Mervyn Pidcock, a Sydney waterside worker, and other Australians the Indonesian strikers broke into the Belvedere and camped there. The Dutch immediately diverted armed guards to the Belvedere. The *Sydney Morning Herald*[10] published a story that the Indonesians had threatened to draw revolvers on the Dutch: this was probably based on an unlikely Dutch claim. The Indonesians did not have guns.

While Indonesian numbers were kept under control by gaolings and camp detentions, the Indian seamen who began to pour ashore from the beginning of October 1945, waiting on wharves with pots, pans, bed-rolls and prayer-mats, posed a frightening accommodation problem. By the first week in October 700 Indian seamen had struck in alliance with the Indonesian Republicans. Well-filled planes arrived from India and British ships turned out to have "spares" or surplus Indian crewmen to be dumped in Australia for the Dutch. Deportations and gaolings of Indians were not sufficient to keep numbers ashore within existing trade union capacities.

The Lido, a private North Sydney hotel allotted to the Dutch as a wartime hostel for Indonesians, was nearly empty after the *Esperance Bay* left on 13 October with the first Indonesian repatriates. Indonesian, Indian and Australian union representatives reconnoitred the Lido, found a Dutch Army captain of immense physique in charge, with an Indonesian petty-officer as deputy. They got the Indonesian on his own; he agreed to leave the catch off a side window to allow breaking and entering, without involving him.

Three five-ton trucks were obtained, free, in the city, Indians and Indonesians — mostly Indians — were loaded aboard with their belongings and drivers took them to the Harbour Bridge toll-gates. Threepence per head toll was then required under regulations. The toll-keepers were told that the Indians and Indonesians crowded in the trucks were boycotting the Dutch; the toll-keepers turned their backs as the toll-free Asians went through. It was about 9 pm on 22 October and dark.

The trucks stopped about 50 yards from the Lido, Australians scouted to see that grounds were clear, then prised open the unlatched window and opened the front door from inside. The Indonesian petty-officer had kept his promise. As the seamen streamed in the petty-officer looked blankly surprised, said it was his duty to ring the Dutch officer in charge and did so. The Dutch captain, arriving posthaste, wanted the Indians evicted, but he was half-placated by Australians present, who told him the Indians could not sleep on the road. The captain grudgingly agreed they could stay for one night only.

Instead of evacuation there was a new influx each day: the TLC Indonesian Sub-Committee transported striking Indians from the *Japara* and *General Verspijck* to the Lido. The arrival of 74 Indians with their baggage was a new shock to the Dutch captain's strained nerves. He told the Australians present that the Indian occupation was "not cricket".

The Police and the Law

Soon three busloads of Dutch guards — 59 were counted — came along Berry Street, North Sydney, to the Lido. The Dutch captain called on the Indians to leave; the Australians present called for reinforcements and groups of waterside workers and seamen arrived. The Dutch guards took over the second floor; the Indians, Indonesians and some Malay strikers remained on the top and bottom floors. The Dutch captain-manager in desperation went to North Sydney police station. The police had some understanding of the political implications and perhaps some sympathy with the Indians and Indonesians. They told the Dutch manager that if he wanted to get the Asians out he would have to comply with Australian law by prosecuting for trespass or seeking an eviction order in court. (There are shorter cuts than this to eviction of illegal occupants, but the police did not mention them.) Dutch troops were withdrawn from the Lido next day, their bayonets unbloodied.

Pathan seamen walked off the *Pahud* on 26 October. They were denied a customs clearance, but Australian union representatives cut through red tape and transported the Pathans from the wharf to the Lido. Harbour Bridge toll collectors were again unable to see the strikers crowded into the trucks. The Dutch locked Lido doors against the Pathans. The tall, turbaned men hammered on the door from the outside. Indians and Australians rushing down from the top floor brushed the Dutch aside and threw open the front door of Australia's most remarkable boarding house, where the boarders were non-paying illegal immigrants, deserters and mutineers, and where armed landlords were powerless to collect rents or resume lawful control of their premises.

The Dutch could not rely on normal processes of law. They called the police again, and the police failed to evict. The Sydney Branch Secretary of the Seamen's Union, Mr Barney Smith,[11] said that the police made a patrol at the Lido each night. They interrogated him at his home about the illegal occupation, but seemed to feel that there was no other solution. The police night patrol to the Lido was more to protect Indians and Indonesians against the Dutch than to uphold Dutch legal rights.

An Indian stokehold crew leader disappeared from the Lido. The Indians rated him as a potential collaborator with the Dutch. They spirited him away and kept him in "protective custody". The Indians would not tell Australians at the Lido where they kept the prisoner. The Australians never found out.

Before they were repatriated the Indians and Indonesians at the Lido cooked a wide range of their national dishes for a farewell dinner to the Australian benefactors.

Extra-Territorial Powers Under Fire

While Indonesians at the Lido enjoyed national dishes, their mutinous colleagues crowded into cells at Melbourne's Pentridge and Geelong Gaols were eating more frugal fare. Dutch use of extra-territorial powers, granted to them, as to other Allied forces in Australia, by the Labor Government, sometimes evoked strong protest, particularly from the Council for Civil Liberties in Melbourne. The late Mr Brian Fitzpatrick, the Australian historian and civil libertarian, made strong and influentially backed representations to the Chifley Government against Dutch actions under the cloak of extra-territorial rights. A Council for Civil Liberties statement said that the extra-territorial powers had "caused embarrassment to Australia" and added:

132

The Council had to spend much of its time in the Spring of 1945 watching the Dutch treatment of their rebellious Indonesian employees in Australia, and helping to get Indonesians returned to their country.

Reports of Dutch military police breaking into an Australian's home in Casino, NSW, without any warrant, of Dutch shooting at Indonesians at Australian aerodromes to compel them to get into planes, and of bad conditions at the Casino Dutch internment camp gave some indication of the dangers of voting any but the barest of extra-territorial rights to foreign (even if Allied) armies on Australian territory.[12]

The Waterside Workers' Federation, through its *Maritime Worker*,[13] also criticised the Labor Government on this issue:

Our own Australian Government's fingers are anything but clean on this issue. It appears it has extended extra-territorial rights to the Dutch without them granting extra-territorial rights. It has allowed them to build concentration camps in Queensland under complete control of the Dutch Army, and has allowed incarceration of Indonesian seamen in Boggo Road Gaol for merely supporting their people's fight for freedom.

The NSW Trades and Labor Council complained:

These Dutch officials are swaggering about our country, protected by armed tommy-gunners, threatening Australian unionists on Sydney wharves, using brutal methods against democratic Indonesians right here in Sydney.[14]

When Indonesian mutineers were transferred from the custody of friendly Australian soldiers at Camp Lytton to the Dutch internment camp at Casino, NSW, the Waterside Workers' Federation addressed urgent inquiries to the Minister for the Army, Mr Frank M. Forde. The Minister replied:

I am informed that NEI personnel concerned (Indonesians) were held at Lytton by the Australian Military authorities on warrants issued by the Dutch authorities under National Security Regulations, under which the Australian Army authorities hold any NEI Service personnel committed to their custody and release them to the NEI authorities when required. The Dutch authorities have now taken these personnel into their own establishment at Casino. In view of the fact that these Indonesians are NEI service personnel and are not subject to Australian military control, the matter of their disposal is one for determination by Dutch authorities.[11]

The Indonesian Republic had existed for nine months when this letter was written, but to the Labor Minister for the Army, Indonesian Republicans were still "NEI personnel", to be held on criminal charges by Australian provosts until their "disposal" was determined by the Dutch.

Emergency hospitality required for sick Indonesians at Turramurra, Sydney North Shore suburb, indicated to many concerned Australians that Netherlands Indies functionaries were prepared to act out to the end the rituals of colonialism. The Dutch expelled from the Princess Juliana Hospital at Turramurra tuberculosis patients, ex-Tanah Merah, who declared for the Indonesian Republic. Those expelled slept in a shed belonging to a providential farmer-humanitarian near Turramurra, where in those times rural neighbourhoods survived. Before succour arrived patients shivered in light clothes. The Indonesians alleged that this exposure killed Jo-Jo, the railway worker from Java who threw the fateful note from the train at Liverpool station, drawing attention to the Digul camp transplant. Jo-Jo was rushed by an Australian relief party to Sydney Hospital — too late, Sydney Hospital insisted that the Dutch should bury Jo-Jo: he was still their legal responsibility.

The Dutch furnished a plain deal-wood coffin of the kind normally available for paupers. At Rookwood Cemetery, Sydney, the Indonesian mourners, reviving passions transplanted from the Digul River, prised the coffin boards apart. They would not allow Jo-Jo the final indignity of burial in a cheap, begrudged Dutch coffin. Jo-Jo's wasted body was lifted from the broken coffin, wrapped in a blanket and buried to the Republican anthem. The Netherlands Indies Government wrote another line to its own death warrant by casting Jo-Jo and the other tuberculosis victims from the Digul into the cold.

15 Repatriation to the Republic

Sydney Harbour had never known such a farewell . . . As the British liner *Esperance Bay* pulled into the stream, Indonesian soldiers, members till then of an Allied power's armed forces, stood on deck and publicly stripped from their uniforms all buttons and insignia bearing the Netherlands flash or imprint. They flung them into the harbour. The *Esperance Bay* Indonesians were first in the remarkable exodus from Australia. They had been brought to Australia as Dutch subjects in 1942; they sailed as subjects of a Republic in seditious opposition to the Netherlands Government. The Australian Government, committed by treaty to the Dutch cause, paid for the ship that carried them free of Dutch supervision.

The deserting and mutinying Indonesians in Australia presented a unique problem the Chifley Government had to tackle quickly. Indonesian sources[1] claimed that by the end of September, that was, in the six days from the first 24 September walk-offs, 1,400 Indonesian merchant seamen had come ashore in Australian ports. They and the mutineers from the Dutch armed forces were imprisoned in Queensland, New South Wales and Victoria. Protocol demanded that the Chifley Government hand the Indonesians over to the Dutch for deportation. Trade union and other opinion would not permit this; the Indonesians themselves announced that they would not leave by Dutch ships or aircraft for fear of reprisals when they reached Dutch-occupied territory. The Prime Minister's dilemma was obvious. He told parliament on 3 October 1945 that the Indonesians "will be required to leave Australia as soon as shipping can be provided for them". Mr Chifley added:

> The Government's insistence upon their leaving Australia
> has nothing to do with whatever differences exist be-
> tween Indonesians and the Dutch Government. The
> Government's decision that the seamen shall leave Aust-
> ralia is dictated solely by a determination that the immi-
> gration law shall be observed. I admit that there is great
> difficulty in providing ships . . .

Mr Archie Cameron (Liberal, South Australia), aware of the
many strike-bound Dutch ships in Australian ports, inter-
jected: "What about putting them on their own ships?" Mr
Chifley shuffled: "I could say a lot about that, too, but I will
not."[2]

The Prime Minister at this stage was thinking of deportation
rather than repatriation. A couple of days later he said that
"Indonesians in Brisbane, where there have been reports of
disturbances, would be interned, pending their deportation".[3]

Repatriation Spelled Recognition

Mr Brian Fitzpatrick, Secretary of the Council for Civil
Liberties in Victoria, made strong and influentially backed
representations to Immigration Minister Calwell to repatriate
Indonesians to Republican instead of Dutch-held territory,
and in British rather than Dutch ships. Mr Calwell promised
that this would be done; it appears that he needed little assistance in making up his mind on this score. He reminisced to
the writer in April 1971:

> Indonesians were in camps, gaols, hostels, private billets
> or wandering at large. The Dutch only wanted these
> Indonesians in Australia as their prisoners, to be interned
> in the Indies.
>
> I approached Mr Chifley about the Indonesians' re-
> patriation to Republican territory. Mr Chifley said that
> he would approve the chartering of ships to carry the
> Indonesians to areas held by the Republic.

The Prime Minister would have been well aware that repatriation of Indonesians admitted to Australia as Dutch subjects
involved de facto recognition of the Republic of Indonesia.

136

In line with this was the Chifley Government's rejection on 29 October 1945 of an Attlee Government's request to set up an Australian consular establishment in Batavia, accredited to the NEI Government. This rebuff to the British implied official Australian resistance to colonial reinstatement and sympathy for Indonesian aspirations.

Queensland Trades and Labor Council Secretary M. Healy asked the Waterside Workers' Federation leaders in Sydney by telegram[4] to seek protection for the Indonesians against deportation, through the Australian Council of Trade Unions. Mr Healy's telegram said that 470 imprisoned Indonesians at Casino camp and 232 at Lytton camp were "threatened by Dutch deporation to prison camps in Dutch New Guinea".

Shipping was desperately short. Australian prisoners of war had to be repatriated from Burma, Malaya, Indonesia, Japan, China, Germany and Italy. Australian troops in New Guinea and the South Sea Islands, East Indonesia and British and European air bases were impatient to get home. In the reverse direction Australia had to repatriate 14,000 Italian prisoners of war, 1,600 Germans, some 1,000 Japanese and various Formosan, Korean and Chinese held in prisoner of war camps following their puppet services to Japan. In addition there were European refugees who had escaped from Singapore, and other war zones in South-East Asia. Britain and liberated Europe were calling for emergency shipments of food, metals and wool. The British, Americans, French and Dutch all wanted as many ships as they could get for their various postwar operations.

White Australia Reversal

The Dutch and their political supporters in Australia were in full cry against release of trained Indonesian soldiers, technicians and political cadres to the Republic. Ironically, those who customarily sponsored deportation of Asians under the White Australia Policy suddenly opposed removal of a large body of Asians — rather subversive Asians at that — from the country. Opposition Leader Menzies attacked the Labor Government for its decision "to precipitate into the country . . . hundreds of natives who by this time are calculated to be fanatically opposed to Dutch authority" and who were also "fanatically persuaded that Australia is anti-Dutch and anti-British". The "Indonesian natives" in Australia had been "constantly indoctrinated with communist nonsense" and "with a few superficial ideas of a revolutionary kind".[5]

Another former Prime Minister, Mr Arthur Fadden, Country Party leader, saw repatriation as export of communist revolution to Indonesia. He said:

> When searched recently the bags and belongings of Indonesians were found to contain communist literature and propaganda of all descriptions. The root of this evil is the communist movement in Australia.[6]

Revolution, concealed in a sarong, could now be exported from non-revolutionary Australia to revolutionary Asia.

Lord Louis Mountbatten of South-East Asia Command, in enough trouble in his confrontations with the national revolutions of French Indo-China and the Netherlands Indies, was strongly opposed to the release of skilled political agitators for the Republic in troubled Java. He expressed his opposition by removing some of them during the voyage, to prevent their arrival in Java.

However, with South-East Asia Command aid, the Chifley Government chartered the *Esperance Bay*, despite the formidable resistance, to repatriate the Indonesians. (Her sister ship, *Moreton Bay*, was soon taking aboard Dutch troops at Sydney to fight the Indonesian repatriates.) Under the supervision of Immigration Minister Calwell, 1,416 Indonesian men, women and children boarded the *Esperance Bay* at Sydney and Brisbane.

Striking Indonesian seamen and mutinous marines from Melbourne, soldiers and political prisoners released from camps, veterans of Tanah Merah concentration camp in New Guinea and the striking Indonesians from Sydney — a few with Australian wives — marched up the *Esperance Bay* gangways. Early on the morning of Saturday 13 October, before *Esperance Bay* was tugged from the wharf, launches called at all Dutch ships in the harbour, collecting those remaining Indonesians whom the Dutch had prevented from reaching the shore. This time the Indonesians were called off, as illegal strikers, under Australian Government protection, so that they could sail for home. Indications were that not a single Indonesian seaman stayed with the Dutch.

The Dutch were dismayed. While the strikers and mutineers remained in Australia there might be a chance of winning many back to their duties. Once *Esperance Bay* was through Sydney Harbour Heads and hull-down on the horizon, the ships' crews and soldiers were gone for ever. Worse, they would reinforce the Republican enemy. Dutch officials came to the wharf in a last effort to cajole Indonesians back into service. Two Indonesians of aristocratic origin and an Australian Customs officer backed their arguments. The *Esperance Bay*, they said, would never see Java, those aboard her would end in Dutch camps and Australian wives of Indonesians would not be allowed to join their husbands.

The Indonesians due to sail had already held a meeting and resolved to accept Immigration Minister Calwell's pledge that they would be landed in Republican territory. One Dutch agent was threatened with violence and retired from the wharf. When he returned a NSW police sergeant ordered him to leave. The Dutch Consul-General at Sydney and several KPM captains arrived in the hope of retrieving crewmen. The police advised them to leave "for their own safety". *Esperance Bay* sailed from Sydney on 13 October, many Indonesians aboard carrying gifts from Australian friends and rending the air with: "Merdeka! Down with the Dutch!"

Money Left Behind

Of nearly 800 boarding the *Esperance Bay* at Brisbane 214 were from Gaythorne internment camp, about 150 from Casino compound, others from Grovelly, Lytton, Chermside, Wacol and Bundaberg. Some were Tanah Merah exiles about to see Java for the first time in nearly 20 years and there were numbers of women and children to join those who embarked at Sydney. Brisbane women donated fruit, sweets and cakes to these women and children. Australians still had to queue for cigarettes, but the Indonesians sailed well provided. Queensland TLC approached the tobacco combine, WD & HO Wills Ltd, who made available to the Indonesians for cash 50,000 cigarettes. Major Wake, in charge of the Commonwealth police at Brisbane, down on the wharf to keep a close eye on the repatriation, said to Mr Healy: "What will you be up to next — getting cigarettes for Indonesians when nobody else can get them!"[7]

The Indonesians left behind considerable wealth in Australia. As a parting token of gratitude for Australian Government repatriation to the Republic those sailing from Sydney in the *Esperance Bay* subscribed £42,000 to the Fourth Victory Loan. Many Indonesians had Commonwealth Savings Bank deposits. The Indonesian seamen entrusted to NSW and Queensland Labor Councils the collection on their behalf of money owed to them by Dutch shipowners. The Secretary reported to Queensland Trades and Labor Council that the KPM company owed 972 Indonesian seamen a total of £104,000 in current and deferred pay, bonuses and dependants' allowances, while another £30,000 was owed to 207 proceeded against as prohibited immigrants.[8]

Slamet came to Mr M. Healy's home often to work out the money problem. Mr Harvey of the Labor Council was of great help. Slamet, a teacher who had been in Tanah Merah since 1926, returned to become a member of parliament, but died in the massacres that followed the "September 30 Movement" of 1965.

The Australian authorities, wisely, would not let the Indonesians take aboard with them money from their Commonwealth Savings Bank accounts: the money was then difficult to exchange in Indonesia and export of currency was banned by regulation. Bank officials, Trades and Labor Council and Indonesian leaders organised the surrender of bank passbooks aboard ship. The money was banked with Messrs Harvey and Healy of the Labor Council as trustees for the Indonesians. This large hoard of money, according to Mr Healy, caused some difficulties. The trustees had guaranteed the Indonesian owners that no one would touch the money: it would be sent to them or next of kin in Indonesia when conditions were sufficiently settled. The Soekarno Government was anxious to get its hands on the deposits and the first Indonesian Ambassador to Australia, Dr Usman, made repeated attempts to have control transferred to him. After Dr Usman left, calls from Indonesian diplomats persisted. Some owners of money deposited in Australia died fighting the Dutch or in fratricidal

140

strife and next of kin were not easy to trace. It was not until the late 1950s that the last remittances were made to Indonesia. Commonwealth Bank officials, said Mr Healy, went to great pains to see that the right Indonesians got the money.[9]

Some Indonesians did not board the *Esperance Bay*. The Government permitted them to remain temporarily to carry on work for the Republic in Brisbane, Sydney and Melbourne. Bondan, Secretary of the Central Committee of Indonesian Independence, and helpers continued to use Room 25 in Brisbane Trades Hall.[10]

Before the *Esperance Bay* sailed an Indonesian leader from Australia was already busily organising a Republican trade union movement (SOBSI, Central Council of Indonesian Trade Unions) in Java. He was Haryono, sometimes called Harriana. Communist officials in Brisbane advised Haryono, whom they considered an outstanding theoretician and organiser, to pretend that he was loyal to the Dutch, get passage to Java and promote trade unionism. An Indonesian friend was something of a rarity to the Wacol Government. The Dutch accepted Haryono and flew him to Hollandia, then to Batavia. When Messrs M. Healy and E. Roach went as Australian trade union delegates to Indonesia in 1946 they found Haryono had done his work well. Haryono presided over the first SOBSI Congress in 1946. He was killed by Soekarno Government troops at Madiun in 1948.[11]

Mountbatten Interrupted Their Journey

General Sir Philip Christison, leading the British military intervention in Java, saw the *Esperance Bay* voyage as an added threat to his attempts to set the colonial Dutch on their rickety feet again and to modify their flat-earth modes of thought. The fierce Indonesian resistance in the battle of Sourabaya and the Republic's resilience had been a shock. Christison, urged on by the Dutch in Batavia, warned Mountbatten that the revolutionaries would be strengthened if the *Esperance Bay* repatriates were landed. Mountbatten earnestly proposed to Canberra that the *Esperance Bay* should be allowed to disembark the ex-Australia revolutionaries at Dutch Timor or neighbouring small islands. British Premier Clement Attlee, no friend of the Indonesian nationalist revolution,

141

reinforced Mountbatten's representations to the Australian Government. Mr Chifley was able to point out that the Dutch had agreed to this repatriation to Republican territory, and that the Dutch in Australia were fully aware of Immigration Minister Calwell's promise that the ex-Australia Indonesians would not be handed to the Dutch but to Republican administration.

However, Mr Chifley buckled under sustained pressure from the Attlee Government. He agreed to diversion of the *Esperance Bay* to Timor and removal from the ship of Indonesians considered by the Dutch and some of their Australian collaborators to be the most dangerous to the colonial interest.

The Chifley Government had, perhaps unwittingly, ensured that no difficulties stood in the way of "fingering" the most dangerous Indonesians aboard the repatriation ship. The Government had chosen as its representative to take virtual charge of the repatriation Lieutenant K.C. Plumb, who for two years before had been the Australian Intelligence liaison officer with the Dutch Intelligence at Camp Columbia, the headquarters of the Netherlands Indies Government-in-Exile at Wacol, Brisbane. Australian Intelligence shadowing of and reports on Indonesians in Australia were available to the Dutch and vice versa. It is reasonable to assume that the Indonesians marked for expulsion from the *Esperance Bay* at Timor, in violation of the pledge given by Mr Calwell — now driven to great anger by the breach of trust — were chosen on the basis of hard Intelligence reports from both Dutch and Australian sources.

Brigadier-General L.G.H. Dyke, Australian Commander in Dutch Timor, received an order that 40 men were to be taken from the *Esperance Bay* at Koepang, Timor, and held. The 40 were among the most active leaders. When 19[12] had been forcibly removed — including Senan, Soerparmin and Saedyut, former Tanah Merah internees, and Lumanauw (known in Australia as "Jim"), who had addressed a Sydney Town Hall rally and had been a prominent spokesman for the Indonesians in Australia — the other Indonesians held an angry protest meeting aboard the *Esperance Bay*. The meeting's resolutions quoted Mr Calwell's promise that all would reach Java without hindrance. The Indonesians cabled from Koepang to NSW and Queensland Labor Councils, both of which protested against the detention of the 19.

Minister Was "Double-Crossed"

Mr Calwell's recollections of the Timor affair, given to the writer in the 1971 personal interview, were:

> We had assurances from the Netherlands Minister in Canberra, Dr Teppema, that the Dutch would not try to stop the Indonesians being landed in Republican territory. I was again double-crossed by the forcible removals of Indonesians from the *Esperance Bay* at Koepang. I protested vehemently, and intervened to save these Indonesians from falling into Dutch hands.
>
> But for the Labor Government's intervention the Indonesians might all have been transported back to Java under very bad conditions. I insisted that they be treated as human beings, that they should be provided with good standard food and decent bunks to sleep in aboard the *Esperance Bay*.

Mr Calwell recalled a quaint quid pro quo on which the Dutch had insisted for their acceptance under protest of the repatriation of the Indonesians in Australian-chartered ships. The Dutch would allow the Indonesians to go aboard the *Esperance Bay* if some of the trucks held under boycott at the Ford works, Geelong, were also carried to Java in the ship. So the *Esperance Bay* sailed with trucks for the Dutch Army and manpower for the Republican Army.

The Immigration Minister's protests did not get the 19 Indonesians removed at Koepang an immediate passage to Java, but at least they were kept out of Dutch hands. Mr Calwell, replying to Waterside Workers' Federation representations, said that he had sent a "strongly worded cable", demanding that none of the 19 were to be handed over to the Dutch and that, if necessary, the men would be brought back to Darwin by the Australian Government for repatriation.[13]

Lumanauw reported that he was detained "under Australian jurisdiction at the instance of the Allied South-East Asia Command at Koepang, Timor; later in British North Borneo and Singapore".[14] The Central Committee of Indonesian

143

Independence in Brisbane claimed that Lumanauw did not reach Java until a year after he was taken from the *Esperance Bay*.[15] It was difficult to get news about the fate of the 19 for some time. The Australia-Indonesian Association of Sydney reported in August 1946 that the efforts regarding the men removed at Timor "seem to have had good effect, as we hear that these men are now in Java"[16]

The British of SEAC and the Dutch had dubbed *Esperance Bay* "a boatload of trouble". Mr Calwell was still angry over the removal of the 19 when he reviewed in 1949 his repatriation of Asians. "All the trouble we have experienced," he told parliament, "has been made by colonial Dutchmen and colonial Englishmen. They and their supporters in this House are responsible for whatever trouble has been created".[17] Mr Calwell's stand must have been firmer than that of Prime Minister Chifley and Army Minister Forde, because the Australian military at Koepang were permitted to act as custodians of the men taken ashore in violation of official pledges.

Australian Navy Repulses Dutch

HMAS *Manoora*, an Adelaide Steamship Company coastal passenger ship converted to a landing-craft carrier, embarked some 800 Indonesian men, women and children and numbers of Australian-born wives — Aboriginal or part-Aboriginal girls for the most part — and children. The Queensland Labor Council was told on 15 October 1945 that 191 Indonesians who wished to return to their homeland remained in Mackay.[18] The *Manoora* called at Mackay to take Indonesians aboard, most of them Tanah Merah survivors for whom Mackay had been a main centre.

HMAS *Manoora* was still manned by her wartime crew of Australian Navy officers and men. This would make it more difficult for Mountbatten to intervene again and remove any of the much-wanted Tanah Merah survivors. The Central Committee of Indonesian Independence Secretary Bondan had asked that every Indonesian aboard the *Manoora* should be "landed in the care of the Indonesian Republican Government in Java" and that Australian unions should seek conditions to prevent "a repetition of the Koepang incident where Indonesians were detained outside Australia but under the control of the Australian Government".[19]

The *Manoora* for her 1946 voyage to Java was commanded by Captain Alan Paterson Cousin, a Queenslander, who graduated from Royal Australian Navy College, then served 17 years as a merchant skipper. In wartime Captain Cousin became Senior Naval Officer Australian Landing Ships and took part in the assault landings at Hollandia, Morotai, Tarakan, Labuan and Balikpapan and in the Philippines.

Some of *Manoora*'s crew had been merchant seamen and unionists: they regarded Captain Cousin as an arch-conservative, but respected him as an officer of physical and moral courage, never known to break his word. The people whom he had contracted to return to Indonesia, free of Dutch control, ranged from young children to struggle-scarred veterans of Tanah Merah. M. Soekato, a President of the Indonesian Seamen's Union in Australia, wrote back to Australia after his voyage in *Manoora* that Captain Cousin, when he learned it was a little Indonesian girl's birthday, had the ship's cooks bake and decorate a cake for her. The day *Manoora* put into Tanjong Priok, port of what was known as Batavia to one side and Djakarta to the other, he gave a well-endowed farewell party to all Indonesian children aboard.

Unlike certain Australian military commanders in East Indonesia Captain Cousin did not issue any non-fraternisation orders. He encouraged the officers and naval ratings to help the Indonesians and to provide the best of care for the sick and nursing mothers. Facilities were available to the Indonesians for concerts and meetings. When sailors showed interest in the meetings, conducted in Indonesian, the speakers switched to English so the Australians could follow. They talked of the never-to-be-forgotten help from Australians and the acute problems of the future. Captain Cousin was touched when the Indonesians gathered round to hand him, as Tanjong Priok loomed near, magnificent presents in appreciation of his kindness.

The Dutch put Captain Cousin to test at Tanjong Priok. Not long after Indonesians had handed presents to him and to the Australian Government representative aboard, Mr Mungoven, a truckload of armed Dutch hove in sight on the wharf. The Dutch demanded that Captain Cousin hand the Indonesian repatriates over to their jurisdiction. They particularly wanted the Tanah Merah ex-prisoners from Mackay. Captain Cousin's response was to contact a Gurkha regiment landed at Batavia by the British. It was made clear enough to the Dutch that if they persisted, *Manoora* officers would break out small arms to the Australian naval ratings and, if that did not suffice, the Gurkhas would be asked to guard the repatriates.

Ex-Able-Seaman Edward McCormick[20] of the *Manoora* related:

> All the former political prisoners of the Dutch and any others who might be in danger of reprisals were escorted by Gurkhas, at Captain Cousin's request, to Republican territory, about 60 miles from Batavia. Women and children were escorted ashore later.
>
> *Manoora* was the only Australian ship at Batavia. We certainly received no welcome from the Dutch. The Dutch warned British warships' crews that we were Republican sympathisers and that they should avoid association with us. *Manoora* crew members were allowed ashore in groups, escorted by armed naval patrols.

Indonesian Tribute to Captain

Ex-Able-Seaman McCormick's recollections are confirmed by Indonesians who reported back to Australia after repatriation. One of them, C.D. Najoan, said in a letter to Queensland Trades and Labor Council that Captain Cousin would not allow the Dutch to make a customs search of the Indonesians' baggage for literature and arms. Captain Cousin, according to Najoan, told the Dutch at Tanjong Priok:

> I brought these Indonesians from Australia and I have been trusted by our Australian Government to hand them over to the Indonesian Republic and no one else. As regards their luggage a thorough search has been made by the Australian Customs and there is no need for it to be searched again, as I am now convinced these Indonesians are trustworthy persons.[21]

Najoan assured Queensland unionists that Captain Cousin had

146

strictly upheld the pledge that they would get to Republican territory. He wrote:

> We felt safe under the Australian guards against the trigger-happy Dutch MPs with their tommy-guns ready. These Dutch MPs were dominating the wharf, but, due to the ship's captain's (Commander Cousin's) action, the British had them removed from the wharf. This made the Dutch believe that the Australians were helping again the Indonesians, as if Australia had declared war on the Dutch.[22]

After the *Esperance Bay* and *Manoora* embarked the strange band of mutineers, strikers, rebels and lawbreakers, guest travellers provided for by the Government of Australia, many Indonesians still awaited repatriation from Dutch prison camps, military camps and offices. Some remained to work for the Republic in Australia.

Grateful to Calwell

On Australian Government instructions the Dutch were obliged to discharge the Indonesians from the camps into Australian charge as further repatriation ships became available. In addition to the Australian repatriation the Australian Government sent to their homelands 580 Timorese (Portuguese Timor) and 1 800 Chinese. Mr Calwell could say with truth in 1947 (overlooking the Dutch deportations to Tanah Merah in 1945 — and the Timor incident):

> Every Indonesian who left these shores left voluntarily. I did not have to issue a single deportation order against one of them. And when they landed in Indonesia, they were handed over to their own people. They were not delivered into the hands of any persons who might exact revenge upon them because of their political opinions.[23]

Indonesians repatriated in the *Esperance Bay*, Mr Calwell added, sent a message of thanks to the Australian Government for what it had done and officers of the ship were "high in their praise of the manner in which the Indonesians comported themselves". Secretary Bondan of the Independence Central Committee told Mr Calwell that if he had visited Chermside camp, Brisbane, after Indonesians had been transported there from Casino for return home, he would assuredly have been given "no half-hearted welcome". "The men themselves," Bondan said, "have asked that we should convey their very grateful thanks, and tell you of their relief and joy at their release and repatriation".[24] Republican Premier Sjahrir's representative, Pandoe Soeingrat, came down to the *Manoora* at Tanjong Priok to offer official thanks to Captain Cousin on behalf of the Indonesian Republic.

The Indonesians were brought to Australia by the Dutch, as Dutch subjects. It was hardly just that Australian taxpayers should have had to foot the bill for their repatriation to Java, particularly as many of them had served at sea for the Dutch during the war. Mr Calwell complained in 1949:

> The Dutch Government did not pay for the repatriation of any of those whom it asked us to accept. Australia has expended approximately £100,000 in this way . . . The Dutch officials have been playing a tricky game in regard to their nationals. They claim that this is a sort of lend-lease transaction, and even have claimed that we owe them money.[25]

Amplifying in the 1971 interview with the writer, Mr Calwell said that while the Australian Government cared for the refugee Netherlands East Indies Government and Dutch servicemen and civilians reaching Australia, and sheltered, fed, armed and trained NEI military personnel at the Australian taxpayers' expense, the Dutch wanted to avoid compensating Australia for this outlay. "They wanted to get out of every financial obligation, to pay Australia nothing for all the services provided, and in these evasions they had substantial success."[26]

16   Air-Lift of Indian Disloyalists

Prince Henry William Frederick Albert, His Royal Highness the Duke of Gloucester, Colonel of the Scots Guards, Colonel-in-Chief of the 10th Hussars, of Iniskilling Fusiliers, Gloucestershire Regiment, Gordon Highlanders and Royal Army Service Corps, Commodore of the Royal Naval Reserve, Field-Marshal, Marshal of the Royal Air Force, Great Master of the Grand Prior of the Order of Saint John, brother of King George VI and Edward Duke of Windsor, and uncle of Princess Elizabeth (now Elizabeth II), was not accustomed to rousing meetings of strikers to higher pinnacles of militancy. Nor to extending friendly greetings to disloyal subjects of his brother, the King-Emperor, ship deserters, violators of wartime regulations and prohibited immigrants.

The first and last time was in Sydney in 1945.

Indian seamen were flown to Australia in a massive air-lift. by arrangement with the British Viceroy, the Chifley-Evatt Government, The Hague and the Netherlands Indies Government-in-Exile. Other Indian seamen were brought here in British ships. Discreetly, they were put aboard Dutch ships in Melbourne, Sydney and Brisbane to replace Indonesian seamen who had refused to serve the Dutch any longer.

When the Indians discovered why they had been rushed to Australia and put aboard Dutch ships they began to join the Indonesian strikers ashore. The India they had left was in an anti-colonial ferment and most of them needed little persuasion to boycott the Dutch, who had the British Raj's backing. The Indians, like the Indonesians, had to be housed and fed ashore.

All available shelter was soon overcrowded. Those Indians remaining without shelter were taken to the Missions to Seamen building, George Street North, close to Sydney's Circular Quay wharves. Mrs Phyllis Johnson[1] and Mr Clarrie Campbell of the Australia-India Association, who acted as Treasurer to the Indian Seamen's Union in Sydney, accompanied them to the Mission.

The Missions to Seamen was never intended to sustain strikers, and particularly not anti-imperial mutineers. The Mission was founded to care for victims of shipwreck, or to give humble relief to the wants of the disabled and distressed, in a religious atmosphere. Society women gave voluntary service to the Mission.

These women charity workers had little understanding of the significance of the Indian seamen's arrival at the Mission and allowed them to sleep there. In kindly tone they would inquire from Hindus, Muslims and Sikhs: "Are you Christians? Are you married? Have you any little children at home?" The Mission ladies served the Indians cups of tea.

Interpreter for the King's Brother

Unaware that the Missions to Seamen building in Sydney was crowded with striking Indian seamen, law-breakers and dis-loyalists, HRH the Duke of Gloucester, then in the middle of his 1944-1947 term as Governor-General of Australia, arrived on an official courtesy visit. Mr Clarrie Campbell, who acted as a kind of godfather and ideologist to the Indian strikers in Australia, suggested to His Royal Highness that he might like to say a few words to the Indians assembled at the Mission, for they were British subjects.

The Duke of Gloucester, according to both Mrs Johnson and Mr Campbell, was only too pleased to oblige. But he didn't know quite what to say to the Indians. (British royalty, until the acquisition of the Duke of Edinburgh, was not noted for speeches without prepared scripts.) Mr Campbell respect-fully formulated for the Duke a platitudinous form of greeting to the Indians. The Duke then spoke to the Indians, following

150

Mr Campbell's suggestions faithfully. He spoke well without the usual written lines and appeared very pleased with his effort — even thrilled.

The interpreter of the royal speech was Dan Singh, leader of the Indian Seamen's Union in Australia, who chanced to be in the Mission building at the time. This happenstance had consequences unique in British royal history. Dan Singh was a short, handsome, volatile Indian whose mind had been set on fire by the anti-colonial struggle. As more and more Indians joined the boycott of Dutch ships and defied their British and Australian supervisors, Dan Singh's optimism gave way to romancing, to purple oratory. When he translated the Duke's speech from English to Hindi for the Indian seamen he gave them what he felt should have been said at this dizzy turn in history rather than what the Duke had said.

His Royal Highness spoke for about three minutes. He looked puzzled as Dan Singh spoke for five minutes — his English had machine-gun velocity but he was putting lightning into his Hindi. The Duke was obviously bewildered when, at the end of 10 minutes, he could identify, in the quickfire Hindi, English terms like "trade union", "colonialism", "imperialism". The one that puzzled all English-language listeners sounded like "trade union banana". What was "trade union banana"? (Dan Singh's "banana" was obviously, according to an Indian scholar consulted by the writer, *banaana*, of Sanskrit derivation. In the context of Dan Singh's interpretation for the Indian seamen the approximate meaning would be something like: "To bring together into one solid group for a particular purpose.")

Dan Singh wound up an oration lasting nearly 20 minutes with what sounded like slogans of tom-tom beat. Hesitantly, the Duke inquired of Mr Campbell: "Did I say all that?"

After having attributed to a brother of the King-Emperor an impassioned plea for solidarity to overthrow empires, Dan Singh, the peppy little Indian interpreter, left to pull some more of the King-Emperor's subjects off a Dutch ship.

The Indians Came Looking For It

Dan Singh was one of four Indians who, on a Saturday afternoon in October 1945, were hammering on shuttered doors in Sydney streets that were holiday-deserted. The Indians were looking for trade union contacts: by chance they found Mr Les Greenfield of Hunter's Hill and Mr J. Johnson of Padstow — both Sydney suburbs — who put them in touch with the NSW Trades and Labor Council Indonesian Sub-Committee and the main maritime unions.

The Indians were from Dutch ships. Dan Singh, from a Dutch ship's catering department, rapped out the story to trade union officials of the great influx of Indians by air and sea. He was speaking for Indians who sympathised with the Indonesian seamen in their boycotts of the Dutch. Some Indians had already walked off Dutch ships and didn't know what the future held for them, Dan Singh said. More were being transported to Dutch ships to carry munitions and troops to Java. Indians, he said, were determined not to provide the Dutch with armaments to crush the Indonesian Republic; they wanted repatriation to Calcutta or Bombay, where they had been signed on without knowing the purpose to which their labors would be put in Australia.

Dan Singh and the other Indians had come ashore looking for fight — and there was soon plenty of it. This was the beginning of a great Indian seamen's strike in Australia — probably the only major strike of Indian seamen ever to take place outside India.

Indian Unionism in Australia

Plane-load after plane-load of Indian seamen, dressed in cottons, some hatless, some in turbans, were flown into Sydney in 1945-46. They were transferred from British to Dutch control to replace striking Indonesian crews in Sydney, or sent by train or air to Brisbane and Melbourne for the same task. They came from an India torn by strikes and rioting, heeding the tramp of "Quit India" marches, hungering in the aftermath of the Bengal famine. They were flown in for much-prized engagements as merchant seamen, not knowing that they were required to rekindle the embers of the Dutch Empire in Asia. When they discovered that they were to sail Dutch war-supply ships under boycott by Australian trade unionists and Indonesian seamen, these men from Calcutta, Madras, Bombay and Karachi, Hindus, Muslims, Sikhs and

152

WE RUN THIS COUNTRY, SEE BUT YOUSE CAN 'AVE ONE SHIP

AUSTRALIA

TRIAL RUN

Lusby, *Courier-Mail*, 1 February 1946

Albert Graham, WWF Brisbane Branch Assistant Secretary, was another active leader of the first bans on Dutch shipping in September 1945

Edward McCormick who, as an Able Seaman on the Australian Navy's repatriation ship, HMAS *Manoora*, witnessed Dutch attempts to seize Tanah Merah survivors arriving at Batavia

Jim Healy, General Secretary of the WWF, addresses a meeting of Australian watersiders and Indian Seamen at the Sydney Domain. Dan Singh, leader of the Indian seamen, is seen smiling at the extreme left. (*Indonesia Calling*)

Pathans, began to join the battle for the Indonesian Republic on the waterfronts of Australia.

The Indian seamen and their families were to suffer severely for their part in the Australian boycott movement. In Australia they were without diplomatic support, for India and Pakistan were not independent till 1947. While they were on strike in Australia their dependent families were denied remittances from wages. The sum of donations from Australians spread thinly among them.

The new airborne force of Indians was signed on at very low wages, sometimes only 15 shillings a week. Indians of wartime service in Australian waters were getting over £20 a month. Like the Indonesians, Indians had economic as well as political grievances.

Between 700 and 800 Indian seamen in Sydney launched their Australian-based Indian Seamen's Union early in October 1945. They demanded £28 a month and cabled information on their struggles in Australia to the Muslim League President, Mahommed Ali Jinnah, and to the Indian Congress President, Dr Abdul Kalam Azad.

A combined meeting of Indians and Indonesians was held in Sydney Trades Hall on 5 October 1945. It was the first meeting ever conducted in Asian languages in the Trades Hall: speeches were in Indonesian, Bengali and Hindi. The Indonesian spokesman, Soeparmin, a Tanah Merah internee, told the Indians that the Indonesians would fight "till the last Dutchman has left Java"; the Indians pledged their support. Dan Singh was the temporary union secretary; Mr Clarrie Campbell was its treasurer. Mr Campbell noted that the burden would fall more heavily on Indians than on other strikers.

As more and more Indian seamen walked ashore the British began to fly from India, for the Dutch service, men who had never been to sea, as well as unemployed seamen. The Indians were mostly flown in secretly in special charter planes. They were escorted by New South Wales, Victorian or Queensland State police to Dutch ships, not knowing that they were to be used as boycott-breakers. Indian seamen flown to man the *Bontekoe* at Brisbane were unaware that the *Bontekoe*'s Indonesian crewmen were in Boggo Road Gaol. Newly arrived Indians put aboard Royal Netherlands Army transport planes at Sydney did not know they were to replace an Indonesian crew until Dutch armed guards and Victorian police put them aboard the *Karsik* in Victoria Dock, Melbourne.

Indians, transported at heavy expense for the Dutch shipping masters, were told that they would be gaoled for long terms in Australia or India if they refused to sail to Indonesia. Some Indians in the British and Dutch service visited them and, in their own languages, left them in no doubt about the significance of threats to imprison and blacklist them. According to the *Sydney Morning Herald* the Dutch told Indians put aboard the *Karsik* in Melbourne "that British forces were helping to quell the Indonesian Republican movement and that, as they were British subjects, they would get into serious trouble in Australia and India if they left the *Karsik* and did not help the British". The Indians said they were "being paid by the British to man the *Karsik*".[3] The Dutch were liberally interpreting their extra-territorial rights when they threatened British subjects with legal reprisals from British and Australian authorities.

Further anxiety was caused to Indians by the stopping of family remittances. The Indian High Commissioner in Australia, nominated by the British Viceroy as a gesture of growing Indian independence, replied when Australian trade union officials asked him to help: "You brought them off; you look after them."[4]

Two-Way Air Lift

Some Indian strikers were gaoled, some were sheltered by Australians and some were speedily flown back to India. The air-lift planes, loaded with Indians, would pass each other in the air, travelling in opposite directions. The *Maritime Worker*, Waterside Workers' Federation organ, asked questions of the Federal Labor Government and three State Labor Governments:

> Why has the KPM Dutch shipping monopoly been given the right to recruit unorganised Indians in Bombay and freely bring them to Australia, put them in a reserve crew pool, while at the same time sending members of the Indian Seamen's Union back to India?

Why are the police forces of New South Wales, Victoria and Queensland — three Labor Governments — forced to collaborate with the Dutch by supervising — Black Marias and all — the shanghai-ing of Indian crews aboard the Dutch vessels, against their will, to enable Dutch ships to be got away to work the ferry service from Singapore to Batavia?[5]

Australian police compulsion of Indian seamen into Dutch service became too much for the moderate leaders of the Australian Council of Trade Unions. A full conference of the ACTU Emergency Committee and of the principal unions concerned in the boycott carried the following resolution on 31 January 1946:

That this conference requests the Federal Government to approach the State Government to prevent the police from shanghai-ing Indian seamen aboard Dutch ships, and that the officials of the Indian Seamen's Union have the right of access to Indian seamen.[6]

A sub-committee of this ACTU-sponsored conference was instructed to interview the Federal Attorney-General, Dr Evatt, and "inform him that the use of police to force the Indian seamen aboard vessels will prejudice the way of overcoming present difficulties . . .". Unless these police methods were immediately discontinued the future running of Dutch ships would be prejudiced, the unions' resolution said.[7] The Dutch, plagued by union boycotts, would have regarded the latter threat as superfluous.

The air-lifted Indians became desperately essential to the Dutch after 13 October 1945 — the day on which they had seen Indonesian seamen shouting imprecations from the decks of *Esperance Bay* as she sailed to Sydney Harbour Heads. The Dutch concentrated on indent of Indians. Some 350 were en route from India to Australia for the KPM Line alone by 30 October 1945.

"Indian Labor Pools" were established in Sydney under the control of British, Dutch and Australian shipping companies. The KPM's Indian Labor Pool was at 17, Harris Street, Pyrmont, close to the Sydney wharves. Here Indians were housed under conditions that would have brought heavy fines

155

and renovation orders on other proprietors, had the tenants been European. Some 20 or 30 Indians were crowded into each room. They shivered on the cold days that sometimes hit Sydney in October and found even the summer heat unpleasant through lack of space.

An "Asiatic Labor Pool" was set up in Lower George Street, or George Street North, close to the wharves. Accommodation provided by the shipowners was so bad that the State Government Health Inspector had to order improvements. Burns Philp & Co, leading South Sea Islands traders and shipowners, the only Australian line that before the war ran regular services to the Netherlands Indies, set up an Indian Labor Pool on an old hulk at No.15 Wharf, Pyrmont. About 180 Indians were packed into the hulk.

British Sailors and Australians Passed Round the Hat

The Indians in Australia faced direful situations, whether or not they agreed to work. They were uncompliant, walking ashore from ship after ship, because they were anxious to hasten the hauling down of union jack in India. The British Government had identified itself with the Dutch cause and had been responsible for air-lifting them to the Dutch service in Australia. The Indians often said that expulsion of the Dutch from Indonesia would soon be followed by British withdrawal from India.

Billets, food and money were urgent problems for the striking Indians. The total of Indian seamen on strike was far greater than the total of Indonesians who had preceded them in the walk-offs because sometimes several Indian crews left the same Dutch ship in succession. A great press of Indians at the Lido hostel, illegally occupied in North Sydney, had joined the Indonesians there.

The Dutch switched off all the refrigerators at the Lido. This made it impossible to store meat and other perishables. The Australians looking after them could not just walk down to the butcher's shop and buy for each meal: they had to order wholesale. Some of the Indians were Muslims who would not eat pork; others were Hindus to whom beef was taboo. Poultry had to be killed according to Muslim rites. Ritually killed meat came from a particular Sydney supplier.

Food was bought in bulk from ships' providores. Indians and Indonesians ate curry that brought tears to Australian eyes and poured condensed milk from cans into tea to produce a sickly brew. The Indians eventually divided into groups and elected a leader to handle food supplies and menus and arrange a roster of cooks. They ate reasonably well until they were repatriated after periods of up to two months at the Lido. The Dutch were forced to restore refrigeration and, strangely, the KPM was induced to donate food for the strikers.

Food had to be paid for and there was the more poignant problem of destitute families in India. Mr J. Johnson and his wife, Mrs Phyllis Johnson, Mr Les Greenfield, Mr Hugh Grant of the Trades and Labor Council Indonesian Sub-Committee, Mr Barney Smith of the Seamen's Union, Mr Mick Ryan, a veteran trade unionist and others organised collections.

Groups of striking Indian seamen went to the waterfront, to ships in port and to factories and construction sites to explain their case. Dan Singh was usually the interpreter: he translated with more fidelity than for the Duke of Gloucester. Within three or four days there was sufficient money to feed the Indians for a week or so. Cash donations from trade unions followed. Early in October the NSW Trades and Labor Council authorised subscription lists for financial support of Indian strikers. Some of the Indonesian strikers, who had savings in Australia, and Chinese seamen donated liberally. The Seamen's Union of Australia raised considerable amounts from its members. Money had to be raised for fares, too. Sometimes Indians, 20 at a time, would board Sydney trams. They wanted to go to the factory, shipboard and wharf meetings.

Australian soldiers and airmen in uniform, some of them with East Indonesia service, visited the Indians at the Lido, bringing gifts. One surprise to the Indians was a visit from a large body of Royal Navy sailors, serving on British warships still in Sydney Harbour after the war, to present large quantities of tobacco, cigarettes and other gifts. The sailors had passed round the hat among the British warships in Sydney Harbour and the response had been generous. In presenting

157

the gifts to the Indians the British sailors' spokesman said: "We are proud of you."[8]

Into Sydney Harbour, while the Indian strikers were in the Lido, sailed a shipload of Indians whose need for gifts was greater. They were Indian soldiers of the British Army, captured in Malaya, Singapore and Hong Kong. They had refused to collaborate with the Japanese and so suffered slave-labor. Australians and Indians from the Lido got comforts aboard to the emaciated survivors of Japanese prison camps.

17 Unpunished Mutiny on the High Seas

Without Australian trade union assistance — and sometimes instigation — the massive desertions of Indian seamen from Dutch ships could not have occurred. Mr Hugh Grant (TLC Indonesian Sub-Committee), Mr Barney Smith (Sydney Branch, Seamen's Union) and other union officials hired launches and took Dan Singh along as an interpreter.[1] Dan Singh's megaphoned slogans caused tumult in some ships and Indians scrambled down ships' sides into the waiting launch. On one Sunday, when holidayers had hired all available passenger launches, the trade unionists hired a steam-powered flat-top barge, used for receiving timber cargoes. The ungainly craft was not easy to manoeuvre in tide and breeze, but it came near enough to Dutch ships to bring down on rope ladders what seemed an avalanche of Indians. The Lower George Street Labor Pool and the Missions to Seamen became babels of tongues, littered with prayer mats, cooking utensils, bedding and bundles. More truckloads of Indians arrived to swell the human press at George Street North, in the Harbour Bridge's shadow.

The Dutch reinforced their guards on ships and at berths. Dutch guards began pointing guns at watersiders who tried to suborn Indians, leading to counter-demonstrations to force withdrawal of armed men from the wharves. The NSW TLC Trade Union Sub-Committee asked: "How long are we going to tolerate a foreign government displaying armed force in Sydney when our Australian soldiers are not allowed to carry arms?"[2]

Dutch plainclothes police trailed Indian leaders around in Sydney and visited the Labor Pools, Missions to Seamen and the Indian Seamen's Club which had just been established. The NSW State Police gave occasional aid to the Dutch in their struggle with the Indian crew replacements. Sixty Indians were taken under NSW police escort to Central Railway Station to entrain for Brisbane. Indian pickets at Central Station were thrust aside by the police and Pathans from the *Pahud* were manhandled. As the Indians were put on the train by police they were heard to call out that they would not sail in Dutch ships. A few days later 35 of the same Indians were walking off the *Both* in Brisbane.

Cutting off Dutch Steam

The Dutch began bringing in soldiers and any spare civilian nationals in Australia to provide skeleton crews for strike-bound ships. They also tried to hold Indian crews under duress. Once outside the Sydney Harbour Heads the Indian crews could be more effectively disciplined than when in direct contact with sedition and incitement at the Sydney waterfront. Newly arrived Indian crews could sometimes be rushed aboard to replace strike-breakers, immune from contact with agitators on shore.

On 20 October Indians aboard *Japara* and *General Verspijck* detected Dutch officers trying to slip the moorings and make a getaway to Java. Both crews escaped ashore. On 26 October KPM offered a newly arrived team of Indians improved conditions if they would leave the Indian Labor Pool at Pyrmont to man *General Verspijck*. Sixty of 62 Indians refused. The Dutch then "borrowed" an Indian crew from Burns Philp & Co, the Australian shipowners and island traders. Once aboard *General Verspijck* the Indians discovered that they were expected to transport military stores. They refused duty, and the Dutch produced arms and threatened to use them and things came near to riot.

Indians of the *General Verspijck*'s engine-room and stoke-hold quietly let down steam at 1 am on 27 October. They then all escaped from *General Verspijck* in a launch provided by the trade unions. The Dutch lost six Indian crews from two ships alone — *General Verspijck* and *Japara*. What shipowners were ever so afflicted by strikes?

El Liberatador got away with a skeleton Dutch crew and some Indians. A launch carrying Australians, Indians and Indonesians followed her down the harbour; appeals were made to the crew to refuse duty. The message obviously got through; there was evidence of trouble aboard *El Liberatador*. The *Swartenhondt*, Dutch wartime troop transport denied repairs by Sydney shipyard unions, was not approached in time to suborn the Indian crew. *Swartenhondt* was later reported as one of the ships in trouble off Newcastle.

Dan Singh, talking in Hindi through the megaphone, regularly followed ships that got away for Java with Indians aboard in a launch. He advised Indians that, if they could not force the ships to turn back in the harbour, they should draw the fires off Newcastle, and try to force the Dutch officers to put into Newcastle Harbour. Several Dutch ships did appear to lose steam off Newcastle; they dropped anchor and rode uncomfortably, sometimes for days, but then struggled away north.[3]

Incitement to mutiny on the high seas, to the endangering of ships by cutting off their steam, carries the direst penalties, particularly when ships are still sailing under naval regulations. But both mutiny and incitement to mutiny went unpunished in Australian waters. The code of the sea gave way to the impulses of the nationalist revolutions. The story of what happened on the Dutch ships that sailed from Sydney with Indians for crewmen is lost, except for the story of the one that came back, turned about by mutineers.

Mutineers without a Chronicler

Indians worked under armed guard aboard the *Patras*, swinging at her moorings in Sydney Harbour. Indian deckhands eluded the Dutch guards and escaped ashore. The deckhands were replaced by Dutch soldiers and a stricter guard was placed over the remaining Indians. *Patras* got up a head of steam and sailed through Sydney Harbour on Saturday, 26 October 1945, carrying munitions. Australians and Asians taking part in the boycott showed their disappointment as *Patras* slipped the net. A few days later they were cheering lustily. *Patras* was on her way back down Sydney Harbour. The *Patras* Indians

161

carried back with them to Sydney wharves a story of mutiny on the high seas that lacked a chronicler. The Indians plotted the *Patras* mutiny under more difficult conditions than Fletcher Christian and his men in Lieutenant William Bligh's *Bounty*, the castaways of Pitcairn Island who became subjects of a spate of novels, histories and films.

Indians in the *Patras* engine-room and stokehold were virtual conscripts, held prisoner by armed Dutch guards. A motor launch had circled *Patras* as she steamed east from near the Harbour Bridge, past Garden Island and the residential suburbs of the harbour front. In the launch were Mr Barney Smith of the Seamen's Union, Dan Singh of the Indian Seamen's Union and other Australians and Indians. Dan Singh appealed to the *Patras* Indians, through a megaphone, to mutiny against the Dutch officers and Dutch military guards. Indians at the ship's rail waved in response but they had to tread warily. Dutch guards were more alert than ever in view of the incitement from the launch. *Patras* ploughed out into the Tasman Sea and became a smudge of coal smoke on the northern horizon.

The Indians knew something of the wartime regulations under which they worked and of the penalties of mutiny on the high seas. They chose mutiny and planned it with consummate skill. By whispers, nods and signals, the engine-room and stokehold crews were enlisted to the conspiracy against the Dutch officers. Suddenly, in an ocean named after the Dutch navigator Abel Janszoon Tasman, the Indians, at a pre-arranged signal, cut off steam.

Patras was adrift, a derelict on the heaving Tasman Sea. Dutch officers and guards found it beyond their capacities to restore steam and get *Patras* under way without the Indian engine-room and stokehold crews. Furiously the Dutch commanded, calmly the Indians disobeyed. Dutch officers looked toward the white surf foaming and pounding on cliffs and sands on the Australian coast between Sydney and Newcastle, where wave and reef had in other days torn many a good ship to flotsam. The Dutch officers could do nothing but accept the Indians' conditions: the stokehold and engine-room crews would provide steam only to sail *Patras* back to Sydney. *Patras* was soon detected, a brooding, grimy ship, moving slowly into Sydney Harbour, past the wharves of Woolloomooloo.

Never in history had a crew of mutineers been welcomed back to a port where the writ of maritime law was supposed to run, to public cheering and a banquet of chicken, fish, lamb, curry stuffs and fruit. Mutiny on the high seas normally excites the interest of police, navy, press, judges, prison governors and sometimes executioners. The rumbling crescendo of the nationalist revolutions in Asia dictated the evasion of criminal trials and the near-suppression of the news of the mutiny, related in voluble Hindi and broken English after *Patras* had swung into her unscheduled berth on Tuesday 29 October.[4]

Patras had been out in the Tasman Sea since the previous Saturday, for most of the time at the mercy of the mutinous crew. In this mutiny off the New South Wales coast in October 1945 men did not rise against their officers to steal a ship, loot treasure, turn pirate, exact revenge on a despot skipper or escape from justice to a desert island. The *Patras* mutiny was plotted and executed without hope of material gain. They were perhaps the first mutineers in history to sail confidently back into a port possessing an efficiently functioning police force, navy and army well able to deal with seamen defying lawful orders from their officers and hazarding a ship on the high seas, and with a legal code that made them subject also to immediate imprisonment as prohibited immigrants. Apart from cheers on the wharves, dramatic shots in Joris Ivens' film *Indonesia Calling*, and acknowledgments in a few Left-wing papers of small circulation, the *Patras* mutineers remained unsung as well as unpunished.

Asians March on Sydney, via Harbour Bridge

The Dutch KPM shipping company withheld wages due to Indians when they deserted its ships — an understandable reprisal. The Indians illegally billeted at the Lido in North Sydney decided to march on the city to demonstrate for their wages. The march followed unsuccessful deputations of Indian spokesmen and Australian trade union supporters to the KPM offices in George Street, city, to the Dutch consular and Indian High Commissioner's offices in Kembla Building,

163

Margaret Street, city. The KPM told the Australian trade unionists who accompanied the Indians that, as they were responsible for the Indians being ashore, they should pay them.

The Indians soon after marched out of the Lido for the first great demonstration of Asians ever seen in the streets of Sydney. Representatives of the Labor Council's Indonesian Sub-Committee and of various trade unions and Australian soldiers and airmen in uniform accompanied the Indians on their march.

The Indians marched on to the pedestrian way of the Sydney Harbour Bridge and then descended on the KPM offices in George Street, arriving just as the typists and girl clerks were being served tea for the morning break. As the vast mass entered the KPM offices, some of the girls screamed and fled. Indians sat down at their vacant desks and sipped the fresh hot tea so hastily abandoned. They fingered typewriter keyboards, which for most of them were a novelty. They danced on KPM office counters and went searching for KPM executives.

Police were called; they tried to cajole and threaten the Indians into leaving, but there were too many to remove and stairs and lifts were blocked with squatting Indians. The marchers from the Lido had been joined by more Indians from the Labor Pool buildings and from temporary billets found for them at Centennial Park, near the city. The KPM executives, somewhat intimidated by this massive demonstration of Asians, agreed to give the Indians their back pay and even to pay some allowances to them while they were on strike, pending deportation.

The Kembla Building in Margaret Street, address of the Indian High Commissioner, was invaded by about a thousand Indians. They were packed side by side on the stairs and landings for a number of floors up, blocking the traffic, and they spilled into the Indian High Commissioner's and other offices. The Treasurer of Sydney Branch of the Waterside Workers' Federation, Mr S. Moran,[5] in the Kembla Building with the Indians, said that they occupied the High Commissioner's room, Gandhi-style, squatting on the floor, chairs and desks. "The police," wrote Mr Moran, "soon gave up the task of

164

carrying Indians to the lifts. The stairs were blocked by the massed Indians. For every Indian ejected from the High Commissioner's office, another would take his place. Finally, the High Commissioner retreated, and all 10 demands laid down were won." Key demand among the 10 was for early repatriation to India. Another was for a guarantee against victimisation in India. The pledge against victimisation was beyond the power of the Indian High Commissioner to enforce.

Hunger Was Their Reward in India

Communal riots flared on the eve of Indian-Pakistan independence. While blood was spilled in Lahore or Calcutta, at the Lido in North Sydney there slept, ate and prayed under one roof Hindus and Muslims, Sikhs, Pathans, Bengalis, Indonesians, Goanese Catholics and a few atheists. Some prayed at the Lido with shoes removed, others with shoes on. Some prostrated themselves on bare boards, others prayed on mats.

Lido trespassers were not all workers. Among them were peasants and petty aristocrats, illiterate former tribesmen and city-educated junior officers. Two of the unrepatriated Indonesians with the Indians at the Lido held princely titles. They were nationalists but had misgivings about consorting with trade unionists and Asians they slighted as "coolies". The princes would not attend union meetings, but went on the deputation to the KPM offices about arrears of pay. One of the princes wrote to an Indonesian aristocrat friend in Brisbane: "Imagine my chagrin at having to go on a deputation with a coolie."[6]

Among the Indians were some whose support for the anti-Dutch strike was qualified. One night at the Lido this handful of Indian waverers suggested that they should return to work on the Dutch ships. A tall, turbaned Indian took the floor and addressed the assembled crowd in Hindi. He said, "We spat on the Dutch ships and on colonialism — and we are not going back to lick it off!"[7]

In Federal Parliament in March 1946 Prime Minister Chifley referred to the Dutch transport of "Lascars" to Australia and their refusal to work Dutch ships.[8] The Central Committee of Indonesian Independence cabled Pandit Nehru, Dr Azad and Dr Jinnah, the two Congress leaders and the Muslim leader,

165

expressing their appreciation of the Indian seamen's strikes.

Pandit Nehru gave political assistance to the Republic, and dockers and seamen in Bombay, Calcutta, Madras and other ports took some action. When Indonesian crews struck aboard Dutch ships in Indian ports, general stoppages were threatened if Indian non-unionists were recruited to strike-bound Dutch ships. However, the boycott movement for the Indonesian Republic was handicapped in India by lack of knowledge and union organisation, and did not achieve the dimensions of the Australian boycott.

Mr Campbell, the Sydney businessman who acted as honorary treasurer to the Indian Seamen's Union in Australia, referred to the prominent part played by Indians: "The withholding of Dutch ships could not have been successful without the cooperation of the Indian seamen."

The effort to get the *Both* away from Brisbane with stores loaded into her by Dutch troops early in 1946 "was only defeated by the Indian crew refusing to sail". Mr Campbell's letter added:

> Throughout the campaign the Indian seamen have played an outstanding part. They led demonstrations on each occasion against the Dutch shipping company. They subscribed many times more cash than did the whole of the Australian trade unions combined.
>
> They sacrificed £20,000 [40,000 dollars] in wages . . . saw their families starve in India rather than assist the Dutch to suppress the Indonesian Republic, and today 500 of these men are starving in Calcutta and Bombay because shipping companies refuse to again employ them with their discharges marked "deserters".
>
> The Indian seamen do not regret the sacrifices they have made in the common struggle; on the contrary, they take pride in being in the vanguard of such an important event in world history. . .[9]

An Indian writer, Sibtey Hassan, in a report to the Seamen's Union of Australia, confirmed Mr Campbell's charge that the Indian strikers repatriated from Australia early in 1946 had been victimised. Sibtey Hassan said that they were now "facing a hard life", as they had been classed as "deserters" and "cannot get employment of any ship". Sibtey Hassan added these lines as their memorial:

They were proud of what they had done — rightly, for they added yet another chapter to the history of India's freedom movement; by their actions, more than any other section of our Indian people, they have told Indonesians that India sympathises with Indonesia's struggle for independence . . .[10]

18 Chinese, Malays, Vietnamese

The Chinese seamen who sailed down to Australia out of South-East Asian battle smoke early in 1942 were probably the first of their race to aid the struggle for the Indonesian Republic.

The Chinese in the Netherlands Indies were a fairly close community, enjoying middlemen's privileges and not popular with Indonesians. Some Chinese among Singapore dockers and seamen gave support and there were a few pro-Republican gestures in the ports of China proper, though none of these had the strength and consistency of the boycotts of the Dutch staged by the Chinese in Australia.

The Chinese in Australia had the union organisation for action against the Dutch. The Chinese Seamen's Union of Australia was formed not long after the fall of Java, to be followed by Australian-based unions of Indonesians, Indians and Malayans. Secretary of the Chinese Seamen's Union was Jong Ngook Bew (Willi Jong). The union was so influential in Australia that the Chiang Kai-shek regime in Chungking awarded it official recognition and thus entitled it to consular services.

The Chinese Seamen's Union appears to have been the first non-Australian trade union ever formed here. It promptly demanded Australian rates of pay and war risk bonus for its members. Strikes yielded substantial interim improvements, then the Curtin Government appointed Mr Justice Ferguson of Sydney to inquire into the conditions of Chinese seamen operating from Australian ports — a unique example of official Australian solicitude for the welfare of Asian aliens. Australian

Seamen's Union Secretary Elliott announced that following Judge Ferguson's findings "all Chinese seamen sailing out of Australia have been granted wages and conditions approximating those of Australian seamen".[1] The support given to Chinese seamen made it easier to bring the Chinese into a common front against the Dutch in 1945.

On Monday 24 September 1945 — the first day of the Indonesian seamen's strike and the Brisbane unionists' boycott — instructions were wired from the head office of the Chinese Seamen's Union, Hay Street, Sydney, ordering every Chinese maritime worker in Australia to regard Dutch ships as black. The Secretary of the Melbourne Branch of the Chinese Seamen's Union, Mr H. Poon, told the press that he had been instructed by his Sydney office that "no Chinese labor was to be supplied on Dutch ships which might be used to crush the Republican movement".[2] Chinese seamen immediately walked off Dutch ships in Australian ports. Several ships had Chinese crews and Chinese served with Indonesians in some of the others.

The Chinese Seamen's Union by October had donated £1,000 to sustain Indonesians and Indians boycotting the Dutch. In Sydney, Brisbane and Melbourne Chinese café proprietors donated occasional meals to Indonesian strikers. Chinese fruit and vegetable wholesalers at Sydney markets and some of the surviving Chinese market gardeners of Sydney's outskirts provided food for strikers billeted in George Street North and the Lido hostel. The Chinese Youth Club in Sydney accommodated strikers in its hall in Dixon Street, Sydney, and paid for treatment to sick Indonesians.

A few of the Chinese seamen who took part in the boycott of the Dutch managed to remain in Australia. The big majority left voluntarily; some were deported under the White Australia Policy, along with Chinese refugees from Singapore and other points in Asia who managed to escape to Australia. There were some 1,800 in the refugee category. A total of 300 Chinese drawn from the refugees and the seamen who had found jobs ashore applied for permanent residence when the war ended. Some had married Australian girls. As soon as enough shipping became available Immigration Minister Calwell served depor-

tation orders on the Chinese who would not leave of their
own volition.

Malays, Vietnamese, Melanesians

Vietnamese, Malays and a few Melanesians from French New
Caledonia and other South Seas islands were manning Allied
merchant ships in South-East Asian waters when the Japanese
troop transports steamed south in late 1941 and early 1942.
They were usually mixed in with Chinese, Indian or Indo-
nesian crews. The Vietnamese, Malays and a few French New
Caledonians were involved in the Dutch ship boycotts. When
Indians deserted the Dutch ship *Japara* at Sydney in October
1945, 24 Malay deckhands, mostly from Singapore and the
Malayan Peninsula, immediately struck and joined the Indians.

The Malays sailing in ships from Australian ports to the
Pacific War fronts staged similar struggles to the Indonesians,
Chinese and Indians for equal pay. They, too, formed a union
in Australia, the Malayan Merchant Navy Association. The
Association's Secretary, Mr J. Abdulla, announced when the
trouble began that Malays would not work Dutch ships bound
for Indonesia. "We are striking in sympathy with Indonesians
and Indians," he said. "We support Indonesian independence
and will not help the Dutch to suppress the Indonesian
nationalists."[3] The Dutch KPM impounded wages and deferred
pay owing to the Malays — as much as £900 in individual
cases. Again, a united Australian-Asian effort was required to
recover the wages.

Numbers of Vietnamese seamen came under British
Admiralty control, either as members of British crews or
through service to Gaullist Free French merchant captains.
Others had joined British ships rather than remain under the
Japanese occupation that coincided with the fall of France in
July 1940. Few Australians could distinguish them from
Chinese, alongside whom they usually served. The Vietnamese
took part in the boycott of Dutch ships in Australia; some
Vietnamese were gaoled at Long Bay, Sydney, for two weeks
for "refusing duty" and "being absent without leave". Vietnamese were in a group of Sydney strikers sentenced to six
weeks' gaol. When a committee of Australians and Asians was

set up to send money to the dependents of Chinese strikers, Singapore, China, Hong Kong and Saigon were among the places mentioned. On a straight economic issue Hanoi and Saigon Vietnamese walked off the French ship *Gia-Long* in Sydney in 1946. The striking Vietnamese from the *Gia-long* were housed, illegally, by Indonesians at the Oranje Clinic, a Dutch medical establishment. Vietnamese did much of the cooking for the Indonesians there.

19   Ten British Mutineers

On the afternoon of 12 November 1945 a lad from West Ham, London, made a wild dash along the deck of the Royal Navy auxiliary vessel *Moreton Bay*, docked at Sydney's waterfront suburb of Woolloomooloo (the 'Loo for short). His name was Ivor Lewis: seven ships had sunk under him during the war, rent by torpedoes and bombs. He had lost his wife and only child in the German air raids on London.

The purpose of Ivor's dash across the *Moreton Bay*'s deck was to reach the 'Loo wharves, via a gangway that British naval officers and Dutch soldiers were already pulling-to. He made it by a split second. As the officers and Dutch troops pulled the gangway Ivor was nearly dashed against the ship's side. A friend, running after Ivor, missed escape to the wharves by a second.

Wilfred Inkins of Cardiff, Wales, was also on the gangway when it began to move. He made a flying leap for the rope, caught it and slid to the wharf. Red-haired Wilfred Palmer of Aberdare, South Wales, ripped his clothes and bruised his hands as he floundered to the wharf. Seven other sailors from the *Moreton Bay* — ten in all — found their way ashore, technically rated as deserters, subject to naval penalties. Some of the ten rushed to the gangway in such haste that they had only shirts and trousers on and coats over their arms. One was stripped to the waist. All ten had to leave personal possessions aboard.

At the deck rails of the *Moreton Bay* throngs of Dutch soldiers jeered as the ten British seamen dashed for the Australian shore. On the wharf a crowd of Australians cheered them. They were witnessing a strange episode in the struggle to forfend military intervention against the Indonesian Republic. The British Navy's auxiliary ship *Moreton Bay* was well known in Australia: she was one of the five Bay class liners in the old Commonwealth Government's merchant fleet, sold to a British shipping company in 1928. *Moreton Bay* was now a troop-carrier, under the orders of South-East Asia Command, transporting 1,600 Dutch soldiers to the Indies. The day before the sailing-eve dash by the ten seamen the 1,600 Dutch troops had been transhipped from the British troopship *Stirling Castle* in Sydney. *Stirling Castle*, a Union Castle Company liner in the pre-war England-South Africa service, could not go to Java because she was under orders to repatriate from Australia members of the British armed forces sent to the Pacific for the war against Japan. The Dutch troops, once transferred to the *Moreton Bay* at Sydney, were rushed to Java.

Stirling Castle, when she berthed at Sydney's Circular Quay early in November, was the first British ship to come under the boycott. The NSW Trades and Labor Council Indonesian Sub-Committee chartered a launch with a megaphone and amplifier to harangue Dutch troops from the sea. A demonstration was organised on Circular Quay. Among those in the launch were Mr Jack Zwolsman, the only anti-colonial Dutchman available in Sydney, it seemed; Mr Newell Carruthers, a Sheetmetal Workers' Union organiser, and an Indonesian, Ray Mongingka. Zwolsman still spoke Dutch reasonably well, though he had been in Australia since before World War I and won the Military Medal while fighting with the 1914-1918 Australian Army. The launch venture was a fiasco. When Zwolsman talked of Atlantic Charter rights the Dutch soldiers' tempers exploded.

Journalists had wind of what was coming: they asked the Trades and Labor Council representatives in the cruising launch to move in closer to the *Stirling Castle* so they could get better pictures. They were not disappointed: the pictures were startling. Dutch soldiers began hurling bottles, garbage, vegetables, iron and wooden objects and crockery from the upper decks. Most missed but there were some hits and uncomfortable near-misses. The Dutch also tipped waste oil

on the launch: Carruthers was smothered and others spat-
tered. Zwolsman, under the rain of engine-room oil and
missiles, forgot his Dutch and shouted advice to his compatriots in impolite Australian. The Dutch played records of
patriotic songs with amplifiers turned up loud, blew bugles,
sang House of Orange songs and waved House of Orange flags.
The rain of bottles and other missiles continued. A solitary
Dutch soldier from the *Stirling Castle* conveyed his disagreement with his fellow-soldiers' conduct to the Labor Council
representatives.[1]

When *Stirling Castle* moved to Woolloomooloo Bay for
transhipment of the Dutch troops to *Moreton Bay*, further
appeals to them were blared from a launch — appeals to allied
troops to lay down arms. Berthed near *Stirling Castle* at
Woolloomooloo was the Dutch hospital ship *Tjitjalengka*, her
Red Cross exempting her from boycott. Dutch officers, from
the decks of the argosy of mercy, threw missiles at the men in
the launch. A girl reporter in the launch was hit with a bottle.
Tjitjalengka carried a Chinese crew. The Chinese shouted in
fury at the Dutch officers, who retired. The Chinese then
collected £158 from among themselves to hand to the Australian trade unionists to intensify the boycott of the Dutch.

Waterside workers, who had both *Stirling Castle* and
Moreton Bay under iron-tight boycott, stopped work on the
Clan Chattan nearby to demonstrate against the Dutch. Transport workers refused to carry food to *Stirling Castle*. Workers
at a big Sydney depot where the Dutch soldiers' meat for the
voyage to Java was stored refused to handle the meat. *Stirling
Castle* and *Moreton Bay*, to which the Australian Government
was host, were under ban by the Australian Council of Trade
Unions, NSW Labor Council and Indian, Indonesian, Chinese
and Malayan unions of seamen.

The demonstration at the wharfside against *Stirling Castle*'s
troop-carrying mission on 7 November made blazing headlines.
Waterfront workers, men from nearby Garden Island naval
dockyard, housewives and young girls took part. Dutch soldiers
and their officers reacted sharply to the sight of Indonesian
independence banners. They yelled, grabbed anything move-
able and bombarded the demonstrators on the wharf. Ship's
crockery, tins, pieces of metal, garbage, wedges and other

174

small carpenters' tools, bottles and blocks of wood rained down, causing some injuries. Then came the ship's firehoses, turned on the wharfside crowd. Most were drenched. The Indian crew of the British *Clan Chattan* added to the pandemonium, hooting, cursing and threatening the Dutch across the water. Everyone, it seemed, was breaking the law with impunity, including the Dutch. Dutch soldiers blocked off the wharf for a time and refused to allow anyone to leave the wharf, not even to ring for an ambulance to carry away the injured. This, too, breached Australian law, but the police took no action.

NSW Trades and Labor Council protests went to Prime Minister Chifley against the visit to an Australian port of a ship carrying Dutch troops for war on the Indonesian Republic, and against "insults" involved in Dutch airmen wearing Australian Air Force uniforms with small "Netherlands" armbands sewn on them. *Stirling Castle* was the last ship to carry troops from Holland to an Australian port.

Disaffected British Sailors

On Saturday 10 November 1945, before the last Dutch soldier had been transhipped from *Stirling Castle* to *Moreton Bay*, the *Bay* liner's crew, after approaches from Australian trade union representatives, decided that they would not sail the Dutch troops to Java. The *Stirling Castle*'s crew had already informed Trades and Labor Council representatives that they did not want to work the ship while Dutch soldiers were aboard, but, as they were under Admiralty orders and in an overseas port, they did not feel able to strike.

Anti-Dutch feeling had penetrated Royal Navy as well as Merchant Navy ranks. Some 30 or 40 British sailors from warships in Sydney Harbour came to the *Stirling Castle* demonstration to express their sympathy with the Australian boycott of Dutch ships. Forty British Navy sailors in Brisbane signed a resolution demanding that British arms should not be used for war on the Republic and donated money to help the boycott. However, other British Navy men, under orders, loaded stores into Dutch and other Java-bound ships to undermine the boycott.

Speakers from the *Moreton Bay* crew, at the meeting held

on the Woolloomooloo wharf on 10 November, pointed out that hundreds of thousands of people in England were short of food, that ships like *Moreton Bay* should be carrying food to the severely rationed British instead of transporting Dutch troops. The Sydney Branch Secretary of the Australian Seamen's Union, Mr Barney Smith (Liverpool-born), appealed to the British seamen to join the boycott and was warmly applauded.

The *Moreton Bay* seamen's representatives informed Admiral Mountbatten's shipping agent in Australia, Sir Thomas Gordon (Director of British Shipping in Australia) and the troopship's captain that the crew would not take the Dutch troops to Indonesia. Sir Thomas Gordon and Mountbatten must have acted quickly. An urgent cable was soon on the way to Woolloomooloo from Mr C. Jarmon, leader of the National Union of Seamen in Great Britain, ordering the *Moreton Bay* seamen that they were on no account to go on strike.

It was little use the Australian Seamen's Union reminding Mr Jarmon by cable that the British seamen were refusing to take Dutch troops to Java "in conformity with the decision of the Australian Council of Trade Unions declaring black any transport of Dutch troops or material to Indonesia".[2] *Moreton Bay*'s captain became very hostile to the boycotting Australian trade unions. He told Mr Barney Smith that, if he had his way, he, Smith, would be "put up against a wall and shot".[3]

The *Moreton Bay* crew's decision of Saturday 10 November brought some 5,000 Australians and Asians on the Sunday to the parkland overlooking the Woolloomooloo berths. The crowd cheered the *Moreton Bay* seamen and hooted the Dutch soldiers, who again produced their House of Orange flags and sang Orange songs — never advisable in the presence of so many Australians and Liverpool and Glasgow seamen of Irish-Catholic origin.

Mutiny of the Moreton Bay

About midday on Sunday 11 November the captain tried to get *Moreton Bay* away for sea, though she was short of meat and other supplies, due to the union bans. The 145 British seamen in the crew refused duty. This refusal of duty was not easy. The *Moreton Bay* was a Royal Navy auxiliary ship. Penalties awaiting deserters under British Navy regulations are severe. The *Moreton Bay* seamen, moreover, had over £300 each, on average, owing to them in deferred pay, which they would forfeit if they deserted the ship and most had dependent families in Britain. Defiance of the National Union of Seamen's order multiplied the hazards. National Union of Seamen's leaders cabled another warning message, confirming their veto of strike, on the morning of 12 November.

The second National Union of Seamen's cable created doubt and division. A majority of the crew met ashore, leaving behind a substantial minority prepared to abide by the National Union of Seamen's order. Over 80 at the meeting decided they would defy both the union and the captain and refuse to transport Dutch troops. Just before 4.30 pm on the Monday they went back aboard to pack their gear. The Australian trade union movement looked like having on its hands, for the first time in its history, a British naval mutiny.

The 80 or so British seamen were not ready for the stratagems of their officers. The officers mobilised Dutch soldiers in readiness, and once the seamen were back aboard and down below packing the officers and Dutchmen began pulling up the gangway, for an immediate cast-off, 20 minutes before the scheduled sailing time of 5 pm. Ten only of the 80 who decided to desert *Moreton Bay* were able to escape in hazardous scrambles and leaps ashore.

The Moreton Bay Ten,[4] who sacrificed more than any Australians in the boycott of the Dutch war on the Republic, were:

Wilfred Inkins, Cardiff, Wales.
Ivor Lewis, West Ham, London.
Wilfred Palmer, Aberdare, South Wales.
John Bacon, Mill Hill, England.
E. Loughlin, Glasgow, Scotland.
George Bennett, Shirehampton near Bristol, Wales.
Ray Goddard, Bristol, England.
Robert Fitzpatrick, Liverpool, England.
Kenneth Hince, Bath, England.
Jim Mack, Perth, Scotland.

Five of them had transported troops under heavy fire for the D-Day invasion of Normandy beaches. All had been in ships bombed or torpedoed. One of them told the writer who had dinner with them the evening they came ashore that the war against the Indonesian Republic was a mockery of the pledges and hopes for which they had seen men bleed, burn and drown. Nearly a quarter of a century later, Mountbatten, against whose orders the Moreton Bay Ten mutinied, came near to agreeing with their sedition. Mountbatten criticised severely the use of British troops and facilities to attempt the restoration of doomed imperial systems in Indonesia and Indo-China.[5]

Australian sympathisers provided the Moreton Bay Ten with clothes, shaving gear and other necessities and food and shelter. Money was raised by donation to support dependent families in Britain. Jobs were found for them all in Sydney and in rural areas of New South Wales. Trade union influence was sufficient to protect these British deserters from trial or from deportation as "prohibited immigrants" — the customary fate of merchant seamen who illegally leave ships in Australia. The Chifley-Evatt Government did not try to prosecute the Moreton Bay Ten.

The *Moreton Bay*, her crew 10 men short, disappeared through Sydney Harbour heads to furnish troops for the unwinnable war. The Dutch soldiers were required to wash off slogans which British seamen had painted round the ship, such as "Dutch Ships for Dutchmen, British Ships for British Food!" and "Food for Britain before Troops for Java!" There were protests by trade unionists in England, including one from the East London Branch of the National Union of Seamen, against the "shanghai-ing" — meaning the premature raising of the gangway and cast-off by officers and troops to prevent seamen walking off — of the 80 or so who had decided not to sail to the Indonesian war zone.

20 Government Help to Both Sides

Replacement of the Churchill Government in 1945 by the Labour Government led by Mr Clement Attlee and Mr Ernest Bevin opened wider channels between London and Canberra. British Foreign Secretary Bevin publicly declared his intention of seeing Dutch rule re-established and, as a Queensland Trades and Labor Council resolution[1] said, Mr Bevin's policy had received "the wholehearted support" of Mr J.A. Beasley, the new Australian Resident Minister in London, who had left the Chifley-Evatt Ministry to take up the post.

Supplementing the pressures from the Attlee-Bevin Government, Mountbatten of SEAC and the British plenipotentiaries handling the Dutch-Indonesian dispute, Lord Inverchapel and Lord Killearn, sought in their representations from South-East Asia the release of Dutch ships held in Australian ports. While Mr Chifley continued to give pledged aid to the Dutch with one hand and wave the boycotters on with the other, the agitations in London and SEAC were not without effect.

Dr Evatt was frequently in Britain and America after the war, on United Nations and other diplomatic missions. The Waterside Workers' Federation felt that anti-boycott representations made to Dr Evatt overseas were not fruitless. Its official organ[2] said:

While on the surface a tacit support is given by the Government to the trade union policy of support to Indonesians, it is quite apparent that some ministers, such as Dr Evatt, are engaged in two-faced dealings, despite statements to the contrary to the trade unions, and are doing everything to assist the Dutch.

It is noteworthy that until Dr Evatt came back from overseas the Government attitude to the ban was fairly good, but since this the situation has deteriorated.

The Liberal Party challenge to the Labor Government to take control of its foreign policy had some effect. Dr Evatt said that he would not allow the foreign policy of the Government to be dictated by the waterfront unions. The *Sydney Morning Herald* editorially praised Dr Evatt:

> It is time somebody in authority took the stand, for in fact the unions have been determining policy in regard to Indonesia during the better part of six months.[3]

The Chifley-Evatt Government added materially to its war-time aid to the Netherlands Indies Government-in-Exile forces. On Canberra direction the Australian armed forces placed in Dutch possession millions of pounds worth of munitions and installations for which Australian taxpayers had footed the bill — roads, aerodromes, wharves, barracks, medical posts, workshops and tools and machines, plus food and clothing in East Indonesia. Early in 1946 the Government handed to the Royal Netherlands Navy the corvettes *Cairns*, *Wollongong*, *Lismore*, *Toowoomba*, *Burnie*, *Ipswich*, *Tamworth* and *Kalgoorlie*, each of 790 tons, built in Australian yards and given new names when they were transferred.

The Government sanctioned the NEI administration's use of Dutch troops and civilians as stevedores to break waterfront strikes in Brisbane, Sydney, Melbourne and Fremantle. The Fremantle WWF Branch Secretary reported that cargo destined for Java was being consigned to Fremantle from Eastern Australian ports and "then loaded in Dutch ships by Dutch naval personnel and Italian POWs".[4]

HMAS *Manoora*, after having safely landed Indonesian repatriates at Tanjong Priok, returned to carry Dutch military stores from Queensland to the Indies. HMAS *Kanimbla*, another naval auxiliary, also carried equipment for the Dutch. HMAS *Kanimbla* carried as ward-room guests to the Indies two Labor Party members of the Queensland Legislative Assembly. They were Messrs John Joseph O'Connor Healy and John Albert Turner. They made passing acquaintance with Balikpapan, Macassar and Ambon and returned with the finding that the Republic did not have popular support. The two Labor MPs attacked Queensland trade unions for their ban on Dutch ships and said that "native independence is dangerous for Australia".[5]

Blockade by Australian Corvettes

The Chifley-Evatt Government's transfer of the eight Australian Navy corvettes led to an upsurge of black bans in shipyards, to heated protests from trade unions, to some irritating Dutch interference with British commerce and to serious damage to the Republic's weak economy. Trade union bans on the corvettes caused Mr Menzies to forget the cautions inherent in his legal training and say: "We could not sell a corvette for which we had no further use because a sub-branch of the Waterside Workers' Federation said no."[6] To which Mr James Healy replied: "The facts are that the corvette had been handed over to the Dutch and a conference of waterfront unions concerned with ship docking repairs at which we weren't represented imposed a ban."[7]

On 13 February 1946 Brisbane WWF Branch telegraphed[8] its Federal Office in Sydney that the corvette *Cairns* had left Brisbane for the Indies three days before "carrying war equipment". Three Indonesian sailors had escaped from the corvette and had been put under Dutch guard. Despite tight trade union black bans at Garden Island and other Sydney dockyards the corvettes all managed to reach Indonesian waters by the middle of 1946. They imposed an effective blockade on Indonesian Republican trade and angered the British, upon whose goodwill the Dutch depended heavily.

The master[9] of one British ship that fell victim to the ex-Australian corvettes' blockade took the extraordinary step of writing to the General Secretary of the Waterside Workers' Federation, blasting the Dutch and lauding the watersiders' boycott of Dutch ships. The tough-minded British salt wrote thus to Mr Healy on the strength of on-the-spot experiences:

The Indonesians are doing their best to trade, in a barter trade or change for change, by exporting rubber, flax, spices, etc., with Singapore, Britain and USA, but in this the Dutch are stopping all trade to and from Indonesia.

The Dutch have armed corvettes recently purchased from Australia patrolling Java and Sumatra ports. Should a British ship be loading or discharging in any Indonesian port, the Dutch patrol immediately enters that part of Indonesia and orders the British ship to leave. If the master does not leave as ordered, the Dutch patrol waits for him outside and makes him proceed with a Dutch boat as escort to a Dutch port.

There, said the British captain, the Dutch searched the ship and confiscated cargo. In addition the British ship master was fined 250 Malayan dollars and fined a further 250 dollars "for not obeying the Dutch corvette's commander" by a court consisting of a Dutch magistrate, a Dutch attorney, a Dutch lawyer and a Dutch corvette commander. The British captain told Mr Healy that "the Dutch are slowly but surely crippling the poor Indonesian people who are sadly in want". He accused the Dutch of "thieving" the Indonesians' produce to sell for Dutch profit in Singapore or the USA.

The Dutch Empire of the East, it might be assumed, was now in senility, inhibiting the commerce of a nation always sensitive about freedom of the seas, and affronting the British flag, though the Dutch urgently required British economic nourishment and diplomatic countenance.

The Dutch, the British captain opined in his letter to Mr Healy, were "just on a pirate mission to seize all they can while the going is good". Indonesians of all classes that he had met and their Republican officials were "very strong-minded level-headed men", but Dutch patrols and intruding planes sought to irritate the Indonesians so that the Indonesians might fire back in defence. "If they do," wrote the captain, "then the Dutch start a massacre, killing everyone in sight."

The Dutch "blamed the British" because they had not "interfered" sufficiently with the Republic, but, the British captain said, "the Dutch hate the Australians more." This letter to the Waterside Workers' Federation of Australia would surely only have been penned, in view of the risks to employment, under compulsion of hot indignation. Dutch deport-

182

ment in the sunset of empire stirred the soul of a British merchant skipper so deeply as to convert him to an advocate of maritime strike and boycott against Dutch shipping.

It is a pity his name is given in confidence, for he deserves a place in history as the only British captain ever to hail a strike of Australian dockers. He called on Mr Healy and the union he led to stand fast against attempts to induce them to end the boycott of the Dutch:

> No, Mr Healy! Your union is right in refusing to load Dutch ships in Australia for the East . . . Please do not use my name, as I do not want publicity. You are at liberty and at your discretion in making known my views on this question of Indonesia and the Dutch, as a master of a British ship.

Mr Healy made the British captain's views known to Mr Chifley.[10] They may have helped him to a realisation that Indonesians and not Dutchmen would provide the future market for Australian goods in the Near North.

The Trade Future

The Labor Government's supply of corvettes drew attention to the agonising contradictions now racking Australian policy toward Asia. The Government made it possible for the Netherlands Navy to deliver blows at Republican commerce, and at the same time looked for export solutions in the greener market vistas of a self-governing Asia. While a campaign suggesting that trade union boycotts were denying Australia millions in export sales to the Indies was causing some difficulties for the unions, Mr Chifley kept his commercial sights set beyond the tumbledown European colonial establishments.

A mushroom organisation known as CEIGOA Ltd, with token capital but generous funds, began to publish full-page advertisements in the press and to sponsor other propaganda against the boycott, on the plea that Australia's trade with the Indies was in jeopardy. Mr Latham Withall, Director of the Associated Chambers of Manufactures, claimed that the Netherlands Indies was "one of the best markets — if not the best market in the world — for Australian manufactured products and its loss would react against Australian secondary industries".[11] However, Australian-NEI trade in its peak years, 1934-39, aggregated only £6 684 826 in exports, the majority of farm and factory origin. Australia bought from the NEI in return over the 1934-39 years some £30 145 031 worth, leaving Australia with a deficit of nearly £23½ millions.

The Sydney *Sun*[12] headlined a story that the NEI had cancelled £6 million in Australian orders and that Mr Van Der Noorda, Chief of the Netherlands Government Export Organisation, had sent 250 letters of cancellation to Australian firms. Shipping hold-ups, the *Sun* claimed, made Dutch-Australian commerce impossible. The *Sydney Daily Telegraph*[13] said that Dutch cancellation of £6 million in orders for Australian goods "should bring home to the Commonwealth and the public the mischief waterside workers have done to this country".

Mr Chifley inferred that the Dutch, if they ruled the Indies, would not buy much from Australia: they were not prepared to accept Australian prices for goods in the past and "they would not place their orders with Australia if they could get them cheaper somewhere else". "That," added Mr Chifley, "is a sound commercial proposition and I have no quarrel with it".[14] One explanation of his demurring response to demands that he deal with trade unions disrupting Australian-Dutch trade was in his statement to parliament:

I should think that 70 million Indonesians might be good customers. The Indonesians are the great mass population of Indonesia: in one area there are 40 million Indonesians and a very limited number of other people.[15]

Despite the pricking of the lost multi-million market fable, it was bound to produce hostility to the boycott among business people, demobilised soldiers and workers displaced from war industries, anxious to see economic growth and more employment opportunities.

Some spice was added to the lost trade campaign by press reports that communists were forming a company to monopolise Australian-Indonesian trade. The story was accorded banner headlines and editorial comment. The name of Mr Clarrie Campbell was mentioned as one of those behind the scheme. Dr Evatt branded the story of the "Communist trade

SLAVE OF THE LAMP
When Dutch officials in Australia approached unions to lift the shipping ban, they were told that the
unions would do this only on the personal instruction of the republican government headed by
Sutan Sjahrir

Australian and Indonesian servicemen in 1945 head the march across Sydney Harbour Bridge from
the Lido Hotel, occupied by Indonesian and Indian seamen, to the city offices of the Dutch shipping
firm KPM. (*Indonesia Calling*)

DAILY MIRROR

Penfold's Port

ARMS, MUNITIONS LOADED ON "MERCY" SHIPS, SAYS CHIFLEY

Action Over Indonesians

ARMS and ammunition had been loaded on four "so-called 'mercy' ships," the Prime Minister (Mr. Chifley) said in Canberra today.

"The Government will see that 'mercy' ships do not carry arms and munitions," he said.

Seamen Caused Delay

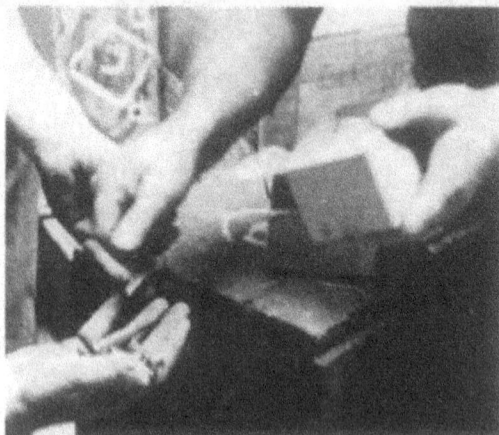

Waterside workers displaying bullets from a broken crate, part of Dutch 'mercy' cargo. The clipping from the *Daily Mirror* reports the Labor government's reaction to this discovery. (*Indonesia Calling*)

Indian seamen from the *Patras* bringing their belongings ashore at Man o'War Steps, near the Sydney Harbour Bridge, after forcing the ship's Dutch officers to return to port in October 1945. (*Indonesia Calling*)

company" as a "pretty elaborate hoax".[16] There was a small flicker of fire behind the dense cloud of propaganda smoke. Mr Campbell, whose association with the Indonesians was extremely close and who later went to South-East Asia, did try to organise a fleet or war-surplus Catalina flying-boats to fly down to Sydney certain lightweight Indies commodities in short supply and fetching high prices.[17] Charity was mingled with commerce to accelerate erosion of public sympathy for the boycotters.

The press and the Liberal-Country Party Opposition ran a fierce campaign against the hold-up of "mercy ships" — those carrying medical and other relief supplies to areas brought near to famine by the war and to released internees and prisoners-of-war. Dutch hospital ships like the *Oranje* and *Tasman* were exempted from the boycott from its start on 24 September 1945. Others not bearing the red cross were described as "mercy ships" by the Dutch. Queensland Trades and Labor Council said that watersiders were "willing and eager" to work hospital ships, but not the other Dutch ships declared black:

> The Dutch Government glibly protests that the black ships were not carrying arms or personnel for the suppression of the Indonesians, but supplies for the relief of prisoners-of-war and other war victims. Yet boxes labelled "Comforts" have been found to contain phosphorus bombs and tommy-guns.[18]

The troopship *Balikpapan* was, according to Brisbane WWF Branch Secretary Englart, described as a carrier of "mercy and medical supplies", but actually carried "large quantities of ammunition and war equipment".[19] Though watersiders had loaded arms before 24 September and were asked to load more on that day and after, a Dutch spokesman said: "We have told waterside workers that no arms will be loaded."[20] WWF Secretary Healy said: "The Dutch assured us that they did not have any war materials aboard, and we found tommy-guns in one of their 'mercy' ships."[21]

The *Tasman* was exempted from boycott as a hospital ship and allowed to sail to Java. Indonesian crew members reported to Sydney maritime unionists on their return that the Dutch officers had told them that when they reached Batavia they would be given courses in engineering. Instead, they were held aboard *Tasman* to ensure that they sailed her back to Sydney. Dutch military officers in mufti, alleged WWF Assistant General Secretary Roach,[22] took passage to Java in the *Tasman*. More Dutch officers went aboard at Sydney on her return from Java to Sydney. Indonesian hospital staff in the ship stopped work not only because of the presence of military officers aboard but because the ship's officers refused to open a package marked with the Red Cross, suspected of holding munitions. A Red Cross package fell from a sling going aboard *Tasman*. A Dutch officer blamed an Indonesian for the accident and scuffled with him. Watersiders were by this time only too anxious to intervene against the Dutch. They protected the Indonesian and examined the broken package's contents. They were machine-gun parts.

Tasman, though bearing the Red Cross insignia, thereupon joined the Black Armada. As Dutch passengers returning to Java lined *Tasman*'s decks 22 Indonesian firemen and greasers suddenly rushed from below with their baggage, shinned over the ship's side and thudded on to the wharf. Two Indonesian engineers, not informed of the escape, heard the commotion and quickly shot over the side when the opportunity came. These 24 who deserted the *Tasman* in March 1946 were the last Indonesian mutineers to come ashore in Australia.

Prime Minister's Confirmation

Mr Chifley refused to put on a threadbare compassion as a protective vestment. From the beginning the Prime Minister confirmed trade union charges about "mercy" deception. He said:

> Inquiries about four so-called mercy ships showed that all of them had arms and ammunition aboard in addition to mercy supplies.[23]

Mr Chifley's exposure of Dutch gun-running in relief ships dropped like cold rain on the "mercy" campaign, but it did not repair all the damage to the boycott movement.

To settle the "mercy" issue the Federal Government had Conciliation Commissioner D.V. Morrison of the Commonwealth Aribtration Court, late in February and early in March 1946, test evidence. Lieutenant A.M. Denboer, Sea Transport Officer at Sydney for the Netherlands Indies Government Sea Transport Bureau (Bureau Zeevervoer) claimed to the court that 1,649 tons of medicine were being held up at Sydney and 500 tons at Melbourne. Conciliation Commissioner Morrison was of a sufficiently mathematical turn of mind to translate the massive weight of medicines into penicillin, smallpox, cholera and typhoid shots, eye-drops and anti-malarial pills. Of the 1,649 tons Lieutenant Denboer claimed were held by boycott in Sydney, he said, "That is enough medicine to cure or kill half the world".[24]

The vestments of mercy became more and more ragged. The Dutch shot down an Indian Red Cross Dakota as it was about to land at Djogjakarta with medical supplies donated in India. The pilot, Wing-Commander Alexander Noel Constantine, a NSW man, his wife Beryl, Squadron-Leader L.C. Hazelhurst of Bolton, Lancs., England, Indian Flight-Engineer Rida Den and five Indonesian crewmen were killed.

An Indonesian Medical Appeal was launched in Australia, but its Secretary, Mr V.L. Matchett, wrote[25] that medicines sent on the *Tjibesar* to Java were confiscated by the Dutch and "not one ounce reached Republican territory". Medicine consigned to Bantam, West Java, arrived at Tanjong Priok, but the Dutch refused transit rights, and the medicines spoiled in the heat of the ship's hold.[26]

Mr Chifley tried to persuade the Dutch into the simon-simple tactics of isolating relief cargoes from munitions and thus releasing their ships from the Brisbane River and Sydney Harbour. Puzzled by the unbending, undiscerning attitude of Dutch leaders, he expressed public regret that it had not been possible to arrange with the Dutch "the loading of purely mercy supplies". He told parliament that it was clear that, when conferences were being held, some Dutch ships were being loaded with arms and ammunition.

Sir Frederick Stewart (Liberal, NSW): Did not the Government itself sell arms to the Dutch?
Mr Chifley: I shall answer the question if it is put to me at the proper time.[27]

The proper time was never. This was too sensitive a contradiction. In their centuries as waggoners of the sea and traders in all lands and climes the Dutch burgherdom had never encountered before a Prime Minister who would sell them arms, then advise them that they should leave the arms to rust on the wharves and take aboard only food and medicines.

21   Anti-Boycott Offensive
in the Unions

By December 1945 the trade union boycott front was being fissured. Early in 1946 leaders of the maritime unions and the Australian Council of Trade Unions were hurling epithets at each other. The ACTU leaders wanted "relief ships" loaded for Java. The Netherlands Federation of Trade Unions and Dr Evatt were urging the unions to do this while Mr Chifley remained discreetly in the background or gave occasional crumbs of comfort to the boycotters.

The Australian Council of Trade Unions full executive, meeting in Melbourne on 9 to 12 October 1945, had endorsed the black bans already applied by unions on Dutch shipping and supplies, declaring that the bans accorded with the Atlantic Charter and that "no war or other material that can in any way be utilised by the Dutch Government against the Indonesian people shall be supplied or transported from Australian territory for use by the Dutch Government".[1]

The ACTU Secretary, Mr Albert Monk, made several trips overseas at the war's end. He interviewed in Amsterdam during November 1945 President Kupers of the Netherlands Federation of Trade Unions, the more moderate of the Dutch trade union federations. Mr Monk cabled the ACTU Emergency Committee that Mr Kupers had urged him that relief ships be loaded for Java on the understanding that no war material was included.[2] British Foreign Secretary Bevin was also anxious to free the Dutch ships. Mr Monk had discussions with British trade union leaders on whom Mr Bevin, for many years a Trade Union Congress leader, exerted much influence.

Australian trade unions in all States were divided on the issue. Only in Queensland was there a decisive majority for boycott continuation. Queensland TLC would not agree to free ships unless United Nations Relief and Rehabilitation Association (UNRRA) and Australian trade union representatives supervised relief shipments to the Indies.[3]

Mr Bevin authorised General Christison, Mountbatten's military commander in Java, to find a formula which the Australian Government could use to end the boycott. One significant result of this British intervention was the despatch by ACTU Secretary Monk of a telegram[4] to WWF General Secretary Healy on 23 January 1946:

Doctor Evatt informed me this afternoon he has had conference with Dutch East Indies Minister relative passage Dutch ships to Java.

Dutch Minister has given personal assurance of acceptance conditions laid down by unions for absolutely no discrimination in distribution of foodstuffs in supplies landed there and that General Christison will be responsible for distribution of supplies.

Dutch Minister making press statement to this effect this afternoon. He has given guarantee that there will be no molestation of Indonesian crews on any vessel.

Dr. Evatt anxious that ships in Brisbane should be bunkered and got away as early as possible to prevent further difficulties.

Notified Healy, Brisbane Labor Council.

Emergency Committee hopes ships will be loaded to permit sailing as early as possible in accordance with this undertaking.

Mr Healy happened to be out of Sydney. The WWF Assistant General Secretary, Mr Roach, replied to Mr Monk that the requirements of the unions had not yet been met in the negotiations. Mr Roach's telegram[5] added:

Must insist satisfactory and direct assurance from Indonesian Premier to Indonesian Seamen's Union. Until such time these assurances received Indonesian seamen insist continuation strike. Waterside workers cannot load ships whilst involved in strike. Solution to this problem urgent.

Within the Australian Council of Trade Unions, nominally a united federation, a system of dual power was given de facto recognition. The ACTU Secretary, Mr Monk, and ACTU President, Mr P.J. Clarey, could propose but the militant unions could often dispose. And, as Mr Roach's telegram indicated, a new power shape had appeared on the Australian horizon: the Indonesian Republic. On 29 January the ACTU Emergency Committee convened a conference of leading trade unions involved in cargo and shipyard boycotts. Deliberations continued till 1 February. Maritime, ship repair and land transport unions stood fast against ACTU leaders' appeals, which had the authority of Australian, British and Dutch Governments. The unions' conference reaffirmed the black ban on Dutch ships.

Though rebuffed at the 29 January-1 February conference, the ACTU leaders, Messrs Monk and Clarey, called a meeting on 9 February of the ACTU Emergency Committee to pursue the drive to lift the black bans on the Dutch. The ACTU Emergency Committee called on the unions involved to man and load relief vessels for Java "on the assurance given to the Commonwealth Government by the Netherlands East Indies Minister". The ACTU full executive endorsed this decision.[6]

However, the atmosphere was becoming less favorable for those demanding an end to the boycott. The departure of the corvette *Cairns*, handed to a Dutch crew by Australian officers and ratings at Brisbane and carrying war equipment to Java, the Dutch sea blockade of the Indonesian Republic, the fiercer battles that raged in Java as more Dutch troops landed from Holland and disturbances in the Dutch internment camp at Casino did not help the anti-boycott cause.

From Java, repatriated Indonesians were keeping the unions informed. Tony Maramis, who went home in the *Esperance Bay* from Brisbane, reported to Queensland Trades and Labor Council that in Batavia Dutch NICA soldiers were "wandering around fully armed, holding up all red-and-white flagged cars, shooting at innocent, unarmed Indonesian men, women and children. There are many cases of gangsterism and banditry by Dutch boys not more than 14 years old".[7] Whether true or exaggerated or false, these reports from Java influenced the maritime unions.

On 26 February Dr Evatt, as Attorney-General, promoted a compulsory conference of unions involved to end "the deadlock over the hold-up of Dutch ships in Australia". Commonwealth Conciliation Commissioner Morrison, the arbitration commissioner responsible for waterfront affairs, was magisterial in tone. According to Mr Roach he issued "some quiet threats" that there would be a dissolution of the Stevedoring Commission, the body controlling waterfront labor on which the Waterside Workers' Federation had representation with the shipowners and the Federal Government, if unionists did not work the Dutch ships. This threat, said Mr Roach, was a bargaining weapon "in an endeavour to force us into supporting the Dutch against the Indonesians" and it carried "the obvious Evatt touch".[8]

Commissioner Morrison indicated that the anti-boycott propaganda campaign had considerable public support. He said:

> The continued hold-up of these Dutch ships in Australia has been a subject of criticism from time to time of the Commonwealth Government. Therein lies the concern of the Government that everything possible which may be achieved to show how unwarranted is such criticism should be done without delay . . .
>
> It may be said that the intervention of the Waterside Workers' Federation into the affairs of the Dutch and Indonesians is unwarranted, but this is not the first time that body has concerned itself with placing a ban on something which seems to them to be all wrong.
>
> I say nothing on that score. But I would point out with all the emphasis of which I am capable that while the ban on the Dutch ships is on Australia is likely to suffer in her trade relations.[9]

Commissioner Morrison spoke with the voice of Dr Evatt rather than the voice of Mr Chifley. He placed the most liberal interpretations on his role as "independent arbitrator". He came forward as a lobbyist for the Australian agricultural implements industry which had already contacted Indonesians awaiting repatriation.[10] Stressing the aid that could be given in modernising the agriculture of Indonesia with Australian-

192

made implements, he said, "The East wants agricultural implements which is a big industry in Australia . . . We cannot afford to lose that trade".[11]

They were not ploughshares that the Dutch ships' holds carried. The Dutch had hardly ever bought a spade or hoe in Australia.

The Commissioner warned that continued boycott would be "in direct defiance of the law of the Commonwealth". He called four compulsory conferences in this period to force if he could the servicing of Dutch ships: instead, the corvettes sold to the Dutch and needing repairs came under bans in the shipyards, and the *Tasman*, alleged to have violated hospital ship conditions, joined the Black Armada.

Unionists Tried to Police Dutch Voyages

One of the most controversial proposals put forward by Communist union officials was that they should have the right to sail on Dutch ships to Java to police the distribution of their cargoes. Communist union leaders at the ACTU-sponsored conference of 29 January-1 February indicated that they were prepared to load a trial shipment of foodstuffs and non-military goods provided a representative of the trade union movement accompanied the Dutch ship to Java. There the Australian trade union observer would check that relief cargo was distributed to those in need, without discrimination, and not used for military purposes.

The ACTU-sponsored unions' conference appointed a sub-committee to investigate the problems of loading, manning and policing a trial vessel, comprising officials of the Waterside Workers' Federation, Seamen's Union and Federated Ironworkers' Association (all then communist-led). The sub-committee recommended that the trial ship should be the *Van Outhoorn*, held in Brisbane for over four months, that *Van Outhoorn* should be manned by her original Indonesian crew if possible; if not, the offer of striking Indian seamen ashore to supply a crew should be accepted.

The communist union officials on the sub-committee were anything but deferential: they proposed that the trade union observer sailing in *Van Outhoorn* as supervisor of Dutch conduct should "be given the right of entry to Java by Lord

Mountbatten and that a representative of the Indonesians be permitted to meet the Australian observer".[11] The 29 January-1 February conference was adamant that *Van Outhoorn* would sail only if an observer acceptable to the sub-committee from the three unions was appointed by the Commonwealth Government to sail in the trial ship and if a definite guarantee was given by the Dutch "that the *Van Outhoorn* returns to Australia with the crew on which she sails from this country".[12] This latter was felt necessary as a safeguard against arrest of the crew at Batavia.

Mr Monk had a theory that the Communist Party wanted an observer from its own ranks so that he could bring back first-hand information about conditions in Indonesia. So did Dr Evatt. Dr Evatt told waterfront unions that he would not agree to Mr Roach from the WWF accompanying a trial Dutch vessel "to ensure that neither the vessel nor its cargo were used against the Indonesians".[13] The unions concerned claimed they would accept Mr J.V. Barry, King's Counsel and later a Victorian Supreme Court Judge, or Mr J.F. Chapple, Federal Secretary of the Australian Railways Union and a Labor Party supporter. Not surprisingly, the Netherlands Minister in Australia, Baron Van Aerssen, declared on 14 February that the proposal to place an Australian trade union observer on a Dutch ship was "scandalous and insulting".

A tense conference of unions involved, reconvened by the ACTU, assembled in Sydney Trades Hall on 27 February. ACTU President Clarey moved for the lifting of the boycott on Dutch ships. The main boycotting unions sponsored an amendment to Mr Clarey's motion, demanding the most specific guarantees that the food and medical supplies sent by Dutch ships released from boycott would be distributed "without regard to nationality or political persuasion, with first priority to women and children". The Australian Government, the amendment proposed, should instruct the General Officer Commanding in Java along these lines "to ensure the carrying out of conditions agreed to without interference by the Dutch". Under these safeguards the union boycotters were prepared to release a trial ship "conditionally upon a representative of the trade union movement being permitted to proceed to Java to act as an observer". The loading of further

Dutch ships would remain in abeyance "until the report is received from the trade union observer".[14]

This amendment was carried on a delegate vote by 13 to 2 — a setback to the ACTU leaders. But they made some progress early in March when the NSW Trades and Labor Council, largest component of the ACTU, voted by a narrow majority of 11 in a total of 137 to accept the ACTU leaders' recommendation that the ban be lifted on assurances given by the Dutch.

Mr J.J. Graves, Member of the NSW Legislative Council, who had enjoyed some notoriety as a member of the "Inner Group" operating under the direction of former NSW Premier J.T. Lang (controversial depression-time Premier, 1930-32) in Sydney Trades Hall politics, was proposed as observer in Java. Mr Roach said that Mr Graves "would no doubt fit admirably into the plans of the Dutch" and that "the report of a person like Graves could be written before he left Australia".[15]

"More Chicanery . . ."

On 12 March Mr Monk fired a heavier broadside against the boycotting unions. The *Sydney Morning Herald*[16] gave Mr Monk 27 inches of column space for an attack on the boycotters, mostly directed at the Waterside Workers' Federation. Mr Monk said that there had been "more chicanery in this dispute" than he had experienced in any other. The *Sydney Morning Herald* published a cartoon, depicting a waterside worker, labelled "Communist agent", standing alongside a "mercy ship for Java" and saying to Messrs Clarey and Monk of the ACTU: "She don't go unless I go with her." The Leader of the Liberal Party Opposition in NSW Parliament, Mr Alexander Mair, a former Premier, called the boycott of the Dutch "Communist blackguardism".[17]

Mr Roach, in a statement of reply, fell back on the "trade union solidarity" defence. The Indonesian Seamen's Union, he said, had never declared the Dutch ships "white" and the decision to end the boycott was "tantamount to asking our members to 'scab' on the Indonesian Seamen's Union. No amount of collaboration on the part of Rightwingers in the ACTU will force members of our Federation to 'scab' on other workers".[18] But the ACTU was ready to get tough.

195

"ACTU May Expel Waterside Workers" said a Sydney *Sunday Telegraph*[19] headline. An anonymous ACTU spokesman was quoted in the article: "We realise that disaffiliation of the Waterside Workers' Federation may completely split the trade union movement." A NSW Labor Council leader was quoted: "Disaffiliation would cause the communist leaders of the Waterside Workers' Federation far more concern than would deregistration by the Commonwealth Arbitration Court".

The *Sydney Morning Herald* said:

> The Commonwealth Government cannot in decency delay any longer active intervention in the matter of the Dutch steamers lying idle in Sydney and Brisbane. The largely Communist blockade of these vessels has extended over more than six months. . . So far they have got away with it, but the time is over-ripe for real intervention by the Government, with the backing of the non-Communist trade unions.[20]

"Real intervention" was already on the agenda. On 16 March Mr Monk said the ACTU Emergency Committee had been called together "to consider the attitude adopted by several unions and a suggestion that might enable food to be sent to Java without the need of assistance from waterside workers in loading ships".[21]

For the Waterside Workers' Federation, Mr Roach replied angrily, accusing Mr Monk of having "suggested a method of breaking the wharfies' strike by either civilian scabbery or the use of armed forces".[22] On the same day that Mr Monk made this suggestion the Sydney morning press[23] reported that the Federal Government was considering a proposal that the Australian Navy should carry Dutch supplies to Indonesia. Mr Roach contended that plans to employ the Navy fitted in with Mr Monk's statement that the ACTU Emergency Committee was considering a suggestion that might enable food to be sent to Java "without the need of assistance from waterside workers loading the ships".[24]

Though under rising attack from within and without the trade union movement the boycott held. Mr Chifley was in no mood to attempt to reflesh the skeleton of the Dutch Empire at the price of internal disorder and the ACTU leaders could not make a wide enough breach in the trade union front to allow the Dutch ships outward passage.

A brighter panoplied presence, a more winsome voice were required. On 30 March 1946 the *Sydney Morning Herald* was confident that the Dutch ships "may sail soon as the result of the dramatic intervention by the Supreme Allied Commander in South-East Asia, Lord Louis Mountbatten, soon after he arrived yesterday". Mountbatten was to apply his uncommon talents before trade union officials at a conference on the boycott called in Sydney on his initiative.

22   Mountbatten Asked the Communists

Lord Louis Mountbatten arrived in Canberra from Singapore on 24 March 1946 in a four-engined York transport aircraft of South-East Asia Command. With him were Lady Mountbatten and his chief aide, Rear-Admiral C. Douglas-Pennant. In the previous week Mountbatten had talked at Singapore with Pandit Nehru, who in 1947 would accept the Mountbatten award dividing the Indian sub-continent into self-governing India and Pakistan. Nehru no doubt made known his views on Dutch as well as British colonialism. Mountbatten and his wife were guests at Government House, Canberra, of the Duke and Duchess of Gloucester. It was not Mountbatten's first visit to Australia: he was aide to the Prince of Wales (later Edward VIII and Duke of Windsor) for his 1920 royal tour.

The Mountbatten mission was a reluctant tribute to the power of the boycotting unions. The Commonwealth Government and the ACTU had failed to release the Dutch ships from the unions' grip and so the SEAC Supremo flew down from South-East Asia to apply his considerable lobbying power. On 25 March Lord Mountbatten interviewed Prime Minister Chifley for two hours and gave a private speech to a Cabinet luncheon in his honour, mostly on problems of colonial revolution in South-East Asia. He was confident. In an interview with the *Sydney Morning Herald*[1] he forecast that the troubles in Indonesia might soon end. He said the British aim was to "find a formula which would satisfy both sides".

The SEAC Supreme Commander flew to Sydney on the morning of Friday 29 March. The Duke and Duchess of

Gloucester came to Sydney, too, so they could be hosts to Lord Louis and his wife at Admiralty House, Kirribilli. Lady Mountbatten was a leader of RAPWI (Release of Allied Prisoners of War and Internees) and her duties took her to Indonesia where there were Dutch, Australian, British and American prisoners to be freed and helped.

Lord Mountbatten was polished, disarming in a courtesy without condescension when he came at 3 pm on 29 March to a conference in the Sydney General Post Office Building, Martin Place, between Pitt and George Streets, to ask Australian trade union leaders to lift the ban on Dutch ships. The conference room was the suite of the Minister for Shipping, Senator Ashley. Lord Louis arrived in a limousine — an open one for the convenience of the viewing public who cheered this descendant of the morganatic Battenburg branch of the House of Hesse-Cassel, adorned with the gold braid of an Admiral of the Fleet and six rows of ribbons.

Plain Louis Mountbatten

In the conference room Lord Louis was welcomed by representatives of the Commonwealth Government, Australian Council of Trade Unions and NSW Trades and Labor Council. As the communist Federal Secretary of the Seamen's Union of Australia, Mr E.V. Elliott, walked in, Lord Louis strolled over, stretched out his hand and said: "Good afternoon, Elliott, I'm glad you were able to come."[2] To the communist Assistant General Secretary of the Waterside Workers' Federation he addressed himself as plain Louis Mountbatten.[3]

Both Mr Elliott and Mr Roach got the impression that Mountbatten, in pressing for the lifting of the trade union boycott on Dutch ships, directed his appeals and arguments to them in the main. They represented the key maritime unions and called the boycott tune despite the efforts of the ACTU and NSW Labor Council leaders. Mountbatten would have been briefed, perhaps by Mr Chifley himself, on who held the levers of power on the Australian waterfronts.

From the conference room Lord Louis was able to look out the window at his wife being besieged by office girls as she arrived for a ceremony in Martin Place. He was also able to quote his wife's views on Indonesia, formed during her RAPWI

199

tasks. His wife had told him, the SEAC Supreme Commander related to the assembled Commonwealth Government and trade union representatives, that she had concluded from her observations during RAPWI work that the Indonesian Republic represented "a genuine independence movement, widely supported".[4]

Some of the Mountbatten conference in Sydney was steno-grammed and the Commonwealth later supplied a precis of discussions — "Notes of Conference . . ." — to the Waterside Workers' Federation. Present at this conference in the Sydney GPO Building on the afternoon of 29 March 1946 were:

> Lord Louis Mountbatten, Supreme Allied Commander South-East Asia.
>
> Rear-Admiral C. Douglas-Pennant, Mountbatten's chief aide.
>
> Senator W.P. Ashley, Minister for Supply and Shipping in the Federal Labor Government.
>
> Mr G.T. (later Sir Giles) Chippindall, Secretary of the Department of Supply and Shipping.
>
> Mr Raymond A. Hetherington, Commonwealth Director of Shipping.
>
> Mr Albert E. Monk, Secretary, Australian Council of Trade Unions.
>
> Mr R.A. King, Vice-President, ACTU; Secretary, NSW Trades and Labor Council and Member of NSW Legis-lative Council.
>
> Mr Frank Kelly, Interstate Executive Member, ACTU; Assistant Secretary, NSW Trades and Labor Council, and MLC.
>
> Mr E.V. Elliott, Federal Secretary, Seamen's Union of Australia.
>
> Mr E.C. Roach, Assistant General Secretary, Waterside Workers' Federation of Australia.

The Aide Exceeded His Brief

Seven Dutch merchant ships were held under boycott in Aus-tralia at this stage. Though the boycott tally had been reduced to seven, each of these seven ships seemed to Mountbatten more important than a battalion of troops or a park of artillery because of the acute postwar shortage of tonnage. Of the seven ships three were in Sydney — *Stagen*, *Van Swoll* and *Merak* — and three were in the Brisbane River — *Bontekoe*, *Van Outhoorn* and *Both*.[5] The release of seven merchant ships would have created a better atmosphere for despatch from Australia of even more essential craft. There were hundreds of Dutch power and dumb barges and landing craft needed in shallow Indonesian waters and estuaries and large numbers of oil-carrying vessels, plus the military trucks, jeeps and arms and munitions which the Dutch could not move from Australia unless the black bans were lifted.

Mountbatten let his aide, Rear-Admiral Douglas-Pennant, open the conference and put the Anglo-Dutch case for ending the boycott. In the notes or precis of minutes[6] supplied to the Waterside Workers' Federation after the conference the remarks of the Rear-Admiral rather than those of Mountbatten were reported. Mountbatten was much more frank.

Rear-Admiral Douglas-Pennant, in putting his Supreme Commander's views as he saw them, placed the hold-up of Dutch ships in Australian ports first among the "three things holding us up" in operations designed to establish British control and then hand over to the Dutch. These Dutch ships under boycott were, he told the conference, "urgently re-required in the Netherlands East Indies to relieve British ships which are at present working there". Among the tasks in which these British ships assisted was "generally helping to maintain law and order". To bring relief in the shipping shortage, Rear-Admiral Douglas-Pennant said, "We want those British ships back at Singapore in our shipping pool".[7]

Mountbatten affirmed that the Dutch ships were needed to replace British ships which could then be diverted to meet British requirements. Messrs Roach and Elliott knew that the Dutch ships which had already escaped from the Australian trade union blockade were being used to carry Dutch troops and arms from Singapore. Mr Roach asked the first question:

Was it a fact that Lord Louis Mountbatten required the Dutch ships held by boycott in Australia as war transport ships for the Dutch forces?

"Frankly, yes," replied Mountbatten. He said British ships

occupied in the shuttle service from Asian ports to Indonesia were wanted elsewhere.[8]

Rear-Admiral Douglas-Pennant obviously went beyond his brief from Mountbatten in his report to the conference, for his thesis sometimes contradicted Mountbatten's expressed views. The aide claimed that while Indonesians were in general a perfectly law-abiding community the main problem was the "fascist-trained and fascist-minded youths . . . who have determined to make trouble". He submitted that "the only trouble is in Java, which is the centre of this movement". There was "very limited trouble in Sumatra" and "virtually none" in other areas. This was at variance with facts, as Australians in Borneo, the Celebes and Moluccas knew.

Rear-Admiral Douglas-Pennant's explanation of the British armed attack on the Indonesian Republic was unoriginal, but as good as any yet devised for denial of self-determination. He said:

> We have been criticised for fighting them. The only reason why we had to fight them is because they have got in our way when we were trying to carry out the tasks laid down for us by the Combined Chiefs-of-Staff.[9]

The Indonesians were still in the way. The job of pushing aside the vexedly increased numbers who bestrode the path was beyond the British Empire's capacities. The aide said:

> The time has come when we have got to withdraw British and Indian troops. We can't go on policing the world forever. So we have started to introduce Dutch troops.

He was not flattering to Dutch warriors for whom the British furnished a precarious shield against the Republic. The reason the British had not introduced the Dutch earlier was "because the Dutch troops themselves are untrained and are quite definitely unreliable".[10] The Rear-Admiral did not add that Indian troops were even less reliable: a storm had broken in India against their deployment in this war. British troops were clashing with the Dutch in Batavia and elsewhere.

Rear-Admiral Douglas-Pennant also rated the Australian trade union leaders as naive when he protested to them:

> Let me say that we have never attempted to take sides in

the Netherlands East Indies. Our sole object in being there was to get control of the Japanese and get out our prisoners and in the course of doing that we bumped up on a number of occasions against the Indonesian forces...

As both Mountbatten and his aide knew, the British Government had given pledges for military and material aid to restore Dutch rule. The Rear-Admiral went on:

> We have done virtually nothing without consulting the Indonesians first, and I think I am right in saying that we have never done anything to embarrass the Indonesian Cabinet who represent the majority of Indonesians except those extremists who are not under the control of Dr Sjahrir or anybody else.[11]

Mountbatten had come to Australia "for the specific purpose of getting the black ban on Dutch ships lifted".[12] His demeanour indicated that he did not want his chances spoiled by his aide's reflections on the political sagacity of Australian trade union leaders. According to Mr Roach, he brushed aside Rear-Admiral Douglas-Pennant's interpretations of the Indonesian situation as rather too threadbare for that audience to wear.[13] Nor would he go along with his aide's grumbling alibi about total lack of Intelligence. The Rear-Admiral had told the conference:

> As you know we immediately came up against this Indonesian independence movement. We did not know anything about it before for the simple reason that Java and the outer Netherlands East Indies nearest Australia were in General MacArthur's theatre of war. They were only turned over to us the day the war ended. He gave us no Intelligence – no information.
> We walked into Sumatra and Java with small forces, hoping to round up the Japanese, get out our prisoners-of-war quickly – and we found this strong independence movement.[14]

The British Intelligence record had no such blank page. True, the retreating Dutch left no Intelligence services behind them and Muslim priests sent from Egypt by the British to report were soon in Kempei-tai hands. But, even if General

MacArthur had held the cards close to his chest, the Australian armed forces Intelligence had information about Indonesian attitudes, freely available to the British. The landings at Morotai in the Halmaheras (Moluccas archipelago) began on 15 September 1944. The Australian Ninth Division began Borneo penetrations at Tarakan on 1 May 1945. When the war ended Australian Intelligence had been operating some time in East Indonesia. NICA men were there, too. While Republican activity in East Indonesia was neither as widespread or as well organised as in Java, it was clearly a force to be reckoned with. The Australian Army expected to be out of East Indonesia by early November but the task of handing over to the Dutch in face of opposition kept them there till March 1946. Before the British landed in Java to begin reinstalling the Dutch, RAPWI representatives − including Lady Mountbatten − had been to Japanese prison camps, British agents had reported the independence movement to Mountbatten by 18 August, the first British paratroops after their Batavia landing of 8 September.

Mountbatten Was More Liberal

At the Sydney conference it was obvious, in Mr Elliott's view,[15] that Mountbatten was not specially concerned with the contents of the Dutch ships' holds; they could sail away empty as far as he was concerned. He badly needed the ships for his SEAC operations. Mr Roach asked Mountbatten the reasons for the refusal to allow a trade union observer to accompany a trial shipment of relief food, clothing and medical supplies to Java to ensure distribution without favour. Mountbatten replied: "You can send a whole shipload of observers if you wish."[16]

"We told Mountbatten," said Mr Elliott,[17] "that we wouldn't release the ships unless Premier Sjahrir approved. When he wanted to know how this could be done, he was told it was simple: Fly one of us to Indonesia to have discussions with Republican leaders and, if they approved, the ships would be released.

"Mountbatten assured us that he would have no hesitation in putting this up to the appropriate authorities. But if there were difficulties in the way, we should tell him just what information we wanted from the Republican leaders."

Mountbatten said that he would get in touch with Lieutenant-General Sir Philip Christison, his field commander in Java, who would put the Australian trade union inquiries to Premier Sjahrir in Java. This was service and international recognition seldom accorded Australian communist union officials. Ironically, Lord Louis Mountbatten, a relative and confidant of kings, now commanding formidable imperial forces, was prepared to go further in conciliation of Leftwing law-breaking unions than were the Chifley-Evatt Labor Government or leaders of the ACTU.

Mountbatten directed more of his remarks at the Sydney conference to Messrs Elliott and Roach than was pleasing to Messrs Monk, King and Kelly of the ACTU. In fact, when Mountbatten agreed to the Leftwingers' proposal for observers, Mr Frank Kelly turned to them and said: "We'll fix that in another place." Mr Kelly meant that the moderate leaders would decide the future course of action once Mountbatten was out of the way.

Mountbatten went all the distance in meeting Leftwing trade union conditions for observers to check on distribution of cargoes in Java. Perhaps it was rather strong meat for the Dutch Empire to swallow — that foreign trade union officials, maybe communists, dedicated to sabotage of Dutch colonial rule, should travel on Dutch ships with overriding supervisory powers to ensure that Dutch captains and government officials did not dishonour their word.

Baron Van Aerssen, the Dutch Minister in Australia, suffered an ailment common to those of the fading *ancien régime*, pretending to power that existed only in a dream. Mountbatten was related to fallen emperors: he had a keener eye for the quicksands of imperial history. The time had come to compromise with the Republic, to limit its influence if that were within British capacity. But the Netherlands Ministers continued along the way they seemed to feel that providence had dictated, and with the faint echo of Cornelius Van Houtman's opening cannonades in the Indies Spiceries three hundred and fifty years before, Baron Van Aerssen shot down Mountbatten's *ballon d'essai*. Baron Van Aerssen had previously denounced the proposal to send trade union observers "as they mean a control on actions" of the Netherlands Government and South-East Asia Command.[18] He now scorned the Mountbatten intervention, firmly declaring that the Royal Netherlands Government which he represented had laid down "the only basis upon which negotiations for the lifting of the ban could be held". Mr Roach's retort had a certain inevitability: "I would remind the Netherlands Minister that he does not happen to be in a position to issue any ultimatums as the basis of settlement . . ."[19]

Dr Sjahrir Remained Suspicious

Lord Mountbatten's next move was to cable a request to Sir Archibald Clark-Kerr, British Government Commissioner in Java, "to make every effort to get Sjahrir to send a message through this office* to the Prime Minister and the unions". The message from Sjahrir was "to state, firstly, that he had no objection to the use of ships in question in Netherlands East Indies waters; secondly, and not necessarily linked with the first point, to get Sjahrir to agree that the ships should bring stores".[20] This latter was in line with Mountbatten's proposition to the trade unions in Sydney: his main interest was in ships, not cargoes.

The Australian Representative[21] accompanied Sir Archibald Clark-Kerr when he called on Sjahrir, and he reported to Canberra that when asked for a message to Australian unions indicating that he supported the lifting of the boycott on Dutch ships, Sjahrir raised the following points:

(1) He felt that, as the goods were not his, the matter was no business of his.

(2) He felt that any overture on his part at the present delicate state of negotiations with the Dutch was unwise.

(3) He wished to know precise details of the goods and their manner of distribution. He was not satisfied

---

*Office of the Australian Government Representative, Batavia.

that this should be handled by Stopford* without knowing what were the proposed points of distribution. He was suspicious that, as the Dutch had bought the stores, they would ultimately claim the right to dispose of them as they thought fit.

(4) If the goods were to be sold, he felt that this would bolster up the Dutch currency, which in fact it would.[22]

Further information, as required by Premier Sjahrir, was obtained from the Dutch, "but in the meantime," reported the Australian Representative in Batavia, "Sjahrir decided that he was not prepared to send a personal message for reasons (1), (2) and (4) given above. Despite considerable pressure brought to bear by British contacts Sjahrir has remained adamant." And the Dutch, while supplying details, had "completely washed their hands of the matter".

Dr Sjahrir obviously did not want to break the Australian boycott. "Sjahrir," added the Australian Representative's cable, "is not prepared to move in the matter until the major question of Dutch and Indonesian relations is settled."[23] Mountbatten, for all his charisma and diplomatic tonnage, failed to break the boycott in Sydney and his Batavia envoys failed to win over Indonesian Premier Sjahrir.

The Australian trade unions' boycott was now more than six months old and Dutch ships lay semi-derelict in Sydney and Brisbane ports. Barges, landing and oil-carrying craft, vehicles, munitions and stores owned by the Dutch in Australia were still denied to the war effort against the Indonesian Republic. The boycott had withstood the attacks in Federal and State Parliaments and the press, the manoeuvres of the Dutch emigre regime and Hague diplomats in Australia, the weighty and well-directed pressures of British diplomacy and the official leadership of the Australian Council of Trade Unions.

But there were last reserves to call to action, an Achilles

---

*British military commander at Batavia, Lieutenant General Sir Montague Stopford.

heel of the boycott movement that could be pierced. Both Mountbatten and the communist representatives of maritime unions that had converted the Dutch war-supply ships to the Black Armada under-estimated Mr Albert Monk and Mr Frank Kelly.

23 Forgotten Union Broke the Boycott

It was like the mouse gnawing the thongs to free the lion . . .
The smallest union on Sydney waterfront, not listed in the
telephone directory or having paid officials, was able to get
the boycott-bound ships away, under semi-secret urgings from
NSW Trades and Labor Council and ACTU leaders. It was a
union that covered those remaining in a fast-dying occupation,
coal-lumping to bunker ships.

Up to this time the barriers to Dutch ship sailings had been
whittled down by stratagems of various kinds, but seven
valuable Dutch coal-burners remained in thrall. The best laid
plans of three governments — Australian, Netherlands, British
— had been of no avail. Lord Louis Mountbatten, the ACTU
Executive and the Arbitration Court failed to get the ban
lifted, as did the cumulative pressures of parliament, press,
the shipowners and associated employers. Flight after flight
of Indian seamen had come to Australian airports to replace
Indonesian mutineers, but most had declined service with the
Dutch. Chinese were cajoled in vain.

The Dutch could not be blamed for thinking that Australians had little sense of humour. In April 1946, after the
Mountbatten mission's failure, the Dutch offered the ships
under boycott as "bride ships", to transport to Australia girls
of other nations who had become wartime brides of Australian
soldiers serving abroad. If only the unions would lift the boycott, the Dutch would forget emergencies in South-East Asia
and speed the foreign brides to the arms of their waiting
Australian husbands. The brides could have been certain of a

rough trip. The remaining seven ships were coal-burning freighters. The Waterside Workers' Federation official organ[1] referred to "the stupidity of using tramp steamers for such a purpose".

By mid-1946 the Dutch had freed the greater number of their ships from stormy Australian waters, using their army and navy men and ex-internees flown in from Japanese camps as stevedores and skeleton crews, under-manning them in contravention of navigation laws, and finding their way into the blue water without tugs and occasionally with firewood stoking boilers for far enough to reach waiting colliers.

The late Benito Mussolini's troops, captured by Australians in North Africa and wearing POW patches, involuntarily contributed to the Netherlands armed forces' offensive against the Indonesian Republic. A lone protest against employment of Italian prisoners-of-war to break a strike of Australian trade unionists is contained in the message[2] from the Fremantle WWF Branch Secretary, Mr N. McKenzie. In parliament the Labor Government was never asked how the Australian command to captive Fascist troops to act as strike-breakers squared with Labor policy, or whether the Geneva Convention permitted governments in a state of war with Italy since 1940 to compel Italian prisoners-of-war to lift munitions from Fremantle wharves to be fired by one of those governments in a colonial war.

Australians were not unanimously reluctant to face the hazards of strike-breaking in the maritime industry. In Brisbane the Returned Servicemen's League sent volunteers to the wharves to load Dutch war cargoes and some non-union seamen sailed Dutch ships out of Australian ports. The *Maritime Worker* made reference to the modesty of these boycott-breaking Australians:

> Twenty-eight Australian seamen, who helped to beat the waterfront blockade by getting Dutch ships away nearly three months ago, on their return to this country the other day asked the press to give them no publicity so that they could slip into their former jobs without arousing the suspicions of their fellow workers.[3]

Some Australian soldiers, before their discharge from the

army, helped to stevedore Dutch ships. Brisbane WWF Branch Assistant Secretary Albert Graham reported that, with Trades and Labor Council officers, he went to Pinkenbah wharves where soldiers were working the *Tasman*, which by now had been listed as a munitions ship rather than a hospital ship.

"These soldiers said they had been sent to the job by the RSSAILA*," Mr Graham said.[4] A Brisbane watersiders' general meeting recommended to the WWF Federal Office in Sydney that there be a 24-hour protest stoppage on the waterfront unless soldiers were withdrawn from the stevedoring of Dutch ships. Later, on 7 September 1947, the Waterside Workers' Federal Executive was criticising the Chifley Government for allowing Australian soldiers to join Dutch Army men in loading two Dutch ships.

Instructions to the "Coalies"

A man who died at Hobart in 1969 was the last Australian survivor of that band of grimy toilers to bunker steamers by baskets of coal carried up a gangplank. Coal-lumping was steadily mechanised from early in the twentieth century, but enough trimming and other manual work remained to maintain in the postwar years a dwindling force of "coalies". In most ports the "coalies" were in the Waterside Workers' Federation. In Sydney the coal-lumpers were in a separate organisation, not affiliated with the Trades and Labor Council and attracting little attention because of its small membership. The maritime unions had temporarily forgotten this strategic group.

The Dutch ships held by boycott in Sydney and Brisbane had used what little coal they could get for heating and cooking. Their bunkers were empty. Coal was hard to buy, even on the black market. Power-houses were experiencing black-outs and there was a barrage of measured abuse of coal-miners who by occasional strikes kept reserves sparse.

Early in July 1946 the Sydney coal-lumpers, who had up

---

*Returned Sailors, Soldiers and Airmen's Imperial League of Australia, called Returned Servicemen's League (RSL) today.

till then carried out trade union boycott policy, received instructions from Mr Frank Kelly, New South Wales TLC Assistant Secretary and ACTU Interstate Executive member, to coal the black-banned Dutch ship *Stagen*. The coal-lumpers were under no obligation to obey, but they bunkered the *Stagen* with a thousand tons of coal. Their excuse, given to protesting waterside workers, was: ACTU and Labor Council policy. The reason was plausible. New South Wales TLC not long before had voted by a narrow majority to lift the boycott of Java-bound ships on the strength of Dutch assurances of equitable distribution of relief to Indies war victims. The ACTU Executive strenuously demanded that the maritime unions adopt the same stance.

The maritime unionists, now going it alone, along with several shipyard unions, were dismayed to see *Stagen*, billowing black smoke, churn her way into the stream without tugs and disappear toward the harbour heads. *Van Swoll* and *Merak* followed: they also got coal from the lumpers. The three ships sailed with scratch crews of Dutchmen and non-union Australians, most of them of little or no training in seamanship, but the officers were competent navigators.

Bontekoe, Both and *Van Outhoorn*, held in the Brisbane River since September 1945, had no coal to maintain power or cooking facilities aboard, so the unions turned a blind eye when the Dutch brought wood to the wharves for the ships' galleys. The unions failed to note, early in July, the insatiable appetite of Dutch stoves for wood. The smell of burning eucalyptus wood wafted to the Brisbane River's banks as *Bontekoe*, *Both* and *Van Outhoorn* weighed anchor and lumbered along the current toward Moreton Bay. The firewood served to fuel the boilers for the short run down the river. In Moreton Bay the three Dutch ships stopped spouting white smoke as they rendezvoused with *Stagen* and took some of her coal. The Dutch ships now had enough fuel to sail on to another coaling rendezvous and then Java.

The *Tribune*'s anger could do nothing to halt the Dutch ships, disenthralled from boycott after nine months. The *Tribune* asked for official explanations that were not given:

.

How did the Dutch ship *Stagen* get excessive quantities

of coal, some of it to be loaded on other Dutch ships at sea, when Australian transport, factories and other services are desperately short? . . . .

Officialdom cries out that there is not enough coal for Bunnerong power-house, not enough for our railways, trams and factories.

Yet Dutch ships, under an Australian labor movement black ban, can get surplus coal to fuel other ships at sea!

The great Dutch coal mystery certainly calls for an official inquiry.[5]

The ships were not "under an Australian labor movement black ban" and the *Maritime Worker* overreached in calling the coaling of the *Stagen* "a piece of working-class treachery". The boycott no longer had official ACTU and NSW TLC endorsement.

The *Maritime Worker* claimed that members of the Waterside Workers' Federation "were responsible for initiating the ban" and that this ban on Dutch ships "has been responsible for rallying world-wide moral and practical assistance to the Indonesian cause".[6]

Last of the NEI Navy

Seven Royal Netherlands Indies Navy submarine-chasers were under trade union black ban at a temporary British naval base established before the Pacific War ended on the south side of Sydney Harbour, at Beach Road, Rushcutters' Bay. Three of them, loaded with arms by British naval ratings, left for Java on the nights of 4 and 5 July, 1946.

On 11 July the President of the Indonesian Seamen's Union in Australia, Mr H. Mailangkay — one of the few Indonesian leaders remaining unrepatriated — warned that four more Dutch submarine-chasers — RP-105, RP-106, RP-107 and one not identified — were being loaded at night with arms for the Dutch troops in Indonesia. Mr Mailangkay said that arms for the Dutch were being smuggled through certain points on the Sydney waterfront. "The Maritime Services Board, Water Police and Customs should be made aware that these dangerous activities are being carried out . . ." He also claimed that

"Dutch evacuees from Japanese camps" had loaded arms in No.4 hold of the *Van Swoll*.

The seven submarine-chasers sailed for Java in July, loaded, according to Mr Mailangkay, with Oerlikon machine-guns and other arms.[7] The last of the NEI Navy was gone, 11 months after the war ended, except for a submarine at Fremantle.

As for the boycott of Dutch merchant ships, the Brisbane WWF Branch Secretary, Mr Englart, read into coaling from *Stagen* in Moreton Bay of *Bontekoe*, *Both* and *Van Outhoorn* clear evidence that "the ban is still effective as far as the Australian maritime workers are concerned". These three ships had to make their way into Moreton Bay "under their own steam and fuelled with firewood, because the workers would handle neither the tugs to tow them nor the coal for the boilers".[8]

The maritime unions, though still in fighting mood, could now only apply token boycott to Dutch ships far beyond their reach. A few Dutch ships made return journeys from Java to Australian ports and were loaded by Dutch soldiers and ex-internees. Oil vessels and barges remained without labor.

A year after the Dutch ships escaped from Sydney and Brisbane, the Netherlands Army's attempt to smash the Indonesian Republic by armed force caused a dramatic escalation of Australian boycott movements against the Dutch.

24 Police Actions Revive Australia's Blockade

The escape to open sea of the last Dutch merchantman in July 1946 and general confusion in Java caused some sag of trade union interest in the boycott of Dutch instrumentalities and services. While Indonesia-bound ships remained under black ban if they sought to transport materials useful for war, Mr Chifley succeeded in his steady pressures to induce the maritime unions to handle foodstuffs, clothing, medicines and other non-military goods for Java. In the first half of 1947 waterside workers were, by agreement between their union and the Prime Minister, loading non-military cargoes for the Indies.

The Dutch, however, did not abandon attempts to rescue military supplies from continuing boycott. On 3 July 1947 WWF General Secretary Healy warned that the loading by Dutch soldiers of army trucks painted jungle-green into the *Tjibesar* at Williamstown, Melbourne, might interfere with the loading of 40,000 tons of non-military goods held since September 1945 and now released from black bans. The Dutch not only made up Mr Healy's mind for him: their dramatic escalation of war in Java pushed the Australian Government into active participation in a boycott revival.

On 20-21 July 1947 the Dutch Army Commander, General Simon H. Spoor, and Admiral Helfrich, commanding ex-Australian corvettes, ex-British and ex-American and some Dutch warships, ordered bombardments, amphibious landings and assaults meant to compress the Indonesian Republic and deprive it of vital Java rice and Sumatran oil areas.

215

This First Police Action, as it was called, was launched from British-won bases in Java and Sumatra. While food lands and trade centres were wrenched from the Republic, the First Police Action was staged before a world knowing a new sensitivity to colonialism. Pandit Nehru could now speak with an independent voice: he told the Dutch that their attack was "an astounding thing that the new spirit of Asia will not tolerate. Foreign armies on Asian soil are an outrage to Asian sentiment."[1]

An RAAF officer in Brisbane said after the First Police Action that the Air Force had been instructed not to supply petrol to Dutch planes. The officer added that this instruction came from RAAF Headquarters in Melbourne and applied "for the moment".[2] The ban grounded three Dutch planes at Archerfield aerodrome, Brisbane.

The Federal Parliamentary Leader of the Country Party and former Prime Minister, Mr Arthur Fadden, said:

> If this ban has not the approval of the Chifley Government, it seems as though the Royal Australian Air Force is receiving its instructions from the ACTU, and is obeying the dictates of a body which is completely unofficial.[3]

Mr Fadden at this stage remained confident that the Dutch would win. He warned that the Dutch could ban Australian planes in the Netherlands East Indies in retaliation for the boycott of Dutch planes at the RAAF Archerfield station.

The Labor Government's Minister for Air, Mr Arthur Drakeford, made the rather puzzling statement to Parliament that "there appears to be no reason why the Dutch authorities should not refuel their own aircraft".[4]

If the Royal Australian Air Force was boycotting the Dutch by cutting off their aviation fuel, the atmosphere in Australia following the First Police Action was obviously so anti-Dutch that the moderate ACTU leaders could no longer stand aside.

"Plain Intervention . . ."

The unions did not have so many Dutch ships or Dutchmen available, but, with resurrected ACTU endorsement, they set out to make up for the lack of boycott targets in intensity

216

Anti-colonial Netherlander Jack Zwolsman, with microphone, urging Dutch troops aboard the *Stirling Castle* to refuse to sail for Indonesia. He, the Australian soldiers on board, and the union official received missiles and abuse for their troubles. (*Indonesia Calling*)

BRIEFING

Lusby. *Courier-Mail*. 28 August 1947

Demonstrators against Dutch troops on the *Stirling Castle* were drenched by fire hoses and had rubbish thrown at them

and extension of anti-Dutch activity. The Building Workers' Industrial Union, covering carpenters, bricklayers and various other construction tradesmen, instructed members not only to refuse any repair work on Dutch ships, but to refuse building jobs ashore for the Dutch armed forces and Dutch companies like the KPM. The Amalgamated Engineering Union threatened to make all ship repair work in Melbourne black if the *Tjibesar* continued loading military supplies at Williamstown docks. The Victorian Secretary of the Seamen's Union, Mr William Bird, gave notice that any pilot taking *Tjibesar* to sea would be declared black by all Seamen's Union members. This meant that offending pilots would be denied pilot-boat crews.

Tjibesar was something of a nuisance to authorities interested in keeping shipping free of unions bans. Someone may have told *Tjibesar*'s captain to depart the port. *Tjibesar*, partly loaded, slipped her cables and sailed through the risky rip of Port Phillip Heads without a pilot, and found her way some days later, without tugs, to a berth in the Brisbane River. *Tjikkampek* was already there; she had been partly loaded by watersiders with food and other non-military goods for Java under the agreement with the Government and came under ban immediately after the First Police Action.

When the Dutch ships were originally boycotted at Brisbane, the Stevedoring Industry Commission, controlling waterfront employment, had placed the banned ships first for labor pick-up. The refusal to man the Dutch ships had led to temporary lock-out of the whole port. In July 1947 the Commonwealth Government's Stevedoring Industry Commission instructed its Brisbane Ports Committee Chairman, Mr N. Boyd, not to receive orders for labor from stevedoring employers wishing to work the two Dutch ships in dispute. This official refusal to call labor for the *Tjibesar* and *Tjikkampek* was positive evidence of Chifley Government aid and comfort to those sponsoring punitive action in Australia against authors of the First Police Action. Mr Menzies complained that the Stevedoring Industry Commission's refusal to call labor for the Dutch ships at Brisbane was "plain intervention in favour of the anti-Dutch section of Indonesians".[5]

Tjikkampek and *Tjibesar* were stevedored by Dutch soldiers transported from Wacol. The fact that Dutch soldiers remained at Wacol in July 1947, instead of being engaged in the Java war, was a symptom of the strains which Indonesian mutinies and Australian boycotts had imposed on resources. In Fremantle, members of the Docks Union refused orders to the Dutch ship *Roepat*. The *Roepat* automatically came under the maritime unions' Police Action ban.

"Trading with the Enemy"

On 5 August 1947 the ACTU called a Conference of Federal Unions, chaired by the ACTU President, Mr P.J. Clarey. The 17 unions represented called on all Australian trade unionists "to refuse to assist in any way whatever the movement of any Dutch goods or the repair, refuelling and/or movement of any Dutch transport, vessel, vehicle or aircraft in or adjacent to the Commonwealth until the ACTU in consultation with the federal unions concerned again considers the question in the light of any decision of the United Nations and until some change of policy is desired by the Indonesian trade union movement".[6]

The ACTU was banning everything Dutch that moved and recognising the new Indonesian trade union movement. On 7 August, though *Ceronia* was only to unload oil and return to Borneo with empty tanks, Amalgamated Engineering Union members and Federated Ironworkers' Association members refused orders to work on the tanker. The Prime Minister intervened. *Ceronia* was freed of the impetuous black ban.

Metal trades and maritime unions also over-reached in banning Holland-Australia Line ships trading between Europe, the Middle East, India and Australia. Though few Dutch ships braved the trade union blockade to pick up Indies-destined goods in Australia after the last seven of the Black Armada escaped in July 1946, the Holland-Australia Line (subsidiary of Vereenigde Nederlandsche Scheevaartmaatschappij NV of The Hague) maintained a busy Europe-Australia trade.

The boycott was extended to five Holland-Australia Line ships — *Grootekerk*, *Meliskerk*, *Gastekerk* and two others — much to the concern of Mr Chifley. He immediately sent a telegram[8] of protest and appeal — over 500 words — to the ACTU. These ships, the Prime Minister pointed out, carried

218

Australian mineral concentrates and millet seed for Antwerp, sheepskins for France, rolled oats for Allied soldiers in Europe, flour for Port Said, apples for Aden. They brought back to Australia glass, potash, olive oil, talc, jute and linseed from India, cheese-making machinery from Switzerland and so on. Mr Chifley warned that the union's ban on Holland-Australia Line ships would seriously jeopardise Australia's prospects of getting the necessary shipping tonnage for her trade.

Grootekerk was the only one of the five in port at the time of General Spoor's offensive. Under black ban, she slipped her cables at Sydney and sailed for Europe, leaving behind scheduled cargo at Port Kembla, Melbourne and Adelaide.

The Holland-Australia Line advertised[9] its apologies to Australian clients for its inability to handle their cargo. The General Manager of the Line, Mr J.M. Lamens, explained:

> For almost half a century the ships of this company have sailed freely in and out of Australian ports as trusted carriers between the old world and the new . . . Now certain Australian trade unions have placed a boycott on them and, if they enter Australian ports, they will be locked up there.

The *Sydney Morning Herald*, noting that in the "industrial warfare" against the Dutch in Australia the unions' ban had been extended and tightened, said:

> Now the boycott of all Dutch ships, not merely trading to the Netherlands East Indies, is to be enlarged to include a complete prohibition on the movement of Dutch goods in Australia.
>
> "Trading with the enemy" is barred, as in wartime, but not by Commonwealth enactment. That function has been usurped by the unions concerned . . .[10]

The ACTU Executive and unions concerned heeded Mr Chifley's appeal. Mr Chifley was able to tell Parliament that he had made "strong representations" and the ban was lifted.[11]

The WWF Assistant General Secretary, Mr Roach, wrote an intriguing letter[12] to the President of the Indonesian Trade Union Federation (SOBSI), Dr Setyadit:

You may have heard that we extended the ban to cover all Dutch ships and then reconsidered this decision and exempted those five ships for tactical reasons . . .

The "tactical reasons" interpreted by Mr Roach to the Indonesians were the necessity to consider the Prime Minister's views, thus avoiding any change in his attitude and keeping the trade union boycott movement strong. "Had we not done this," Mr Roach advised the Indonesian unions' leader, "he would have made a declaration that would have somewhat weakened our position."

Dutch Misreading of Madiun

In the year after the First Police Action it seemed to Australian trade unions that the Republic was making sufficient international headway and that Dr Van Mook was making sufficient compromises to allow easement of the anti-Dutch bans. Early in June 1948 the Commonwealth Government pledged to the unions that permits would not be issued to export war materials to Java and claimed that the Dutch blockade which had prevented normal trade by British and Australian vessels "was not now operating".[13] While this was an exaggeration, the unions accepted Government assurances and an ACTU-sponsored conference lifted the bans, except on weapons of war.

To the Australian Left forces that were then so influential in union policies, the Indonesian Left appeared ready to make spectacular political gains. They had visions of an Indonesian People's Republic emerging. In March 1948 an Indonesian People's Democratic Front was formed, including in its ranks leaders of Indonesian organisations that had recently operated in Australia. Dr Sjarifuddin led an important sector of the Socialist Party into alliance with the Communists and other Left groups. The advice Indonesian exiles had carried from the Australian Left — to support the Republic, to manoeuvre for advantages while the Dutch remained and then, after the final expulsion of the colonial regime, seize opportunities expected to arise for establishment of a People's Republic — was in discard. The Indonesian People's Democratic Front wanted an end to negotiations with the Dutch, military solutions and a harder line against the Republican Government of President Soekarno and Prime Minister Hatta.

The Soekarno-Hatta Government reacted sharply. On 19 September the Republican Government declared martial law. On 20 September raids and arrests of Front sympathisers began in Djogjakarta. Military attack was launched on the Front's concentration in Madiun, Java. By 30 September the Madiun resistance had been overwhelmed. Among the dead were Tanah Merah men from Australian, including Sardjono.

The Dutch fatally misinterpreted Madiun. This internal strife and schism, they deduced, would make relatively easy the demolition of the Republic. The reality was that the military action against the left forces at Madiun caused Washington to look more sympathetically on the Soekarno-Hatta administration. Washington's readjusted diplomacy gave the Republic a greater durability in face of the Hollanders' sightless strategies.

Neither at The Hague nor in the colonial capital of a name so soon to disappear from the atlas — Batavia — would the majority of Dutch leaders study the lessons of history — not even their own national history. From its own liberation struggles against the French or the Duke of Alba the Dutch should have been warned that no sword inflicts so mortal a wound as one beaten from a ploughshare. Those who held sway at The Hague would not concede that social reparation was the only alternative to Indonesians forging this kind of sword and carrying it to victory. They, like the British and French, had breached in 1941-42 the classical reciprocal contract which the Europeans themselves drafted: the metropolitan country to defend the colony and the colony to meet the bill in obedience and tribute.

The contract was turned to ashes in the fires of Singapore and Bandung and the ignominy of French Indo-China. Cervantes, as Byron read him, smiled Spain's chivalry away. The Dutch *colons* were not to be moved on at so slight an expenditure. The colonial lobby remained impervious to advice, allergic to criticism. Australian Prime Minister Chifley, deeply disturbed by Dutch obstinacy, was still offering himself as cartographer, but the successors to Dirk Hartog and Abel Tasman in these seas never learned to steer by the wind.

221

In 1948 he continued to advise the Dutch that reform and concessions were essential salvage operations. Instead of heeding they sniped at him. The answer to Java's unsubdued commotions was the Second Police Action, which sounded the knell of the Dutch Empire of the East.

Second Police Action Responses

After Madiun, the Dutch went on closing down Republican schools and newspapers, banning assemblies of more than six people, intimidating Republican delegations entitled to United Nations protection and transporting troops and arms. The compromiser Van Mook, one of the very few to detect the unknitting of the Dutch administrative fabric before he turned his back on flaming Bandung in 1942, was now rated as "too lenient". He was out of Java by November 1948, replaced by Dr Louis J.M. Beel, former Prime Minister, bearing the title of High Commissioner of the Crown. Dr Van Mook's resignation was reported as "the result of reported differences between the Netherlands Government and Dr Van Mook."[14] His dismissal accelerated the Dutch exodus.

The new Dutch administration refused Republican requests for elections and on 11 December announced that they would form a government without the Republic. In Batavia, the Dutch told the UN Committee of Good Offices at 11.30 pm on 18 December that they were resuming freedom of action at midnight.

The first most of those attached to the Committee of Good Offices at Djogjakarta knew of the Second Police Action was when bombs and rockets began to fly around them and Republican leaders were arrested. Dutch Foreign Minister Dirk Stikker's assessment of Republican life-span was that the military operation would not require "more than a couple of days".

Hell broke loose in the international diplomatic world and boycotts were imposed on Dutch ships and aircraft in a number of countries. The *Manchester Guardian* appealed to the UN Security Council to "save the Netherlands Government from its own folly".[15] The appeal was too late. The Second Police Action made boycott resumption in Australia an easy political exercise. The Waterside Workers' Federation immediately notified Mr Chifley that a new boycott movement was proposed. Mr Chifley registered no contrary appeal. Under ACTU endorsement, Dutch ships, aircraft, vehicles and services were banned once more.

Only two Dutch ships were in Australian waters when Djogjakarta was blasted by the Dutch Air Force and the Republican leaders kidnapped and flown away. They were the passenger-liners *Nieuw Holland*, denied tugs and labor at Melbourne, and the *Maetsuycker*, treated likewise by Fremantle unions. Between the Second Police Action of December 1948 and The Hague Agreement, negotiated between 23 August and 2 November 1949, Dutch ships gave the stormy anchorages of Australian harbours a miss, except in rare instances.

The Dutch, having denied their viceroy Van Mook enough straw to make the bricks of a reformed order, refused under The Hague Agreement to grant Indonesia the same degree of independence that Britain, more than two years before, had conceded India. The Raj could easily read writing on the wall that was now in poster-size script; the British hauled down the flag and allowed the natives to auction off the statues of Queen Victoria, to help save London's investments in India. The Netherlands stayed faithful to the iconography of empire and retained in The Hague Agreement restrictive controls over their *untermenschen*, thickening the pall of distrust and guaranteeing total loss of the Indies. Tanks could never climb the ancient rice terraces and forested mountains; guerillas would defy annihilation by General Spoor and his half-trained Dutch troops and Ambonese Cossacks in the jungles, swamps and overgrown plantations. The resisting peoples of some 3,000 islands could never be held under the waning shadows of Dutch power.

The Hague Agreement inhibitions were finally repudiated by the Indonesian Republic in 1956, and colonial treasures that had been in Dutch hands for 300 years fell away like apples from a tree. Though the cold war and the McCarthyite witch-hunt had arrived in Australia, weakening their muscle, the Australian trade unions and the Chifley-Evatt Government had been able to lend a helping hand in the final military phase of the Republic's struggle for survival.

25   Trade Union Influence on Foreign Policy

In the first black armada years, 1945-46, the power of militant unions to intervene in the nation's foreign policies was at its peak. The unions were assisted by the democratic surge generated in the war waged by an alliance of diverse forces on Axis Fascism, which gave birth to the Atlantic Charter and the Universal Declaration of Human Rights. Fewer and fewer people were swayed by slogans from a rusting colonial arsenal: the beliefs were gaining ground that all people should be free to govern themselves, and that Asian independence could reduce international frictions and benefit Australia.

Adequate answers have not been found to explain the unique contributions of Australian trade unions to the struggles of oppressed and shackled peoples in Asia, nor will the answers be easy to find in a country not celebrated for internationalism of outlook and tolerances toward humans of different skin pigmentation.

Trade union intervention in foreign policy is seldom a problem which governments in Europe, Asia, Africa, the Middle East and the Americas have to face. This Australian trade union capacity for intervention in a wide range of issues, from Greek and Chilean juntas to apartheid in South Africa and sub-standard wages paid to seamen in Liberian, Panamanian and other flags-of-convenience ships, has caused deep concern to politicians and corporations both here and abroad. As Attorney-General in the Lyons-Latham Government, Mr R.G. Menzies tried in vain to kill the habit before it took hold, during the 1938-39 Port Kembla waterside workers' ban on

224

pig-iron shipments to the Japanese invaders of China. In 1945-49, anger and frustration over this exceptional capacity of Australian trade unions to influence the course of international affairs was extended to The Hague, London and Washington.

Sussex Street Diplomacy

Australian newspapers – not a single daily paper failed to assail the boycott of Dutch ships – testily referred to "Sussex Street diplomacy" and "the Foreign Ministers of Miller's Point"; Sussex Street, known in harsher days as "the Hungry Mile" then being the best known wharves area on Sydney Harbour, and Miller's Point ("the Rocks") being a traditional watersiders' residential zone. The titles were not without relevance. Waterside workers were officially conceded a role in international diplomacy during the boycott of the Dutch.

Prime Minister Chifley always respected the General Secretary of the Waterside Workers' Federation, Mr James Healy, as a man of his word, despite serious political differences. The Royal Netherlands Government Minister in Canberra enjoyed less Prime Ministerial trust than this Manchester-born Irish Home-Ruler, an immigrant to Australia who left part of a leg and hand in France, when he was Private Healy, Argyll and Sutherland Highlanders, wounded by the same shell that killed Scots comedian Harry Lauder's son.

After Mr Healy had taken up with Mr Chifley the need for Australian pressures to have the Dutch naval blockade of Republican-held ports lifted, the Prime Minister made representations to the Netherlands Minister, Mr Petrus Ephrem Teppema. On 22 May 1948 Mr Chifley sent to Mr Healy on Prime-Ministerial notepaper a letter[1] showing that Chifley-Healy consultations on twisting Dutch arms were based on mutual confidence:

Dear Jim,
I attach a copy of a second paper which I received from Mr Teppema regarding the blockade. This is the one I mentioned to you on Friday night. I don't know that it is much clearer than the previous one, but perhaps it is

225

well that you should see what further he had to say.
Yours sincerely,
J.B. CHIFLEY

The Netherlands Minister in Canberra might make representations to the Australian Government about freeing Indiesbound Dutch ships from the unions' boycott, but the plenipotentiary's proposals would have to be submitted to the Waterside Workers' Federation for consideration.

Mr Healy was called to a top level conference with Mr Chifley, Shipping Minister Ashley and the Secretary of the Department of Supply and Shipping, Mr G.G. Sutcliffe, at Canberra on 5 May 1948. Standard Oil of New Jersey, Socony Mobil and Shell had a keen interest in the conference, because they wanted their oil-carrying vessels freed from boycott in Australian ports. The conference also discussed the fruit trade carried on by KPM vessels from Adelaide and Tasmania to Singapore and Malaya, the import of urgently needed timber from Borneo to Western Australia in Dutch ships and the Dutch blockade of Indonesian ports. Mr Chifley wanted the ban removed from fruit cargoes in Dutch ships. Mr Healy pointed out that the Blue Funnel Line of Great Britain was prepared to undertake the fruit traffic in place of the Dutch. He proposed to the conference use of British rather than Dutch ships.

Mr Healy was not giving much away, nor was Mr Chifley in an unconditional frame of mind, as this conference decision shows:

> That the existing barrier to shipment of weapons and munitions from Australia should not be affected by these present conversations or any action arising out of them . . .
>
> Lifting of the ban should involve a raising of the Dutch blockade of Indonesian ports.[2]

Union Arbiters of Shipping Routes

Sir Thomas Gordon, representative in Australia of the United Kingdom Ministry of Transport and of the Allied Consultative Shipping Council, Director of Shipping for the Commonwealth Government, Member of the Shipping Control Board and an executive of the Peninsular and Oriental SN Co.'s vast Australian enterprises, was not briefed when he accepted the posts on how to tender written assurances to Australian trade union leaders that he would not permit ships to depart the ports on routes of which they did not approve. Nor did the master of a Royal Packet Navigation Co. (KPM) vessel anticipate that he would be required to put pen to his company's notepaper to provide the Waterside Workers' Federation of Australia with a pledge that he would not cheat those illegally boycotting his nation's ships.

Sir Thomas Gordon, given to firm responses to maritime unions, slipped into pliant mood in his correspondence with Mr Healy on the boycott. In a letter[3] to the WWF General Secretary dated 28 February 1946 Sir Thomas wrote:

> *Straat Malakka* — Flour for Colombo
> Referring to our telephone conversation — on behalf of the Ministry I wish to give you an assurance that this vessel, in accordance with charter instructions to the Captain, is loading flour at Sydney for Colombo on behalf of the British Ministry of Food.
>
> This flour is urgently required at Colombo and I trust that no further delay will occur with the despatch of this urgent vessel to Colombo — I repeat the word Colombo.
> Yours faithfully,
> T.S. GORDON

The skipper of the *Straat Malakka* should have envisioned bold Dutch navigators of old turning in their shrouds as he signed this undertaking[4] to gain Waterside Workers' Federation permission to sail his ship through the union blockade:

> The undersigned, J.M. VAN NOORDEN, Master of the mv *Straat Malakka*, declares that he will, according to his instructions, proceed as laid down in his charter party to Colombo and not divert his destination.
> J.M. VAN NOORDEN, Master.

Written pledges like these from ships' captains, to sail only on high seas routes approved by the Waterside Workers' Federation of Australia and to divert to no other, must be without parallel in maritime history.

The Dutch ship *Curacao* furnished further evidence that ships could only move freely from Australian ports if watersiders were convinced that their cargoes and routes would not be to the Indonesian Republic's disadvantage. The Commonwealth Government Ships Chartering Committee, before wartime regulations awarding it control of shipping movements had been annulled, recognised a situation of dual power. The Government Chartering Committee under date of 19 October 1945 addressed from its Melbourne head office this letter[5] to the Waterside Workers' Federation General Secretary in Sydney, to secure *Curacao*'s release:

Dear Mr Healy,
I was speaking to the Director of Shipping in Sydney by telephone this morning and he asked me to advise you that ss *Curacao* has been fixed to load stores for the Australian troops in New Guinea.
W. ASHBURN, Executive Director.

Australian Government wheat and flour marketing authorities were obliged to talk over export arrangements with Mr Healy, and certify that shipments would not aid the Dutch. The Australian Wheat Board General Manager, Mr C.J. Perrett, discussed with the WWF General Secretary, in Mr Healy's office, the importance of reviving the Australian flour trade with the Indies. A flour surplus was threatened. Mr Perrett expressed to Mr Healy in a letter[6] of 8 February 1949 his fear that the Americans might capture the Indonesian market unless Australian flour was shipped there. Shipping space for 10,000 tons of flour ordered by the Netherlands Indies Government had to be cancelled because of the watersiders' boycott, Mr Perrett said. His letter asked the WWF to modify its ban "so as to enable the flour to be shipped".

Encouragement to World Boycott

The Australian union boycotters of the Netherlands war supply services not only made their weight felt in foreign policy and international trading arrangements; they also inspired and incited moves against the Dutch in other countries.

The walk-off from Dutch ships at the Brisbane wharves on

24 September 1945 was only a day old when the Australian-born President of the International Longshoremen's and Warehousemen's Union, Mr Harry Bridges, cabled[7] the WWF from San Francisco, offering "wholehearted commendation" to Australian watersiders for refusing to assist the Dutch re-impose their rule in the Indies and giving assurances that US West Coast longshoremen would not load cargoes likely to help Dutch counter-moves against the Indonesian Republic.

Mr Toby Hill, leader of New Zealand waterside workers, rang the WWF Federal Office from Auckland immediately news of the Australian boycott reached the New Zealand waterfront. He pledged that Dutch ships would be black in New Zealand ports and the pledge was quickly carried out. Mr Hill informed the WWF Assistant General Secretary, Mr Roach, who took the phone call,[8] that the National Executive of the NZ Federation of Labor (the central trade union body) had acknowledged the correctness of the Australian boycott. Mr Hill added that "if this policy statement is questioned let the Dutch send a ship and we will quickly disillusion them". The Dutch did try to find an alternate source of supply in NZ, but this was denied them by waterfront black bans. The *Sydney Morning Herald* reported from Auckland that NZ watersiders had unanimously endorsed the boycott policy of Australian watersiders.[9]

Trade unions in Holland, Britain, India and other countries cabled Australia for further information on the boycott. There was inherent recognition that Australia was the world centre of union action against the Dutch in the sending of an expensively long circular cable[10] to leaders of all dockers' unions in Europe, Asia, the Americas and Africa — where unions' addresses were known — conveying a WWF appeal for international banning of Dutch shipping in retaliation for the First Police Action of July 1947. Though Canada had little responsibility in the Dutch-Indonesian affair, Vancouver longshoremen and seamen responded to the Australian appeal. Mr H. Murphy, of the Seafarers' International Union of North America, cabled from Vancouver: "Your recent wire concurred in by our membership. Have two Dutch vessels tied up at this port."[11]

Egyptian workers banned passage of the Dutch troopship

Hollandem through the Suez Canal. Independent India, after the 1947 First Police Action, denied passage to Dutch ships and aircraft. Pakistan and Thailand temporarily applied similar bans. Dockers had already taken initiatives against the Dutch in Burma, Ceylon, Singapore, the Philippines, Bombay and other Indian ports. Despite the throes of civil war bans were imposed on the Dutch in a few Chinese ports.

Premier Sutan Sjahrir, who met Indonesians repatriated from Australia aboard HMAS *Manoora* at Batavia in 1946, said that the stand taken by the Australian trade unions, beginning on the waterfront, "has drawn international attention to the Indonesian question which the Dutch have tried to prevent".[12]

In fizzy disagreement with Australian trade union initiatives on behalf of the Indonesian Republic were those forces, then strongly represented on the Melbourne waterfront, which became known as the ALP Industrial Groups and which, after the 1955 expulsions that followed attacks on Dr Evatt's leadership, were incorporated in the Democratic Labor Party. In a pamphlet issued in the late 1950s (undated), titled *Communism on the Waterfront*, the "National Vigilance Committee of the Waterside Workers' Federation" — an Industrial Groups' agency — depicted the bans on Dutch ships as a response to "the orders of International Communism". "These actions," said the Industrial Groups' pamphlet, "were impudent attempts to dictate policy to a Labor Government, for the Communists were then at the height of their arrogant power over the trade union movement . . ."

The Waterside Workers' Federation and the Seamen's Union, first among trade unions acting to strike off the shackles of the old semi-colonial vassalage and to swivel foreign policy around from European "umbrella" and rising-tide-of-color obsessions, were obviously in Mr Menzies' sights when he returned to the Prime Ministership in December 1949. His Communist Party Dissolution Bill of 1950 sought to "declare", to expel from office and virtually outlaw union officials blacklisted by the Australian Security Intelligence Organisation. WWF and Seamen's Union officials were among the 53 "declared" before Parliament in 1950. These two unions needed no second ringing of alarm bells. It was, logically, the

Waterside Workers' Federation, remembering Mr Menzies' fierce responses to waterfront bans on loading pig-iron for the Japanese war machine and to the shock waves created by the boycott of Dutch ships, that briefed Dr Evatt, Queen's Counsel and ex-High Court Judge, to challenge, successfully to Mr Menzies' chagrin, the "Red Bill" before the High Court, which found the legislation invalid in every clause. The WWF and Seamen's Union contributed money and services in generous measure to the campaign, in which Dr Evatt was so active, to ensure the defeat of the Government's McCarthvite proposals in the 1951 referendum.

Although penal laws passed by the Menzies Government severely abridged trade union rights the Waterside Workers' and the Seamen's Union continued to intervene in foreign policy under Liberal-Country Party rule. Australian seamen would not man ships serving the wars in Korea, Malaya and Indo-China. Sydney watersiders in 1954 walked off the *Radnor*, loading arms for the French in Indo-China, and eventually black-banned the *Jeparit*, regular carrier of supplies to Australian troops in Vietnam. Also before the ALP electoral victory of December 1972 seagoing and waterfront unions held protest stoppages on South African ships, to demonstrate their abhorrence of apartheid, and on ships from junta-ruled Greece.

Future historians may resolve that in this era the conscience of the Australian people found expression more often on the waterfront than in the nation's legislatures.

26 Australian Army Wouldn't March

While the dishevelled Dutch command waited fretfully for ships, troops and munitions, and the British interventionists squandered goodwill and morale in Java, formidable Australian Army, Navy and Air Force units idled in East Indonesia. In Australian ranks were sympathisers with the boycott of Dutch ships and the Indonesian Republic. Though most officers were pro-Dutch, quite a number of them came to a healthy dislike of the NICA colonials.

The Australian forces in East Indonesia and adjoining Melanesia must have appeared far more attractive to South-East Asia Command than the motley army available in the last months of 1945. Mountbatten had the Fifth Indian Division, the last Indian troops ever to serve Britain in a colonial war and deserting to the Indonesians in impressive numbers, some companies of Gurkhas, the reluctant British regiments impatient for home and family, and Dutch contingents trickling in from Australia or Europe or recruited in poor psychological shape from the Japanese prison camps in the Indies, Singapore-Malaya, Thailand and Japan. Protest clamour in India soon compelled withdrawal of Indian troops. Mountbatten, to make up his deficiencies, came to use the Japanese for bloody assaults in Java and thus corrode further the morale and repute of the reoccupiers.

The British command ran into far greater difficulties than it anticipated as it tried to reoccupy key centres for the Dutch in Java. The Indonesians at Sourabaya resisted British and Indian troops, who held far superior weight of arms, for a

232

month. The Sourabaya assault was costly in lives — Brigadier Mallaby of the British Army was killed on 19 October 1945 and other officers were among the dead — and the Indian and British troops became more disaffected.

Terror warfare did not work. The British used petrol to wipe out Bekassi, and Tjibadak was ripped to pieces by Mosquito bombers and Lend-Lease P47s, firing rockets and incendiaries to allow NICA officers and their Ambonese mercenaries to enter. Ambarawa and various other towns and kampongs were burned. The Royal Air Force bombed Djogjakarta and Surakarta and the Royal Navy threw shells into coastal areas. But SEAC, despite frequent deployment of Japanese troops, did not have the resources to subdue the Republic and make Java safe for Dutchmen. The British could neither win the war nor push the Dutch far enough along the road to an uneasy accommodation with the Republic. The taut stretch of British military control in South-East Asia presented intractable problems.

The battle-toughened Australians nearby should, by all the rules of war, have been able to overrun every main Republican centre with expedition. The Ninth and Seventh Australian Divisions, mostly veterans of Middle East campaigns against Field-Marshal Rommel's Germans, Mussolini's Italians and Vichy French (Syria-Lebanon), had taken Tarakan, Brunei and Sarawak. The Seventh Division stormed ashore at Balikpapan. The five Australian forces holding East Indonesia immediately after Japan's surrender — Macassar, Ambon, Menado, Ternate and Timor Forces as they were known — and the Headquarters troops at Morotai included many of campaign experience. In the Solomon Islands, New Guinea, New Britain and adjacent islands and in North Australia there were also substantial concentrations of Australian troops. Some of the Australian units were expert in amphibious landings and had the craft and armaments to mount attacks in strength against Republican strongholds. Others had learned jungle warfare the hardest way, on the New Guinea mountains.

None of these closeby Australian troops were to stand to arms beside the British, Indians, Gurkhas, Dutchmen, Ambonese and Japanese. This Australian non-involvement in a British-led war, right at the country's front-door, was a turning point in relations between England and a loyalist Commonwealth member, and a signal that the "Asian hordes" syndrome was losing potency.

This first Australian rejection of a British war was not because Australian troops would have been unwelcome. Notices were posted at certain Royal Australian Air Force stations, seeking volunteers at high pay to serve with what was described as the "Component for Duty with the Netherlands Indies Air Force". Australian Air Force men protested against their commanding officers permitting display of a recruiting poster for Australian mercenaries to serve the Dutch. Some of them took the unusual step of informing the trade unions,[1] who acted firmly and quickly. NSW Trades and Labor Council demanded that the Chifley Government take urgent steps to prevent any use of Australian troops against the Indonesian Republic. The TLC Disputes Committee declared:

> Any recruiting will be resolutely opposed by the Australian trade union movement and will mean a counter-demand that volunteers be recruited in Australia for service with the Indonesian Army.[2]

"Australian Brigade" Counter-Threat

Recruitment for the Dutch and counter-recruitment of Australians to fight with the Indonesian Republican Army would have created tensions and problems without precedent in Australian society. If the Dutch had been allowed to recruit mercenaries, or if Australian soldiers from East Indonesia had been placed at Mountbatten's disposal in Java, there no doubt would have been, in the fervid atmosphere of the times, a massive response to the call to join an Australian brigade to fight beside the Republicans. Australians would have been shedding each other's blood on a foreign battlefield. No Australian Government was likely to encourage such schism and confrontation. The recruiting notices for the "Component for Duty with the Netherlands Indies Air Force" were torn from RAAF notice boards on ministerial instructions. The Minister for Air, Mr Drakeford, announced on 12 November 1945 that no RAAF men would be sent to Java.[3]

SEAC had already launched the Java invasion when Mr

Chifley announced that Australian troops would not be used in the Dutch-Indonesian conflict.[4] Professor Crisp of the Australian National University who, in writing the late Prime Minister's biography,[5] had better access than most to relevant documents, said that Mr Chifley "would not agree to the sending of Australian troops to Indonesia". Professor Crisp referred to the Java war: Australian troops had already intervened to restore Dutch rule in East Indonesia.

Mr Chifley had to sprag some extra-curricular empire-building efforts by Dr Evatt. Dr Evatt proposed by cable from London in November 1945 that an Australian force should be landed in Java. Ostensibly, the Australian invasion would be directed to peace-keeping and to induce a compromise settlement between the Indonesian Republic and the Dutch, who were still anything but reform-oriented. Dr Evatt's real aim was to promote in postwar Indonesia those Australian interests he had already defined, somewhat raggedly and inconsistently. For good measure Dr Evatt included in the responsibilities of the Australian invasion force the removal of all Japanese and Allied prisoners of war. (This would have deprived SEAC of those Japanese soldiers who had taken the Indies from the Dutch and were now slaughtering Indonesians to restore the Dutch, and the Dutch command of the released prisoners of war rushed into police and military service against the Republic.)

Mr Chifley replied to Dr Evatt from Canberra that he was sure Cabinet would not agree to this additional commitment of Australian forces. It would be difficult enough, he argued, to keep the Australians in Borneo for an extended period. Mr Chifley was strongly supported by Mr William Macmahon Ball, sent to Java in October 1945 as Australian Political Representative to the Allied Commander, NEI. The Macmahon Ball report from on the spot in Java was before a December War Cabinet meeting. Australia, it said, would have little chance of being accepted as mediator by the Dutch and even if the Dutch did accept Australia "for fear worse might befall them," this would imply obligations to back Australia's intervention with military force. The report warned:

If the impressions I gained on my flying visits to Morotai

and Borneo are correct, then any Australian Government which sought to transfer our troops to Java instead of bringing them home would be faced by a major political crisis.[6]

Mr Chifley was, according to official war historian Paul Hasluck, "against any initiative by Australia". He quoted a War Cabinet minute of 18 December 1945:

It was the wish of the Government that the Australian forces in the Netherlands East Indies should avoid, as far as possible, participation in Indonesian strife.

Paul Hasluck concluded that "the decision of the War Cabinet was a decision for non-intervention and for withdrawal as quickly as possible from the risk of additional commitments in the Netherlands Indies".[7]

Professor Macmahon Ball — as he became in 1949, at the University of Melbourne — referred to Dr Evatt's plan to have the invading Australians settle the conflict in Java when he spoke at an Australian-Indonesian relations seminar at Monash University, on 11-12 November 1972. The writer, one of the speakers at the seminar, asked Professor Macmahon Ball what the Australian soldiers would have done if ordered to invade Java. His verdict was definite: "They wouldn't have gone."

The reasons why the decisive Australian military strength was not brought to Java and into conflict with the fledgling Indonesian Republic bore close relationship to the anti-colonial manifestations in Australian ports and repercussions among servicemen in East Indonesia.

The Impossible Neutrality

When General MacArthur's South-West Pacific Command came to an end on 2 September 1945, control of Australian armed forces reverted to the Commonwealth Government. Mr Chifley indicated in his statement on the war's ending that Australia had responsibility for East Indonesian islands stretching from Borneo to Timor, and that the Dutch would take over from the Australian military. This was something more than a walk-on part for the Australian armed forces.

The Minister for Defence, Mr J.A. Beasley, said that the

Government desired relief of Australian troops to be completed by the end of October, and that responsibility for civil affairs should be taken over by the British and Dutch authorities "with the least delay". In addition to accepting the Second Japanese Army's surrender in East Indonesia, Australia had responsibility for Portuguese as well as Dutch Timor, "in concert with the Portuguese Government". Mr Beasley served notice of Australia's "special interest" in Netherlands New Guinea, where Hollandia and Biak were Australian Air Force staging bases.[8] There were Dutch suspicions of a "special interest" in Timor, too, where the official Australian neglect to invite Netherlands representatives to the Japanese surrender ceremony caused comment.

The Australian armed forces had never before been ordered into such an operation — to take over from a defeated enemy a substantial and rich segment of its colonial war booty and hand the possessions back to the displaced empire. The political consciousness and experience required to meet Indonesian nationalist opposition was not at a high level. The Australian command, in restoring the Dutch to a toppling throne, kept backs turned to the future.

Ironically, the Australian command's task of transferring what authority they were still able to exert to the Dutch was made less difficult by the trade unions' boycott of Dutch ships in Brisbane, Sydney, Melbourne, Fremantle and other ports. Private George Bliss[9] (known as Jim Bliss in the Army), 2/14 Battalion, Seventh Division, with service in Morotai, Balikpapan and in Macassar Force in the Celebes (Macassar and Pari Pari), reported on his repatriation to Sydney in 1946 that when the Australians launched their transfer-of-power operation in the Celebes the Indonesians already knew of the trade unions' boycott of Dutch shipping. "The Indonesians," said Private Bliss, "used to make their own very rough paper and produce a news-sheet on the only typewriter available to them. Copies were carried by couriers to different localities and in some towns that possessed typewriters more of the news-sheets would be typed out. The contents were read to meetings to overcome the illiteracy problem. In this way the Indonesians in the Celebes were informed that the Australian unions were supporting in action the Indonesian Republic.

237

Wherever we went Indonesians linked Australia with their word *bagus*, meaning good or fine — in this case, something more".

Not well instructed in the permitted dissidences of societies enjoying some democratic rights, Indonesians felt that if Australian trade unions were for the Republic then the Australian Army must be for the Republic. Australian officers, publicly resenting maritime unions that interfered in political and strategic affairs, found themselves taking advantage of the high repute that the union boycott of Dutch ships had conferred on Australia among Indonesians. It took Indonesians some weeks to become finally convinced that the Australian Army's mission was to place them in bondage to the Dutch again.

The Australian Army command's proclaimed "neutrality" in the Dutch-Indonesian dispute immediately became a mockery. Instructions[10] on which the Australian military were to act read:

> The Australian Military Forces are not concerned with the eventual form of government to be set up in the NEI and will maintain a completely impartial attitude on that question. Thus it is no concern of ours if Indonesians express a desire for a Republican or any other form of government.

As these instructions were being pasted up NICA camp-followers were emerging from behind Australian Army tent-flaps. The wording of the proclamation[11] issued by the Australian Commander-in-Chief, General Sir Thomas Blamey, serving as Allied Commander in East Indonesia, was less cosmetic. General Blamey warned the Indonesians in English, Dutch and Malay that "until such time as the lawful Government of the Netherlands East Indies is once again functioning" and the NEI laws were enforced by officers of NICA, the Australian forces would maintain law and order.

The Australian command did not take seriously its own pretensions of "impartiality". It banned Republican flags, badges, newspapers, processions and meetings when it could, and re-imposed the rule of the Republic's enemies. Republicans faced heavy penalties for carrying arms, while the Australian Government, through its military officers in East

Indonesia, was handing millions worth of armaments and installations to the Royal Netherlands Indies Army.

Private Bliss said that his commander at Macassar, Brigadier I.N. Dougherty, appointed Major Wegner as NEI Government man, and, finding Indonesian cooperation lacking, had to use Japanese for some administrative tasks. Brigadier Dougherty tried to ignore Republican transport boycotts. "I went out on patrols led by officers whose aim was to take from the Indonesians arms they had managed to acquire," Private Bliss said. "Once we went from Pari Pari to Palopo, six or seven hours' drive, to seize some guilders from a pro-Republican Rajah to hand them to the Dutch. The weight in silver was six to seven hundredweight. On that long drive, no matter how small the village, the red and white Republican flag was flying and the sight of Australian uniforms brought the usual *bagus*. They did not know that we were on a mission to grab guilders for the Dutch."[12]

Indonesian Republicans occupied many points in the sprawling islands system of East Indonesia when the Australians began introducing the NICA men. Indonesians had rounded up the small Japanese garrisons and set up their own Republican administration. In some of the more remote islands and inland areas there had only been the thinnest Japanese garrisoning. The Republicans reluctantly came to the conclusion that they had been betrayed by the Australian command, though this command had made no commital to Republican power. The Australian command was, in the Indonesian view, dislodging Republicans from their rightful places of power. Ambonese soldiers under NICA command began to tear down Republican flags and assault and sometimes kill Republicans. Bloody brawls developed, in which Australian soldiers sometimes intervened against the Ambonese. The Australian command had to take measures to curb the more provocative of the Ambonese mercenaries. Some rabidly pro-Dutch Australian officers, according to Private Bliss, harassed and humiliated Republicans.

These officers staged marches by Australian soldiers to display superior and intimidatory armed strength. Later at Pari Pari, headquarters of the 14th Battalion in which Private Bliss served, machine guns were put on public view in large numbers for no other purpose than to discourage the independence movement. The quickening Celebes turmoil was threatening serious bloodshed just before Brigadier F. O. Chilton took over Macassar Force from Brigadier Dougherty on 18 October 1945. While investing the Dutch with licence for violence the Australian Army was arresting Republicans. "I am sure," said Private Bliss, "that if it had not been for the tremendous Indonesian goodwill toward Australians, created by the boycott of Dutch ships and by some evidence of Australian Government sympathy for the Republic, the activities of an army major from Melbourne would have led to bloody clashes. I and other sympathetic Australian soldiers were able to persuade Indonesians to break it off. Not many knew that the Republicans actually set a date for retaliatory attack on contingents of Macassar Force. This plan of attack resulted from anti-Indonesian connivings and provocations by certain officers of the 2/14 Infantry Battalion in which I served. The Republicans fixed Christmas Day 1945 to launch their offensive against Australian troops. Again, we were able to draw upon goodwill flowing from action against the Dutch in Australia and dissuade the Republicans from military confrontation of grave consequences. The rapport established between sympathetic Australian soldiers and Republicans was yielding important results, helping to cancel out the threat of armed Republican retaliation which would have sparked all kinds of trouble for both the Australian command and the Republicans. Divisions in the Australian Army on the Dutch-Indonesian conflict would have been widened and it would have been in poor morale if called on to cope with Indonesian guerilla warfare in East Indonesia."

Republic's Allies in Australian Army

The contradiction puzzled Dr Van Mook: while Australian forces in East Indonesia "contributed materially" to restoration of "law and order" the Australian Government "followed an increasingly anti-Dutch policy as time went on".[14] A subsidiary factor in the Chifley Government's scaling down of support to the Dutch cause was evidence of sympathy for the Indonesian Republic and antipathy to NICA among a significant minority of Australian servicemen.

240

Australian Army Education Service distributed printed propaganda among troops that challenged Dutch propaganda. The Army Education Service journal issued to the forces in East Indonesia just after the Republic's proclamation what was in essence an appeal to Australians to be nice to the Indonesians:

Australians who have been fortunate enough to gain some insight into the habits, customs and modes of living of the native peoples of the Balikpapan area will . . . be agreed that they are an attractive race, kindly, hospitable, clean, hard-working and intelligent.

Though subjected to the usual hardships and atrocities of vicious Japanese militarism, they have emerged with honour as a people who, with few exceptions, did not collaborate with the invader and who are now carrying on cheerfully in the difficult transition period of resettlement.[15]

Despite discouragements from officers, Australian soldiers accepted this implied invitation to fraternise with the Indonesians. An Australian command order against fraternisation was widely ignored.

NICA and the Royal Netherlands Army advance units, when they began to trickle in, intervened actively against Australian-Indonesian fraternisation. Armed Dutch arrived in jeeps to prevent Indonesians receiving medical care at Australian posts, according to an Indonesian who wrote from the Australian-occupied zone to Sydney:

The Indonesians were not allowed to talk to the Australians. Many times the Australians gave medicines and food, but the Dutch took them away and put us in gaol with hard labor. If they knew we were doing favours for the Aussies they put us in gaol for five days with hard labor. The opinion of the Indonesians is that the Dutch hate the Australians in Indonesia.[16]

Friction between the Australians and Dutch grew as the Anglo-Dutch military intervention in Java demanded more and more shipping. Soldiers blamed diversion of shipping to Java for delay in their repatriation. As irritation mounted, so did some Australian soldiers' support for the Republic. Corporal S. Tapper, who served in Borneo, reported that Australian soldiers were chalking up on buildings and old tanks signs like: "We fought for freedom — let's give it to the Indonesians!", "Hands off Java!" and "Freedom for Indonesia!"[17]

Return of Australian armed forces from Indonesia — the last regiments got away in March 1946 instead of October 1945 — did not come any too soon. As the danger of their being caught in Dutch-Indonesian crossfire mounted, so did the evidence that not all Australian soldiers would have pointed their guns in the same direction. Hostility to the Dutch led many Australian soldiers to back the Republic. They got into fights with Dutch soldiers, particularly if they saw them maltreating Indonesians. In one fight witnessed by Private Bliss,[18] bottles, fists and boots were used, until Australian provosts moved in. The Dutch came off second best.

Illegal Services to the Republic

Within days of the August 17 proclamation a pro-Republican organisation began to take shape in the Australian Army and Air Force. The organisation was originally dependent on Communist Party members, quickly spreading to soldiers who were not communists but favoured national independence or merely detested the colonial Dutch.

To the writer's knowledge there were 4,000 members of the Communist Party, in round figures, serving in the Australian armed forces in 1945. Of the 4,000 some 1,400 were in East Indonesia—a substantial reservoir of cadres. They were mostly in the Seventh and Ninth Divisions; others were scattered in occupation units and headquarters and education staffs and Air Force stations. Air Force crewmen of Communist Party membership or leanings or of independent sympathies with the Republic or antipathies to the colonial Dutch performed vital services as couriers. They carried by air both written and word-of-mouth instructions from the Indonesian organisations operating in Australia to the East Indonesian Republicans. Many bundles of leaflets and pamphlets were delivered by air, in the kits of RAAF crewmen or of air-transported military personnel. The RAAF was taking part in seditious missions to aid war on Dutch allies, unknown to the air-marshals.

Australian servicemen helped in distribution of Republican propaganda printed in Australia. This distribution was sometimes so open that NICA protested to the Australian command. The distribution was particularly extensive at Balikpapan, where there was a strong Communist Party branch. At Macassar, the several Australian Communist Party members in and around the headquarters staff and in the Army Education Service had to work circumspectly. The Sydney *Bulletin*[19] charged that soon after Australian troops landed in Pontianak, Republican propaganda in Indonesian, printed at Melbourne, was being circulated among the populace.

Pamphlets bearing the imprint of the Indonesian Committee of Independence, Brisbane, were located in Labuan.

It was not unknown for Australian soldiers to incite Indonesians to action against the Dutch. The official Australian war history reports that at Balikpapan on 14 November between 6,000 and 8,000 Indonesians demonstrated in the NICA compound, wearing Republican emblems, and that "from 10 to 15 Australian soldiers were reported to have been present, inciting those Indonesians". Some Indonesians were arrested, "but the Australians had disappeared before the Australian military police arrived".[20] Australian soldiers also gave advice on political and military tactics to the Republicans.[21]

Australian Arms for Republicans

Australian Army Public Relations Department conceded that Dutch charges that Australians were providing arms to the Indonesians contained more than an element of truth.[22]

Some of the Australian arms in Indonesia were jettisoned. Other dumps were transferred to the Netherlands Indies Army. The war was over: the Australian Command was not meticulous about inventories, and guards on munitions stockpiles were of relaxed vigilance. A few appear to have suffered defective vision when Republicans marched off with light arms.

243

The Netherlands Indies authorities lodged charges that Australians were supplying arms to Indonesian revolutionaries. Some Australian soldiers interviewed by the writer on their return to Sydney in 1946 claimed that substantial quantities of light arms and ammunition went to the Republicans from Australian stockpiles.

Soldiers' letters from East Indonesia reflected a sufficient intensity of pro-Republican feeling to facilitate a flow of arms to the Republicans. Although every vessel tied up aggravated the postwar shipping shortage and delayed eagerly-awaited repatriation — pro-Dutch Australian officers labored this point in talks to the troops, angled against the trade union boycotters — a significant section of servicemen continued to give illicit aid to the Republic and to hail the unions for immobilising the Dutch war armada. The Waterside Workers' Federation Indonesian File has remarkable letters from Australian soldiers in East Indonesia — letters that do not always accord with Army Regulations. Eighty signed a letter forwarded on their behalf by a soldier from Victoria, addressed the WWF General Secretary James Healy:

> Please find enclosed the total of 80 signatories from Australian soldiers in Balikpapan, supporting the action taken not only by your men but men of all trades on the Indonesian situation.
>
> The overwhelming majority of our chaps have a tremendous amount of sympathy for these people here, whose life is one of continuous squalor under the imperialists. To quote the most freely used phrase among our chaps, "The Dutch are a mob of bastards", meaning, of course, those who are tools of imperialism. Almost all the Indonesians here, though mostly illiterate, know of the Javanese situation; there is no need to tell you where their sympathies lie . . . .

A corporal of Engineers, 18th Field Company, Labuan Island, North Borneo, wrote to the WWF on behalf of a number of soldiers:

> During the past few weeks we have read of the action taken by waterside workers in connection with the load-

ing of Dutch ships intended to convey war materials for the suppression of the newly proclaimed Indonesian Republic. I have been urged to write applauding the action taken.

We of the Services are proud of the action taken by your union and we here on Labuan Island, possessing some first-hand knowledge of their people and their conditions, are sure their claims are reasonable . . . .

Almost to a man the Australians have found the Indonesian people eager and intelligent and determined to continue the demand for democratic government . . . . A democratic government in Indonesia means a friendly neighbour — a vital asset strategically to Australia.[23]

A telegram to the WWF head office in Sydney from a group of Australian soldiers in East Indonesia said: "Convey congratulations workers' stand taken in Indonesian struggle (for) Atlantic Charter principles."[24]

A member of the RAAF wrote from Tarakan:

NICA won't let the natives trade with the Australians direct, but only through NICA at exhorbitant prices. There is much fraternisation going on between Australians and Indonesians, though there is in fact a non-fraternisation ban. We could get 20 days' field punishment for fraternising with Indonesians — but most Diggers don't pay any attention to this undemocratic regulation.[25]

The airman, like many other Australian servicemen, lauded the waterside workers for denying labor to Dutch ships. Professor Macmahon Ball's theory that the Australian soldiers, if given marching orders for Java battlefields, would have voted No with their feet, was well founded.

27   Australian Dreams of Empire

The Netherlands Indies Government-in-Exile had no suspicion of strings attached to Australia's hospitable welcome of March 1942. The Dutch were staggered when Australia, which hadn't seemed to have a soul of its own in the arena of world politics, revealed pretensions to imperial grandeur. Before the Dutch had time to settle down in their temporary base the Netherlands Minister in Canberra, Baron Van Aerssen, was reporting to the Royal Government in London that, at an Allied Political Warfare Committee in Canberra on 30 June 1942, Dr Evatt suggested that the people of the NEI should not be told that the war was being fought to regain Indonesia for the Dutch. The Dutch had given up their territories without resistance; it was unlikely that they would govern after the war. According to Van Aerssen, Dr Evatt claimed that Australia should govern the islands or at least they should be a condominium.[1]

Dr Evatt's bunyip messianism — for want of a better definition — must have bewildered the Dutch all the more, because he was publicly emphasising that Australia was the base from which the Dutch would recover the Indies.

On 3 September 1942 Dr Evatt made an anti-colonial speech in parliament, obviously with the Dutch in mind, laying down Australia's right to expand economic relations with near neighbours and opposing the return of colonial economic exclusivism — a particular Dutch vice. He said that "our postwar aims in the Pacific must not be for the benefit of one power or group of powers".[2]

246

Dr Van Der Plas perhaps flattered the aspiring Canberra empire-builders when in December 1942, while serving as Netherlands Indies Chief Commissioner here, he warned the Royal Government that Australian ambitions could be a threat to Dutch control of the Indies. He noted Australian talk of a madate over the NEI.[3]

Early in 1943 Dr Evatt would have struck a chord among Australia's rising manufacturing and agricultural interests when he said:

North of Australia, in South-East Asia and in the Pacific, there are enormous markets practically untapped. There are millions of people who must be provided with improved standards of life. Close to Australia there is a very special zone suitable for the performance of our obligations toward the United Nations in the postwar world.[4]

In April and May 1943 Dr Evatt was in Washington pressing Australian claims under the slogan of "trusteeship for the benefit of all Pacific peoples". The Americans had other ideas about the future of European colonies in Asia. In November 1943 he was at it again, calling on the Australian High Commissioner in London, Mr Stanley Melbourne (later Lord) Bruce, to ask the Dutch for a long-term lease of Dutch Timor and Dutch New Guinea.[5] This lobbying in London and Washington lent some colour to the complaint by the Batavia paper *Java Bode* years later that while Dr Evatt was in America in 1943 he had proposed to the State Department that Australia should be allotted postwar control of Dutch Timor, Dutch New Guinea and the Kai, Aru and Tanimbar Islands in the Arafura Sea (from which the Japanese bombed Darwin in 1942). Dr Evatt denied the *Java Bode* story.[6]

While Prime Minister Curtin's ambitions did not bolt as fast as those of Dr Evatt, he, too, wanted a place for Australia in the Indies sun. Mr Curtin, addressing the Australian Labor Party Commonwealth Conference in Sydney and Canberra in 1943, described Australia and New Zealand as "autonomous nations in proximity to the colonies of the powers whose seats of government are located in other continents" and as nations "in a pre-eminent position to speak with authority on

247

the problems of the Pacific and have a primary interest in their solutions".[7]

The same confident modes in diplomacy and design were evident in the Opposition's South-East Asian policies. Mr Menzies rated the Netherlands East Indies as "among our first regional responsibilities". Doing some violence to recent history Mr Menzies said that the Netherlands East Indies represented "not only a military and political barrier reef to north-west Australia but also, in the future trading of the world, they represent great possibilities of friendly association and mutual development. I would never exclude them from even the smallest picture of the responsibilities and interests of Australia".[8]

Mr P.C. Spender, then Advisory War Council member, a former Minister for the Army and to become Minister for External Affairs in the Menzies Government when it returned to office late in 1949, saw an Australian "overriding interest" in the islands to the north. He went further than his colleagues, hinting at demissions of Dutch power and a more decisive role for Indonesian subjects:

> We must remember that the native inhabitants have a civilisation two thousand years old. They have survived invasions by Mohammedans and Hindus and intrusions by the Chinese. As a nation those people are of vital importance to Australia; and I emphasise the importance of our developing a recognition and understanding of their problems.

Mr Spender, in the same speech, called on the Australian Government "to assert our interest" in South-East Asia "at every possible opportunity".[9]

MacArthur versus Australian Imperialists

The precocity of Canberra's South-East Asian aspirations concerned both the Americans and the Dutch. General MacArthur was reported to have told Dr Van Der Plas on 14 August 1944 that the Australian military command had pressed him insistently to use the Australian Army and RAN for the reconquest campaign in the NEI. General MacArthur was in accord with Dr Van Der Plas's conviction that the Australian

ORDERS IS ORDERS

Lusby, *Courier-Mail*, 10 September 1947

THE FIGUREHEAD

Frith. *Sydney Morning Herald*. 28 M

'Yeah, it looks beaut, and wot's more it doesn't affect the steering.' Federal transport and waterside unions
decided to life the ban on Dutch shipping imposed in September 1945, while Sydney seamen have impose
ban on Greek ships

attempt to remove the NEI from his (MacArthur's) South-West Pacific Area Command "had been engineered by an annexationist group linked with Blamey". He told Dr Van Der Plas that he had made a stern complaint to Prime Minister Curtin, in which he indicated that he discerned sinister intentions in the attempt. General MacArthur promised to assist Dr Van Der Plas to counter Australian political meddling. He also suggested that Dutch troops would be better served by US control of Australian ground troops within the SWPA Command "rather than their transfer to a British command".[10]

Dr Van Der Plas chronicled this alleged design by a 7-million nation for sovereignty over 70 million:

> With regard to the campaign against the Indonesian islands the Australian military command persistently urged the United States commander to use Commonwealth ground and naval forces ...
>
> According to MacArthur the attitude of the Australians stemmed from designs of annexation vis-a-vis the Indies, fostered by a powerful group centred around the Australian Commander-in-Chief, General Sir Thomas Blamey. It was suggested that to leave the richest of all Asian colonies in the hands of a nation as weak as the Netherlands was tantamount to inviting another aggression in the future.[11]

South Pacific Empire

These plottings for a kangaroo-leap forward into an islands empire had not the faintest resonance of reality. They apparently embraced, at one stage, Polynesian and Melanesian colonies of Britain and France in the South Pacific, as well as the substantial south-of-the-equator sector of the Netherlands Indies and, doubtless, Portuguese Timor. President Roosevelt treated Australian imperial appetites seriously enough to declare, to a Washington Cabinet meeting that discussed, on 9 March 1945, just before his death, postwar disposal of Pacific Ocean territories that "the Australians had advanced the thesis that they would take by direct acquisition everything south of the equator, leaving to us those islands north of the line". This Australian claim was dismissed by President Roosevelt as "unacceptable".[12]

Canberra's hopes of Indies footholds at Dutch expense either dampened hostility or promoted sympathy for trade union boycotters dedicated to sabotage of the Dutch restoration. Dutch awareness that among their Australian allies in the Cabinet and Army General Staff were candidate-imperialists anxious to force at least a division of Indies spoils worsened relations with representatives of metropolitan Holland's Government, like the Far East Commander-in-Chief, Admiral Helfrich, and Baron Van Aerssen. Velvety diplomacy was missing when Dr Evatt met the Dutch envoys at the first United Nations Conference in San Francisco. Dr Evatt and the Dutch were soon trading uncomplimentary remarks in a dispute over trusteeship for colonial territories, fervently advocated by Dr Evatt for the NEI. The Dutch wouldn't have a bar of it. In Canberra relations between the Chifley-Evatt Government and the Netherlands Legation became glacial.

Separatism and Partnership Designs

Because the Indies-orientated Dutch, led by Dr Van Mook, had good grounds for suspecting that certain Australian leaders were would-be hijackers of their islands, they had to abandon ideas of a Batavia-Canberra partnership. Dr Van Mook represented *colon* cravings for more autonomy. The iron hold of the metropolitans would have to be broken, and fresh winds sent through colonial institutions. Dr Van Mook, as a former police functionary, had detected the lava of disaffection bubbling in Java; he knew the Dutch were smitten in their prestige, that they retained only the shadow of power and dwelled in a kind of no man's land between the Great Powers and an unpredictable Asia. Infusions of more Indonesian administrators and economic partnerships with the British, the Americans and the Australians would have to be accepted, in place of the old exclusivism retained since Dutch East India Company days. He could make little impression on the unamiable States-General, but found an occasional friend at The Hague.

The unrepaired paternalist Gerbrandy spoke bitterly of a force of Netherlands Indies officials "who did not envisage a new nation, based on a synthesis of East and West, as part of

250

the Kingdom. They aimed instead at the formation of an independent state which would be basically Eastern and independent of the rest of the Kingdom. They did not favour an integration of the Netherlands Indies with the Kingdom, but preached separation".[13]

The Dutch in Indonesia were not, as a rule, temporary residents, like the British in India, the African colonies, Malaya or the China concessions. Generation after generation of Hollanders had been born in the Indies. Not all the colonial-born were satisfied with their salaries or the heavy drain of wealth to Holland.

Dr Van Mook's cautious separatist probings found echoes in Holland among business groups more interested in the Indies markets than in the mystique of empire and among Dutch statesmen of Indies background. Professor Gerbrandy named as allies of Dr Van Mook in separatist designs Professor J.H.A. Logemann (Minister for Overseas Territories in liberated Holland; NEI service, 1921-39) and Dr J.A. Jonkman (successor to Professor Logemann, as Minister for Overseas Territories, 1946; NEI service, 1919-39).

The Chifley-Evatt Government and some members of the Opposition, like Mr Spender, moved toward the Van Mook camp, feeling that The Hague's inflexibilities would draw uncrossable lines between the Europeans generally and Indonesian nationalism. So did sectors of the Australian business community canvassing for new markets in Asia.

Dr Van Mook was prepared for closer cooperation between Australia and an Indies of limited liberalisation, freed from metropolitan dictates. He was, however, to identify Australian imperial calculations that prejudiced both colonial and metropolitan Dutch interest. After the warmth of his welcome in March 1942 Dr Van Mook was conscious of a cooling in relations. While the NEI Government-in-Exile had de facto authority from 1942, Dr Evatt stalled on official recognition, which was not awarded till 14 September 1944. Dr Evatt was doing quite a bit of arm-twisting for an Australian share in post-war Indonesia and Dr Van Mook became wary. Dr Evatt's reluctance to recognise the Van Mook emigre regime as the future government of Indonesia reflected power-sharing aims.

Dreams of empire exploded like a toy balloon in the firestorms that followed the fall of the Japanese Co-Prosperity Sphere. But they lasted long enough to prevent a partnership developing between Australian politicians keen on Indies economic opportunities and Dr Van Mook's colonial Dutch. Had the partnership evolved, the Chifley-Evatt Government would probably have evoked sanctions against the boycotters.

28 Boycott Therapy for National Neurosis

The Netherlands Indies Government's presence in the Wacol scrub, the mingling of restless Indonesian subjects with the Australian population and the boycott of Dutch shipping and other war services provoked confrontation and dialogue on an issue born of a political neurosis peculiar to White Australia.

The dogma, correlated with White Australia ideology and "our empty, undefended north" syndrome, that Australia could only be militarily secure if European colonial regimes remained in Asia, came under the first serious assault from defenders of the Indonesian Republic. They could not exorcise the demon altogether, for some leading statesmen remained possessed, but they provided evidence that Australians were beginning to acclimatise to an entirely new Asian environment.

Strategic interest in what later became known as "the island ramparts", "the umbrella", or "the Malay Barrier" of World War II — Singapore-Indies-North Australia — became apparent as soon as the original New South Wales colony was proved viable. Sir Stamford Raffles, seizing Java temporarily in the Napoleonic era and founding British Singapore, wanted Britain to possess the Indonesian islands to form an India-Malay-Australia defence triangle. The first garrisoned British settlements established in North Australia had the Dutch-ruled islands in focus. As Dutch power became dependent on British, defence understandings were reached between Batavia and Singapore.

The Netherlands East Indies were accorded a silent partnership in the Anglo-Australian strategic zone and "ramparts" status by speakers in the Australian national parliament. The white flags raised with much speed and little dignity by French, British, Dutch and Portuguese regimes in South-East Asia to Japanese forces should have entombed this faith in European regimes to guard Australia's empty north. For many politicians the ignominy of the French transfer, without warfare, of power to the Japanese in Indo-China, to prepare the area as a base for assault on Malaya-Singapore, the Netherlands Indies, Thailand, Burma and India, and the lightning conquest of South-East Asia, including Australian-ruled Rabaul, carried little corrective force. The dying twitches of the Dutch Empire in Java produced even more strident dedication to the "ramparts" theory. The theory lingered pervasively into the 1950s and 1960s when Holland tried to exclude Netherlands New Guinea from the territorial transfer to Indonesia and pursue a Katanga-type subversion of the Republic. In 1942 the Dutch had not thrown so much as a wooden shoe at the Japanese invading Hollandia nor broken a bottle of Bols gin to reduce the takeover of booty. Yet Australians were asked to believe by both Government and Opposition speakers that unless a tired regime of Hollanders, of notorious military incapacity, now badly concussed by their collision with the twentieth century, held the western half of New Guinea, they would be engulfed by Asia.

By no means all Australians, however, were wearing the old-cut clothing from off the White Australia peg. The climate of ideas changed between the Singapore-Indies collapse and the marshalling in Australian ports of the Dutch armada in 1945. A new consciousness of the misery and mayhem of Asia and the refusal of Asian peoples to take arms in defence of colonial regimes was born. Australian foreign policy was, painfully and belatedly, acquiring a sense of ecology and an adult vocabulary. To these dramatic shifts of course the Dutch and Indonesian wartime influx, the trade union boycotts of the Dutch and the width of public sympathy for pro-Republican action contributed. But the still formidable groupings of traditionalists could not shake off the fantasies of imperial rebirth, nor their indifference to Asian sufferings.

Asia should retain pukka sahibs and tuan besars, rickshas and rice-bowls.

A favourite theme of the traditionalists was that if the Indonesians won independence peoples in British, Australian and other colonies of the Near North would also demand freedom and thus the "ramparts" would be totally demolished. The domino theory was popular in Australia long before Washington posed it as a justification for the Vietnam intervention. The well known World War I Commander-in-Chief of Australian forces in France, General Sir John Monash, told the Constitutional Club in Melbourne in 1931 that "if India left the Empire it would be goodbye to Australia, because it would mean that we would have a potential enemy on our trade route".[1]

"A Very Lonely Country"

Mr Menzies was the chief exponent of the domino theory. He warned immediately the boycott began that if Australia supported the expulsion of the Dutch and other "friends here and there" then "we shall be a very lonely country".[2] The White Australia policy itself was at stake, in Mr Menzies' view. He saw dangerous precedent in Dr Evatt's acceptance of the Indonesian request to place the Dutch Army's First Police Action on the UN Security Council agenda. Chapter VI of the UN Charter (the "domestic clause") made the internal affairs of any country the business of that country. That clause, Mr Menzies submitted, was "designed to safeguard Australia's right to maintain the White Australia policy". He commended Dr Evatt for his fight at San Francisco to have the White Australia policy protected by the UN Charter against outside intervention.

Mr Menzies contended that both Dutch rule over the Indies and the White Australia policy were protected by the Charter's "domestic clause" — an invitation to a layman to tell the constitutional lawyer and King's Counsel that the UN Charter was not as bendable as all that. The Dutch-Indonesian dispute, Mr Menzies added, was "entirely internal". It was "a matter between the Dutch, who have been in the Netherlands East Indies for 350 years, and a great number of Indonesians who are loyal to them, on the one hand, and a certain number of

Indonesians who are in rebellion against them, on the other hand".

Mr Menzies blamed "a handful of malcontents on the Australian waterfront" as the influence behind the Chifley-Evatt Government's intervention at the United Nations "in a problem of domestic jurisdiction in the Netherlands East Indies". Included in this considered 1947 Menzies statement on the Dutch-Indonesian dispute and Australia's role were these premonitory rumblings:

> The day will come when we will regret that we have succeeded. The day will come when some ingenious theorist in some other country will say, "Ah, there is the White Australia policy!" or perhaps he will refer to the way Australia is treating the natives of Papua or New Guinea and the problem will be taken to the Security Council . . . .[3]

"A Few Skunks . . . ."

The national political neurosis, spawned of the White Australia policy, the spectre of the brown flood breaking through the dykes if the Dutch finger was pulled out, no doubt contributed to the divisions, vacillations and contradictions within the Labor Party and the ACTU and to the violence of Liberal-Country Party epithets thrown at the boycotters in black armada years.

The steam had not stopped hissing from the boilers of the first boycotted Dutch ships in the Brisbane River before Opposition Leader Menzies threw down the gauntlet to the Chifley-Evatt Government on control of foreign policy. Unhindered direction of foreign policy by the government in power was fundamental to Mr Menzies' philosophy. Ever since Port Kembla watersiders boycotted pig-iron manifested for Japan in 1938-39, Mr Menzies had insisted that he would not tolerate "trade union dictation' of foreign policy.

On 25 September 1945, the day after the Brisbane walk-off from Dutch ships, Mr Menzies moved the adjournment of the House of Representatives to censure the Labor Government. He described the boycott as the "impudent attempt by Communists in the Waterside Workers' Federation to intervene in the domestic affairs of a foreign country, namely, the Netherlands East Indies", and went on:

In the last 24 hours insult has been added to injury by the fact that the Waterside Workers' Federation, Communist-led, has decided, as it did on a prior occasion, to intervene in foreign policy. It has now undertaken to see that certain Dutch ships shall not be loaded for transport to the Netherlands East Indies unless forsooth, the men on the waterfront are given a guarantee that the goods are used by a so-called "People's Government", which is a revolutionary movement in the Netherlands Indies operated and controlled by a man who was the puppet Premier of the country under Japanese rule, the one man who was the Quisling of Java.[4]

Next day Mr Menzies challenged the Chifley-Evatt Government to decide whether it recognised Dutch rule or the revolutionary Indonesian Government: "The Australian Government must settle that point. It cannot leave it to the Waterside Workers' Federation in Sydney".[5] To a meeting of the Liberal Party in Brighton Town Hall, Melbourne, late in February 1946, Mr Menzies branded the anti-Dutch and pro-Indonesian boycotts in Australia as the work of "a few skunks on the waterfront".[6] The wharfies, seasoned in combat with Mr Menzies, bore up under this latest intemperance with their customary fortitude.

A week later Mr Menzies' hauteur might have been too much even for Dr Van Mook, busy promising Indonesians he would take large numbers of them into the postwar administration. The Opposition Leader unwittingly placed Dutch colonial education policy in a worse light than it deserved. Assailing those who advocated self-government for Indonesians — an "extraordinarily false" doctrine — Mr Menzies said:

It acts on the assumption that all these people are fit for self-government . . . the truth is that in the Netherlands East Indies those who, by reason of intellectual development, are fit to cope with the democratic instrument

257

could probably be numbered by hundreds, certainly not by millions.[7]

The policy of "driving the white man out of the Netherlands East Indies" and out of Asia generally was, Mr Menzies declared, "what a great commentator once described as the very ecstacy of suicide . . . ."[8] He seemed as sure as the millenarians prone to paint "Eternity" signs at hazardous hairpin bends on mountain roads that the end was near — unless Dutch tuans and British sahibs stayed on as our friendly neighbourhood frontier guards. The doctrine which some people, including the waterside workers, thought good enough to justify the eviction of the Dutch with the assistance of Australia, he said, would "completely justify the eviction of the British from India, Burma and the Malay Peninsula. When we have, in this absurd frenzy, cleared our powerful friends out of places that are vital to us, Australia will know all about isolation. I hope this time will never come".[9]

"The Very Existence of Australia . . ."

Mr William Morris Hughes, the Prime Minister who represented Australia at the Peace Conference following Germany's surrender in World War I and obtained the mandate over ex-German New Guinea and Buka and Bougainville in the Solomon Islands, was usually awarded oracular status when he spoke of the "ramparts". At Versailles in 1919 he had demanded that "the world should at least see that those islands which lie like ramparts along our coast should not be in the hands of an actual or potential enemy". The 1945 proclamation of the Indonesian Republic led him to declare that the Netherlands Indies islands were "just as much bastions of Australia as New Guinea itself. Those who hold Java and Sumatra occupy a position which holds the free people of Australia to existence on sufferance".[10]

Mr Hughes was a Labor Prime Minister before he crossed to the conservatives in World War I, and, early in the century, had been President of the Waterside Workers' Federation and one of its founders. When Indonesian independence was mentioned no trace of his union background surfaced. His rejection of rights for Asians was enough to give the lady who inquired why the breadless mob couldn't eat cake a reformist colouration. Mr Hughes told Parliament that the people of Indonesia had "no greater right to govern themselves than the Aborigines of Australia". "Where are the Aborigines now?" Mr Hughes asked. "One has to go to the far distant parts of Australia even to see one. We have settled their pretensions to self-government." Like Mr Menzies he was fiercely opposed to handing over "vital outposts of our country to the natives who, without training, experience or aptitude for self-government, are demanding the right to govern themselves".[11] By 1952 Mr Hughes was advocating military action to support Dutch retention of West New Guinea — an islands zone "vital to the very existence of Australia".[12]

Former External Affairs Minister Spender — created Sir Percival Spender in 1952 — paraded the national neurosis before the UN General Assembly on 24 November 1954. As leader of the Australian UN delegation, backing the Dutch effort to hold on to West New Guinea, Sir Percival said: "New Guinea has been shown to present the very key to Australia's defence".[13]

Sir Percy's successor as External Affairs Minister, Mr R.G. Casey, added a little cold war jargon: "the major threat to Australian security is the southward movement of Communism, and the Dutch administration in West New Guinea is the best guarantee of its exclusion from the area".[14] This nightmarish stuff was bi-partisan. Dr Evatt, Leader of the Opposition, thought, like the Liberals, that "the defence of New Guinea is really integral to the defence of Australia".[15]

Deputy Opposition Leader Calwell's sudden anti-Indonesian hysteria puzzled Mr Menzies. He had accused Mr Calwell, as Minister for Immigration in 1949, of "a scream of undiluted hatred against the Dutch". Mr Calwell's theme, according to Mr Menzies, was: "I hate the Dutch, I hate the Dutch, I hate the Dutch."[16] In a year the last Dutch pro-consuls, trying to rule the Melanesian remnant of their empire, in between sipping gin pahits in the palatial residence built at Hollandia for General MacArthur, and shouting orders to servants above the music of a splashing courtyard

259

fountain, became our saviours from "the hordes". Mr Calwell said:

> Any Government that did not immediately indicate to the Javanese that if they intended to walk into Dutch New Guinea we shall walk in before them does not deserve to last five minutes.[17]

Outbidding Mr Menzies in apocalyptic oratory he added:

> If we allow the Indonesians into Dutch New Guinea there will be no hope of holding the northern portion of Australia and the fate of this country will be sealed and certain.[18]

Mr Calwell made our fate "sealed and certain" again in a 1958 speech. The Indonesians made the Dutch colony Irian Barat in 1962 and neglected to relieve him of the mantle of false prophet.

The neurosis was of such deep seepage into ALP ranks that the more progressive Dr J.F. Cairns (elected Deputy Prime Minister in 1974) endorsed the Calwell campaign. Dr Cairns protested against limited US supplies of arms to Indonesia in 1960 in terms that drove the conservative Country Party Leader and Deputy Prime Minister, Mr John McEwen, to rebuke him. Mr McEwen rejected the hysterical anti-Indonesian campaign. He told Dr Cairns that it was not Government policy "to pick a quarrel and become bad friends with a great populous country which it is our destiny to live beside forever". The Indonesian Government as the constituted power in the country, was "entitled to cast around to equip itself to handle an internal situation".[19]

A study of the Australian attitude to its own New Guinea island "ramparts" in 1942, what were called "the umbrella" by Mr Hughes at Versailles in 1919 and "the very key to Australia's defence" during the Indonesian dispute, might make the national neurosis label inadequate. Defence of "the very key" was not seriously considered until after Pearl Harbour. Panic reinforcements by small air and military forces, many of them not properly trained or hardly trained at all, endangered men without offering protection of Australia.

When the Japanese struck, poorly equipped and small garrisons, like that at Rabaul, New Britain, suffered massacre and torture. Australia's New Guinea colonials behaved no differently to the Dutch in the Indies. They did not consider themselves defenders of island ramparts, and most of them fled to Australia, along with the Dutch.

Mr J.V. Barry, King's Counsel (later Mr Justice Barry of the Victorian Supreme Court) was appointed by the Curtin Labor Government in 1944 to investigate the collapse — the pre-invasion collapse — of Australian administration in Papua. The flight from the Mandated Territory above Papua, former German New Guinea, apparently did not bear investigation. "Repeated attempts in Parliament to obtain an investigation were not fruitful," said Dr W.E.H. Stanner, then Reader in Comparative History, Australian National University, Canberra. He referred to "the almost holus-bolus abandonment of the Mandated Territory". Dr Stanner, in reviewing the Barry Report said:

There was rapid administrative disintegration . . . . In Papua civil government came to an end in somewhat confused circumstances on 14 February. On the next day the Administrator and members of Legislative Council left for Australia by flying-boat at the direction of the Military Commandant.[20]

The date — 14 February — of the administrative collapse in Port Moresby, Papuan capital, has some significance. Singapore surrendered on 15 February; the end came in Java on 7 March; the Japanese did not start moving up the Buna track to Kokoda, aiming for Port Moresby, until about 22 July; they reached the limit of their drive down the Kokoda Trail, 40 miles from Port Moresby, on 14 September, and were defeated by the Australian Army.

It was not because of the white man's presence in any South-East Asian area, including New Guinea, that the Japanese were stopped. Everywhere, colonial regimes collapsed ignominiously, and the easily conquered colonies became stepping stones for attack on Australia. Invasion did not take place because the Japanese grossly over-reached themselves and American naval, military and air forces arrived in great strength to support the beleaguered Australians.

By the time the West New Guinea crisis broke the development of long range missiles had changed "Asian hordes" paranoia to political infantilism and demolished the claim that Australia's fate hinged on a thin garrison under the House of Orange tricolour at Hollandia. Led by officers and some veterans of 1942 who had been unable to crush guerilla bands in Java, glory at the cannon's mouth was eschewed in favour of an arranged evacuation to Broome.

Mr Edward Gough Whitlam was one of the select minority who tried to pose rationality against neurosis. Two years before he became Deputy Leader of the Opposition, restively under Mr Calwell's leadership, Mr Whitlam told a 1958 seminar in Canberra:

> Strategically, it is maintained, it is necessary for us or some like-minded power to occupy West New Guinea in order that we may be safe in any future war. No one has pointed out, however, that Indonesia already occupies the islands between West New Guinea and Arnhem Land in Northern Australia, namely, the Kai, Tanimbar and Aru Islands which during the last war were used by the Japanese as a base for operations against Australia. The fact that they are at present in Indonesian hands must bring second thoughts to those who say that Indonesia must at all costs be excluded from West New Guinea.[21]

Had Mr Chifley lived the ALP forces represented by Mr Whitlam might have gone a long way toward submerging the national neurosis. In his first parliamentary session as Opposition Leader in 1950 Mr Chifley vainly tried to clip the wings of his party hawks:

> It has been said that the Government of the United States of Indonesia desires to possess Dutch New Guinea. That, surely, is a matter for the Indonesians and Dutch to settle.[22]

Mr Calwell on the same day called for a pre-emptive strike in West New Guinea. His addictive reliance on the white man's solidarity against Asia continued right into 1962, the year of decision. He presumed that if Australia and Holland fought the Indonesian Republic — the latter solidly supported by Afro-Asian and socialist nations and supplied with modern arms by the Soviet Government — the two most powerful white powers would be compelled to extricate Australia from the bloody mess. Mr Calwell said:

> Only if Britain and the United States consider us expend-able could they refuse to agree to our point of view and that I do not believe for a moment. This is a moment in our history when bold and decisive action is not only the proper course but the safe course . . . We shall not be left alone, for, if we are, then friendship is a mockery and the principles of international law are mere shibbo-leths.[23]

But Australia was left alone. Australia, Mr Whitlam said, had failed to realise "how isolated we are internationally on this issue".[24]

Mr Menzies at last began to sense the claustrophobic isolation. The British and Americans were now arming the Indonesian Republic and had lost interest in the overblown Dutch military establishment at Hollandia. Mr Menzies conceded that though Australia recognised Dutch sovereignty "every nation in Asia supports the Indonesian claim".[25] The Hague, in disabling diplomatic purdah, signed on 15 August 1962 the United Nations Agreement to transfer Netherlands New Guinea to Indonesia as Irian Barat. Faced with growing revolt in his own party Mr Calwell disengaged. The Australian people, he lamented, did not want war with Indonesia. The black armada period should have reminded him earlier of this. He cast aside the new tablets of international law he had inscribed to fit the Irian case, and made mockery of his plan to send marching from Eastern New Guinea across an un-surveyed frontier a conquering army bearing the armorial bearings of the kangaroo and emu by saying that Australia had "nothing to fight a war with".[26]

The flag of Papua Barat, woven of Dutch cloth and cere-moniously run up on 1 December 1961, was hauled down — the briefest life for any emblem in the history of colonial heraldry in Asia. Indonesians who marched in to acquire the last rags and ruin of the Dutch Empire of the East failed to feed the national neurosis by spreading the moth-wing sails of their praus to the monsoon *bara*, blowing down to North Australia, just as the French arquebusiers confounded the prophets of doom by neglecting to tramp up the Dover Road when Mary Tudor lost Calais.

29 Dirty Tricks Under the American Umbrella

Mr Menzies' sweeping election victory in December 1949 coincided with transfer of sovereignty to the "United States of Indonesia" under The Hague Agreement. The Dutch were supposed to begin a leisurely folding of tents in South-East Asia. The Australian Government did not want them to hurry the issue of demob suits.

European reductions of strength in Asia inspired the old mechanical metaphors. Not able to read, as did the British Raj, the signal from Congress, Muslim and Communist flags fluttering side by side in the 1946 Bombay naval mutiny, Mr Menzies was "surprised and dismayed"[1] at the Mountbatten award of independence to India and Pakistan. Canberra exerted all possible influence for the maintenance of white garrisons in the "United States of Indonesia" and in Singapore-Malaya. By 1955 Australian Army and Air Force units were stationed in Singapore-Malaya, with a naval presence also. Well before this a restorationist coup in Indonesia had been placed on the agenda by several foreign governments.

The return of white soldiers to the scenes of recent military humiliations could not hide the symptoms of decline and fall. Uncertainties over the Anglo-European future in Asia weakened London's gravitational pull in Australian foreign policy. Like Labor Prime Minister Curtin after Japanese bombers dashed hopes that the British Navy would guard our shores by sinking the battleships *Prince of Wales* and *Repulse* off Singapore in December 1941, Mr Menzies quieted pangs of kinship — more acute than those of Mr Curtin — and solicited an alternate "umbrella" from the United States. It was no longer the America of Franklin D. Roosevelt and Henry Wallace but of the Truman Doctrine and John Foster Dulles' brinkmanship, designed in part to salvage the imperial stake in Asia.

Reorientation was patent in the Menzies Government's inaugural foreign policy statement to Parliament in March 1950, delivered by External Affairs Minister Spender. Mr Spender recognised that Australia's and Britain's old positions in relation to Asia had gone, following independence for India, Pakistan, Ceylon and Indonesia, the emergence of Communist China and of nationalist movements in other areas. He forecast a pact with the United States and "a common military effort".

Mr Spender outlined as a major objective the build-up between Australia and the United States of "somewhat the same relationship as exists within the British Commonwealth".[2] In June 1950 he foreshadowed Australian partnership with America — without Britain — in a Pacific Pact. This Pacific Pact would be of great importance to "the stability of the area in which we are geographically placed".[3] "Stability" had the old "restoring law and order" ring.

The Menzies Government was not sparing in its demonstrations of anxiety to acquire from America a stouter shield than the British, French, Dutch and Portuguese had offered. It was not intended to hover in any borderland between British and American empires. Mr Menzies offered obeisance to Washington policies without reservation: "The benevolent commands of a great empire are good for mankind. If that is American imperialism, let us have more of it".[4] National independence was becoming a seditious foreign doctrine: the Menzies Government's Minister for the Interior, Mr Wilfrid S. Kent Hughes, spurned it. "Australia," he said, "must become the 49th State of America".[5] The same willingness to serve Amerca was expressed by later Prime Ministers in such declarations as "All the way with L.B.J.", "Where you go we will go" and "We'll go waltzing Matilda with you". The American "umbrella" was sought as an alternative to cooperation with Asian nationalism.

Mr Calwell got in before the Menzies Government in rejecting cooperation with independent Indonesia in favour of the American "umbrella", with perhaps some resplicing of the unravelling link with Britain. Soon after the new Parliament assembled in 1950, with the ALP on the Opposition benches again, Mr Calwell said:

> I do not believe we can cooperate with such people in any matter concerning the safety of this country. The only way to ensure our safety is to make sure our relationships with the British and American Governments are sound.[6]

The ANZUS (Australia, New Zealand, United States) Treaty was signed at San Francisco on 1 September 1951 and John Foster Dulles also had Australia's signature on his Japanese Peace Treaty in the same month. Neither were pleasing to the British, serving notice as they did of the switch of allegiance. The British were admitted in 1954 at Manila as co-junior partners with Australia in Mr Dulles' South-East Asia Treaty Organisation (SEATO).

Dirty Tricks in Indonesia

The Indonesian Republic's takeover of 3,000 odd islands — 7,000 odd if uninhabited islets are included — traditionally regarded in Australia as "ramparts" or the "umbrella" was a vital influence in Canberra's swing from Britain to America. The "umbrella" had proved as useful as Sherlock Holmes' dog that did not bark, but the Menzies Government could not rid itself of old fixations. And so, aiming to reverse the irreversible, Canberra collaborated with the Americans, Dutch and British in conspiracies for overthrow of the Indonesian Republic.

The ramshackle federal system called the "United States of Indonesia" to which qualified sovereignty was transferred under The Hague Agreement was vulnerable to separatist plottings. The unreconstructed colonialists promptly embarked on operations designed to disintegrate the "United States of Indonesia". Captain Paul (Turco) Westerling, Dutch officer trained by the British in commando tactics and much else, transferred to the Netherlands Indies Army and early in 1950 launched a bloody expedition. With an army of Dutch officers and soldiers, police inspectors and Indonesian mercenaries Westerling entered Bandung on 23 January 1950. Massacre, arson and looting ensued. Then Westerling's agents infiltrated Djakarta. Popular resistance was strong and Westerling found it convenient to flee to Singapore in a Dutch aircraft. The British and Dutch refused Indonesian extradition demands.

In the Celebes-Moluccas archipelagos the colonialists' restoration efforts made more headway. Dutch officers seized Macassar, with the aid of Ambonese. The Indonesians claimed 40,000 died in the massacre. A Dutch officer was flown to Ambon to assist in organising a breakaway from the Republic. When the rebel flag of the "Republic of South Moluccas" was hoisted over the Royal Netherlands Indies Army barracks, a Dutch colonel in uniform took a leading part in the ceremonies.

The Indonesians organised counter-strikes with difficulty, due to the continued presence of the well-armed Dutch and chaotic transport. However, Indonesian troops recaptured Macassar on 21 April 1950. The federal system, of which Dr Van Mook had been chief architect, was falling to pieces and the Republic was consolidating a central authority.

The breakaway "Republic of South Moluccas" remained a thorn in the Indonesians' side. Many Ambonese were still of Hessian mentality, and feudal survivals in this zone were strong. The Australian Intelligence and Security Services were proven guilty of aid and comfort to the colonial puppet regime of the South Moluccas. The full extent of Australian dirty tricks against the Indonesian Republic would still be hidden in a jungle of classified files: it was only by the accident of a conscientious Australian Government quarantine officer's discoveries that a corner of the curtain was lifted on illegal gun-running from Darwin to the "Republic of South Moluccas".

"Stick to the Fishing Story"

Before a court of the Commonwealth-ruled Northern Territory in 1952, William Edwards, master of the forty-foot Darwin vessel *Tiki*, pleaded guilty to having misled a quarantine officer about a voyage of the *Tiki* to the South Moluccas and back to Darwin. Edwards was acquitted, though regulations governing visitors from areas where certain contagious diseases are often endemic are customarily enforced strictly.

Evidence in court showed that the *Tiki* left Darwin on 30 January 1952 with seven persons aboard and returned on 14 February. One of the seven was Peter Lokollo, who said he was Minister for Food and Supply in the rebel "Republican Government of the South Moluccas". Lokollo, according to witnesses in the Darwin court, said that he was making this trip via Darwin to contact his "government" on the island of Ceram. (Ceram is a large island, about a thousand kilometres north of Darwin, past Tanimbar, the Bandas and Ambon and adjacent to Netherlands New Guinea as it then was, where the Dutch had naval, air and military bases). Captain Edwards took Lokollo to Masool, 50 kilometres from Ceram. At Masool he was told by the Dutch not to go to Ceram because it was heavily patrolled by Indonesian ships and aircraft.

The *Sydney Morning Herald* report of the Darwin court case began:

> Army and Navy Intelligence officers in Darwin and the Security Service had full knowledge of the voyage of the Darwin vessel *Tiki* to Masool Island before the trip started, it was alleged in the Northern Territory Supreme Court today.[7]

Edwards, according to the *Herald* report of the case, said a man named Merelovitch approached him about making a trip in the *Tiki*. "The story sounded a bit funny at the beginning . . ." said Edwards. "I contacted Mr Charles Mooney of the Security Department". Edwards added that he later had discussions with Mooney and Lieutenant Eric Einhuus, of Army Headquarters, Darwin. At another conference before the *Tiki* sailed, Lieutenant Einhuus of the Army was again present with a Lieutenant-Commander J. Toulouse of the Navy. On his return to Darwin Edwards had further talks with Lieutenant Einhuus. Edwards testified that when he asked Einhuus whether he should tell people where he had been Einhuus replied, "Definitely not. Don't tell anyone around here the whereabouts of your trip. Stick to the fishing story".[8]

The "fishing story" was that Edwards had been on a fishing expedition to the Wessel Islands off the North Australian coast and had not been out of Australian waters. There was good reason for the "fishing story", related to Commonwealth authorities' desire to avoid publicity: anyone going outside Australian waters comes under quarantine and customs laws and must make due declarations. Edwards told Dr Alfred H. Humphrey, Quarantine Officer, clearly a dedicated guardian of health, who smelt something other than fish. Dr Humphrey initiated prosecution of Edwards for contravention of Commonwealth quarantine regulations. The press report included these intriguing revelations:

> Edwards said in evidence that police helped him secure small arms to take on the trip. He said he had discussed the trip with members of the Security Service.
>
> Mr Justice Kriewaldt ruled that details of discussions with Security officials would not be admissable as evidence.[9]

Before the *Tiki* affair came before the Supreme Court in Darwin, External Affairs Minister Casey stated that he had informed the Indonesian Government that the *Tiki* voyage was "unauthorised".[10] If this gun-running to a "government" in treasonable revolt against an Indonesian Government with which Australia had diplomatic relations was "unauthorised", surely the External Affairs Minister should have insisted on an inquiry into charges that the Commonwealth-controlled Security Service, Northern Territory Police and Army and Navy Intelligence officers had collaborated in arms supply to the South Moluccas "Republic"? Evidence would have been readily available: journalists and others in Darwin knew all about the *Tiki* expedition. Some local interest was aroused when two Ambonese, flown to Darwin via Sydney, stayed at the Hotel Darwin, not celebrated for red-carpet welcomes to non-whites. Arms were loaded into the *Tiki* at Doctor's Gully beach. A lively party — girls, grog and all — was organised nearby to divert attention from the stevedoring of .303 rifles and other small arms. One Northern Territory police executive, not taken into Security's confidence, acted on a tip-off about illicit arms-running out of Darwin and had a bomber sent out, under a standing arrangement between police and Air Force, to search for the law-breaking craft. But visibility was too poor over the Timor Sea, as in the External Affairs Department at Canberra.

Australian contacts with the South Moluccas rebels appear to have been maintained after the exposure of gun-running from Darwin in 1952. Leslie H. Palmier, who wrote under the auspices of the Institute of Race Relations, London, related that in November 1954 a revival of rebel activity in the South Moluccas was reported and that "the insurgents had been making several attempts to obtain arms from Australia".[11] Leaders of the "Republic of South Moluccas" were tried and imprisoned in March 1955.

Australia's Role in 1958 Rebellion

U.S. State Secretary John Foster Dulles, to a 1954 Senate Committee session in Washington, listed Indonesia among the South East Asian countries he considered in danger of "subversion". The task of meeting the threat of subversion, he said, "will tax our resources and ingenuity to the utmost". Subversion had been dealt with in the SEATO Treaty "more specifically than we have in any other treaty".[12] Naturally, "subversion" in Indonesia did not come from those taking up arms against the Republic.

A SEATO "anti-subversion school" was set up in the Philippines, for exchange of intelligence, "analysis and exchange of operational techniques for combating subversion on a multilateral basis". Dr Kerry Young, an American chronicler of SEATO activities, said that SEATO Pact members "agreed to periodic but discreet meetings" to work out the plans for combating subversion on a multilateral basis. "The nature of the threat of subversion and of United States policy problems resulting from the threat may be illustrated by the present situations in Indonesia, Singapore, Laos and Thailand."[13]

Australia, as a SEATO member, participated in this "anti-subversion" activities, which were certainly on a multilateral basis when they were directed against the Indonesian Republic in 1958. The full story of Australian involvement in the 1958 "Permesta" rebellion remains untold. There were uprisings against the Republic in East Indonesia and Sumatra, where the "Revolutionary Government of the Indonesian

Republic" was proclaimed. As Dr George Modeleski showed in studies of SEATO activities, published under the auspices of the Australian National University in 1962, "Permesta" rebels against the Indonesian Republic sent emissaries to a SEATO Council meeting in Manila, seeking aid and de facto recognition, and pledging support to SEATO objectives.[14]

American pilots bombed Indonesia from what were in fact SEATO air bases in the Philippines. This could not be denied, for one of them was brought down, captured and tried by the Republic. Mr Casey flatly denied that SEATO played any role in the 1958 insurrection. "Any attempt to connect SEATO in any way with the present occurrences in Indonesia is foolish," he said.[15]

Britain, second most important SEATO member, did not hesitate to intervene on behalf of the "Permesta" rebels — an intervention costly in Indonesian blood and treasure. Dr Justus Van Der Kroef, Visiting Professor, South-East Asian Studies, Nanyang University, Singapore, not usually noted for sympathy to the Republic, gave a reminder in 1963 that Indonesian Army commanders who fought the prolonged campaign against the "Revolutionary Government of the Indonesian Republic" in Sumatra "cannot forget that Malaya and Singapore, notwithstanding Indonesian protests, provided important sources of supply as well as sanctuary to rebel leaders . . .".[16]

As the junior partner of Britain in the military, air and naval garrisoning of Singapore-Malaya — still colonially controlled — the Menzies Government must have been consulted and in agreement with use of the area as an operational base for an armed attack on the Indonesian Republic. Australian assistance to the rebels would have been consistent with Menzies Government policy. Certainly, the Indonesian Government was in no doubt that Australia was aiding the rebellion of 1958. One Indonesian charge was that the RAAF was dropping arms to the rebels from the air. The Minister for Air, Mr F.M. Osborne, denied the report.[17]

Labor Opposition Leader Evatt referred in 1958 to Indonesian charges, quoted by Radio Australia, that "Australians are taking an active part in fomenting rebellion". Dr Evatt expressed concern for the safety of Australian citizens in Indonesia. External Affairs Minister Casey estimated that there were only 280 to 290 Australians in Indonesia, of whom about 17 were in the Sumatran war zone. There had been no action of any sort against Australian citizens or Australian property since the troubles began, he said.[18]

Before Mr Casey left for a SEATO conference in March 1958, Dr Evatt proposed that Australia should seek United Nations intervention to end fighting in the Indonesian rebellion. UN intervention in 1958 conditions could have only prejudiced the right of the Republic to suppress a foreign-inspired and foreign-armed counter-revolution.

Two leading Australian newspaper correspondents, James Mossman *(Sydney Morning Herald)* and Denis Warner, writing for leading Sydney and Melbourne dailies, were received at rebel headquarters in Sumatra, suggesting that the rebels had no cause for grievance against Australia. In influential Canberra circles at this stage there was a willingness to go to war with the Indonesian Republic if it tried to expel the Dutch from West New Guinea. This was not calculated to engender a pacifist neutrality in the 1958 counter-revolution. The deep secrecy with which the Menzies Government surrounded the activities of its armed services agencies in Malaya-Singapore during the rebellion and the vehemence of its denials of intervention were signs of official recognition that the reservior of popular goodwill for the Indonesian Republic had not altogether dried up since black armada days.

The depth of secrecy that covered Australia's dirty tricks in Indonesia before the coup of September-October 1965 is shallowing. Washington is much kinder to chroniclers of these dirty tricks than Canberra. Evan Whitton, Assistant Editor of the *National Times,* in his series of articles on the history and causes of the Vietnam war, opened up the question of a "trade' being sought by the Menzies Government, of which Sir Paul Hasluck, later Governor-General of Australia, was then (1964-65) External Affairs Minister, under which Australian troops should extend the military intervention in Vietnam and America should intervene militarily against the Indonesian Republic. Quoting official Washington sources claimed to be unimpeachable, Evan Whitton records meetings between the Australian Ambassador, Sir Keith Waller, and Presidential Adviser William McGeorge Bundy, Assistant Secretary of State for East Asian and Pacific Affairs, in Washington. On 21 January 1965 Mr Bundy seemed to have got the idea that the Australian Ambassador was "suggesting that the US might like to consider taking an active role in Indonesia, as they were in South Vietnam". The Australian Ambassador proposed "a joint examination of the South Vietnam and Indonesian-Malaysia situation".

Evan Whitton concluded that "there seemed to be just a hint that Australia's leading officials were suggesting that the US might care to embroil itself in Indonesia (in which case, no doubt, it would have meant in due course total mobilisation for Australia, rather than a battalion). But the thought of working a trade-off with the US on Vietnam in return for US force in Indonesia was not a new issue".[19] There had been previous discussions.

Providentially, Washington at this stage was not so addicted to hallucinogenic tripping into spice-laden trade winds as Canberra. It would be coming down too heavily on the side of charity to describe as irresponsible the mere thought of a second Vietnam in Indonesia, with Australians fighting alongside Americans and British over much more formidable terrain. Oceans and frontiers separated the invaders' homelands from Indo-China, placing them beyond reach of Vietnamese retaliation. The Indonesian archipeligo could not be invaded to loud-hailer slogans like "Better to stop them there than here". Australia and Indonesia had a common frontier in New Guinea, with virtually no troops in the Australian half. For Indonesian commandos the Kai, Tanimbar and Aru Islands between New Guinea and undefended North Australia were a short monsoon-ride distant. Little wonder the *National Times* writer talked of "total mobilisation".

The unshrouding of the noisome remains of Canberra's dottily conceived anti-Indonesian conspiracies of 1950-65 had only just begun.

30 Boycott Forced Debate on New Policies toward Asia

Some of Mr Chifley's speeches explaining or defending the trade unions' boycott of Dutch ships were harbingers of dramatic policy readjustments impelled by the crisis facing colonial empires in Asia. The black armada persuaded Australian Government leaders into the first rational definitions of the policy changes forced on Australia by the Asian nationalist revolutions.

Before the advent of the Indonesian Republic the right of Asians to independence had never been officially recognised. An Australian Government had never been in direct conflict with Britain in the diplomatic arena. The Dutch-Indonesian dispute was also to evoke Canberra's first significant difference with Washington, the new senior patron.

Australia had been the land of the faithful ditto. Its troops were willingly offered to sustain the imperial interest against challenge — in the Sudan, in China's Boxer Rebellion, in the Boer War and, by seconding Australian officers to British forces, in India and the Chinese treaty ports. Mr Chifley did not lead a Government of anti-colonialists: this was made very clear in the outbursts of some of his ex-Ministers in the Dutch cause during the confrontation over West New Guinea. The Chifley Government's tolerance of illegal boycott and mutiny against a colonial ally in 1945-49 was born of a realisation that the old order in South-East Asia was beyond recall. Guarantees from the British naval base at Singapore proved much less than copper-bottomed and the guardians of the Indies "ramparts" became the "Flying Dutchmen" of 1942.

To Mr Thomas White, a Minister in the first and second Menzies Governments, the boycott of Dutch ships was "this infamy" and to Mr M.F. Bruxner, Country Party Leader in NSW, anti-Dutch demonstrators were "miserable, noisy, useless curs and mongrels". Mr Menzies had given the cue for this all-stops-out tirade against the boycotters by his finding that they comprised "a few skunks on the waterfront". To Mr Chifley, on the other hand, the waterfront boycott and the wide public sympathy and responses it aroused were the opportunity to bring into the realm of practical politics an acceptance of the new governments of national independence in Asia. It should be underscored, however, that the Prime Minister did not have to make up his mind suddenly on 24 September 1945 – the day the trade union bans first applied to Dutch ships in Brisbane – on the need to chart new courses in foreign policy. The arrival in Australia of the Netherlands Indies administration and its armed forces leaders and thousands of Indonesian subjects had given Mr Chifley and other Cabinet Ministers their first intimate contact with the men who ruled and with the resentments of the ruled. The Dutch colonials, almost tone-deaf to the raised voice of Asia, made an unwitting contribution to the cause of their Indonesian and Australian enemies: they helped to persuade Mr Chifley and some of his Ministers that the system which produced them must lack social health. To these Ministers and many others who met them the title, "colonial Dutch", was soon one of denigration.

The Netherlands Indies establishment arrived in 1942 with built-in weaknesses. The legend of benevolent and enlightened Dutch colonial rule, though it employed many artisans, was inclined to be fragile in any country inheriting the English language. The Dutch image was wantonly disfigured in bygone days at the hands of English commerical rivals of great sophistication in reducing the repute of continentals interfering with their interests. The Hollanders, for long superior in navigational and marketing skills, had been "masters of the sea wide and large" as King James I called them, and such formidable maritime opponents that "Dutch" qualified for dirty word status in English conversation. If a mouse when sober and a lion when drunk, that was "Dutch courage". Too mean to buy a friend a drink and preferring to pay only for oneself: "a Dutch treat". Gibberish was "double Dutch". Unpopular: "in Dutch". "That's right or I'm a Dutchman", meaning a fool. The proverbial "Dutch uncle" was harshly paternalist. When the writer tossed sweatily in Singapore's equatorial nights he had for company the standard long pillow. The English called the long pillow "a Dutch wife" — dumb and sexless. They conceded that the Dutch ladies were capable of sex by calling a contraceptive device "a Dutch cap".

The Dutch image might be lacquered over in the expediencies of wartime alliance, but the covering began to peel when the colonial Dutch in Australia rejected any idea that this was the world of freedom charters and not of Cornelius Van Houtman's cannonades. Mr Chifley, Dr Evatt, Lords Mountbatten, Killearn and Inverchapel all advised in varying emphasis the very elementary line laid down by Lawrence of Arabia — that half a calamity is better than a whole one. Most of the Dutch favoured no half-way descent from the heights of imperial power.

Rebukes to the Dutch

Instead of recognising wisdom derived from experience in the Australian trade union movement and the whirl of Labor politics the Dutch, almost completely uninformed on such things, chose to organise attacks on Mr Chifley through press and Parliament. Baron Van Aerssen and his successor at the Netherlands Legation in Canberra, Dr P.E. Teppema, had semi-public brawls with the Prime Minister and fed anti-Government ammunition to press proprietors like Sir Keith Murdoch (Melbourne *Herald* group), Sir Frank Packer (*Daily Telegraph* group, Sydney) and executives of Associated Newspapers *(Sun, Sunday Sun, Sydney)* and the Melbourne *Argus*. For a time during the war the writer was employed on the mass circulation *Sunday Sun* in Sydney, for feature-writing mostly on international affairs. It was quite apparent that the

277

Dutch enjoyed a productive liaison with this Sydney newspaper group. Among the Dutch contacts were Dr Van Mook and Admiral Helfrich. The Chifley-Evatt Government was not at all pleased when Mr Tom Gurr, Editor-in-Chief of the *Sunday Sun,* and Brigadier Errol G. Knox, Editor-in-Chief of the Melbourne *Argus,* became the guests of the Dutch in Java on initiatives from Baron Van Aerssen and Mr Menzies, aimed at countering rising anti-Dutch feeling in Australia. They returned to publicise the Dutch case against the Indonesian Republic.

Mr Chifley became so incensed at Dutch intrigues and orchestrated attacks on his Government that he rebuked the Netherlands Legation in Canberra:

> I would have thought that diplomats would have been serving their country much better by trying to settle the differences that exist between the Dutch Government and its own subjects than by engaging in newspaper controversy in another country.[1]

Dutch inelasticity and contempt for his advice helped to enhance Dr Evatt's aid to the Indonesian Republic. The External Affairs Minister who in 1942 publicly committed himself to restoration of Dutch sovereignty was in 1946 recognising that it was "important to establish good relations with the Indonesian and other peoples who were advancing toward more self-government",[2] while in 1947 he was near enough to being the Indonesian Republic's de facto ambassador to the United Nations.

Mr Calwell's fixations about colonial "ramparts", his misty obsessions about white racial purity and his abiding bias against coloured Asians as migrants to Australia might conceivably have made him an ally of the colonial Dutch in 1945-49 confrontations with the Republic, as he was in the 1950-62 Dutch campaign to retain West New Guinea. But Mr Calwell could find no concordance with the unchastened representatives of the defeated Dutch Empire of the East. The colonial Dutch in Australia so fouled their cause that Mr Calwell was drawn to the Indonesian independence movement in 1945-49. Looking back to his wartime and postwar experiences with the emigre Dutch, as Minister in the Curtin and Chifley Governments, Mr Calwell told the writer in 1971:

> Relations between the wartime and postwar Australian Governments and the NEI Government-in-Exile were never very good. The Netherlands Minister to Australia, Baron Van Aerssen, was aristocratic of manner, but not to the point of the colonial Dutch officers' offensiveness. The colonial Dutch we knew in Australia bore certain resemblances to English pukka sahibs from India. Whether they were worse or better than the sahibs I'm not prepared to say.
>
> In our day in Canberra the Australian armed services people had some contempt for officers of the NEI, which I shared. I have heard the colonial Dutch referred to by Australian Army officers as "a race of fair men and brave women". The colonial Dutch were not highly regarded by Members of Parliament and Cabinet Ministers who had dealings with them.[3]

Resemblances between Colonial Dutch and English sahibs were more expedient to discern. An archetypal "colonial Australian" awaits depiction. If overseers and recruiters of indentured labor evacuated from Australian New Guinea before the Japanese landings and North Australian officials accustomed to govern the lives of Aborigines had been visited upon a metropolitan Dutch community, exhibiting to them unfamiliar manners, lushly superior privileges and arrogant racism, the ruffled Hollanders might have been tempted into less flattering equations. The pot always knows how to describe the kettle.

"A Considerable Body of Opinion"

Thus the Dutch themselves had softened up the Chifley Government before it was called on to face what was tantamount to a declaration of "war without shooting", to borrow Mr Menzies' formulation, by Australian boycotters and Indonesian mutineers. The Prime Minister at first fell back on the alibi of trade union solidarity to counter the Menzies-led Opposition's cry that he was permitting the unions to dictate

279

foreign policy. On 25 September 1945, the day after the first Brisbane ban on Dutch ships, he replied to Mr Menzies' heated denunciations in Parliament:

> The hold-up of ships bound for Javanese ports is a matter between the Dutch authorities and their own subjects. Indonesians refused to work these ships. If the Dutch authorities cannot make their subjects do the job I can easily imagine that the subjects of another country are not likely to take action which might be regarded as "scabbing".[4]

Coming from the veteran trade unionist who, as striking engine-driver of the Forbes Mail in 1917, had himself been scabbed on, this alibi was calculated to have appeal. It also underlined the tactical success gained for the anti-Dutch movement by the linking of Indonesian seamen's genuine economic demands with what was predominantly a political strike or mutiny. However, the "no scabbing" alibi fell well below the credibility line. Mr Chifley would have been aware that some hours before he spoke ship-repair unionists had walked off the *Swartenhondt* in Sydney. The *Swartenhondt* was in dock and there was no Indonesian crew aboard to strike or desert. The Australians' walk-off was a demonstration exclusively in support of the Indonesian Republic. The "no scabbing" alibi was finally cancelled out when Mr Chifley had the Australian crew of HMAS *Bungaree* — "the subjects of another country" — to carry the Netherlands Indies guilders to Java after Melbourne and Bowen unionists and Indonesian seamen had black-banned the Dutch ship *Karsik* and its cargo of reoccupation currency. Before that Mr Chifley allowed the Dutch to break waterfront strikes with their own and Italian soldiers. The explanations of Government tolerance of the anti-Dutch boycott did not lie in a Prime Minister's memories of a scab-broken general transport strike back in 1917.

Mr Chifley was more sensitive to the problems posed for Australia by the revolutionary storm that must transform relations with a neighbour nation of tenfold more population, and to a popular sentiment for Asian independence, new to the Australian political scene, that ran far beyond trade union

Sydney University students demonstrate outside the Netherlands Consulate against the 'First Police Action' by Dutch forces in July 1947

Frith. *Sydney Morning Herald*. 22 December 1948

ONE-ARMED STRONG MAN

Australia will call for a cease-fire in Indonesia and demand that the Dutch forces retreat to the lines held before their latest attack (the 'Second Police Action')

Frith, *Sydney Morning Herald*, 21 Dece

'Are you coming in, or have I got to rescue you?' A Dutch spokesman says Dutch forces have taken 'police action'
purpose of 'liberating' Indonesian Republican territory

membership. In a later debate, he appealed to Mr Menzies to appreciate the extent of public support to the Indonesians in their struggle with the Dutch: he told the Opposition Leader that it was useless to deny "that a great deal of feeling exists over this incident", that "a considerable body of opinion" felt that "a great deal of reformation" was required in the Netherlands East Indies.[5]

However, his tactic was to frighten off the Opposition from boycott-wrecking exercises with the spectre of a great industrial upheaval that would have prejudiced postwar rehabilitation and reconstruction. He suggested that direct Government intervention, as proposed by Mr Menzies, would lead to a flare-up "that would have involved the whole industrial movement and the whole of the shipping trade of this country".[6] The Minister for Shipping, Senator William Ashley, also set his face against counter-boycott action "which would have the effect of embroiling the whole of the waterfront of Australia in a dispute arising out of trouble which had occurred in another country".[7]

Australia as the Republic's Spokesman

In the tense days that followed the 1947 Dutch military offensive the Chifley-Evatt Government recorded a first for Australia in her relations with Asia. The anti-colonial movement in Australia, with the ship-banners still in the van, furnished sufficient protection to the Chifley Government's tradition-shattering policies that it could accept nomination from the Indonesian Republic to act as its international spokesman.

The Republic appealed to Australia to represent it in United Nations negotiations, designed to curb Dutch military pressures that threatened to be crippling. The Australian Government agreed and referred the First Police Action to the UN Security Council, charging a Dutch breach of peace. The UN Security Council on 25 August 1947 authorised the setting up of the UN Good Offices Committee on Indonesia, in the hope that it could halt the bloodshed. Indonesia selected Australia as its representative on the Good Offices Committee and Mr Justice Richard C. Kirby of the Commonwealth Court of Conciliation and Arbitration was appointed to this post by Dr Evatt. It was logical that Holland should choose Belgium to represent it on the Committee: much capital sucked from the Indies had been invested in the Belgian economy and transferred Indonesian profits helped Belgians to colonise, bloodily, the Congo. Paul Van Zeeland of Belgium was chosen by The Hague. Dr Frank P. Graham, President of the University of South Carolina, served as third member for the USA, at a time when America was arming the Dutch.

Australia, though cold war language had come to UNO, was lining up with the Soviet Union against Britain and America, so strongly did the Chifley Government feel about the Dutch attempt to annihilate the Republic. On the UN Security Council Britain, America, Holland, France and Belgium labored to re-establish substantial Dutch suzerainty. While Mr Chifley and Dr Evatt favoured some kind of "commonwealth" link for Indonesia with Holland, Australia voted on the Republican side in the Security Council, along with the Soviet Union and Poland.

The atmosphere in Australia was changing in favour of accommodation with a self-governing Indonesia. The *Sydney Morning Herald* strongly critisised the First Police Action; so did leading churchmen like Bishop Moyes of Armidale, Canon E.J. Davidson, the Rev. W.G. Coughlan (Church of England), the Rev. Alan Walker and the Rev. Ralph Sutton (Methodist). Australian universities, rated as citadels of conservatism by radicals, began to march in step with the times. Sydney University students poured in a vast throng to Wynyard Square and Margaret Street, Sydney, to demonstrate to the Netherlands Consulate in protest against the First Police Action. This founding demonstration was violently charged by 21 Division of the NSW Police, so brutally and illegally that press and other public protests followed and arrested students were successfully defended by Mr J. (later Mr Justice) McClemens.

Between the Police Actions of July 1947 and December 1948 Mr Chifley and Dr Evatt stepped up diplomatic aid to the Republic and stretched their tolerances of the boycotters at home. They felt that Batavia still carried a heavy cargo of prejudice against Indonesian self-government and that anti-compromise leaders held sway at The Hague. Mr Chifley wrote to a high British envoy in South-East Asia after the Second Police Action:

> I had a heart-to-heart talk with Teppema (Dutch Minister) in Canberra recently and told him that I thought his Government had made a colossal blunder and that they were only assisting the upsurge of nationalism in the East.[8]

Dr Evatt's man at the United Nations, Colonel W.R. Hodgson, compared the Second Police Action to Hitler's attack on Holland in 1940 and urged that Holland should be expelled from UNO if the ceasefire was not obeyed. Dr Evatt himself was so angered by the final Dutch effort to strangle the Republic that he criticised those American interests whose arms and other aid made the Second Police Action possible. He probably incurred enduring Washington suspicions. US Under-Secretary of State Robert A. Lovett, as the *Forrestal Diaries*[9] revealed, raised the matter with some warmth at a Cabinet meeting in Washington on 20 December 1948:

> He (Lovett) expressed annoyance at the gratuitous interference of Dr Evatt, the Foreign Minister of Australia, who had, although not a member of the Security Council (they are a member of the Good Offices Commission) addressed a communication to the Security Council expressing the view that if the US had taken firm and preventive action with respect to the intent of the Dutch Government to intervene in the affairs of the Republic the present situation might not have arisen.

The US Under-Secretary of State expressed to the Australian Ambassador in Washington, Mr Norman J. Makin, "in the strongest terms" the US Government's dissatisfaction with "this unilateral action on the part of Dr Evatt".[10]

New Image in Asia

Australia, because of the boycott of the Dutch war organisation in 1945-49 and the friendly diplomatic services rendered to the Indonesian Republic in its hour of need, enjoyed until the fall of the Chifley-Evatt Government in December 1949 an image that was outside the foresight of the White Australia Policy's architects.

Dr Evatt accepted an invitation from Indian Premier Pandit Nehru to a conference of Asian nations in New Delhi on 20-23 January 1949 to sponsor more united action against Dutch colonialism. The invitation and acceptance to an Asian anti-colonial conference represented for the Australian Government a break with history, never to be repeated. Dr Evatt also contributed to the calling of The Hague Conference later in the year — a conference which weakened the Dutch hold sufficiently for the Republic to assert full sovereignty and nationalise Dutch enterprises in 1957.

The London *Economist* was about the only conservative organ in this era to acknowledge that the Chifley-Evatt Government had served Australian national interest in defending the Indonesian Republic. The *Economist* concluded that the outcome of The Hague Conference at the end of 1949 was that "the confidence which Australia has now won in most Asian countries" justified Australian Government actions. Australia, the *Economist* said, "also showed its new power at the Asian conference in Delhi . . ."[11]

In one of his first speeches after the defeat of his Government Mr Chifley gave from Opposition benches reasons for his Ministry's support to the Indonesian Republic:

> The Labor Government realised that 80 million Indonesians could not continue to be governed by 10 million Europeans whose sole interest in Indonesia was to extract from the country as much wealth as they could and give in return as little as possible.[12]

Here was striking resemblance to the reasons put forward by Australian trade unionists for immobilising the black armada.

Indonesian Gratitude

Neither Liberal-Country Party hostility in Opposition and in the first decade of 23 years in Government, nor the noisy rattling of skeletons in the White Australia cupboard during

Mr Calwell's pre-emptive strike ambitions in West Irian could dry up the goodwill created by the trade unions' boycott and the Chifley-Evatt Government's helping hand. The Indonesians put their gratitude on the record in the first weeks of the bans that clogged Dutch war-supply arteries. President Soekarno paid tribute early in October 1945 to the important aid given the Republic by "the magnificent, freedom-loving stand" of the Australian trade unions.[13]

As the first Indonesian repatriates were about to sail from Australia to Republican territory in October 1945 the Central Committee of Indonesian Independence said in a manifesto issued in Brisbane:

The understanding and support given us by the Australian people will never be forgotten, and we will convey this history of our struggle in your land to our countrymen at home. We hope that the friendship between our two peoples may become stronger and endure in the best interests of democracy.[14]

Many Indonesians wrote back to Australian friends after their return. "We will never forget what the Australian workers have done for us," said a letter from Willi Mongawal, President of the Indonesian Club in Sydney.[15] To the Australian Council of Trade Unions the Secretary of SOBSI (All-Indonesian Central Council of Trade Unions), Suronyo, and the General President, Haryono, described the Australian unions' boycott of the Dutch as "a deed of historic importance and an example to the world".[16] Suronyo and Haryono came to these leading posts in the new Republican trade union federation after study of union organisation in Australia 1942-45. The Indonesian Independence Committee President in Sydney, Jan Walandouw, told a Sydney Town Hall rally before his repatriation that in Indonesia "the name of Australia would long be remembered".[17]

At the Government level Indonesia thanked the Chifley-Evatt Government for its uncompromising defence of the Republic at the United Nations following the 1947 First Police Action. Dr Amir Sjarifuddin, Premier at Djogjakarta, the temporary Republican capital, cabled Prime Minister Chifley expressing "deep gratitude to the Government and people of Australia who have repeatedly proved their sympathy with the Indonesian people and who have always held high the principles of freedom and democracy". The Indonesian Premier's cable added:

> I have no doubt whatever that these principles we have in common will strenghten the ties which bind us together and will favourably influence relations between our two peoples in every possible field for the benefit of both our nations and for the maintenance of everlasting peace.[18]

Another Republic Premier, Dr Sutan Sjahrir, officially thanked the Australian Government and the trade unions.

Following the boycotts and demonstrations evoked by the 1948 Second Police Action the Director of the Indonesian Republic's New York Information Office, Mr C. Thamboe, credited Australians, rather unselectively, with leadership in "constructive action for democracy in South-East Asia," and said that "the people of Australia, as represented by the wharf-laborers, supported the Republic and action against the Dutch".[19] To which the *West Australian* of Perth gave the predictable reply: "It is pertinent to tell the Indonesian Republicans that wharf-laborers do not represent the people of Australia . . ."[20]

An Indonesian delegation which came to Australia in March 1963 — Brigadier-General Latief Hendraningrat, Chairman, Foreign Affairs Committee, Republican Parliament, Mrs Jo. Chaerul Saleh, wife of the Deputy Prime Minister and active in women's and youth organisations, and Mr Suroto, Editorial Board member, Antara news agency — had this question put to them by the Sydney *Daily Mirror*:[21] "Do Indonesians still remember Australia's early support for their independence?" The Indonesian delegates answered: "We shall never forget. If we had only one thing to say to the Australian people on this mission it would be: 'Thank you' ".

Australian students visiting Indonesia in the 'seventies confirmed that the Australian contribution to the Republic's victory continues to influence favourably the Indonesian view of Australia, despite recurring political difficulties. General

Suharto, Indonesian leader, and Liberal Government hosts
also recalled — rather incongruously on the latter's part —
Australia's post-natal services to the Republic during the
General's visit here in February 1972.

Indonesia Calling, in Australian Accents

The Waterside Workers' Federation, the Seamen's Union and
13 other Australian waterfront and maritime unions sponsored
a film, *Indonesia Calling*, which played a role in defeating the
Dutch censorship and by getting the story of Australian
trade union aid to the Republic to vast numbers of Indonesians.

Indonesia Calling was produced by a famous Dutch maker
of documentary films, Joris Ivens. He came to Australia as
Film Commissioner of the Netherlands Indies Government-in-
Exile; his main task was to film the Dutch reoccupation of
the Indies. Immediately the Indonesian Republic was proclaimed Ivens breached his contract with the NEI Government and, illegally using its equipment, put on film the
chronicle of Australian boycotts and demonstrations and
Indonesian and Indian seamen's mutinies. Ivens' chief assistant, as camera-operator, editor and production manager, was
an American girl, Marion Michelle. Harry Watt, the well
known British producer, was in Australia at the time, filming
The Overlanders, starring Chips Rafferty. Harry Watt shot
some of the scenes for *Indonesia Calling.* The commentary
was written by Catherine Duncan, an Australian actress.
Peter Finch, later one of the world's most renowned actors,
was commentator. Mr Edmund Allison, now Manager of
Quality Films, Sydney, headed the Austral-Asia Syndicate,
formed for the express purpose of making *Indonesia Calling.*
Bondan, one of the leaders of the Central Committee of
Indonesian Independence at Brisbane, who returned to Java
to write a book on experiences in Australia, was the Indonesian
representative on the Syndicate.

A Commonwealth Film Censor's ban on *Indonesia Calling*
for export, on the grounds that it would offend a friendly
nation, the Dutch, was a setback to the Republic in its
propaganda battle abroad. Abroad, propaganda odds were
heavily weighted in favor of the Dutch in most countries.

287

WWF General Secretary James Healy made representations to the Chifley-Evatt Government: Prime Minister Chifley, along with other Ministers, saw a screening and on 5 November 1946 announced that his Customs Minister, Senator J.M. Fraser, "had overruled the decision of the Commonwealth Film Censor". The film was shown to millions throughout the world and to Indonesians, despite the Dutch ban.

It was probably not unknown to Mr Chifley that *Indonesia Calling* was carried to Java aboard a repatriation ship and smuggled through the Dutch lines at Batavia. The film gave a boost to Indonesian morale. Republican areas were rather isolated from the world; communications were hampered seriously by the Dutch who spread suggestions that the Republic was virtually without friends in the world. *Indonesia Calling* was given publicity in the Republican press and by Antara news agency. According to Marion Michelle, the camera girl, the film was shown in village after village of Republican Java on open-air screens.[22] Javanese watching Joris Ivens' exciting portrayal of Australians as standard-bearers of Indonesian liberation could have been forgiven some bewilderment. Australia was never a land of interest to them, except for its complicity in subjection of neighbours to alien rule and rigid exclusion of people with pigmentation like theirs. Australia was the pallidly pliant extension of Great Britain in this South-East Asian environment, an imperial echoland. Why had all this changed, almost overnight? The Australian Government, formed of a party that once ranted apocalyptically about the looming descent of Asian hordes and demanded the shield of the white men's battleships, was the dynamic ally of Asians whittling down the European power. Australian trade unionists, often given to repellent obsessions about "coloured labor" were the first white volunteers in the battle of brown men against white overlords, denying passage to colonialist ships and munitions of war. The boycott of Dutch ships and the Chifley-Evatt Government's rising resistance to Dutch, British and American efforts to bring down the Indonesian Republic meant that Labor Party foreign policy could never be pushed back into the old furrows, despite aberrations over West Irian.

31 Last of the Black Armada

Despite anti-Republican exercises in the first decade following its 1949 election victory, the Menzies Government was compelled by the domestic and international pressures of 1945-49 to expand the contours of tolerance and treat with Republican leaders as equals. Early in 1959 the Indonesian Foreign Minister, Dr Subandrio, was invited to Canberra for talks on West Irian. A joint communique issued by Dr Subandrio and External Affairs Minister Casey indicated a Government retreat from belligerence. Australia undertook to accept peaceful and legal transfer of West Irian to Indonesia if this were mutually agreed upon by Holland and the Republic. The Subandrio-Casey communique incurred pledges that Australia would remain neutral and not stand in the way of a settlement.

The ties of retrospective traditionalism were too strong for the Menzies Government. The pledges were not taken seriously. Agitation on behalf of the Dutch, steps toward Dutch-Australian administrative cooperation continued in press and Parliament. Mr Menzies, visiting Indonesia to back Dutch claims to West Irian, had a long and lively discussion with President Soekarno at Bogor, Java, on 6 December 1959. Mr Menzies remained unacclimatised, as Australian correspondent Bruce Grant found:

> Asia is not Mr Menzies' field. It is too hot for a start, but it is also too emotional for a man with an ironic and conservative judgment . . . . It will probably be another

generation before Australia produces a leader who can approach some of the new nations of Asia with any certainty or understanding.[1]

The Netherlands Government in 1960 embarked on a last-ditch stand at its Hollandia and Biak bases. The aircraft-carrier *Karel Doorman* and her destroyer escorts, *Groningen* and *Limburg*, were ordered to Hollandia, with Washington and North Atlantic Treaty Organisation approval. Egypt denied the Netherlands warships passage through the Suez Canal, now nationalised Egyptian property despite the combined efforts of Britain, France, Israel and Mr Menzies in 1956. Thus they had to take the long haul via the South African Cape and Western Australia. Distant relatives of the the Dutch at the Cape and friends in Canberra offered the aircraft-carrier and her escorts refreshment.

The Indonesian Government warned that it would not remain idle if this Dutch force continued to West Irian; the naval reinforcement was branded as dangerous and "highly hot-headed and provocative"; in Djakarta Captain K.A. Matjik, spokesman for the National Front for the Liberation of West Irian described the naval mission as "an act of war".[2] Some Indonesian leaders advocated sinking *Karel Doorman* and escorts if they entered Indonesian territorial waters. The voyage of these warships was one of the main causes of Indonesia's diplomatic breach with Holland of August 1960. Indonesian warnings and diplomatic isolation in Asia could not deter the Menzies Government from offering the hospitality of the Swan River estuary to the Royal Netherlands Navy. Louder appeals were heard for a Dutch-Australian military alliance to resist an Indonesian takeover in West Irian. A scent of battle smoke was over the old Dutch East India Company route to the Spiceries via the Cape and Western Australia.

This offer of refreshment at Fremantle, seeming to Indonesians to augur an Australian Netherlands alliance in arms, caused the *Times of Indonesia* to claim that "the intransigence of the Netherlands has only been made possible by overt Australian backing and covert American support". Australia, said the Republican paper, seemed "more pro-Dutch than the Dutch".[3]

On 31 May 1960, the day *Karel Doorman* and destroyer escorts *Groningen* and *Limburg* sailed from home ports for Fremantle and Hollandia, the Indonesian Government officially made known its displeasure at Australian collaboration. Dr Subandrio said in Singapore that he would look into the possibility that the Dutch warships' proposed call at Fremantle "affected Australia's neutrality on West Irian".[4]

External Affairs Minister Sir Garfield Barwick thought it wise to explain "carefully" to Indonesian representatives in Canberra and Djakarta that refuelling of Dutch warships in an Australian port "did not mean any change of policy towards Indonesia". These "routine courtesies" and "routine facilities" for the warships were not "an unfriendly gesture towards Indonesia".[5] The Dutch newspaper *Trouw* had already mentioned an Australian invitation to send the Dutch warships.[6] A week after Sir Garfield Barwick's explanation it was announced that the *Piet Hein*, a Dutch warship well known to Australian dockyard boycotters, would call at Port Moresby, New Guinea.

Indonesia closed eastern air spaces from Morotai south to islands about 100 miles from West Irian. The main airline affected was Qantas of Australia.

Karel Doorman, Groningen and *Limburg* appeared off Fremantle early in July. The *West Australian*[7] announced that the three warships, carrying 1850 officers and men, would stay six days at Fremantle. *Karel Doorman* sailed past Rottnest Island and thrust her ungainly silhouette through the winter mists and rain that engloomed the Swan River estuary on the morning of 12 July 1960.

Final Act in the Boycott Drama

Fremantle trade unionists, though facing joint Government and Opposition committals to the Dutch retention of this imperial anachronism and official trade union leadership resentments against any anti-Dutch action in their own State, prepared for boycott when they first heard, in June 1960, that the warships were coming.

291

Members of the old Docks Union — reconstituted as the Western Australian Branch of the Federated Ship Painters' and Dockers' Union — mostly had their minds made up when they met at Fremantle Trades Hall on 4 July. The dockers were under the leadership of Mr Paddy Troy, veteran of the 1945-49 boycotts of the Dutch. Union members Tarbutt and Trantham moved a protest, carried unanimously by the meeting, against the stationing of Dutch warships in West Irian waters, calling this "a danger to peace in South-East Asia" and "a menace to the security of Australia".[8]

The *West Australian* on 12 July reported a Seamen's Union black ban on the three warships. This meant no tug or pilot boat crews for the warships. A Seamen's Union spokesman said the action was "because the union felt that the purpose of their voyage could lead to war".[9] The paper also reported further that Dutch forces would be sent to West New Guinea in August and September and that Dutch peace supporters staged a three-hour sitdown demonstration outside the Ministry of Defence at The Hague in protest against the despatch of reinforcements.[10]

Attacking the boycotters editorially, this most influential of the State's papers observed that the Seamen's Union had "arrogantly tried to dictate the foreign policy of the Federal Government". The Australian Government had offered facilities to the Dutch warships "and could not in justice have done otherwise". The editorial added:

By its temporary intrusion into foreign politics the union has exposed itself to the charge that its real reason is not to help Indonesia but to support the Communist line on the New Guinea question.[11]

Only one Seamen's Union member was aboard the little pilot-boat ordered out to *Karel Doorman* in the Swan estuary. He refused duty. The pilot-boat seaman was peremptorily sacked. He had 35 years' service with Fremantle Harbour Trust. Sacking meant that he would lose all retirement pay and other privileges.

None could deny the Dutch their navigation skills. *Karel Doorman*, without tugs or pilot, was in foul weather. As she reached Fremantle wharves driving rain came in on a nor'-west

292

gale. For her nimble destroyer escorts manoeuvre was relatively easy. *Karel Doorman* could not berth without external power aids. Her captain sent pilots into the cockpits of warplanes lined up on the flight-deck. Engines were revved up. The wind generated by the air-screws competed with the nor'-west gale and got the lumbering aircraft-carrier near enough to the wharf for the sailors to get lines ashore.

The warships were denied shipyard repairs and various services. Mr Troy claimed that the boycott had repercussions throughout the world, so much so that Japanese unions later denied *Karel Doorman* right of entry to the ports of Japan.[12]

Away on the Man-Made Wind

The lone seaman actively involved in the boycott was before the State Arbitration Court (Judge Neville), appealing against his dismissal, while the Dutch warships were still in Fremantle. The Seamen's Union, knowing that no further labor would be called for the warships, claimed that the boycott had been temporarily lifted. This allowed Judge Neville to reinstate him and save his retirement benefits.

Karel Doorman needed a new man-made wind, stronger than the steady beat of the trades that once carried Dutch Indiamen to the Spiceries, to get out into the stream. On the morning of 18 July 1960, approaching the fifteenth anniversary of the first boycott of Dutch ships in Australia, the gale created by the propellors of Dutch aircraft on the flight-deck announced for miles around the Black Armada finale.

The boycotters — seamen, painters and dockers, waterside workers, engineers, boilermakers, shipwrights, carpenters and harbour staffs — paused at their jobs and ships' passengers and crews gathered at rails in wonderment. Seven war-planes on *Karel Doorman* were roaring their propellors. Workers reeled back as the whirlwind blew over Fremantle wharf. The propellors of the fighter and bomber aircraft aboard slowly blew *Karel Doorman* out from the wharf. To supplement the push of the screws the Dutch sailors ran lines out to buoys in the harbour to get pull.

As the Dutch warships disappeared over the horizon no other Dutch ship came as a candidate-member of the Black Armada.

Conclusion: The Sum of Australian Boycott Aid

Australian boycotters did not give much thought in 1945 to the domino effect of the casualties they inflicted on the Dutch military machine — to the interlocking ramifications, for example, of landing barges immobilised by Churchillian preoccupations in the Adriatic and barges detained by trade union black bans at Port Kembla and Townsville.

The addled planning associated with strategies of the dawning cold war, power rivalries, thickening fogs of suspicion and efforts to salvage more of the status quo than was possible in Asia caused spreadeagled deployments of armies, navies and air forces at the war's end. These were destined to sap Anglo-American contributions to the Dutch and to make the havoc of the Australian boycott of Dutch ships, barges, vehicles and armaments cumulative in effect. The criss-crossing web of delays, dispersals and strategic strains of the postwar months aggravated the malfunction of the Dutch reconquest apparatus based in Australia.

There were less tangible measures of the boycott's impact on the Netherlands Empire in the wane of its power than ships at sagging mooring ropes in the Brisbane, Yarra and Swan Rivers and Sydney Harbour. The boycott generated political passions beyond Australian shores and encouraged the Chifley-Evatt Government to diplomatic services to the Indonesian Republic in the international arena, further weakening on occasions the imperial diplomacy that had been pushed on to slippery ground by the Asian revolutions.

The Netherlands armed forces, despite the bridgeheads won

for them in Java by the British, had no chance of immediate or effective offensives against the Republic without the 450 barges, lighters and surf-boats and the fuel transport craft held in the hammerlock of the Australian boycott. At very few ports in the Indies could ships tie up at wharves. Estuaries, inland waterways and beach approaches are customarily shallow. Indies inter-islands and overseas trade relied heavily on light craft for stevedoring and shallow-water navigation. The Japanese expropriated many of these small vessels for their South Pacific war operations and losses to Allied air, naval and shore fire were serious. In addition, the inadequate Indies harbour and dock installations suffered war damage. Without power and dumb barges the Dutch could not handle war cargoes, except at Batavia and a few other points, and could not use canals and streams to penetrate inland and prevent consolidation of Republican bases.

The NEI Sea Transport Officer at Sydney, Lieutenant A.M. Denboer, emphasised before the Commonwealth Arbitration Court on 1 March 1946 that the 450 small vessels owned by the Dutch in Australia and ready for shipment or towage were urgently needed to unload ships in the Indies and for river and canal transport. "That is an essential part of our program," he said.[1]

Holland's allies knew no shortage of the barges the NEI Sea Transport Officer rated as vital to Dutch reoccupation. The greatest fleets of troop, cargo and oil barges ever known were immobilised against Hitler's Fortress Europe and General MacArthur had thousands in the Pacific.

In the last stages of the European war, Mr Churchill was anxious to divert amphibious forces to South-East Asia. He did not want British, French and Dutch armies to find Resistance movements in power or to receive colonies back on an American platter. The Americans, for their part, were nervy about postwar dispositions in Japan, China and the Philippines. But for both powers, the main fixation was Europe, over which the Red Army marshals were driving a demoralised German Army.

Mr Churchill wanted British troops in Vienna and Budapest before the Red Army. This Churchillian pursuit of phantoms delayed despatch of troops and equipment to South-East Asia. The US-built landing craft that could have been so helpful in Java seas for Anglo-Dutch occupation of key points were handed to Field-Marshal Alexander for "a right-handed movement to give Germany a stab in the Adriatic armpit", to reach Vienna and resist "the rapid spread of Soviet influence".[2] For these cold war eve obsessions the Indonesian Republic and its Australian allies could be grateful.

With the battle-weary Red Army halted at its treaty frontiers on the Elbe the United States, now led by President Truman, gave considerable attention to China, where for years the partisan armies led by Mao Tse-tung and Marshal Chu Teh had borne the brunt of action against Japan and commanded more popular support than Generalissimo Chiang Kai-shek's Government. Into China America poured bombing and fighter planes, tanks, trucks, jeeps, ships, barges, artillery, rifles and ammunition in vast quantities. This American support to Chiang Kai-shek was not only for a doomed cause but, in Dr Van Mook's view, betokened neglect of Dutch needs at a decisive stage. While the West was "trying to adapt its policy to the hopeless task of staving off dissolution in China, it failed to observe that South-East Asia was slowly degenerating into a state of permanent convulsion".[3] The barges that Dr Van Mook thought should have been on the Java coast and waterways helped Chiang's troops to retreat across China's rivers, there to be abandoned to the People's Liberation Army.

Rockefeller Courtesies to Boycotters

The Dutch could not move around convulsed Indonesia without oil, one of the most severely rationed of postwar commodities. Under boycott at Townsville and Brisbane in Queensland, Sydney and Port Kembla in NSW and at Melbourne were 36 oil-transport craft, ranging from tankers to 50-ton barges. These craft were needed to serve the restored Royal Dutch Shell refinery in Borneo and the American refinery in Sumatra and to carry petroleum from Netherlands New Guinea, to fuel the war in Java.

A tanker was tied up at Brisbane, along with 18 200-ton oil barges and two 50-ton barges. At Sydney the unions held the motor-lighter *Chelmer*, the tug *Hampshire* and four 50-ton barges. At Townsville there were two 50-ton barges (a third sank off Townsville while being towed from Sydney); at Port Kembla the unions held the small motor vessel *Plym* and at Melbourne five 100-ton barges. These oil-transport craft remained immobilised in Australia till 1948.

They were owned by three of the world's corporate giants — Standard Oil of New Jersey, Socony Mobil of New York and the Anglo-Dutch Shell Co. The Rockefeller and Shell combines have been credited — not only in Leftwing publications — with power to topple thrones and governments. Jersey Standard's international business turnover exceeded the gross national product of Australia. The courtesies extended to Australian maritime union leaders by a corporation greater in economic terms than Australia and of fabled political muscle, and by the other two oil giants suffering boycott, merit notice.

Jersey Standard, Socony Mobil and Shell compiled a document innocuously headed, "Notes for Discussion", which was passed to Waterside Workers' Federation leaders.[4] The three companies proposed that a tanker held under ban at Brisbane should tow a 200-ton barge to northern waters where it might be picked up by a Dutch tug. Brisbane unionists had consistently refused to handle the tanker lines unless a firm assurance was provided that barges would not be towed by Dutch tugs or come into Dutch possession.

The Notes for Discussion showed the international oil combines were in no doubt about the capacity of Australian unions to deny essential services to the Dutch. The Notes said:

> Endeavours have been made to have the barges towed from Australia to destination by outside firms but without success . . . Endeavours have been made to transfer craft from southern locations in Australia to northern ports where they could be picked up by Dutch tugs from NEI but difficulty has been experienced in moving craft along the coast.
>
> The possibility of towing by tanker to Singapore or NEI has been considered but is regarded as impracticable.

297

Furthermore, any political reaction by the unions to such a course might involve tying up of a whole tanker fleet, which would be so serious as to be beyond contemplation.

The oil companies' Notes for Discussion noted that the Brisbane Branch Secretary, Mr E. Englart, had taken a "leading part in preventing the movement of craft". They revealed that an attempt had been made to ship barges from Sydney and Melbourne direct to the Indies. Space had been offered for barges on a ship leaving Sydney "but the booking for two barges had to be cancelled as difficulties were expected by the shipping company as well as by Shell, inasmuch as it was known that barges moving along the coast are specially watched by the unions".[5]

The three oil corporations approached the Chifley Government for help in getting the ban on their craft lifted. The Government called a conference on 5 May 1948, attended by the Minister for Shipping, Senator Ashley; the Secretary of his Department of Shipping, Mr G.G. Sutcliffe, and the WWF General Secretary, Mr Healy. Cast-iron assurances were required by the unions that if the oil vessels were released from boycott they would not supply fuel to the Dutch armed forces or go near the Java war zone. Mr Justice Kirby of the Commonwealth Arbitration Court told Mr Healy before the conference assembled that the Government was anxious that the WWF should agree to working non-military cargoes for Netherlands New Guinea in these craft, which would bring back to Australia oil produced by the Netherlands New Guinea Petroleum Company.

The oil companies put into writing a pledge to the Waterside Workers' Federation that the vessels would be restricted to the Netherlands New Guinea-Australia run. The powered craft and barges in tow, some loaded with non-military goods and some ballasted with sand, were allowed to leave Australian ports in mid-1948 and return with petroleum. For the first and only time in their history Rockefeller oil corporations and Royal Dutch Shell agreed to operate only on routes sanctioned by Australian trade union officials.

Fuel stocks in Java were low when Japan surrendered, and

298

Borneo and Sumatran refineries were war-damaged. The trade union denial of oil-transport vessels to the Dutch during the immediate postwar scarcities was, like the boycott of landing and cargo barges in Australia, a wounding blow to the Dutch and an award of time and space to the Republic.

The Quality and Quantity of Mercy

As part of the Dutch effort to have the trade union ban on certain cargoes lifted, the NEI Sea Transport Officer, Lieutenant Denboer, made available to the Commonwealth Arbitration Court in Sydney on 1 March 1946 a list of "relief" or "mercy" goods under ban. The quality of mercy was strained: barges, trucks and cement were included. No accounting was provided on guns, ammunition, aircraft, components and other military stores coming under boycott.

Lieutenant Denboer testified that 25,272 tons of "relief" goods were under union black bans — 10,900 tons in Melbourne, 1,700 in Adelaide and most of the remainder at Sydney and Brisbane. These were goods bought and paid for by the Dutch: perhaps more important were goods bought but not yet paid for. As Lieutenant Denboer pointed out to the court, Dutch-leased storehouses were already filled with boycotted stocks and the manufacturers could not deliver any more.

The paid-for goods included textiles, ready-made clothing and medicines, 10,972 tons designated as "miscellaneous" and 5,177 tons of canned foods. The long list of unpaid-for "mercy" goods that could not be delivered from factories because the boycott had jammed up all space available to the Dutch comprised such items as cement, fish-hooks and fish-lines, household utensils and so on. Mr E.C. Roach (for the WWF) was not prepared to believe that Dutchmen in Java were such keen fishermen, or that the large order of cement would be used to replace atap huts. The unions indicated to the court that they would continue to keep cement away from Dutch pillbox sites.

Dutch postwar opportunities to acquire barges and trucks were apparently so limited, due to war devastation of industry and transport, that in 1947 the NEI authorities were still placing orders for them in Australia. Mr Albert Monk, ACTU President, told the September 1947 ACTU Full Executive meeting that he had warned the Minister for Shipping, Senator Ashley, and Mr Healy (WWF) that the Dutch were still buying in Australia and that cargoes were being loaded by Dutch soldiers. Mr Monk complained to Senator Ashley that "in no other country would Dutch soldiers be allowed to load ships with merchandise" and protested that this was "provocative". Dutch army stevedoring was only partially successful. Lieutenant Denboer admitted to the Arbitration Court that ships loaded by soldiers had to sail away without much of the required freight. The Dutch, he said, did not have sufficient "military volunteers" for cargo loading.

Waterside workers at Geelong, Mr Monk reported to the September 1947 ACTU Full Executive meeting, had drawn his attention to attempts to load lorries from the Ford Company works on to a Dutch ship. Mr Monk found on inquiry that not only lorries but steel towing barges were loaded for the Indies. Geelong waterside workers imposed a tight ban. Union members at Ford's Geelong plant held up oiling and greasing the new Ford lorries built for the Dutch. The ACTU then authorised lubrication of the trucks for their preservation while the ban continued. Lieutenant Denboer on 1 March 1946 gave the Arbitration Court a figure of 1,000 trucks tied up by the unions. Obviously, the Dutch need for Australian-built trucks in Java was acute.

Frustrated Java Rendezvous

Australian boycott delays of Dutch tonnage, troops and firepower meshed perfectly with American-ordered postponements of European restorations in South-East Asia.

Mountbatten relied confidently on Dutch troops from Brisbane, Sydney, Melbourne and Fremantle when he fixed 4 October for rendezvous with the Dutch at Batavia and the launching of joint landing operations.[6] First he had to move his armada from Ceylon to Singapore to take the Japanese surrender. General MacArthur sent him a sudden order while his force was at sea that no British landings or occupations were to begin until Japan signed the articles of surrender. This

300

order covered Java. The Japanese did not sign the surrender aboard USS *Missouri* till 2 September.

The monsoon was pelting across the Bay of Bengal. Mountbatten found it impossible to turn back to Trincomalee or Colombo. His ships had to be supplied at sea, in the lee of the Nicobar Islands. Eighteen days passed after the war's end. Mountbatten's force, kept forward afloat, consumed food, fuel, patience and Indies reoccupation potential. The Dutch were in near-frenzy. Dr Van Mook and Dr Van Der Plas pleaded and protested. The surrender delay in Tokio Bay till 2 September was, Professor Gerbrandy, the ex-Prime Minister of Holland, said, "at a moment when the situation called for the utmost expedition. It is a bald statement of fact that the delay was vital".[7] Mountbatten's Intelligence Officer David Wehl agreed: "It is impossible to stress too much the importance of this hiatus in the rule of Indonesia".[8]

Britain's South-East Asia tasks, Mr Churchill noted, demanded "much more shipping than Mountbatten possessed".[9] Acting State Secretary Sumner Welles considered that "the British troops available for the task were far inferior in number to what was required" and that they arrived six weeks too late.[10]

The absence of sufficient British troops and the union blockade on Dutch military movements out of Australian bases led SEAC and the Dutch into improvisations and excesses that engendered deeper Indonesian hostility. They threw into battle against the Republic Japanese troops, detested for their anti-Indonesian atrocities, and Dutch ex-internees, many of them warped psychologically by concentration camp existence. Trade union interference with transport from Australia and the Indonesian troop mutinies played their part in pushing the British and Dutch to these excesses. In addition to the delays to troopships, Dutch soldiers were required for stevedoring, and, along with loyal Ambonese and West Indians, for police duties in situations of mutiny.

No Hospitality for New Dutch Army

The Hollanders were greatly concerned to recruit and transport from liberated metropolitan Netherlands a sizable new

301

army. This was needed to extend the controls after the Indies empire had been exhumed by the Netherlands Indies armed forces from Australia. The presence of a strong Dutch army would also prevent the Australians from East Indonesia gaining footholds, if suspected Canberra ambitions were acted upon, that might lead to postwar political and economic intervention in Java. Fears that the British and Americans desired to share their Indies wealth were known to tincture Dutch calculations.

Holland, with industry, transport and housing in disorder, was not a suitable place to train an army for service in the tropics. Australian military camps, being vacated by troops moving north, and the climate and geography were ideal for the project.

The metropolitan government in the second half of 1943 began to strengthen the NEI apparatus in Australia. The royal Government-in-Exile in London chose Lieutenant-General L.H. Van Oyen as Commander-in-Chief in October 1943. Discourteously, the London Government overlooked notification of his appointment to the post in Australia to the Curtin Government. Soon after, the General approached the Australian Government for facilities to house, train and equip the large force of Dutch troops that would become available after the Germans were driven from the Netherlands. The troops trained and partially armed in Australia would move to the NEI at the war's end. Dr Van Mook made similar representations.

From London the Dutch Government officially asked the Australian Government for troop training facilities in August 1944, naming a figure of 30,000. A War Cabinett meeting favourably considered the Dutch request in September 1944, with the condition that the Dutch Army should be established here without detriment to Australian needs. Dr Van Mook was definite about the Australian commitment: he wrote on 29 May 1943 to Admiral Sir James Somerville, British Naval Member, Combined Chiefs of Staff, Washington, that the "very helpful" Australian Army was putting at Dutch disposal "camps, equipment and training facilities" which were "ideally suited for the training of the light battalions we need".[11]

Major-General L.P. Van Temmen, who served with the NEI Army in Australia under General Van Oyen, claimed some three weeks later that 100,000 Dutch troops would soon be arriving in Australia. Navy personnel were already training in England and the Dutch Air Force would be augmented. All would come to Australia as soon as ships were provided. Major-General Van Temmen added his hope that Australia would equip most of this Dutch force.[12]

The Department of External Affairs then wrote to the Netherlands Minister, Baron Van Aerssen, submitting that the proposal had been to admit 30,000 not 100,000. The Department now cast doubts on Australia's capacity to take 30,000 "in the light of existing and prospective commitments".[13]

Mr Menzies, obviously aware of the contents of the External Affairs letter to Baron Van Aerssen, challenged the Government in Parliament about the agreement to accommodate, train and partially equip 30,000 Dutch troops, charging breach of faith. Mr Chifley acknowledged there was such a proposal in 1944, but he also raised doubts about "the capacity of the Australian nation to meet the physical requirements of troops based in Australia".[14] Next Baron Van Aerssen divulged the External Affairs letter[15] and also alleged breach of faith against the Australian Government. The Prime Minister thereupon accused the Netherlands envoy of "highly improper" behaviour.

Mr Chifley was already somewhat disenchanted with his Dutch allies and was looking for escape clauses in the contract to accept 30,000 troops from Holland. The shift in SWPA priorities in March 1945 — from NEI operations to the Philippines invasion — aided him in this. The Allied Chiefs of Staff, short of shipping, resisted the plan for early despatch of the 30,000, but in April 1945 agreed that a first instalment of 5,600 Dutch troops should be landed in Australia. At the Potsdam Conference that followed immediately on Germany's defeat, the Dutch lobbied President Truman and the British for more or less emergency transport of 27,000 soldiers from Holland to Australia. The Allied Chiefs of Staff could see no way at this stage of getting the Dutch Army on its long journey to Australia. Too many ships were at the bottom of the sea and they had more urgent priorities.

Again, the compound sum of delays was adding up to make the coming boycott of the Dutch in Australian ports all the more disruptive. The anti-Dutch campaign in Australia was also to make the country far too inhospitable as a training base for Dutch troops destined for transhipment to the Indies. War dislocation meant that the first Dutch troops could not reach Australia from Holland until November 1945, aboard the *Stirling Castle*, sailing under British Admiralty orders.

Dutch soldiers lining the *Stirling Castle*'s decks at Circular Quay, Sydney, to hurl missiles at Australian demonstrators for Indonesian independence were nearly all untrained recruits. They were not ready for Java where the battle lines were now drawn. Before they went into action these young men anticipated training and equipment in Australia. It could have been that the decision not to disembark them in Australia was taken before they reached Sydney, due to mounting hostility to the Dutch cause and the danger of violent confrontations. The riotous responses to the Dutch soldiers' arrival by the *Stirling Castle* and the demonstrations at the *Moreton Bay*, to which the Dutch soldiers were transferred at Sydney, were enough to get the Australian Government off the hook. The campaign against the colonial Dutch prevented the conversion of Australia to an important *place d'armes* for war on the first significant ex-colonial regime ever established in South-East Asia. Mr Chifley may not have been displeased at the *Stirling Castle-Moreton Bay* disturbances, or at the Dutch command's estimate that Australian public opinion was so hostile that the Dutch troops could not be allowed shore leave after their long voyage for fear of mayhem in Sydney's streets. No more was heard of the plan to train and equip the Dutch Army in Australia. The future movement of Dutch troops was outward only, and that seldom according to plan. After the Sydney demonstrations against the Dutch Army's arrival, Air Minister Drakeford pledged that no Australian airmen would be allowed to go to Java. A prior arrangement by the Government to "lend" 250 Australians to staff a Dutch air base until Dutch reinforcements arrived was cancelled following the Sydney wharf riot.

304

Toll of Easy Living

Import of colonial habits from the Hotel des Indes to Brisbane fostered a masterly inactivity in face of onrushing emergencies. The Netherlands commanders responsible for the Indies operation also failed to address the problem of rational Intelligence analysis of the nationalist movement in Java. While the Australian boycott gave the Indonesian Republic time to get traction, the unamended habits of the Dutch emigres gave the unions time to beaver away to build the dykes against passage to Batavia.

Neither the reinstated Government at The Hague nor Drs Van Mook and Van Der Plas took kindly to being asked to march to the discordant rhythms of their allies. They pressed Mountbatten to make all haste to Java, but the same high-tuned admonitions do not seem to have been despatched to Government-in-Exile executives charged with the movement of Dutch personnel and supplies out of Australian ports. No high noon tensions intruded on the social gatherings in specially constructed beer gardens and officers' messes. The generosity of the Curtin Government to Dutch guests unwittingly served the boycotters.

Dr Van Mook, addressing at Pangkalpinang, Java, in 1946, a conference of minority groups likely to assist a compromise settlement for Indonesia, was called on to answer criticism that the "Brisbane Government" had spent too much time in soft-living and diversions to allow study of Indies developments. The criticism was not baseless. While waiting, in contemplation of the gilded existence ahead, the Allied liberation of the NEI Dutch officialdom in Australia became slothful. Between the Japanese surrender of 15 August and the weekend of 22-23 September 1945, when the boycott snares were set, the Netherlands Indies Government-in-Exile was dilatory in preparing removal to Java. The troopship *Van Heutz*, designated to carry key administrative and military leaders and documentation from the Camp Colombia headquarters at Wacol, had not completed loading by 24 September, the day on which Indonesian seamen and Australian waterfront unionists immobilised her in the Brisbane River.

Similar delay occurred with the loading of the new guilder

notes and coins minted in America and shipped to Australia, though a Dutch currency system was vital to resumption of rule. The chests of postwar NEI currency, stored in Melbourne bank vaults for months to revive the Dutch-supervised Indies economy, had barely been loaded in full when the Indonesian crew, on Sunday, 23 September, served notice that they would not sail the *Karisk*, the chosen currency transport, out of Melbourne's Yarra River.

Admittedly, demands on services were heavy in the immediate postwar months, but there were not sufficient encumbrances to justify the Government-in-Exile's failure to despatch the *Van Heutz* and the *Karsik* weeks earlier.

Deaf Ear to Intelligence Warnings

The Dutch Intelligence in Australia had informers among the Indonesians. Australian Intelligence services, fairly well informed on moves by the Australian left and militant unions and on Indonesian contacts with them, passed on their reports to the Dutch Intelligence. The Dutch, as brilliant linguists, did not lack staff able to read the portents in the leftwing press.

Intelligence reports from Java, far more foreboding, were available to the Government-in-Exile's leaders before the walk-offs from the Dutch ships in Australian ports. Mountbatten revealed at his Sydney conference with trade union leaders and Australian Government representatives in 1946 that his agents had reported to him on 18 August, three days after Japan's surrender, that there was then in Indonesia "a strong, widespread, legitimate independence movement".[16]

Though Colonel Simon H. Spoor's Australian-based Intelligence operations yielded scanty results — Captain G.C.M. Van Arcken and two others, landing in Java from a submarine, learned little and most other secret landing parties were lost to the Japanese — the Dutch had the same opportunities as Indonesians in their Australian offices to monitor radio broadcasts from Japanese-occupied Java. These had provided the Indonesians with clues to postwar developments. The NICA Intelligence units would have found it difficult to ignore

306

Republican manifestations in the Moluccas following the Allied presence there in 1944.

Dr Evatt claimed that Australian special representatives were in the Netherlands Indies "since VJ-Day".[17] In that event they must have been on the spot when the Republic was proclaimed on 17 August. The Australian agents' reports would have been available to the Dutch. As Dr Van Der Plas was by then at Mountbatten's side, acting as liaison for the Netherlands Indies Government-in-Exile at the SEAC Ceylon base, the Mountbatten Intelligence report would surely have been known to him and relayed to Camp Columbia.

If Dr Van Der Plas needed confirmation of the 18 August report from Mountbatten's agent he got it on 16 September on arrival at Tanjong Priok aboard the first British warship to make a Java port, HMS *Cumberland* (Rear-Admiral W.R. Patterson). Margueritte Harmon Bro, wife of an American diplomat who served in Indonesia after the war, wrote[18] that the British arrived in Batavia to find red-and-white Republican flags flying from Government buildings, Indonesian signs on the ministries and *merdeka* on every tongue. Indonesian police, she said, patrolled a peaceful city.

The seven officers who formed the advance party of the first Allied Mission to the NEI, parachuted to Kemajoran (Batavia) airport on 8 September 1945, reported that the political problem was "most acute in Batavia" and that there was "intense anti-Dutch propaganda among the natives".[19] No directives came to Brisbane and Melbourne stevedoring companies to seek labor priorities for loading Dutch ships selected to carry administrators and currency.

The Lonely Viceroy

Australian news correspondents were in Batavia before *Van Heutz*, *Karisk* and other urgently required ships were held by union black bans and Indonesian mutinies. The correspondents reported that the British were asking the Japanese Commander-in-Chief, Major-General Yamaguchi, to keep order. One correspondent cabled that the British and Dutch of the Allied

Mission were "quartered in the Hotel des Indes as guests of senior Japanese officers".[20]

The condominium of *Pax Japonica*, *Pax Britannica* and *Pax Neerlandica* was a gift to propagandists of the Australian boycott movement against the colonial restoration. Reliance on Japanese troops and then on SEAC reinforcements told the world that so strong was Indonesian Republican resistance that only by support of the hated enemy, Japan, and the armed forces of the old imperial rival in the East, the British, could the Dutch ever hope to reimpose control.

Dr Van Mook, as Acting Governor-General, landed in Java, his native earth, on 3 October 1945. Instead of shiploads of troops, civil servants and munitions from Australia Dr Van Mook found Republican soldiers and policemen running a city they called Djakarta and a new flag flapping in the trade wind. Where once batik-saronged Javanese waited his command not a soul came forward to lift the Viceroy's bags. He and his staff carried their own luggage to the vice-regal palace. Footfalls sounded hollowly in the deserted expanses, larders were empty and no servants were at hand to procure or serve him a bowl of rice, let alone a rijs-taffel. It took some days to find Indonesian servants daring enough to serve the Dutch leader whose name was now a dirty word on the capital's walls.

One slogan cried: ' Van Mook — What Are You Doing Here?" His spectacles, another story went, were not good enough to read the next slogan, so he asked his secretary. The secretary whispered it: "Death to Van Mook!"

The lonely Emperor had no clothes . . .

Threat of Indo-China Fate

The boycotts and mutinies in Australia and the effects of delays to the Dutch war plans before the 1949 Hague Agreement can have no precise measures in territorial or diplomatic gains for the Indonesian Republic. However, it is marginally ahead of an educated guess that the black armada and the spinoffs from the anti-colonial movement in Australia siphoned away sufficient Dutch capacity to prevent occu-

308

pation of the vital north-western areas of Java, embracing Batavia and Bandung, following Japan's collapse, and the speedy setting up of a more plausible regime in Batavia. These would have augmented significantly Dutch military clout and diplomatic bargaining power against the Republic.

The value of Australian assistance was given wider dimension by the onset of the cold war and US State Secretary Dulles' brinkmanship. By the time of The Hague Agreement the fogs were closing down on UN-chartered hopes for an end to foreign interference in Asian nations' affairs. The Republic just made the high ground in time; hence the warmth of Indonesian appreciation of the schedule-wrecking delays inflicted on the Dutch by Australian boycotters. If the Indonesians had not been able to reach in a short five years, in face of bloody disorders, commotions and confusions, adequate administrative and military organisation and political resources, the archipelago could well have become another Indo-China.

Washington's hostility to the Soekarno Government was modified by the crushing of the left forces at Madiun in Java and by the black discredit which befell the Dutch after their December 1948 Police Action. In 1949 the Americans began throwing their weight about again in the Dutch interest. Margueritte Harmon Bro, observing from US diplomatic offices in Java, described how, when pre-Hague discussions opened at Djakarta, American envoy Cochran "continually pressed" Indonesian delegate Roem "to give in to Dutch demands" voiced by Holland's Van Royen.[21] The State Department under Mr Dulles was doing its best to push Indonesian independence into the swamps. Asia's upsurge shadowed all judgments in Washington. The Hague Agreement creating the vulnerable "United States of Indonesia" was signed only three months after the last remnants of the Kuomintang Government fled to Taiwan. American arms and money flowed in a swollen stream to French Indo-China. Sustenance also went to a Kuomintang military rabble in Burma and means were canvassed for a Chiang Kai-shek restoration in China. Aggressive lobbies came to the forefront in Washington, particularly the "China Lobby" advocates of armed intervention to stem the Asian tides. Senator Joseph

McCarthy was subduing all in the State Department bold enough to suggest that colonialism's maladies in Asia were terminal. Enthusiasm for UN Charter rights could not easily be kindled, as foreign policy became indexed to cold war escalations. Britain, deploying troops against a Communist-led uprising in Malaya, and Australia, soon to have troops in East and South-East Asia, gave obeisance to the charmless John Foster Dulles. The Communist Party of Indonesia was showing symptoms of recuperation after the Madiun hecatomb: there were "red menace" overtones to the old "Asian hordes" neurosis.

In June 1950 the Korean War signalled America's intention to intervene massively in Asia and to mobilise as many partners as possible. Australian airmen and soldiers were General MacArthur's first allies on the Korean battlefield. President Truman ordered immediate Seventh Fleet occupation of Taiwan and acceleration of arms flow to the Philippines Government to fight internal opponents. Nuclear bases were established in Japan. The Joint Chiefs of Staff advised all US commanders of troops abroad ' to increase their readiness without creating an atmosphere of tension"[22] — an order that carried a contradiction. Tension was already the rule. US invasion on the side of Saigon friends followed the French debacle of Dien Bien Phu and the Indo-China War flared into one of the most devastating in Asia's history. Efforts to reverse historical processes under the slogans of "counter-insurgency" and "anti-subversion" now had top place on Washington's agenda and the expected support from London, The Hague and Canberra.

The course of events in Indonesia during the 1950s invoked loose definitions of "subversion". The time-bombs set by The Hague Agreement were ticking audibly. The Dutch-monitored "United States of Indonesia" carried the seeds of bloody discord, not by accident. The archipelago was carved into "autonomous" regions, prey to local prejudices, separatist ambitions and cultural divisions. The sprawl of some 3,000 inhabited islands and some 4,000 uninhabited islets offered countless lairs for guerillas to assail a Republic that lacked naval and air strength. The USI's wobbly scaffolding looked easy to dismantle. The islands around Java could be gradually

310

stripped away and the main Republican base encircled, the primitive economy cast into the quagmire and the Government compressed and subverted. Supply bases for anti-Republican forces at Singapore, British Borneo, Darwin and in the Philippines could tighten the noose.

Amok is an Indonesian word: it was the Dutch who earned its application. Holland's Captain Turco Westerling was guilty of massacres; the Republic could not but draw lessons from America's failure to protest and British and Dutch refusal of Indonesian requests for Westerling's extradition to be tried for his crimes. Dutch unravelling of the USI was to begin at the hems. They nibbled away at the Moluccas, main recruiting area for mercenaries. The Dutch slotted in their puppets, schooled to behave as "brown Dutchmen", for the "Republic of the South Moluccas", which was able to buy arms in Australia. Various Republican officials were assassinated in this decade and attempts were made on President Soekarno's life.

American, British, Dutch and — allegedly — Australian support to the 1958 "Permesta" insurrection, for which rebel leaders were moved from Singapore-Malaya to Sumatra, was evidence that a serious decision had been taken to supplant the Republican Government with a collaborationist leadership. Central Intelligence Agency involvement in the insurrection could have only one meaning. CIA activities have been sufficiently demisted to reveal that a US aircraft shot down on a bombing mission against the Republic was flown by a CIA pilot.[23] It was a fair estimate that he was not the only CIA operative engaged against the Indonesian Republic.

President Soekarno's adventurous confrontation with Malaysia later on was due in part to use of Malayan territories, where Australian troops were stationed with British, as a base for the anti-Republican insurgents.

The foreign-promoted carnage and disorder of the 1950s and Anglo-American-Australian backing, until late 1961 or early 1962, of the revanchiste Hollanders' hold on the powerfully equipped ex-American bases at Hollandia and Biak would have been more than sufficient to convince the Republic that the time and space won for it by the 1945-49 boycotts of

311

Dutch war-supply services were precious. Though hit between wind and water by foreign and puppet armed forces, by blockade and insurrection, the Republicans, able to create in time a viable central system, avoided a Vietnam price in blood and ashes. The "brown Dutchmen" required to invite foreign invasion on the Saigon model could not be found in adequate weight. The scenarios of alien subversion were many, but the Indonesians, when faced by the "United States of Indonesia" system, spuriously mandated by American muscle, were in possession of the administrative capacity to weather the storms. Threats of a Vietnam-style intervention evaporated like the steam from ships' boilers made cold by black bans in Australian ports. Except for the brutal interruptions in the South Moluccas and Sumatra, Republican central authority was accepted all over the former Netherlands East Indies, excluding West New Guinea, from 1951.

Underlined in Red

Dutch and Ambonese troops were no match for Republican guerillas in an archipelago of myriads of islands, terraced slopes, mountain and jungle retreats and hostile millions. The Dutch soldiery found the drum-beat in their hearts fainter and many were glad to be shot of their country's dirty war. By 1957 most Dutch enterprises were nationalised and 50,000 Dutch nationals received expulsion orders. The colonial Dutch, along with their bedraggled sepoy detachments, mostly returned to Holland. A few thousand came to Australia, ranging from a former commandant of the Casino camp where Indonesian mutineers were interned to airmen who rocketed Djogjakarta. Unlike the Dutch who huffed and puffed in 1942-45, they were shrinking violets — "New Australians" to the indigenes.

So strong were interventionary moods in Washington, Canberra and Asian capitals with rulers under American patronage — as the Vietnam holocaust was soon to underline — that the death throes of the Dutch Empire of the East came none too early for the Republic's survival. The Australian boycotts and mutinies were certainly not decisive, but they were an historic contribution to the scales that tipped against

Gall, *Courier-Mail*, 22 December 1948

RIGHT ON OUR DOORSTEP

Gall, *Courier-Mail*, 29 December 1949

THINGS ARE HAPPENING NEXT DOOR

KEEP IT DARK

Gall, *Courier-Mail*, 21 January 1949

Eyre Jr, *Sydney Morning Herald*, 24 January 1949

DR EVATT AND MR HYDE

There is a widespread conviction that Australia can have no possible place at the
New Delhi conference on Indonesia

the Dutch and their allies and allowed the Republic of Indonesia, first represented before the nations at UNO by the Australian Government of 1947, to step on to the world stage.

Australia, from whose ports troopships sailed to uphold colonial rule in Africa and Asia, blockaded colonialist troopships in those same ports in 1945-49 and for the first time in her history won a place on the national liberation record. This independence, so assisted, came to the world's second greatest colony. It was not relevant then to forecast the traumas that must arise for newly independent Indonesia, flowing from inexperience in government and foreign relations, illiteracy and the withering of much cultural flora, an economy filleted by centuries of wealth extraction, with pathetically low industrial, financial and technological bases and a faltering plantation and peasant agriculture; breathtaking problems of transport and communication and, in common with most other Third World nations, a vulnerability to military coups. Independence, despite all this, was a thousand times better than the humiliation of colonial subjection.

Australian Air Force Prisoner-of War Relief Officers, travelling between Batavia and Sourabaya not long after Japan's capitulation, noted that prominent everywhere on the roads of Java were bulletins issued by Indonesian nationalists. These bulletins reported the Australian trade unions' boycott of the Dutch in the cause of Indonesian independence. The news from Australia was underlined in red.

As for the Dutch, they reached to the ultimate in acknowledgment of the place won in Indonesian hearts by Australians responsible for the black armada. The first Australian newspaper despatches from postwar Java recorded that the small advance party of Dutchmen wore Australian Army "Digger" hats and uniforms as insurance against Indonesian wrath in the streets of Batavia.

313

Appendix

The Boycott List

Royal Netherlands Navy

Karel Doorman, aircraft-carrier

Groningen, destroyer

Limburg, destroyer

Piet Hein, corvette

K15, submarine

Submarine (not identified) kept in disrepair and eventually used as a breakwater in Fremantle

RP-105, RP-106, RP-107 and four other submarine-chasers not identified

(*Tromp*, heavily armed cruiser, badly damaged in the Lombok Strait in 1942, got away in September 1945 with some of her crew mutinous, before trade unions had begun the boycott)

Australian Corvettes Transferred to Royal Netherlands Navy

Ambon (ex-*Cairns*)

Banda (ex-*Wollongong*)

Batjan (ex-*Lismore*)

Boeroe (ex-*Toowoomba*)

314

Ceram (ex-*Burnie*)

Morotai (ex-*Ipswich*)

Ternate (ex-*Tamworth*)

Tidore (ex-*Kalgoorlie*)

(These eight corvettes of 790 tons displacement (full load), all built in Australian yards during the war, were sold by the Chifley Government to the Dutch early in 1946. Some were delayed in shipyards: they all came under both shipyard and maritime unions' bans. Munitions and other war supplies were put into them by Dutch and Australian Services personnel. *Jane's Fighting Ships*, 1947-48 edition, described the eight corvettes as "all serving in the East Indies".

Royal (British) Navy

Moreton Bay, troopship

Stirling Castle, troopship

Royal Australian Navy

Bungaree, sloop

Kanimbla, naval auxiliary transport

Manoora, naval auxiliary cruiser

(No call was made for trade union labor for these three RAN ships; they were automatically declared black when union-banned cargoes were loaded into them for Java by naval ratings or Dutch military personnel.)

MERCHANT SHIPS

Balikpapan

Bonaire

Bontekoe

Both

Cawra

Curacao

El Liberatador

Fort Renselaár (US-owned, Dutch crew)

General Verspijck

*Grootekerk**

Janssens

Japara

Karsik

Khoen Hoea

Kota Gedeh

Maetsuycker

Merak

Minjak Tanah

Nieuw Holland

Pahud

Patras

Roepat

Stagen

Straat Malakka

Swartenhondt

Tarakan

Tasman

Tjibesar

Tjikampek

Tosari

Van Der Lin

Van Den Bosch

Van Heutz

316

Van Outhoorn

Van Spilbergen

Wewak

*Meliskerk, *Gastekerk* and two other ships of the same Holland Australia Line as *Grootekerk* were announced as under black ban, but they were not in Australian ports at the time. The ban on them was lifted before it could become operative.

Oil Vessels

Ceronia, tanker

Tanker, not identified

Chelmer, motor-lighter

Hampshire, oil company tug

Plym, motor-launch

18 200-ton barges

5 100-ton barges

9 50-ton barges

Barges, Lighters, Landing Craft

450 small vessels ready for shipment or towage were mentioned by Lieutenant A.M. Denboer, Netherlands Indies Government Sea Transport Officer, before the Arbitration Court at Sydney early in March 1946. They were power and dumb barges, lighters, surf-landing-craft.

Australian Trade Unions With Members Involved in Boycott

Amalgamated Engineering Union
Australasian Society of Engineers
Australian Federation of Locomotive Enginemen
Australian Meat Industry Employees' Union
Australian Railways Union

Blacksmiths' Society
Boilermakers' Society
Breadcarters' Union
Building Workers' Industrial Union

Electrical Trades Union

Federated Clerks' Union
Federated Enginedrivers and Firemen's Association
Federated Ironworkers' Association
Federated Ship Painters and Dockers' Union
Firemen and Deckhands' Association

Hotel, Club and Restaurant Employees' Union

Marine Stewards and Pantrymen's Union
Merchant Service Guild
Miners' Federation
Moulders' Union

Operative Painters' Union

Plumbers' Union

Seamen's Union
Sheet Metal Workers' Union
Shipwrights' Union
Storemen and Packers' Union

Transport Workers' Union

Vehicle Builders' Union

Waterside Workers' Federation
West Australian Docks', Rivers and Harbour Workers' Union
West Australian Carpenters and Joiners' Union

Trade Unions of Asian Seamen, Temporarily Established in Australia and Participating in the Boycott

Chinese Seamen's Union in Australia
Indonesian Seamen's Union in Australia
Indian Seamen's Union in Australia
Malayan Merchant Navy Association

Countries Where Boycotts Were Imposed on the Dutch Following Boycott Action in Australia

Burma	China	India	Pakistan	United States
Canada	Egypt	Japan*	Singapore	of America
Ceylon	Holland	New Zealand	Thailand	(West Coast)

(Assistance to the Dutch war in Indonesia was prohibited in the Soviet Union and associated countries at government level.)

*Refusal of entry to *Karel Doorman* and escorts during West Irian crisis.

References

Introduction

1. *Sydney Morning Herald*, 7 August 1947.
2. *The Stakes of Democracy in South-East Asia* by H.J. Van Mook, London, 1950.
3. *Courier-Mail*, Brisbane, 13 October 1945.
4. *Commonwealth Parliamentary Debates*, 6 March 1946.
5. *Commonwealth Parliamentary Debates*, 26 June 1945.
6. Australian Associated Press, Singapore, 4 November 1948; in *Courier-Mail*, Brisbane, 5 November 1948.
7. *Commonwealth Parliamentary Debates*, 18 July 1944.
8. See 7.
9. See 7.

Chapter 1

1. The note tossed ashore from the *Both* at Bowen was delivered to Mr J.C. Henry, then Queensland State leader of the Communist Party of Australia, in Brisbane. He personally took the note to Sydney. Mr Henry gave to the writer in two personal interviews at Sydney in February 1974 his account of events associated with the Tanah Merah prisoners' arrival, of their political activities and their ideological conflicts and tactics, of which he had intimate knowledge.
2. *Dutch Imperialism Exposed: The Green Hell of Tanah Merah*, published by the Indonesian Independence Committee, Melbourne, 1946.

3. *Out of Exile*, by Sutan Sjahrir, New York, 1949.
4. *Indonesian Introduction*, by Gerald Peel, Sydney, 1945.
5. Abdul Rachman was a student at an English-language class for Indonesians conducted by Mrs Gwyn Williams, of Darlinghurst, Sydney. Mrs Williams noted the stories her Indonesian students had to tell of their experiences. She gave considerable information to the writer, including Abdul Rachman's account of his escape from Tanah Merah and deportation from Australia, in a personal interview at Sydney in May 1964.
6. *Australia in the War of 1939-45: the Japanese Thrust*, by Lionel Wigmore; Series I, Army, Vol. IV, Australian War Memorial, Canberra, 1957.
7. See 2.
8. Mrs Laura Gapp, of Narrabeen North, Sydney, related in two personal interviews in May 1961 her discussions, experiences and work among the Tanah Merah exiles and other Indonesians.
9. The writer had several personal interviews with Sardjono at Sydney in October and November 1945, and also interviewed other Tanah Merah ex-prisoners.
10. Bulletin, Committee of Indonesian Independence, Brisbane, 16 October 1945.

Chapter 2

1. *Out of Exile*, by Sutan Sjahrir, New York, 1949.
2. The accounts given in this chapter of the Tanah Merah exiles' political attitudes, evolution and strategies and of their contacts and cooperation with the Australian Left are based on personal interviews with Sardjono at Sydney in October and November 1945 and with other deportees from the Digul during 1944-45; and on two personal interviews in February 1974 with Mr J.C. Henry. Mr Henry was given the main responsibility from the Communist Party of Australia for work among the Indonesians and he acquired a considerable knowledge of the Indonesian revolutionary movement's history. The writer, as Associate Editor of the Communist *Tribune*, organ of the CPA Central Committee, in this period, also had personal acquaintance with Indonesian activities.
3. See 2 for references to J.C. Henry.

Chapter 3

1. *Australia in the War of 1939-45, Royal Australian Air Force, 1939-45*, by Douglas Gillison; Series I, Air, Vol. I, Australian War Memorial, Canberra, 1962.
2. See 1.
3. See 1.

4. *The Story of the 2/2nd. Pioneer Battalion*, by E.F. Aiken, Melbourne, 1953.
5. Lewis Hillier, now an official of the Melbourne Branch, Waterside Workers' Federation of Australia, described the escape of his party from Singapore and Tjilatjap to the writer in personal interviews during October 1974.
6. *Sydney Morning Herald*, 10 March 1942.

Chapter 4

1. *Current Notes on International Affairs*, Vol. 12, No. 3, Department of External Affairs, Canberra, March 1942.
2. *Commonwealth Parliamentary Debates*, 29 April 1942.
3. *Commonwealth Parliamentary Debates*, 14 October 1943.
4. John Quinlem, letter to *Bulletin* editor, *23 June 1962.*

Chapter 5

1. *Australia in the War of 1939-45: The Japanese Thrust*, by Lionel Wigmore; Series I, Army, Vol. IV, Australian War Memorial, Canberra, 1957.
2. *Commonwealth Parliamentary Debates*, 9 February 1949.
3. Estimate given to the writer by the late Mr James Healy, then General Secretary, Waterside Workers' Federation, in May 1961.
4. Mr Elliott described the *Swartenhondt* dispute in a personal interview with the writer at Sydney in June 1964.
5. *Sydney Morning Herald*, 25 September 1945.
6. *Seamen's Journal*, Sydney, September 1945.
7. *Commonwealth Parliamentary Debates*, 14 May 1942.

Chapter 6

1. *The Stakes of Democracy in South-East Asia*, by H.J. Van Mook, London, 1950.
2. *Commonwealth Parliamentary Debates*, 18 May 1945.
3. See 2.
4. Personal interview with Mrs Williams, May 1964.
5. Personal interview with Mrs Gapp, May 1964.
6. The petty-officer related the incident to Mrs Williams (see 4).
7. Quoted, *Merdeka*, pamphlet issued by the Central Committee of Indonesian Independence, Brisbane, on the first anniversary of the Republic's proclamation, 17 August 1946.
8. See 7.
9. "Australia and the Indonesians", *Communist Review*, Sydney, December 1944.

Chapter   7

1. *The Stakes of Democracy in South-East Asia*, by H.J. Van Mook, London, 1950.
2. Minutes, Queensland Trades and Labor Council, Brisbane: Meeting 22 August 1945.
3. *Tribune*, Sydney, 23 August 1945.
4. *Civil Liberty*, organ of the Council for Civil Liberties, Melbourne, March 1946.
5. Minutes, Queensland Trades and Labor Council, Brisbane: Executive meeting 12 November 1945.
6. See 5.

Chapter   8

1. Manifesto (roneo-ed), in Waterside Workers' Federation Indonesian File.
2. Quoted, *Tribune*, Sydney, 25 September 1945.
3. Leaflet authorised by M. Healy, for Queensland Trades and Labor Council, September 1945.
4. Bulletin, Committee of Indonesian Independence, Brisbane, 16 October 1945.
5. Minutes, Queensland Trades and Labor Council: Executive Meeting 17 September, Council meeting 19 September 1945.
6. *Tribune*, Sydney, 26 October 1945.
7. Minutes, Queensland TLC: meeting 17 October 1945.
8. See 7.
9. The two released internees, Rakiman and Soebardi, reported this to Queensland TLC Secretary M. Healy, who was interviewed by the writer at Brisbane in January 1970.
10. 18 April 1946.
11. Quoted, *Merdeka* (pamphlet), Central Committee of Indonesian Independence, Brisbane, August 1946.
12. The late Mr James Healy, General Secretary, WWF, and other trade union leaders who made representations to Mr Calwell were the source of this account of the cable to The Hague.

Chapter   9

1. Personal interview with Mrs Williams, May 1964.
2. Australian maritime unions who were in touch with Subianto have heard nothing of him since the massacres that followed the "September 30 Movement" of 1965. He is missing, believed dead.
3. Personal interview with Mr E.V. Elliott, Federal Secretary, Seaman's Union of Australia, June 1964.
4. See 3.
5. Mr Healy described to the writer the events leading to the walk-

offs of Indonesian seamen and subsequent actions in a personal interview at Brisbane, January 1970.

6. Minutes, Queensland TLC: Report by M. Healy to Disputes Committee meeting, 24 September 1945.

7. Leaflet, authorised by M. Healy for Queensland Trades and Labor Council, September 1945.

8. Quoted, *Merdeka*, pamphlet issued by the Central Committee of Indonesian Independence on the first anniversary of the Republic's proclamation, Brisbane, 17 August 1946.

9. The roneo-ed circular bore the imprint, "Waterside Workers' Federation Branch of the Communist Party," and was first distributed to Sydney waterside workers on 22 September 1945.

Chapter 10

1. Minutes, Brisbane Branch, Waterside Workers' Federation: Meeting, 1 October 1945.

2. Minutes, Queensland TLC: Meeting, 3 October 1945.

3. Copy of Mr Englart's telegram in WWF Indonesian File.

4. See 3.

5. Copies of messages and protests in WWF Indonesian File.

6. Minutes, Queensland TLC Disputes Committee: Meeting, 27 September 1945.

7. See 6.

8. Minutes, Queensland TLC Disputes Committee: Meeting, 29 September 1945.

Chapter 11

1. This was the opinion of the late Mr Charles Young, WWF Federal Councillor, who made personal representations to the *Karsik*'s crew: personal interview with the writer, September 1962.

2. Mr Young (see 1) gave all assistance possible, but pointed out that those controlling Melbourne WWF Branch at the time "kept no files other than press cuttings" on the boycott of Dutch ships. The writer inspected these and found the cuttings of little value. The Victorian Branch of the Seamen's Union has no records whatever in its Melbourne office that related to the 1945-49 period.

3. Mr Young gave a written report on the Melbourne events, additional to the personal account of the previous year's interview, in a letter to the writer dated 18 October 1963.

4. 3 October 1945.

5. See 4.

6. Mr Little's telegram in WWF Indonesian File.

7. Australian Associated Press despatch from Batavia, *Sydney Morning Herald*, 7 March 1946.

8. See 7.

9.   *Sydney Morning Herald*, 11 March 1946.

Chapter   12

1.   *Sydney Morning Herald*, 28 September 1945.
2.   *Boycott the Dutch*, issued by Frank Kelly for NSW Trades and Labor Council, October 1945.
3.   Correspondence, 1945 files of Federated Ship Painters and Dockers' Union, Sydney.

Chapter   13

1.   Minutes, Western Australian Docks, Rivers and Harbour Workers' Union, Fremantle, 1945.
2.   See 1.
3.   *Quarterly Report*, organ of Federal Council, Boilermakers' Society of Australia, No. 37, Vol. III, Sydney, July 1946.
4.   See 1.
5.   Letter to the author from P. Troy, Trades Hall, Fremantle, 9 December 1963.
6.   2 April 1946.
7.   *West Australian*, Perth, 15 April 1946.
8.   Minutes, Brisbane Branch, Waterside Workers' Federation: Executive meeting, 6 November 1946.

Chapter   14

1.   Mr Healy described the arrangements to accommodate Indonesian seamen in a personal interview with the writer at Brisbane in January 1970.
2.   Interview with Mr Healy (see 1).
3.   See 2.
4.   *Sydney Morning Herald*, 4 October 1945.
5.   *Commonwealth Parliamentary Debates*, 25 September 1945.
6.   6 October 1945.
7.   The language test or dictation test under the Commonwealth Immigration Act was, before its abolition after World War II, a transparent legal device to allow the Australian Government to claim that it banned certain migrants on "educational" grounds and not because of skin pigmentation (or, in some cases, politics). Unwanted migrants were customarily examined in a language they were unlikely to understand.
8.   *Telegraph*, Brisbane, 14 November 1945.
9.   Quoted, *Merdeka*, pamphlet issued by the Central Committee of Indonesian Independence, on the first anniversary of the Republic's proclamation, 17 August 1946.
10. 29 October 1945.

11. Mr Smith described the Lido incidents in a personal interview with the writer at Sydney in October 1964.
12. *Civil Liberty*, organ of the Council for Civil Liberties, Melbourne, March 1946.
13. 18 April 1946.
14. *Boycott the Dutch*, leaflet issued by the NSW Trades and Labor Council, October 1945.
15. Letter from the Minister for the Army to General Secretary, Waterside Workers' Federation, 22 May 1946; in WWF Indonesian File. The Dutch exercised territorial rights in dealing with their nominal Indonesian subjects, without due legal authorisation from but with the connivance of the Australian Government, up till the end of 1943. It was not until 24 November 1943, long after Indonesian seamen and Digul internees had been put into Australian prisons and camps that the Minister for the Army, Mr F.M. Forde, formally authorised the incarceration of the Dutch Empire's subjects who broke Dutch laws.

Chapter   15

1. "Outline of the Struggle in Australia," by the Central Committee of Independence, in *Republic of Indonesia* (pamphlet), Brisbane, February 1946.
2. *Commonwealth Parliamentary Debates*, 3 October 1945.
3. *Sydney Morning Herald*, 6 October 1945.
4. Telegram in WWF Indonesian File; date obscured.
5. *Commonwealth Parliamentary Debates*, 6 March 1946.
6. See 5.
7. Personal interview with M. Healy, Brisbane, 15 January 1970.
8. Minutes, Trades and Labor Council: Executive meeting, 15 October 1945.
9. See 7.
10. See 8.
11. The Haryono arrangement was described by M. Healy (see 7).
12. The Central Committee of Indonesian Independence (roneo-ed bulletin, Brisbane, 23 July 1947) refers to "27 persons detained under Australian jurisdiction at the instance of the Allied South-East Asia Command at Koepang, Timor, later in British Borneo and Singapore."
13. From typewritten notes in WWF Indonesian File of discussion between Mr Calwell and WWF Assistant General Secretary E. Roach, 8 February 1946.
14. Letter dated 6 April 1946 in files of Sydney Branch, Boilermakers' Society of Australia.
15. Bulletin (roneo-ed), by Information Service, Central Committee of Indonesian Independence, Brisbane, 23 July 1947.
16. Quoted, *Merdeka* (pamphlet), issued by the Central Committee of

Indonesian Independence, Brisbane, on the first anniversary of the Republic's proclamation, 17 August 1946.

17. *Commonwealth Parliamentary Debates*, 9 February 1949.
18. Minutes, Queensland Trades and Labor Council Executive.
19. Letter to Mr H. Grant, Chairman, NSW Trades and Labor Council Indonesian Sub-Committee, 6 April 1946; in files of Sydney Branch, Boilermakers' Society of Australia.
20. Ex-Able-Seaman McCormick, then a Federal Councillor of the WWF, described the *Manoora* voyage and incidents at Batavia in an interview with the writer, Sydney, October 1964.
21. Quoted, *Labor News*, organ of Federated Ironworkers' Association, Sydney, April 1946.
22. See 21.
23. *Commonwealth Parliamentary Debates*, 7 March 1947.
24. Letter dated 23 November 1946: copy in WWF Indonesian File.
25. *Commonwealth Parliamentary Debates*, 9 February 1949.
26. Personal interview with Mr Arthur Calwell, former Minister for Information (1943-49) and Immigration (1945-49), later Leader of Federal Parliamentary Opposition; 9 April 1971.

Chapter   16

1. Mrs Phyllis Johnson, who was active in organising relief ashore for Indonesian and Indian strikers during the boycott of Dutch ships, and who now lives at Padstow, Sydney, gave her recollections to the writer in July 1964.
2. Mr Clarrie (sometimes called Steve) Campbell was a Sydney businessman involved in semi-secret trade deals with the Indonesian Republic in its founding years. He played a considerable part in assistance to Indonesian and Indian strikers ashore in Sydney. He gave frequent accounts of boycott happenings to the writer in 1945-46. Later Mr Campbell went to South-East Asia: his present whereabouts are not known to the writer.
3. *Sydney Morning Herald*, 28 September 1945.
4. Written report supplied in December 1963 by Mr S. Moran, then Treasurer, Sydney Branch, Waterside Workers' Federation, and now retired. Mr Moran took a prominent part in demonstrations and deputations involving Indian seamen.
5. 23 February 1946.
6. Minutes of ACTU-sponsored conference, in WWF Indonesian File.
7. See 6.
8. *Seamen's Journal*, organ of the Seamen's Union of Australia, May 1946.

Chapter   17

1. Messrs H. Grant, B. Smith, L. Greenfield, J. Johnson and M. Ryan,

main organisers of this operation to get Indians off Dutch ships, all gave their accounts to the writer in 1964. Dan Singh gave his versions to the writer almost daily in 1945.

2. *Tribune*, Sydney, 9 October 1945.
3. Report from Mr L. Greenfield, personal interview with the writer, June 1964.
4. The writer interviewed some of the *Patras* mutineers on their return to Sydney.
5. Mr Moran gave a written report to the writer on events concerning the Indian seamen, December 1963.
6. From a written report given to the writer by Mr M. Ryan, formerly of Sydney, then at New Lambton, Newcastle, December 1963.
7. See 6. The translation was by Dan Singh and the statement would have lost nothing in his interpretation.
8. *Commonwealth Parliamentary Debates*, 6 March 1946.
9. *Seamen's Journal*, August 1946.
10. *Seamen's Journal*, May 1946.

Chapter 18

1. *Merchant Seamen in the War* (pamphlet), by E.V. Elliott, Sydney, 1944.
2. *Sydney Morning Herald*, 27 September 1945.
3. Statement to Waterside Workers' Federation by Mr Abdulla, recorded in WWF Indonesian File.

Chapter 19

1. This sole expression of disagreement was noted by Mr Les Greenfield of Hunter's Hill, Sydney, who took part in the demonstration and gave an interview to the writer in July 1964. The writer personally witnessed events at the *Stirling Castle* and *Moreton Bay*.
2. Information from a personal interview with Mr Barney Smith in June 1964.
3. See 2.
4. The writer interviewed all of the *Moreton Bay* Ten after they came ashore, 12 November 1945.
5. BBC interview with Mountbatten, shown on ABC television, Sydney, 7 December 1969.

Chapter 20

1. Minutes, Queensland Trades and Labor Council: Meeting 12 December 1945.

2. *Maritime Worker*, 23 September 1946.
3. 12 March 1946.
4. Letter from Mr N. McKenzie, Secretary, Fremantle Branch, WWF, to Federal Office, Sydney, 23 December 1948; in WWF Indonesian File.
5. Quoted, "Indonesia — Fact and Fancy", (roneo-ed bulletin), issued by E.A. Laurie, Research Officer, Queensland TLC, 8 February 1946.
6. *Daily Telegraph*, Sydney, 28 February 1946.
7. Press statement, 28 February 1946; in WWF Indonesian File.
8. Telegram signed E. Englart, Secretary, in WWF Indonesian File.
9. Letter from c/o Hong Kong and Shanghai Banking Corporation, Singapore, 23 May 1947; in WWF Indonesian File. The captain signed his name, but this is suppressed in accord with his request.
10. Mr Healy told the writer in 1960 that he had shown this letter to Mr Chifley.
11. *Sydney Morning Herald*, 10 April 1946.
12. 10 April 1946.
13. 11 April 1946.
14. *Sun*, 11 April 1946.
15. *Tribune*, Sydney, 2 April 1946.
16. *Sydney Morning Herald*, 23 May 1946.
17. Mr Campbell told the writer of the trade-by-air project early in 1946. The press campaign and pressure on pilots about to be engaged made the project impracticable.
18. Leaflet, authorised by M. Healy for Queensland TLC, issued at the end of September 1945.
19. Minutes, Queensland TLC Disputes Committee: Meeting with unions involved in the boycott, 25 September 1945.
20. *Sydney Morning Herald*, 28 September 1945.
21. See 20.
22. Mr Roach described the *Tasman* events to the writer in November 1964.
23. *Sydney Morning Herald*, 29 September 1945.
24. Transcript, "A Conference re the Working of Dutch Ships," Proceedings in the Commonwealth Court of Conciliation and Arbitration, Sydney 1 March 1946.
25. Copy of Mr Matchett's letter in WWF Indonesian File.
26. Indonesian Information Service in Australia, the Republic of Indonesia Office, Canberra, July 1948.
27. *Commonwealth Parliamentary Debates*, 3 August 1946.

Chapter 21

1. Minutes, ACTU Executive.
2. Minutes, Queensland Trades and Labor Council Executive meeting, 4 December 1945.

3. See 2.
4. Telegram in WWF Indonesian File.
5. Telegram in WWF Indonesian File.
6. Minutes, ACTU Full Executive meeting, 18 to 22 February 1946.
7. Quoted, "Indonesia — Fact and Fancy" (roneo-ed bulletin), issued by E.A. Laurie, Research Officer, Queensland Trades and Labor Council, 8 February 1946.
8. Press statement (undated), in WWF Indonesian File.
9. Transcript, "A Conference re the Working of Dutch Ships," Proceedings in the Commonwealth Court of Conciliation and Arbitration, Sydney.
10. Two leading Indonesian Republicans in Australia personally recounted to the writer approaches from well known Victorian agricultural implements manufacturers and a visit to their works.
11. From a report of the meeting in WWF Indonesian File.
12. See 11.
13. *Sydney Morning Herald*, 12 March 1946.
14. See 11.
15. WWF press statement, 13 March 1946, in WWF Indonesian File.
16. 13 March 1946.
17. *Sydney Morning Herald*, 14 March 1946.
18. See 15.
19. 21 March 1946.
20. 23 March 1946.
21. *Maritime Worker*, Sydney, 23 March 1946.
22. See 21.
23. *Sydney Morning Herald* and *Daily Telegraph*, 16 March 1946.
24. See 15.

Chapter   22

1. 26 March 1946.
2. Mr Elliott described conversations with Mountbatten and other events at the conference in a personal interview with the writer, June 1964.
3. Mr Roach similarly described conversations and conference events in a personal interview with the writer, November 1964.
4. See 2.
5. The writer could not identify the seventh Dutch ship. It was perhaps in a ship-repair dock.
6. "Notes of Conference", held to discuss the release of ships for the Netherlands East Indies, Sydney, 29 March, as supplied to the Waterside Workers' Federation; in WWF Indonesian File.
7. See 6.
8. See 3.
9. See 6.
10. See 6.

11. See 6.
12. See 2. Based on a statement by Mountbatten to Elliott.
13. See 3.
14. See 6.
15. See 2.
16. See 3.
17. See 2.
18. Netherlands Indies Government Information Service, Melbourne, 20 March 1946.
19. Press statement (undated), in WWF Indonesian File.
20. Included in cable from the Australian Representative, Batavia, dated 3 April 1946, to the Australian Government in Canberra; copy of cable, supplied by Government for information of unions most concerned in boycott negotiations with Mountbatten, in WWF Indonesian File.
21. The copy of the cable in WWF Indonesian File is "from Brooks" and addressed to Canberra for the attention of Dr Evatt and his External Affairs Department. The cable was in fact from Mr A.D. Brookes, Assistant Australian Political Representative at Singapore and Batavia — a strong advocate of Australian support to the Indonesian Republic, of which the moderate Dr Sjahrir was then Premier.
22. See 20, 21.
23. See 20, 21.

Chapter   23

1. *Maritime Worker*, 20 April 1946.
2. Letter to WWF Federal Office, dated 23 December 1948.
3. 23 November 1946.
4. Brisbane WWF Branch Minutes: Meeting 9 October 1946.
5. 19 July 1946.
6. 20 July 1946.
7. Indonesian Seamen's Union press statement, Sydney, 11 July 1946.
8. Quoted, *Merdeka* (pamphlet), issued by the Central Committee of Indonesian Independence, Brisbane, on the first anniversary of the Republic's proclamation, 17 August 1946.

Chapter   24

1. *Sun*, 25 July 1947.
2. *Sydney Morning Herald*, 26 August 1947.
3. *Sydney Morning Herald*, 23 August 1947.
4. *Commonwealth Parliamentary Debates*, 19 September 1947.
5. *Sydney Morning Herald*, 30 July 1947.
6. *Maritime Worker*, Sydney, 9 August 1947.
7. The writer could not identify the other two.

8. Minutes, ACTU Interstate Executive: Meeting 11 August 1947.
9. *Sydney Morning Herald*, 31 July 1947.
10. 6 August 1947.
11. *Commonwealth Parliamentary Debates*, 24 September 1947.
12. Copy of Mr Roach's letter, posted in September 1947, in WWF Indonesian File.
13. Circular from General Secretary J. Healy to WWF Branches and Federal Councillors, 4 June 1948.
14. Australian Associated Press-Reuter message from The Hague, *Courier-Mail*, Brisbane, 18 October 1948.
15. 20 December 1948.

Chapter   25

1. Letter in WWF Indonesian File.
2. "Notes for Discussion," including conference decisions, officially supplied to the WWF after talks between Messrs Chifley, Ashley and Healy; in WWF Indonesian File.
3. See 1.
4. See 1.
5. See 1.
6. See 1.
7. Bridges' cable in WWF Indonesian File.
8. WWF Assistant General Secretary E.C. Roach issued a press statement (undated, in WWF Indonesian File), containing the report on the NZ telephone call.
9. 28 September 1945.
10. In WWF Indonesian File.
11. Murphy cable in WWF Indonesian File.
12. Letter from C.J. Najoan, Djakarta, one of the Indonesian leaders repatriated in HMAS *Manoora*; quoted, *Labor News*, organ of the Federated Ironworkers' Association, Sydney, April 1946.

Chapter   26

1. Mr R.A. King, then Secretary, NSW Trades and Labor Council, told the writer in October 1945 of approaches by RAAF men for support against this Dutch recruiting effort.
2. *Tribune*, Sydney, 23 October 1945.
3. *Argus*, Melbourne, 13 November 1945.
4. See 2.
5. *Ben Chifley*, by L.F. Crisp, Adelaide, 1960.
6. *Australia in the War of 1939-1945: The Government and The People*, by Paul Hasluck, Series IV, Civil, Vol. II; Australian War Memorial, Canberra, 1970.
7. See 6.
8. *Commonwealth Parliamentary Debates*, 7 September 1945.

9. The writer personally interviewed Private Bliss in March 1946, soon after his return from Macassar.

10. Instructions to Macassar Force in Connection with the Roels of the Australian Military Forces and Netherlands Indies Civil Administration in the South Celebes, November 1945; quoted, *Australia and the Indonesian Nationalist Movement 1942-45*, M.A. (Preliminary) Thesis, by Beverley M. Male, Australian National University, Canberra, 1965.

11. *Australia in the War of 1939-1945: The Final Campaigns*, by Gavin Long, Series I, Army, Vol. VII; Australian War Memorial, Canberra, 1963.

12. See 9.

13. See 9.

14. *The Stakes of Democracy in South-East Asia*, by H.J. Van Mook, London, 1950.

15. *Tropicana*, Army Education Service journal for South-West Pacific Area, September 1945.

16. WWF Indonesian File.

17. See 16.

18. See 9.

19. 28 November 1945.

20. See 11.

21. See 9.

22. *Argus*, Melbourne, 28 November 1945.

23. WWF Indonesian File. Number of soldiers involved was not given.

24. See 23.

25. WWF Indonesian File.

Chapter 27

1. Secretary General for the Netherlands Minister for Foreign Affairs to the Minister for Colonies, London, 17 November 1942, in *Londens Archief* (Netherlands Government in London); quoted, *Australian Attitudes and Policies Towards the Netherlands East Indies and Indonesian Independence, 1942-49*, by Margaret George, Doctor of Philosophy thesis, Department of International Relations, Research School of Pacific Studies, Australian National University, Canberra, 1973.

2. *Commonwealth Parliamentary Debates*, 3 September 1942.

3. Note for the Minister for Foreign Affairs, Royal Netherlands Government, 29 December 1942, quoted, Margaret George's thesis (see 1).

4. Radio Talk, ABC, January 1943.

5. Margaret George's thesis (see 1).

6. *Sydney Morning Herald*, 7 November 1949.

7. Quoted, *ALP: The Story of the Labor Party*, by George Healey, Brisbane, 1955.

8. *Commonwealth Parliamentary Debates*, 18 July 1944.
9. See 8.
10. Quoted, Margaret George's thesis (see 1), from official Netherlands documents.
11. Notes and Reports of Dr Van Der Plas, from Enquete Commissie Regeningsbelied 1940-45, quoted in Idrus Nasir Djajadiningrat, *The Beginnings of the Indonesian-Dutch Negotiations and the Hoge Veluwe Talks*, Monograph Series, Modern Indonesia Project, South-East Asia Program, Department of Far Eastern Studies, Cornell University, Ithaca, New York, 1958, p.10-11; quoted, *Australia and the Indonesian Nationalist Movement 1942-45*, M.A. (Preliminary) Thesis, by Beverley M. Male, Australian National University, Canberra, 1965.
12. *The Forrestal Diaries: The Inner History of the Cold War*, edited by Walter Millis, London, 1952.
13. *Indonesia*, by P.S. Gerbrandy, London, 1950.

Chapter 28

1. Quoted, "The Australian-Japanese Disputes of the Nineteen-Thirties", by I.M. Cumpston, *The Australian Quarterly*, Sydney, June 1957.
2. *Commonwealth Parliamentary Debates*, 25 September 1945.
3. *Commonwealth Parliamentary Debates*, 24 September 1947.
4. See 2.
5. *Commonwealth Parliamentary Debates*, 26 September 1945.
6. *Daily Telegraph*, Sydney, 28 February 1946.
7. *Commonwealth Parliamentary Debates*, 6 March 1946.
8. See 2.
9. See 7.
10. See 5.
11. See 5.
12. *Sunday Sun*, Sydney, 10 February 1952.
13. Quoted, "New Guinea and Australia's Defence Policy", paper by Dr John Andrews to 24th Summer School, Australian Institute of Pacific Relations, Canberra, 1958; published in *New Guinea and Australia*, edited by John Wilkes, Sydney, 1958.
14. See 13.
15. See 13.
16. *Commonwealth Parliamentary Debates*, 9 February 1949.
17. *Commonwealth Parliamentary Debates*, 23 February 1950.
18. See 17.
19. *Commonwealth Parliamentary Debates*, 5 October 1960.
20. *The South Seas in Transition*, by W.E.H. Stanner, Australian Institute of International Affairs, Sydney, 1953.
21. In discussion on Dr John Andrews' paper, "New Guinea and Australia's Defence Policy" (see 13).

22. *Commonwealth Parliamentary Debates*, 23 March 1950.
23. *Sydney Morning Herald*, 9 February 1962.
24. See 21 and 13.
25. *Sydney Morning Herald*, 12 February 1962.
26. *Sydney Morning Herald*, 13 February 1962.

Chapter 29

1. *Commonwealth Parliamentary Debates*, 16 February 1949.
2. *Commonwealth Parliamentary Debates*, 12 March 1950.
3. *Commonwealth Parliamentary Debates*, 8 June 1950.
4. *Boston Christian Science Monitor*, 24 September 1952.
5. *Argus*, Melbourne, 24 March 1950.
6. *Commonwealth Parliamentary Debates*, 23 February 1950.
7. *Sydney Morning Herald*, 14 June 1952.
8. See 7.
9. *Daily Telegraph*, Sydney, 14 June 1952.
10. See 9.
11. *Indonesia and the Dutch* by L.H. Palmier, London, 1962.
12. Hearings before the Committee on Foreign Relations, US Senate, 11 November 1954.
13. *South-East Asia in Perspective*, by Dr John Kerry Young, New York, 1959.
14. *SEATO: Six Studies*, edited by George Modeleski, Canberra, 1962.
15. *Commonwealth Parliamentary Debates*, 26 March 1958.
16. "Indonesia and the Confrontation: Compelling Reasons for the Anti-Malaysian Campaign," *Bulletin*, Sydney, 14 December 1963.
17. *Commonwealth Parliamentary Debates*, 18 March 1958.
18. See 17.
19. *The National Times*, Sydney, 5-10 May 1975.

Chapter 30

1. *Commonwealth Parliamentary Debates*, 25 September 1945.
2. *Sydney Morning Herald*, 14 March 1946.
3. Personal interview with Mr Arthur Calwell, former Minister for Information (1943-49) and Immigration (1945-49), later Leader of the Federal Parliamentary Opposition; 9 April 1971.
4. *Commonwealth Parliamentary Debates*, 25 September 1945.
5. *Commonwealth Parliamentary Debates*, 6 March 1946.
6. See 4.
7. *Commonwealth Parliamentary Debates*, 26 September 1945.
8. Quoted, *Ben Chifley*, by Professor L.F. Crisp, Adelaide, 1960.
9. *The Forrestal Diaries: The Inner History of the Cold War*, edited by Walter Millis, London, 1952.
10. See 9.
11. 3 December 1949.

12. *Commonwealth Parliamentary Debates*, 23 March 1950.
13. Broadcast, Republican Radio, Batavia, 9 October 1945.
14. "To Our Friends," issued from Trades Hall, Brisbane, 16 October 1945.
15. Letter to Mrs L. Byrnes, of the Australia-Indonesia Association, sent from Java in November 1945.
16. Copy of letter, addressed "Australian Trades and Labor Council," in WWF Indonesian File.
17. *Maritime Worker*, Sydney, 20 April 1946.
18. Copy of Dr Sjarifuddin's cable from Djogjakarta supplied to WWF and printed in its *Maritime Worker*, 13 September 1947.
19. *West Australian*, Perth, 31 December 1948.
20. See 19.
21. 13 March 1963.
22. "Indonesia Calling," chapter by Marion Michelle in *Le Cinema Pendant La Guerre*, Vol. IV, edited by Georges Sadoul, Paris, 1962.

Chapter 31

1. *Sydney Morning Herald*, 14 December 1959.
2. Australian Associated Press-Reuter from Djakarta; *Daily Telegraph*, Sydney, 28 April 1960.
3. 2 July 1960.
4. *Daily Telegraph*, Sydney, 1 June 1960.
5. *Sydney Morning Herald*, 2 June 1960.
6. Australian Associated Press-Reuter message from The Hague to *Courier-Mail*, Brisbane, 1 April 1960.
7. 6 July 1960.
8. Minutes, Federated Ship Painters and Dockers' Union of Australia, Western Australian Branch; annual report to members at meeting, Trades Hall, Fremantle, 9 January 1961.
9. *West Australian*, Perth, 12 July 1960.
10. See 9.
11. 13 July 1960.
12. See 8.

Conclusion

1. Transcript, "A Conference on the Working of Dutch Ships," Proceedings of the Commonwealth Court of Conciliation and Arbitration, 1 March 1946.
2. *The Second World War and an Epilogue on the Years 1945 to 1947*, by Winston S. Churchill, London, 1959.
3. *The Stakes of Democracy in South-East Asia*, by H.J. Van Mook, London, 1950.
4. WWF Indonesian File.

5. See 4.
6. *The Birth of Indonesia*, by David Wehl, London, 1948.
7. *Indonesia*, by P.S. Gerbrandy, London, 1950.
8. See 6.
9. *The Second World War, Triumph and Tragedy*, Vol. IV, by Winston S. Churchill, London, 1954.
10. *Where Are We Heading?*, by Sumner Welles, New York, 1946.
11. See 3.
12. *Argus*, Melbourne, 22 June 1945.
13. *Argus*, Melbourne, 8 August 1945.
14. *Commonwealth Parliamentary Debates*, 1 August 1945.
15. See 13.
16. Mr E.V. Elliott, Federal Secretary, Seamen's Union of Australia, quoted this Mountbatten statement, made to him at the 1946 Sydney discussions on Dutch ships, in a personal interview with the writer, June 1964.
17. *Commonwealth Parliamentary Debates*, 13 March 1946.
18. *Indonesia: Land of Challenge*, London, 1955.
19. See 6. David Wehl was Mountbatten's Intelligence Officer in Java.
20. C.C. Eager, despatch from Batavia to *Sydney Morning Herald*, 25 September 1945.
21. See 18.
22. Military Situation in the Far East: Hearings, Before the Senate Armed Services Foreign Relations Committee, 82nd Congress, 1st Session, Washington, 1951; quoted, *The United States in World Affairs*, by Richard P. Stebbins, New York, 1951.
23. *The C.I.A. and the Cult of Intelligence*, by Victor Marchetti and John D. Marks, New York, 1974.

Index

340

Hill, Toby: 229.
Hillier, Sapper Lewis: 44-5.
Hince, Kenneth: 177.
Hindus: 150-2, 156, 248.
Hitler: 28, 30, 283. Hitler's Fortress Europe: 295.
Hodgson, Colonel W. R.: 283.
Holland: 4, 7, 9, 13, 37, 53, 56, 59, 70, 87, 175, 191, 251, 254, 263, 282-3, 289-90, 295, 301-4, 310, 312.
Holland-Australia Line: 218-9.
Hollandem, ship: 229.
Hollandia: 20, 67, 77, 141, 145, 237, 254, 259, 262-3, 290-1, 311.
Hong Kong: 59, 158, 171.
Hotel Darwin: 270.
Hotel des Indes: 304, 307.
Hughes, William Morris: 258-60.
Humbolt Bay: 67.
Humphrey, Dr Alfred H.: 270.

INDIA, INDIANS –
218-9, 232, 251, 254-5, 258, 265-6, 275, 279. Independence struggle: 7, 149, 152-6, 165. Indian High Commissioner: 154, 163-5. Indian Labor Pool in Sydney: 156, 159-60, 164. Indian seamen in Australia: 4, 105-6, 108, 115, 130-2, 149-167, 170, 174, 193, 287. Indian Seamen's Union in Australia (see Trade Unions). Indian Seamen's Club, Sydney: 160. Indian POWs (ex-Singapore); 158. Indian Red Cross Dakota shot down: 187. Indian troops (Fifth Indian Division) in Java: 202, 232-3.
India-Malaya-Australia defence triangle: 253.
Indo-Chinese: 7, 309.
Indo-China War (Australian ship boycott): 231.
INDONESIA, INDONESIANS –
Republic of Indonesia: 1-4, 6-7, 16-7, 59-60, 72-4, 84-8, 91-2, 94-6, 98, 102, 105, 107-11, 115-6, 119, 127, 129, 133, 135-8, 141-4, 146-8, 152-3, 166-8, 173-4, 178, 181-2, 187, 191, 200, 202-7, 210, 214-6, 220-2, 228-30, 232-9, 253, 257-8, 260, 262-3, 265, 267-8, 270-4, 275, 278, 280-91, 294, 296, 298, 301,

305-8, 310-3. Refugees to Australia, 1942: 3, 58-66, 254. Independence Committees in Australia: 3, 21, 36-7, 63, 72-7, 79, 82, 84, 86-7, 141, 143-4, 147, 165, 243, 285, 287. Manifesto for Republic, Central Committee of Indonesian Independence Committees: 84. Mutinies, strikes of Indonesians in Australia: 2-4, 28, 36, 67, 69, 77-9, 80-1, 84-7, 91-7, 98-111, 135, 139, 218, 279-80, 287, 301, 307-8, 312. Indonesian Club, Sydney: 71, 285. Indonesian Petty Officers' Social Club, Sydney: 74. Indonesians' Defence Committee, Casino: 90. Indonesian Technical Battalion, Casino: 64-5, 86-7. Nationalist rebellion in Indies, 1926-7: 16, 22-3, 28-9, 30, 33, 35-6. "People's Republic", "Democratic Front", Madiun clash and Soekarno regime's military response: 220-1. Indonesian Socialist Party: 220. Repatriation of Indonesians from Australia: 60, 91, 110, 135-48, 285. Soekarno, Dr, and Soekarno regime: 37, 140-1, 221, 257, 285, 289, 300. Indonesian Medical Appeal in Australia: 187. Indonesian Seamen's Union (see Trade Unions). Republican Information Office, New York: 286. "Republic of South Moluccas" and gun-running to from Darwin: 268-72, 311. "Revolutionary Government of the Indonesian Republic" and "Permesta" rebellion: 271-2. Communists (see PKI and Tanah Merah).
Indonesia Calling, film: 163, 278.
International Labor Organisation: 127.
Inverchapel, Lord: 277.
Irian Barat (see New Guinea, Indonesian).
Iroot, Willi Pande: 71.
"Island ramparts": 253, 255, 258-9, 260-1, 267.
Israel: 290.
Italy, Italians: 28, 30, 137, 210, 233. Italian POW's in Australia: 6, 21, 23, 137, 180, 210, 280.
Ito, General Takeo: 58.
Ivens, Jorris: 163, 287-8.

345

Docks, Rivers and Harbour Works Union): 119-21, 218. Electrical Trades Union: 17. Federated Clerks' Union: 106, 111. Federated Iron-Workers' Association: 111, 116, 129, 193, 218. Federated Ship Painters and Dockers' Union: 106, 111, 115-6, 119, 292. Fremantle Lumpers' Union: 119. Hotel, Club and Restaurant Employees' Union: 66. Miners' Federation, miners: 104, 108. Painters' Union: 125. Seamen's Union:' 33, 92-3, 106, 111, 122, 127, 132, 140-1, 157, 159, 162, 176, 193, 199-200, 217, 230-1, 287, 292. Sheetmetal Workers' Union: 117, 173. Storemen and Packers' Union: 101. Transport Workers' Union: 106, 111, 117.

Waterside Workers' Federation, waterside workers: 33, 83-4, 92, 97-8, 100-2, 104-6, 111, 119, 123-4, 128, 133, 137, 143, 154, 164, 174, 184-5, 190-6, 199-201, 213, 215, 223, 224-31, 257-8, 286-7, 297-300.

(See also list of trade unions participating in boycott of Dutch in Australia in Appendix, 318-9).

ASIAN UNIONS in Australia – Chinese Seamen's Union: 174. Chinese union activities: 114, 125. Indian Seamen's Union: 114, 174, 209. Indian union activities: 105-6, 108, 114-5, 130-2, 229, 287. (See also under India and Chapter 16 and 17, 149-67). Indonesian Seamen's Union: 74, 92, 114, 125, 168, 190, 195, 213. Indonesian union activities: 69-71, 74, 80, 92, 95-6, 114, 127-8, 219-20. (See also Boycotts, Mutinies, Strikes.) Malayan Merchant Navy Association: 114, 168, 170, 174.

UNIONS OVERSEAS – Britain: National Union of Seamen, 176-7. NUS East London Branch: 178. Trade Union Congress: 189. India: 229. Indonesia (SOBSI): 141. Netherlands: 229. Netherlands Trade Union Federation: 189. Netherlands Seamen's Union Branch, New York: 129. New Zealand Waterside Work-

ers' Federation: 229. NZ Federation of Labour: 229. North America: International Longshoremens and Warehousemen's Association: 229. Seafarers' International Union of North America: 229.
Tribune, Sydney: 68, 93-4, 212-3.
Tromp, warship: 84-5, 97, 119.
Trotsky: 28.
Trouw, Holland: 291.
Troy, Paddy: 120-1, 292-3.
Truman, President: 296, 303, 310. Truman Doctrine: 303.
Truth, Brisbane: 126.
Tudor, (Queen) Mary: 264.
Tukliwon: 92-3.
Turner, John Albert: 181.
Turramurra: 25, 134.

Union Castle SS Co.: 173.
United Nations: 10, 127, 179, 218, 222, 247, 273, 278, 282-3, 285, 309, 312. UN Committee of Good Offices on Indonesia: 22, 281-3. UN Security Council: 222, 255-6, 281-3. UN Agreement for Netherlands New Guinea: 263. UN General Assembly: 259. UN (Australian) delegation: 259. UN Charter: 255. UN Universal Declaration of Human Rights: 224. UN Conference, San Francisco: 250, 255. UNRRA: 190.
"Umbrella" (islands defence screen): 253, 266-7.
United States (see America).
United States of Indonesia (see Indonesia – Republic).
Usman, Dr: 140.

Van Aerssen Beyeren Van Voshol, Baron: 122, 194, 205-6, 245, 250, 277-9.
Van Arcken, Captain G. C. M.: 306.
Van Der Molen: 49.
Van Der Noorda: 184.
Van Der Kroef, Professor Justus: 272.
Van Der Plas, Dr Charles: 13, 21, 28, 49, 247-9, 300, 305-7.
Van Diemen's Land: 10.
Van Haselen, Colonel: 80-2.
Van Heutz, ship: 98-104, 117, 305, 307.
Van Hoogenstraaden, Dr J. E.: 50-1.